AF781424

HUMAN RIGHTS, LEGITIMACY, AND THE USE OF FORCE

406175165
3/10
CAMERON UNIVERSITY LIBRARY
2800 WEST GORE BOULEVARD
LAWTON, OKLAHOMA 73505
WITHDRAWN
KZ
3410
.B828
2010

HUMAN RIGHTS, LEGITIMACY, AND THE USE OF FORCE

ALLEN BUCHANAN

OXFORD
UNIVERSITY PRESS
2010

OXFORD
UNIVERSITY PRESS

Oxford University Press, Inc., publishes works that further
Oxford University's objective of excellence
in research, scholarship, and education.

Oxford New York
Auckland Cape Town Dar es Salaam Hong Kong Karachi
Kuala Lumpur Madrid Melbourne Mexico City Nairobi
New Delhi Shanghai Taipei Toronto

With offices in
Argentina Austria Brazil Chile Czech Republic France Greece
Guatemala Hungary Italy Japan Poland Portugal Singapore
South Korea Switzerland Thailand Turkey Ukraine Vietnam

Copyright © 2010 by Oxford University Press, Inc.

Published by Oxford University Press, Inc.
198 Madison Avenue, New York, New York 10016

www.oup.com

Oxford is a registered trademark of Oxford University Press.

All rights reserved. No part of this publication may be reproduced,
stored in a retrieval system, or transmitted, in any form or by any means,
electronic, mechanical, photocopying, recording, or otherwise,
without the prior permission of Oxford University Press.

Library of Congress Cataloging-in-Publication Data
Buchanan, Allen E., 1948–
Human rights, legitimacy, and the use of force / Allen Buchanan.
p. cm.
ISBN 978-0-19-538965-4
1. International law. 2. Human rights.
3. Humanitarian intervention. 4. International and municipal law.
I. Title.
KZ3410.B828 2010
341—dc22 2009021790

1 3 5 7 9 8 6 4 2

Printed in the United States of America
on acid-free paper

ACKNOWLEDGMENTS

I am indebted to many scholars in philosophy, international law, and international relations, both for their valuable written work and for their generous responses at various conferences to my own efforts. I am especially grateful to Charles Beitz, Hurst Hannum, Jeff Holzgrefe, Robert O. Keohane, James Nickel, Russell Powell, Stephen Ratner, and John Tasioulas. I am especially grateful to Bob Keohane for his generosity and patience in teaching me how to think about international institutions. Peter Ohlin and Molly Wagener have been encouraging and efficient editors and I thank them as well.

Thanks are also due for permissions to republish the chapters in this volume: to Rowman & Littlefield for "Justice, Legitimacy, and Human Rights," which appeared in *The Idea of Political Liberalism*, edited by Victoria Davion and Clark Wolf (2000); to Blackwell Publishing, for "Taking the Human Out of Human Rights," in *Rawls's Law of Peoples: A Realistic Utopia?* edited by Rex Martin and David Reidy (2006); to Sage Publications, for "Equality and Human Rights," in *Philosophy, Politics, and Economics*, vol. 4, no. 1 (2005); to Cambridge University Press for "Human Rights and the Legitimacy of the International Order," in *Legal Theory*, vol. 14, no. 1 (2008); to Blackwell Publishing, for "The Legitimacy of Global Governance Institutions," coauthored with Robert O. Keohane, in *Ethics and International Affairs*, vol. 20, no. 4 (2004); to Oxford University Press for "The Legitimacy of International Law," in *The Philosophy of International Law*, edited by Samantha Besson and John Tasioulas (in press); to the *Georgia Journal of International and Comparative Law* for "Democracy and the Commitment to International Law," coauthored with Russell Powell, in *Georgia Journal of International and Comparative Law*, vol. 34, no. 2 (2006); to Blackwell Publishing for "Survey Article: Constitutional Democracy and International Law: Are They Compatible?" *Journal of Political Philosophy*, vol. 16, no. 3 (2008); to Blackwell Publishing for "The Internal Legitimacy of Humanitarian Intervention," *Journal of Political Philosophy*, vol. 7, no. 1 (1999); to *Philosophical Topics* for "Beyond the National Interest," in *Philosophical Topics: Special Issue on Global Equality*, vol. 30, no. 2 (2002); to Blackwell Publishing for "Institutionalizing the Just War," in *Philosophy and Public Affairs*, vol. 34, no. 1 (2006); to Oxford University Press for "Justifying Preventive War," in *Preemption: Military Action and Moral Justification* (2007); to the University of Chicago Press for "From Nuremburg to Kosovo: The Morality of Illegal International Legal Reform," in *Ethics*, vol. 111 (July 2001).

CONTENTS

HUMAN RIGHTS, LEGITIMACY, AND THE USE OF FORCE

INTRODUCTION

This volume includes thirteen chapters that have appeared in diverse venues over the last nine years and arranges them in a way that makes their systematic interconnections evident. The chapters explore important relationships between the nature and moral grounding of international human rights, the legitimacy of international institutions, and the justifications for the use of force across borders. Taken together, they make the case for a holistic, systematic approach to the issues they examine, articulating close connections between human rights, legitimacy, and humanitarian intervention that have hitherto gone unnoticed because of the tendency to focus exclusively on one or the other of the three topics. A central theme of the volume is that productive thinking about the ethics of international relations must be more attentive to institutional issues. Instead of thinking first about norms and then only about institutions as mechanisms for implementing norms, it is necessary to consider alternative "packages" of norms and institutions. When philosophers make the case for certain norms and reject others, they typically rely tacitly on certain assumptions about the characters of the institutions within which the norms will operate, but too often these assumptions are accepted uncritically and are empirically unsupported. A central conclusion of this volume is that if philosophical thinking about ethics and international relations is to be rigorous, it must be more empirically informed as well as more sensitive to when it is relying on empirical assumptions about institutional resources.

Part I, "Human Rights," contains four chapters. The first, "Justice, Legitimacy, and Human Rights," broaches the topic of human rights with an examination of Rawls's attempt to ground human rights in the account of legitimacy he developed in *Political Liberalism*. I argue that the understanding of toleration on which that account of legitimacy is based is defective because its criteria for a reasonable moral or religious view are too undemanding. In particular, Rawls's notion of reasonableness overemphasizes epistemic humility at the expense of epistemic responsibility, by failing to require that the *empirical assumptions* of a moral or religious view must meet minimal epistemic standards if the view is to count as reasonable in the sense relevant to legitimacy. In addition, by elevating epistemic humility to a principle of the highest priority, Rawls is in effect assuming a highly controversial comprehensive moral view of what it is to show respect for persons, and this violates his own stricture against relying on comprehensive moral views in developing the Law of Peoples. Because he accepts this defective understanding of toleration, Rawls cannot account for a central feature of modern human rights, namely, their egalitarianism, especially as it is evidenced in rights against discrimination on grounds of race, gender, or religion.

Since Rawls's view cannot account for this central feature of modern human rights, it is deeply revisionist. While the possibility that the best philosophical reconstruction of modern human rights doctrine may be deeply revisionist cannot be ruled out in advance, Rawls has given us no good reason to accept such a major revision, because his conception of toleration is both implausible in its own right and at odds with his effort to eschew reliance on comprehensive moral conception.

The second chapter, "Taking the Human Out of Human Rights," deepens the preceding chapter's criticism of Rawls's conception of human rights. It focuses on Rawls's attempt to develop a conception of human rights *without* relying on the traditional philosophical idea that all human beings share some morally relevant characteristics, capacities, or basic interests. I argue that (1) Rawls's reasons for avoiding reliance on this conception of human rights are unsound and that (2) his attempt to ground human rights on the idea of cooperation covertly assumes the traditional philosophical idea that he rejects, because his thesis that only societies that qualify as forms of cooperation are "decent" rests implicitly on the principle that *all* members of society have some shared characteristics that entitle them to be participants in cooperation rather than subjects in a system of coercion.

Although these first two chapters are reflections on Rawls's conception of human rights, they are more than critical exegesis. They are original contributions to the current upsurge of philosophical thinking on human rights. They also help prepare the way for the next two chapters, which explore the connections between human rights and contemporary theories of egalitarian justice and advance a constructive and novel "institutionalist" account of the nature of the task of justifying claims about the existence of human rights. According to the institutionalist account, institutions are important not only for implementing human rights norms but also for helping to determine their content. While Rawls is correct in thinking that a plausible doctrine of human rights cannot be developed solely from a conception of humanity or human nature, he is mistaken in thinking that it can be developed without making some assumptions about the morally relevant common characteristics of human beings.

The third chapter, "Equality and Human Rights," begins by calling attention to the surprising disconnect between the recent work on egalitarian theories of justice and the growing philosophical interest in the moral grounding of human rights. I then outline and defend an account of human rights, the Modest Objectivist View, according to which human rights, when respected, provide valuable protections of basic human interests against what Henry Shue has called "standard threats." The advantage of the Modest Objectivist View is that it can make sense of the idea that human rights are (in a sense) grounded in our humanity, while at the same time acknowledging that which human rights we have can vary over time, as the standard threats to those interests change.

Next, I examine the Modest Objectivist View's egalitarian assumptions and ask whether they are compatible with egalitarian theories of justice at the societal versus the international level. I conclude that the modest egalitarianism of human rights is compatible with robustly egalitarian conceptions of justice at the societal level, given a plausible understanding of the distinctive function of human rights as standards of transnational justice, that is, as principles of justice that it is reasonable for international society to expect each state to satisfy in its treatment of its own citizens.

The final chapter of part 1, "Human Rights and the Legitimacy of the International Legal Order," builds on the analysis in the preceding three chapters. It develops further the Modest Objectivist View of human rights and provides a bridge to part II, by offering an account of the connection between the *justification* of claims about the existence of human rights and challenges to the *legitimacy* of the institutions that implement human rights norms. My main thesis is that whether the current "justification deficit" regarding claims about the existence of human rights can be remedied—and in such a way as to meet challenges to the legitimacy of institutional attempts to implement human rights—depends in part on the *epistemic qualities* of the institutions through which human rights norms are articulated, contested, and revised over time. I argue that although a defensible core philosophical conception of human rights (in particular, the Modest Objectivist View) is necessary, it is not sufficient for remedying the "justification deficit." The justification of claims about the existence of human rights and the legitimacy of institutional efforts to implement human rights is not a once-and-for-all feat of abstract philosophical reasoning; it is an on-going process in which institutionalized, public normative reasoning plays an ineliminable role. This new perspective on the justification of human rights norms curbs the pretentions of philosophical theory in one respect, but expands the philosophers' task in another: while traditional philosophical reasoning is not adequate for fully determining the content of human rights norms, but must be supplemented with institutionalized public reasoning, philosophical reasoning is needed to determine what sorts of epistemic virtues institutions must have if they are to help to determine the content of the norms. To put the same point differently, traditional philosophical theorizing about human rights needs to be augmented by social moral epistemology, understood as the systematic comparative evaluation of alternative social institutions and practices as to their effectiveness and efficiency in forming beliefs that are critical for moral judgment and justification.

Part II, "Legitimacy," contains four chapters. The first, "The Legitimacy of Global Governance Institutions" (cowritten with Robert O. Keohane) examines an issue that philosophers have tended to neglect but that is of urgent practical importance: what *conception* of legitimacy is appropriate for global governance institutions and what *standards* of legitimacy ought to be applied to them? First, we distinguish stronger and weaker conceptions of legitimacy as "the right to rule" and argue that the stronger conceptions, which may be appropriate for states, do not apply to global governance institutions because of their distinctive features. Next, we offer an account of the distinctive social function of legitimacy assessments, distinguishing legitimacy from justice and mutual advantage. The key point here is that legitimacy assessments can help coordinate support or resistance to institutions in the absence of agreement about justice.

Keohane and I then articulate and reject three standards for the legitimacy of global governance institutions: the State Consent or International Legal Pedigree View, the Democratic State Consent View, and the Global Democracy View. By reflecting on the inadequacy of these three standards, we develop a set of desiderata that a standard should meet and then argue that what we call the Complex Standard satisfies them. The substantive elements of the Complex Standard include a minimal moral acceptability condition, spelled out in terms of respect for basic human rights, a comparative benefit condition, and an institutional integrity condition. We then complete our explication of the Complex Standard with an account of the *epistemic* aspects of legitimacy, grounded in the insight that assessments of the legitimacy of global governance institutions, at present, must be made under conditions of both moral disagreement and moral uncertainty about the proper functions of such institutions, including their role in promoting international justice. This last element of the analysis connects this chapter closely with the last chapter of the preceding part, because it emphasizes the epistemic functions of international institutions.

The second chapter, "The Legitimacy of International Law," is a contribution to the burgeoning field of the philosophy of international law, but it also elucidates central connections between that field and political philosophy as it has been traditionally conceived. Here I deepen the analysis of legitimacy offered in the preceding chapter and apply it to international law-making institutions, arguing that the international lawyers' debate about the legitimacy of international legal *norms* should be recast as an inquiry into the conditions that international law-making *institutions* must satisfy if they are to be legitimate. I answer six basic questions about the legitimacy of international law. (1) What is the distinctive character and point of legitimacy judgments about international legal institutions and how do they differ from other kinds of evaluations of those institutions? (2) What concept or conceptions of legitimacy are relevant to international law and what standards of legitimacy ought international law-making institutions (ILIs) meet? (3) What are the chief challenges to the legitimacy of international law? (4) What is at stake in assessments of the legitimacy of international law—more specifically, why does the legitimacy of ILIs matter and to whom? (5) What conditions should a theory of the legitimacy of ILIs satisfy? (6) What are the main rival approaches to the legitimacy of international law and which seem most promising, given an account of the conditions they should satisfy? I conclude by articulating the link between the issue of the legitimacy of ILIs and the problem of justifying claims about the existence of human rights that is developed in more detail in "Human Rights and the International Order." This chapter's discussion of the challenges to the legitimacy of international law provides a bridge to the next chapter in this part.

The third chapter, "Democracy and the Commitment to International Law," is framed as a critical reflection on Eric Posner and Jack Goldsmith's iconoclastic book, *The Limits of International Law*. This discussion deepens the preceding chapter's account of the legitimacy of international law by exploring the nature of the commitment to the project of bringing international relations under the rule of law. I argue that Posner and Goldsmith's view that democratic states should view international legal commitments in a purely instrumental way is based on a flawed conception of democracy and an equally defective conception of what it means to have a moral commitment to the rule of international law. I prepare the way for the final chapter in this part, by broaching the issue of whether the commitment to democracy at the state level and the commitment to international law are compatible. I also lay the groundwork for the first two chapters in part III, which criticize more systematically the unexamined assumptions that underlie the instrumentalist view that Posner and Goldsmith advocate.

The final chapter of part II, "Constitutional Democracy and the Rule of International Law: Are They Compatible?" (cowritten with Russell Powell) provides the most systematic examination currently available of the claim, usually associated with the so-called New Sovereigntist movement in American constitutional and international legal scholarship, that there is a deep tension if not a contradiction between the commitment to constitutional democracy at the level of the state and the commitment to the project of establishing an international legal order that significantly constraints state sovereignty. It is a contribution both to the philosophy of international law and to the contemporary philosophical debate between liberal nationalists (such as David Miller, Ronald Dworkin, the later Rawls, Michael Blake, and Thomas Nagel) and liberal cosmopolitans (such as Thomas Pogge, Martha Nussbaum, David Held, Kok-Chor Tan, and Darrell Moellendorf). This chapter identifies and critically evaluates five different concerns about the compatibility of the two commitments, and argues that, although there is no inherent incompatibility, in practice there can be serious tensions and that resolving them may require significant constitutional changes in democratic states. One important conclusion is that liberal cosmopolitans have conceived of the scope of their theorizing much too narrowly: they need to develop a normative theory of constitutionalism to show how the commitment to democracy at the state level and the project of developing international institutions capable of satisfying cosmopolitan principles of justice can be made compatible.

Part III, "The Use of Force," contains five chapters. The first, "The Internal Legitimacy of Humanitarian Intervention," discusses the philosophical literature on humanitarian intervention, which has focused primarily on the conditions under which it is justifiable for a state or group of states to engage in military action across borders for the sake of protecting human rights. This literature has been assumed that the question is whether an intervening state can justify its actions *to other states or to international agents such as the UN Security Council.* I systematically examine a prior, equally important, and grossly neglected question: what conditions must be satisfied for state leaders to be able to justify humanitarian intervention *to its own citizens*? This is what I call the problem of the internal legitimacy of humanitarian intervention. The attempt to answer this question forces one to examine critically what I call the discretionary association view of the state, namely, the thesis that the state is simply an association for the mutual benefit of its members. I explain the seeming attractions of this thesis, especially to those in the social contract tradition broadly understood, but argue that it is at bottom incoherent, given certain plausible and widely held assumptions about what makes the exercise of coercion on the part of the state legitimate. My central argument connects closely with the exploration of the nature of the commitment to international law in the last two chapters of part II. In particular, I heighten the contrast between the view that a democratic state's commitment to international law is purely instrumental and an understanding of the value of international legal order that is consonant with cosmopolitan moral values. I also prepare the way for the following chapter in this part, which critically examines the assumption that the exclusive goal in foreign policy ought to be the pursuit of the national interest.

The second chapter, "Beyond the National Interest," argues that whether the use of military force across borders is justified depends in part on what the proper role of the pursuit of the national interest is in the state's behavior. In particular, some widely held conceptions of the national interest tightly constrain the permissibility of humanitarian military intervention. In this chapter I distinguish and critically evaluate several different theses about the national interest, including (1) the claim that a state's foreign policy always ought to be determined exclusively by the national interest (the Obligatory Exclusivity Thesis) and (2) the claim that it is always permissible for a state's foreign policy to be determined exclusively by the national interest (the Permissive Exclusivity Thesis). I focus on criticizing the Permissive Exclusivity Thesis because it is more plausible and because if it is refuted then the Obligatory Exclusivity Thesis is refuted *a fortiori*. I argue that if there are any human rights, then there is a weighty burden of argument on those who subscribe to the Permissive Exclusivity Thesis. I then distinguish and reject two attempted justifications for the Permissive Exclusivity Thesis that are associated with the Realist tradition in international relations: the Fiduciary Realist justification and the Instrumental Justification. My criticism of these two justifications provides one of the most systematic attacks available on the implicit normative and empirical assumptions of the Realist approach. Understanding the implausibility of the Permissive Exclusivity Thesis helps to reinforce the case made in the preceding chapters for taking seriously the project of developing legitimate international institutions.

The third chapter, "Institutionalizing the Just War," argues for a radical reorientation of philosophical thinking about the ethics of war. It challenges the assumption that the key question for contemporary just war theory is whether to relax or to qualify the norm according to which war is permissible only in response to an actual or imminent attack. I argue that the proper choice is not between more constraining and more permissive norms but rather between alternative *combinations of norms and institutions*. Focusing only on competing norms rather than on combinations of norms and institutions makes sense only if one assumes (1) that the validity of the norms does not depend upon the institutional context in which they are followed or (2) that existing institutional resources for constraining war are negligible *and* the creation of new institutional resources is either not feasible or not worth the cost. I argue that neither assumption (1) nor (2) is defensible. To help make the case for this reframing of the debate, I explore how the focus on combinations of norms and institutions illuminates two central topics of contemporary just war theory: preventive war and forcible democratization.

The fourth chapter, "Justifying Preventive War," delves more deeply into the ethics of preventive war, identifying and refuting two "consequentialist" objections to the thesis that preventive war is sometimes justifiable, what I call the bad practice objection argument and the irresponsible act objection. According to the former, preventive war is unjustified because the preventive principle could not be generally followed without unacceptable consequences; according to the latter, it is irresponsible for state leaders to justify going to war on preventive grounds because this kind of justification is too subject to abuse and error. I argue that neither objection takes into account the point made in the preceding chapter, namely, that whether a norm governing the use of force is justified cannot be determined *a priori*, in the absence of defensible assumptions about the institutions within which the norm is embedded.

I then go on to identify two more serious, "rights-based" objections to the claim that preventive war is sometimes justifiable: the simple rights-based objection, according to which preventive war is never justifiable because it always involves using force against agents who have *not yet* done wrong or harm, and the failure to discriminate objection, according to which preventive war inevitably involves the use of force against some persons who are not parties to the conspiracy to commit wrongful aggression that the preventive action is intended to thwart. I refute the simple rights-based objection by invoking a qualified analogy with the crime of conspiracy, according to which conspirators can be forcibly prevented from bringing their conspiracy to fruition even if they have not yet begun to inflict harm. My response to the failure to discriminate objection involves what I believe to be a new and important understanding of the role of considerations of *fairness in the distribution of risk* in just war theory and more generally in theorizing about the right of self-defense. The key point here is that an absolute prohibition on preventive war would make innocent parties unduly vulnerable to predation by aggressors.

The final chapter, "From Nuremburg to Kosovo: The Morality of Illegal International Legal Reform," explores the ethics of humanitarian intervention, applying the institutional approach developed in the preceding chapters in this part to the NATO intervention in Kosovo, and criticizes the comfortable assumption that the transition to a more morally acceptable international law concerning humanitarian intervention can be achieved by strictly legal means. Unlike in other philosophical treatments of the ethics of humanitarian intervention, I connect just war theory with the philosophy of international law and with issues concerning the legitimacy of international institutions explored in part II. This chapter occupies a unique position in the voluminous contemporary literature spawned by the NATO intervention. Other contributors to that literature either argue that no significant change in international law regarding the use of force is needed and that any attempt at making humanitarian intervention permissible without Security Council authorization would betray a rejection of the ideal of the rule of law or that reform is needed and can be achieved legally. I show that it is equally simplistic to assume that a concern for the rule of law requires one to support the existing international legal strictures on humanitarian intervention or to assume that reform can be achieved without violating existing law. In some circumstances, a commitment to the rule of law may require violating existing international law—but only if the violation is only one element in a more complex and difficult course of action that includes the building of new, more just legal institutions.

The chapters in part III address the three main concerns of contemporary theorizing on the ethics of going to war: humanitarian intervention, preventive war, and forcible democratization. In addition to offering new insights on each of these topics, these four chapters help flesh out two central theses of the volume as a whole: namely, that philosophical thinking about the ethics of international relations must take institutions seriously and that issues concerning human rights, the legitimacy of international institutions, and the use of force cannot be fruitfully theorized in isolation from one another.

PART I

HUMAN RIGHTS

1

JUSTICE, LEGITIMACY, AND HUMAN RIGHTS

1. THE DISTINCTION BETWEEN JUSTICE AND LEGITIMACY

It has been said that while *A Theory of Justice* is about justice, *Political Liberalism* is about legitimacy—about the conditions that must be satisfied if it is to be morally justifiable to use force to secure compliance with principles of justice.[1] This is almost correct. *Political Liberalism* is about the role that considerations of legitimacy should play in theorizing about justice. By bringing the relationship between justice and legitimacy to center stage, Rawls has launched his second revolution in thinking about justice.

Once the distinction between justice and legitimacy is noticed, it is hard to understand how it could have been so neglected by most who have written about justice until the appearance of *Political Liberalism*. In *A Theory of Justice*, Rawls, like most theorists of justice before and after the book's publication, proceeded as if the task of the political philosopher was to articulate and support principles of justice on the basis of the best moral view available, on the assumption that it is morally justifiable to enforce those principles if need be (for example, to solve the assurance problem—to provide reasonable assurance to those disposed to comply with principles of justice that others will reciprocate or to prevent free riding). Rawls's assumption in *A Theory of Justice* was that one can first determine what justice requires and then ask what the circumstances are that permit enforcement of justice (such as the need to solve collective action problems that would result in noncompliance).

In contrast, in *Political Liberalism*, Rawls shows how a conception of legitimacy can in part determine the content of the principles of justice rather than merely serve as an external constraint on the enforceability of principles of justice that are derived independent of considerations of legitimacy. The significance of this view—which might be called "the primacy of legitimacy"[2]—is perhaps clearest in Rawls's application of his principle of legitimacy to the idea of an international legal order in his paper "The Law of Peoples."[3] Rawls notes that

> not all regimes can reasonably be required to be liberal, otherwise the law of peoples would not express liberalism's own principle of toleration for other reasonable ways of ordering society nor further its attempt to find a shared basis of agreement among reasonable peoples. Just as a citizen in a liberal society must respect other persons' comprehensive religious, philosophical, and moral doctrines provided they are in accordance with a reasonable political conception of justice, so a liberal society must respect other societies organized by comprehensive doctrines, provided their political and social institutions meet certain conditions that lead the society to adhere to a reasonable law of peoples.[4]

In other words, one of Rawls's chief tasks in "The Law of Peoples" is to determine how the constraints of legitimacy determine the content of principles of international justice.

Some have taken strong exception to the results of this endeavor. A number of critics, including some who were generally sympathetic to *A Theory of Justice* and *Political Liberalism*, have charged that the principles for an international legal order derived in "The Law of Peoples" are unacceptably inegalitarian, even regressively illiberal.[5] In particular, they have objected to his conclusion that a reasonable law of peoples would require only that societies respect a proper subset of what liberals usually regard as human rights, that societies should be regarded as fully legitimate even if they lack democratic institutions, make no provisions for distributive justice beyond the guarantee of subsistence for all members, do not recognize freedom of expression or of association, and include serious institutionally sanctioned inequalities between men and women or even between different castes or races. If this criticism should turn out to be valid, it would raise serious questions about the revolutionary strategy of which it is a part, the attempt to take legitimacy seriously in the process of arguing for substantive principles of justice. In order to evaluate this criticism it is necessary to reconstruct Rawls's arguments to make clearer the basis for his claim that a reasonable law of peoples would require only this truncated set of rights.

2. THE REASONABLENESS CRITERION AS A PRINCIPLE OF LEGITIMACY

In the passage cited above, Rawls states that liberalism must recognize reasonable pluralism in formulating a law of peoples: Toleration must be shown to hierarchical, that is illiberal, societies so long as they are ordered by comprehensive conceptions of the good that are reasonable. Thus, a reasonable law of peoples will be a law for reasonable peoples.

In "The Law of Peoples," Rawls says little explicitly about how the notion of reasonableness is to be applied to the comprehensive conceptions of the good that order hierarchical societies. In *Political Liberalism*, in contrast, Rawls explicitly first characterizes reasonableness as applied to persons: "Rather than define the reasonable directly, I specify two of its basic aspects as virtues of persons. Persons are reasonable in one basic aspect when, [(a)] among equals, say, they are ready to propose principles and standards as fair terms of cooperation and to abide by them willingly, given the assurance that others will likewise do so.... and [(b)] they are willing to recognize the burdens of judgment."[6] To recognize the burdens of judgment is to appreciate that there are a number of factors that can lead to reasonable disagreements among persons on matters of value, including questions of justice. Rawls says little about what this appreciation amounts to practically speaking, that is, in efforts to determine whether a conception of the good is reasonable. He does not articulate a set of minimal epistemic conditions—standards of minimal rationality that any acceptable argument for organizing a society according to a conception of the good must satisfy—and then argue that appreciation of the burdens of judgment entails that one not attempt to impose on others any principles of social order that one cannot support by arguments that satisfy those standards.

After characterizing reasonableness as applied to persons, Rawls goes on to connect the idea of the reasonable as applied to persons with that of a society organized by reasonable principles: "The reasonable is an element of the idea of society as a system of fair cooperation and that its fair terms be reasonable for all to accept is part of its idea of reciprocity."[7] It would seem to follow that a society organized according to a comprehensive conception of the good would meet the criterion of reasonableness if, and only if, that comprehensive conception could be consistently held by a reasonable person, one who is willing to propose and accept fair terms of cooperation with others as equals, assuming they are so willing, and who properly acknowledges the burdens of judgment. (We will see that the inclusion of the phrase "as equals" creates difficulties for this interpretation, but more of that later.)

According to this interpretation, Rawls's task in "The Law of Peoples" is to articulate the minimal conditions that any society must satisfy if it is to fall within the domain of the reasonable and hence be entitled to toleration, that is, to noninterference by societies organized according to different principles. And this will require showing that the society is organized according to principles that could be accepted by persons who are reasonable according to the two aspects of reasonableness (a) and (b) noted previously.

There is a striking difficulty with this line of interpretation, however, namely, the inclusion of the phrase "as among equals" in the first aspect of reasonable persons stated in the reasonableness criterion. For Rawls's point in "The Law of Peoples" is that some societies can be reasonable—ordered according to principles that reasonable persons could accept—and yet be quite inegalitarian. Indeed, at times in *Political Liberalism* Rawls seems to restrict the characterization of reasonableness to reasonable persons in a *liberal society*, as when, for example, he equates recognizing the burdens of judgment with accepting the consequences of the burdens of judgment "for the use of public reason in a constitutional [i.e., liberal] regime."[8] Similarly, Rawls sometimes refers to the principle that it is unjustifiable to impose principles upon persons who can reasonably reject them (that is, principles that are inconsistent with their reasonable conceptions of the good) as "the liberal principle of legitimacy."[9]

The difficulty is that if the notion of reasonableness (as including aspects [a] and [b] previously) is only applicable to liberal societies, then that notion cannot be used by Rawls in "The Law of Peoples" to determine which societies are entitled to be regarded as members in good standing of the society of peoples, and hence to noninterference. In other words, if the notion of reasonableness applies only to liberal societies, then it cannot be invoked to distinguish between those illiberal societies that are entitled to toleration and those that are not. But if this is the case, then we may ask, How is the latter distinction to be drawn?

In fact, in "The Law of Peoples" direct references to the notion of reasonableness, understood as including the idea of fair terms among persons as equals, are not in evidence. Instead, in that work Rawls simply sets out two conditions that a society must meet if it is to be entitled to noninterference: respect for what Rawls calls human rights properly speaking and nonexpansionism (refraining from attempting to impose its own conception of the good on other societies). Societies that are illiberal but that meet these two conditions he refers to as "well-ordered hierarchical societies."[10]

If one assumes that "The Law of Peoples" builds consistently on *Political Liberalism*, one will assume that well-ordered societies are entitled to noninterference because they are organized according to comprehensive conceptions of the good which, though illiberal, are reasonable. And one would expect that "The Law of Peoples" would argue that hierarchical comprehensive conceptions of the good can be reasonable. However, this is not how Rawls proceeds in "The Law of Peoples." As I have already suggested, the notion of the reasonable recedes into the background, or drops out of the picture altogether, in the latter work. Instead, Rawls sets out the two conditions that a hierarchical society must meet if it is to be well ordered. These questions naturally arise, then: Where do these two conditions come from? and If they are not supposed to be derivable from the two-aspects criterion of reasonableness set out in *Political Liberalism* (on the assumption that that criterion, with its emphasis on fair cooperation *among equals*, only applies to liberal societies), what reason is there to accept Rawls's two conditions? In particular, what reason is there to conclude that a society that is quite inegalitarian in its treatment of women, say, is entitled to be regarded as a member in good standing in the society of peoples so long as it respects Rawls's truncated set of human rights? The problem is that the notion of reasonableness specified in *Political Liberalism* seems inapplicable to the task of the "Law of Peoples" yet no alternative notion of reasonableness on which to base Rawls's conditions for well-ordered hierarchical societies is presented in that work.

Consider first the nonexpansionism condition. It would be natural to say that reasonable societies will be nonexpansionist because reasonableness includes as one of its aspects a recognition of the burdens of judgment and recognizing the burdens of judgment entails not attempting to impose one's own society's conception of the good on others. But if the reasonableness criterion is only to be applied in liberal societies, then this way of supporting the claim that hierarchical societies are entitled to noninterference is not available. So the question remains: If the reasonableness criterion is only a *liberal* principle of legitimacy, what grounds the nonexpansionism condition?

Next consider Rawls's second condition for well-ordered hierarchical societies in "The Law of Peoples": respect for what he deems human rights proper. This is a much leaner list of rights than those that are generally regarded as human rights. According to Rawls, hierarchical society is entitled to noninterference if (in addition to being nonexpansionist) it respects its members' rights to material subsistence; rights against religious persecution (though this is compatible with there being an established religion); rights against slavery, involuntary servitude, and forced occupations; a right to hold personal property; a right to emigrate; and a limited right to dissent at an appropriate level within what Rawls calls a "consultation hierarchy."[11] For Rawls, the list of human rights proper does not include a right to democratic governance or democratic participation, nor does it include liberal-style rights to freedom of religion, expression, or association.

In "The Law of Peoples," Rawls does offer a reason why these particular rights, and only these, must be respected by a society if that society is to be well ordered and, hence, entitled to noninterference. He asserts that hierarchical societies that are well ordered are those that are organized according to a "common good conception of justice." A common good conception of justice includes three elements: (1) "the system of laws imposes moral duties and obligations on all members of society"; (2) the conception of the good according to which the society is organized "takes impartially into account what it sees not unreasonably as the fundamental interests of all members of society"; and (3) "there is a sincere and not unreasonable belief on the part of judges and other officials who administer the legal order" that the law is indeed guided by a common good conception of justice.[12]

The idea of a common good conception of justice can provide the basis for Rawls's assertion that a hierarchical society is entitled to noninterference if we make the following assumption: The institutional embodiment of a common good conception of justice includes what Rawls calls the human rights properly speaking. The idea is that a society that did not respect those fundamental rights would not be organized by a common good conception of justice. Respecting those rights is necessary, in particular, if everyone's essential good is to be impartially taken into account. This interpretation merely pushes the puzzle back another step, however, for we can now ask, Why should we assume that a society is entitled to noninterference (assuming it is nonexpansionist) if and only if it is organized according to a common good conception of justice?

At this point there seem to be only two candidates for interpreting the structure of Rawls's view: According to interpretation one, there is a radical discontinuity between *Political Liberalism* and "The Law of Peoples." The notion of reasonableness employed in the latter plays no significant role in determining the limits of toleration in the latter, in spite of Rawls's statement at the beginning of "The Law of Peoples" that the task is to develop principles of international order which recognize that societies can be illiberal yet reasonable. Instead, an entirely new notion, that of a common good conception of justice, is foundational for determining which nonliberal societies are entitled to toleration and noninterference. In this first interpretation, the idea of a common good conception of justice and the idea of the human rights proper as the institutional embodiment of a common good conception are not grounded in the notion of reasonableness that is so central to *Political Liberalism*. One gap in Rawls's view, understood according to interpretation one, is that we still have no account of why the nonexpansionist condition is to be included in the conditions for well-ordered hierarchical societies. It appears to be simply stipulated, because there is nothing in the notion of a common good conception of justice that constrains the external relations of a society that embodies it in this or any other way.

According to interpretation two, Rawls's argument in "The Law of Peoples" goes like this:

1. A society is entitled to noninterference (and to be regarded as a member in good standing in the society of peoples) if and only if it is organized by reasonable principles.
2. Principles for organizing a society are reasonable if and only if they could be accepted by reasonable persons, that is, by those who (a) acknowledge the burdens of judgment and (b) are willing to propose and accept fair terms of cooperation.
3. Those who acknowledge the burdens of judgment will not attempt to impose their conception of the good on other societies (i.e., are nonexpansionist).
4. A society is organized on the basis of fair terms of cooperation if and only if it is organized by a common good conception of justice.

5. If a society is organized by a common good conception of justice, it will respect the human rights proper.
6. Therefore, a society is entitled to noninterference (and to be recognized as a member in good standing in the society of peoples) if and only if it is nonexpansionist and respects the human rights proper.

There is much to be said for argument 1–6, whether or not it is supported by the Rawlsian texts. The intuitive idea is that although there are and can be disputes about what counts as fair terms of cooperation, the latter notion has some minimal content that is not reasonably disputable and this minimal content is captured by the idea of a common good conception of justice, whose institutional embodiment in turn requires the human rights proper.

On the face of it, interpretation two is preferable. It not only connects "The Law of Peoples" with its predecessor *Political Liberalism* in a coherent way but also, in so doing, provides an argument (1–6) for the conclusion that there can be reasonable, though illiberal, societies and that reasonable persons will tolerate such societies. In addition, interpretation two, unlike interpretation one, accounts for both the human rights proper condition and the nonexpansionist condition.

Interpretation one, in contrast, portrays a radical discontinuity between *Political Liberalism* and "The Law of Peoples" by severing the idea of reasonableness, so central to the former, from the attempt to derive a law of peoples while supporting only one of the two conditions, respect for the human rights proper, and that only by the seemingly ad hoc stipulation that societies which satisfy the minimal standards of a common good conception of justice are entitled to noninterference. Because interpretation one fails to connect the idea of a common good conception of justice to the notion of reasonableness, it renders mysterious Rawls's introductory remark in "The Law of Peoples," cited above, that his task is to reveal the basis for an agreement "among [the] reasonable peoples of the world," for unless all societies that meet his two conditions for noninterference fall within the domain of the reasonable, this remark would make no sense.

The only difficulty with interpretation two is that it seems to be inconsistent with those passages in *Political Liberalism* in which Rawls appears to regard the "two-aspect" reasonableness criterion as a principle that applies only within liberal societies, as a distinctively liberal principle of legitimacy. If the reasonableness principle's first aspect is understood to include not only the willingness to accept and impose fair terms of cooperation but also the further liberal-sounding specification that cooperation is to be regarded as cooperation "among persons regarded as free and equal," then there is an inconsistency. However, as my formulation of the reasonableness criterion in argument 1–6 indicates, we might instead conclude that what is relevant to the law of peoples is what might be called Rawls's fundamental reasonableness criterion, one that characterizes a more general sense of reasonableness that omits this specification.

On the interpretation I am suggesting, Rawls in effect has two reasonableness criteria: a general one, or the reasonableness criterion proper, and one that includes the particular way reasonableness gets specified within the distinctive political culture of a liberal society. The former speaks only of fair terms of cooperation; the latter, of fair terms of cooperation among persons considered as free and equal. The idea of a common good conception of justice is then understood as providing the minimal content for the idea of fair cooperation—that is, fair cooperation as such, not fair cooperation among persons as free and equal.

The advantages of attributing this distinction between a general and a liberal-specific notion of reasonableness to Rawls are great. It allows us to reconstruct the central argument of "The Law of Peoples" as 1–6 while avoiding any inconsistency with those passages in *Political Liberalism* that seem to restrict the notion of reasonableness to liberal societies. And in so doing, this interpretation both presents the two works as a coherent whole and defends Rawls against the charge that his conditions for legitimate hierarchical societies are ad hoc.

For these reasons, I will proceed on the assumption that interpretation two is correct and that argument 1–6 captures the main outlines of Rawls's central argument in "The Law of Peoples." We are now in a position to see whether Rawls's attempt to introduce considerations of legitimacy into the heart of theorizing about justice is successful.

3. THE DUALITY OF JUSTICE

Perhaps the most striking conclusion Rawls reaches in the execution of this second revolution is what I shall call "the duality of justice thesis," the assertion that there are very significant differences between the principles of justice it is legitimate to enforce in a liberal democratic society and those that may be enforced in an international legal system. More specifically, as we have seen, in "The Law of Peoples" Rawls concludes that while the liberal egalitarian principles of justice he argued for in *A Theory of Justice* and in *Political Liberalism* may be justifiably enforced in a liberal democratic society such as the United States, it would be wrong to attempt to enforce them in international law because they cannot be justifiably imposed on illiberal societies. According to the duality of justice thesis, to require hierarchical societies to comply with the liberal egalitarian principles of justice that comprise Rawls's theory of justice as fairness would be to act illegitimately. The proper standard of justice for the international legal system is far less demanding: Instead of the full list of civil and political rights set out in Rawls's "Equal Liberty Principle" (which includes rights to participate in democratic government and rights to freedom of expression and freedom of religion), "the Principle of Fair Equality of Opportunity," and "the Difference Principle," all that a legitimate international legal order can require of any state is that it be nonaggressive in its foreign relations and that it respect the human rights proper.

It is worth dwelling, for a moment, on just how conservative (or regressive) Rawls's view of international law is. In "The Law of Peoples," Rawls concludes that a proper application of the notion of legitimacy yields the result that it would be wrong to try to use international legal institutions or unilateral action to compel any state to do more than respect the human rights proper in its dealings with its own citizens. This means that even states that prevent women or members of a particular racial or ethnic minority from getting an education, from voting, or from holding public office are to be regarded as fully legitimate so long as they do not threaten the physical security of such persons, provide them with a minimal of material means for subsistence, do not persecute them for their religion, and allow them to voice their views at some "appropriate" level of a consultation hierarchy (and are nonexpansionist). In Rawls's view, a state that used public resources to support a hereditary elite in luxury would be quite legitimate as long as everyone were provided with the means of subsistence.

Rawls would no doubt emphasize that the only hierarchical societies he regards as legitimate are *well-ordered* ones. Well-ordered societies are stable in the sense that their basic principles of justice are public and, when implemented over time, generate their own support. In brief, in a well-ordered society the public order is regarded as legitimate by the members of that society.

"Well-orderedness" rules out gross inequalities that can be sustained over time only by sheer brute force, but it is still compatible with gross inequalities. A sufficiently clever regime, if it lasted long enough, might gradually replace the enforcement of its principles by brute force with popular support for them by effective policies of indoctrination. Such a process would be greatly facilitated by the lack of a right to democratic participation and the lack of the liberal rights of freedom of religion and expression.

The charge that Rawls's view counts as legitimate unacceptably inegalitarian social orders is serious. However, in general, liberal critics of "The Law of Peoples" have done a better job of pointing out what they take to be the regressive implications of Rawls's duality of justice view than in showing how these implications can be avoided while at the same time taking seriously the crucial distinction between justice and legitimacy. In fact, they have neither argued that Rawls is wrong to make so much of the distinction between justice and legitimacy nor provided an alternative account of legitimacy that avoids what they take to be the regressive implications of Rawls's account. Most important, these critics have not challenged—or apparently even noticed—the fundamental theoretical stance on which Rawls's duality of justice view rests, what I have called "the primacy of legitimacy thesis." To that extent, they simply have not engaged the central features of Rawls's current view.[13]

My strategy, in contrast, is to take Rawls's distinction between justice and legitimacy seriously but to argue that Rawls is mistaken as to the implications of this distinction for a morally defensible international legal order. I argue that Rawls's view on the primacy of legitimacy as well as his particular principle of legitimacy (the general reasonableness criterion) can be preserved without the regressive implications concerning human rights that critics of "The Law of Peoples" find so disturbing. To do so, I will have to show that at least the more inegalitarian of what Rawls regards as well-ordered hierarchical societies do *not* pass the test prescribed by his legitimacy principle—or at least I will have to show that it is unwarranted to assume, as Rawls does, that such societies fall within the domain of the reasonable.

4. REASONABLENESS AND HUMAN RIGHTS

To pursue this strategy, we must examine argument 1–6 more closely. Rawls is on solid ground, I believe, when he says that reasonableness requires a common good conception of justice, for it is hard to see how terms of social cooperation that do not include the three elements of a common good conception could be regarded as fair terms of cooperation, even if fairness is understood in the most minimal way. A system of law that exempted some persons from having any moral duties or obligations would not treat those individuals as being minimally equal in the sense required for even the most austere notion of fair cooperation: They would either be above others, occupying a position of godlike privilege, or they would be beneath others (as when slaves are said to be "morally dead"—beings who are not understood to have moral obligations because they are assumed to lack moral personality). Similarly, a comprehensive conception of the good that did not impartially take into account everyone's essential interests would not be a fair basis for cooperation in even the most minimal sense; in such a system the good of some would not count at all, and hence to require their cooperation would not be fair.

Rawls's argument for the crucial premise 5 is rather terse.

> The requirement we laid down [under the idea of a common good conception of justice] was that a society's stem of law must be such as to impose duties and obligations on all its members and be regulated by what judges and other officials reasonably and sincerely believe is a common good conception of justice. We then say that for this condition to hold, the law must at least uphold such basic rights as the right to life and security, to personal property and the elements of the rule of law, as well as the right to a certain liberty of conscience [the right against religious persecution] and freedom of association [within the strictures of the social hierarchy] and the right to emigration. These we refer to as human rights.[14]

Nevertheless, the following seems plausible enough: What Rawls calls human rights appear to be institutional embodiments of the conviction that everyone's essential interests are to count in the organization of society where this, in turn, is understood to be required by the idea of fair terms of cooperation. It would be difficult to argue that a society which did not honor these basic rights could be described as being organized according to a comprehensive conception of the good that is reasonable in the sense of being acceptable to persons who are willing to accept fair terms of cooperation, even according to the least robust interpretation of fair cooperation. The question, then, is, not whether respect for Rawls's truncated list of human rights (along with nonexpansionism) is necessary for a hierarchical society to be justified in enforcing its principles of social order, and to be free from interference by other societies, but whether it is *sufficient*.

If 1–6 is the correct reconstruction of Rawls's argument, then it appears that there are only three ways one can argue that Rawls's standard for membership in the society of peoples is not sufficiently demanding, that it legitimizes unacceptably inegalitarian societies. First, one can argue that a proper acknowledgment of the burdens of judgment is compatible with rejecting as unreasonably inegalitarian some social orders that meet Rawls's minimal requirements. Second, one can argue that Rawls has construed the idea of fair terms of cooperation *too* minimally, that some extremely inegalitarian societies that meet Rawls's minimal requirements do not exemplify fair terms of cooperation. Third, one can argue that even if Rawls is correct in holding that fair terms of cooperation, as such, only require his truncated list of human rights, the secure institutional realization of those rights requires a richer set of rights, including a right to democratic government (not just a consultation hierarchy) as well as liberal-style rights to freedom of expression and freedom of association. Each of these arguments for expanding Rawls's requirements for being a member in good standing of the society of peoples will be considered in turn.

4.1. The Burdens of Judgment

Surprisingly, Rawls does not consider arguments, familiar from discourse about human rights, that gender, racial, ethnic, or caste discrimination is unjust wherever it occurs. Instead, Rawls seems simply to assume that those who offer those arguments fail to recognize the burdens of judgment—that a proper appreciation of the sources of disagreement among reasonable persons entails that all arguments against these forms of discrimination are not compelling. Or, to put the same point differently, Rawls seems to assume, without argument, that those who advocate forms of discrimination that are compatible with his truncated human rights list can support their inegalitarian views by arguments that are not unreasonable, once the burdens of judgment are properly acknowledged.

At this juncture it is important to remember that in the real world of human rights discourse, those who advocate regimes of extreme inequality are quite reasonably expected to provide arguments for those inequalities. Although I cannot of course canvass all of them here, I can indicate some of the more familiar arguments offered by the advocates of extreme inequality and suggest why I think one can criticize them effectively without failing to recognize "the burdens of judgment." On the contrary, I will suggest that the arguments typically given in favor of regimes that discriminate on the basis of race, ethnicity, caste, or gender fail to meet minimal standards for rational argumentation.

Consider a standard argument frequently offered by spokespersons for dictators or authoritarian ruling elites in developing countries: There is no universal that is, human right to democratic governance because in some societies (like this one), democratic government is incompatible with the kind of social discipline needed for effective economic development. This argument, like most if not all arguments for undemocratic institutions, rests on empirical generalizations about what does and what does not facilitate economic development or other dimensions of the common good. The effective reply to such arguments is to challenge the relevant empirical generalizations, and they are very implausible generalizations indeed. For example, there is substantial evidence that undemocratic regimes are plagued by corruption, that corruption severely retards economic development, and that undemocratic states are therefore more prone to economic disasters, such as famines.[15]

To make this point clearer, consider Rawls's conjecture that the reasonableness criterion does not rule out social orders that are deeply sexist, which systematically deprive women of rights that men enjoy without providing anything like compensating privileges for women. Consider the fate of women under the Taliban theocratic regime in Afghanistan. Reportedly, women are not allowed anything beyond the most basic education, if that, nor are they allowed to participate in political processes, to move freely outside the home, or to travel, except under very restrictive conditions. They also have virtually no rights regarding divorce, though men have substantial rights in this regard.

Surely, a proper recognition of the burdens of judgment does not preclude us from requiring that a positive defense of these inequalities be provided, nor from criticizing such a defense by pointing out that it rests either on dubious assumptions to the effect that "the essential interests" of women differ from those of men or that women are not equal to men except in the very minimal sense that their good is to count for something. My surmise is that in general, the defenders of gender, racial, ethnic, or caste inequalities tend to make just these sorts of assumptions and that the assumptions are eminently criticizable—that they fail to meet the minimal standards for moral argument that are quite compatible with, and indeed required by, a proper recognition of the burdens of judgment.

The example of racial inequalities is highly illustrative. It is sometimes said that advocates of racial inequalities believe persons should be treated differently simply because of the color of their skin. This is a gross misunderstanding of racism. Racists believe that a darker skin is merely the external mark of an inward inferiority. When pressed to justify Apartheid or Jim Crow laws, the racist appeals to a web of empirical generalizations about the moral and intellectual inferiority of blacks, assertions about the nature of black people. These generalizations can and ought to be challenged.

This is not to say that the disagreement between racists and antiracists is always purely empirical, only that it invariably includes a significant empirical element without which the racists' justifications fail in their own terms. The racist also may be wrong, not only about his generalizations concerning the intellectual inferiority and moral viciousness of blacks, but about which sorts of differences among individuals or groups are capable of providing a plausible basis for unequal treatment.

As noted earlier, Rawls supplies no account of what a proper recognition of the burdens of judgment requires when it comes to assessing the reasonableness of comprehensive conceptions of the good. He provides no set of epistemic standards for empirical claims used in arguments to justify inequalities nor any minimal standards for reasonable inferences. However, reflections on the sorts of justifications actually given for extremely inegalitarian regimes suggest that any plausible account of the burdens of judgment is likely to rule out much more than Rawls assumes.

It might be objected that some who advocate gender, racial, ethnic, or caste inequalities (or undemocratic regimes) do not defend them in these ways. They simply claim that the inequalities are required by the revealed doctrines of their comprehensive religious conceptions of the good. To this I would reply that however the burdens of judgment are to be understood, it would be implausible, especially for a Rawlsian, to hold that rejecting such a "purely religious" justification for serious inequalities constitutes a failure to recognize the burdens of judgment. On the contrary, it is the person who refuses to give reasons to support such inequalities—beyond claiming that they are required by his religious doctrines—who cannot be regarded as having properly recognized the burdens of judgment and, hence, who cannot be regarded as reasonable.

Properly recognizing the burdens of judgment, in a world containing not only different religious conceptions of the good but secular ones as well, requires that argumentation concerning what counts as "fair terms of cooperation" *among human beings* be framed primarily in terms of the interests of *human beings*, considered in their own right. By asserting that reasonableness requires at least that a comprehensive conception of the good that is to serve as the basis for organizing society must recognize the minimal freedom and equality of persons captured by the idea of a common good conception of justice, Rawls himself admits as much. But once we go this far, the burden of justification lies on those who support inequalities beyond this minimum, and that burden cannot be born simply by making religious claims that are not accessible to those who hold reasonable secular views. Given that what is at issue is fair terms of cooperation among human beings, defenders of ethnic, racial, caste, or gender inequalities must support their views with reasons that engage directly with the interests of those who are expected to participate in such a cooperative scheme.

Rawls's notion of acknowledging the burdens of judgment is unfortunately one-sided. It counsels humility—a clear-eyed recognition that, for a number of reasons, there can be disagreement about values and justice among reasonable persons. Humility is not the only relevant virtue, however. In fact, it is at best only half the story; there is also the need for an acknowledgment of justificatory *responsibility*, for acknowledging that justifications for coercively backed principles of social order must meet minimal standards of argumentation. In other words, reasonableness requires humility as well as responsibility, a recognition that reasonable people can agree but also a recognition that reasonable peoples' arguments meet minimal critical standards. This second, equally crucial, dimension of reasonableness is not discussed by Rawls.

There is another difficulty with Rawls's assumption that well-ordered hierarchical societies that respect his list of human rights proper are reasonably organized. Rawls maintains that all that is necessary for a hierarchical society to be legitimate, so far as religious freedom goes, is that it not persecute religious minorities. It is permissible for there to be a state religion: "A hierarchical society may have an established religion with certain privileges. Still, it is essential to its being well-ordered that no religions are persecuted or denied civic and social conditions that permit their practice in peace and, of course, without fear."[16] The problem is that this limited right to religious freedom appears to be compatible with arrangements that seem to violate the reasonableness criterion—that involve the coercive imposition of rules of public order upon persons who cannot accept them from the standpoint of their reasonable comprehensive religious conceptions.[17] Suppose, for example, there are compulsory holidays according to the state religion or that it is illegal to engage in business activities on Saturday. Or suppose that all women, whether they are Muslim or not, are required by law to wear a veil in public. Such arrangements are compatible with members of minority religions being free to practice their religion without fear (we are assuming that their religious doctrines do not make refraining from work on Saturday or wearing a veil in public *impermissible*). Nonetheless, these tenets of another religion are being imposed by the coercive power of the state. Here, then, is another area in which Rawls has failed to show that social orders that respect what he takes to be the human rights pass his reasonableness test.

4.2. Fair Terms of Cooperation

I have already noted that Rawls is on firm ground when he asserts that respect for his truncated list of human rights is necessary for meeting the standard of fair terms of cooperation. The question, however, is whether it is also sufficient, as he assumes.

It is very important at this point to understand upon whom the burden of argument lies. Given that fair terms of cooperation at least require the minimal equality and freedom embodied in the idea of a common good conception of justice—that everyone's basic interests are to count for something and that everyone is to have moral obligations and duties—the proper question to ask is, How are inequalities (regarding gender, race, ethnicity, caste, or the distribution of political power) compatible with the terms of cooperation being fair?

Notice that Rawls's account of reasonableness is not directed toward those who would deny that they are bound to take the requirements of fair cooperation into account—those who instead say that fairness has nothing to do with it, that only the revealed will of God, or the pursuit of some perfectionist ideal, counts. Rawls is assuming that reasonableness, at least as it applies to conceptions of justice, requires a commitment to finding fair terms of cooperation. This point is extremely important since it implies that if inequalities are to fall within the domain of the reasonable, they must be consistent with the idea of fair cooperation.

However, Rawls seems to be insufficiently appreciative of how difficult it would be to justify the extreme inequalities of the Taliban regime or of the traditional Hindu caste system by appeal to the idea of fair cooperation. It is interesting to note that in general, it is efficiency, or the maximization of social good, that is typically appealed to in order to justify such inequalities when anything beyond purely religious "reasons" are offered in support of them. I have already suggested that such appeals to efficiency or the optimal social good appear invariably to rest on false empirical claims (about what is needed for economic stability or for development or about the natural differences between those at the top and those at the bottom of the social hierarchy). Quite apart from this, however, the crucial point is that if we take Rawls's reasonableness criterion seriously, any attempt to justify inequalities by appeals to efficiency or the maximization of the common good is ruled out as irrelevant if the inequalities in question cannot be shown to be compatible with the terms of cooperation being fair. Rawls is on very shaky ground when he assumes that the extreme forms of discrimination that are compatible with his account of a well-ordered hierarchical society can be reconciled with a commitment to fair terms of cooperation.

Showing that an extremely inegalitarian social order is compatible with fair terms of cooperation would require more than supporting claims about the natural differences between men and women or blacks and whites or untouchables and Brahmins in a way that meets the minimal epistemic standards that are properly included in the idea of acknowledging the burdens of judgment. Thus, for example, even if reasonable empirical support could be mustered for generalizations to the effect that certain racial groups or women rank lower according to objective measures of some desirable "natural" characteristics, the burden would still be on the advocate of racial or gender inequality to show why it is that *these* differences warrant unequal treatment in the social system. And this, in turn, would entail showing how a social system that based unequal treatment on these differences would meet the requirement of being a *fair* system of cooperation—not just one that maximized the good or was efficient or attained some perfectionist ideal.

It is worth emphasizing that nowhere in *Political Liberalism* or in "The Law of Peoples" does Rawls engage actual or possible defenses of inegalitarian social orders. He merely assumes or conjectures that those who recognize the burdens of judgment must concede that such inequalities fall within the domain of the reasonable, that they count as fair terms of cooperation.

I do not presume to have shown that all arguments for hierarchical arrangements are so defective that no departures from the liberal rights Rawls advocates in his theory of justice as fairness can count as reasonable in Rawls's sense. I believe I have shown, however, two things: First, Rawls's assumption that seriously inegalitarian, undemocratic societies fall within the realm of the reasonable is an unsupported conjecture; second, the burden of argument lies on those who contend that such societies can be supported by reasonable comprehensive conceptions of the good. I have also *suggested* that in general, that burden of argument has not been met successfully, though I do not pretend to have justified that generalization.

4.3. The Insecurity of Rawlsian Human Rights

Rawls assumes that his truncated list of human rights makes institutional sense without the addition of other rights typically regarded as human. But this assumption is dubious. Rawls does not address the familiar and plausible view that one cannot consistently advocate what he calls the human rights properly speaking and at the same time deny the right to democratic governance. The familiar claim is that in general and in the long run, the only reliable way to secure Rawlsian human rights is to make the government that is responsible for enforcing them subject to the controls that democratic processes provide.

Rawls assumes, without argument, that a society that includes what he calls a consultation hierarchy will reliably secure what he calls the human rights properly speaking, even in the absence of a multiparty political system, liberal-style freedom of expression and association, and a universal or even broad franchise that empowers citizens to vote at least on who will represent them in the making of the most basic laws. It is hard to evaluate this assumption, in part because Rawls says so little about what a consultative hierarchy includes. He does say that judges and other officials in a consultation hierarchy are bound to listen to voices of dissent. However, the idea that consultation is hierarchical seems to imply that persons are not allowed to address officials at the upper end of the hierarchy directly, and the qualifier "consultative" presumably implies that dissenters have no institutionally recognized power to try to influence social policy, as they would have if they had the right to vote and to form political parties. If this is so, then it appears that the government of a society that includes only a consultative hierarchy is less likely, other things being equal, to be held accountable by its citizens than one that is democratic. Therefore, it would also appear that, other things being equal, Rawlsian human rights will tend to be more secure in a democratic society than in a society that includes only a consultation hierarchy.

Earlier I noted that some who have been sympathetic to Rawls's views have expressed alarm over the apparently regressive character of his current views about human rights, but if my arguments are sound, this concern may be misplaced or at least exaggerated. Critical to my account is a distinction between what Rawls's notion of legitimacy requires and what he assumes it to require. In my view, the notion of reasonableness on which Rawlsian legitimacy rests places more substantial constraints on inequalities than Rawls himself believes it does. A plausible understanding of the burdens of judgment and the idea of fair terms of cooperation carries us beyond the truncated list of Rawlsian human rights and much closer to what might be called the mainstream of contemporary human rights doctrine.

5. THE LAW OF PEOPLES RECONSIDERED

If my analysis is correct, then Rawls's formulation of a rather austere (or regressive) law of peoples is premature at best. He is not entitled to conclude that his principle of legitimacy (the reasonableness criterion) bars international enforcement of anything beyond the extremely lean set of rights he calls the human rights proper. He is not entitled to this conclusion because he has done nothing to show that respect for the "basic" human rights is sufficient, not just necessary, for reasonableness. If this is the case, then recognizing what I have called the primacy of legitimacy may be compatible with a law of peoples that is much more egalitarian than Rawls supposes.

Notes

I am grateful to Thomas Christiano for his helpful comments on an earlier draft of this chapter.

1. David Estlund, "The Survival of Egalitarian Justice in John Rawls's *Political Liberalism*," *Journal of Political Philosophy* 4, no. 1 (1996): 68.

2. The phrase "primacy of legitimacy" is not intended to mean that considerations of legitimacy have priority over considerations of justice; it is simply a denial of the claim that what is just can be determined independent of considerations of legitimacy.

3. John Rawls, "The Law of Peoples," in *On Human Rights: The Oxford Amnesty Lectures 1993*, ed. Stephen Shute and Susan Hurley (New York: Basic Books, 1993), 42–82. Rawls expanded his views in a work entitled *The Law of Peoples* published by Harvard University Press in 1999.

4. Ibid., 43.

5. Fernando R. Tesón, *A Philosophy of International Law* (Boulder, Colo.: Westview Press, 1998), 107–21; Darrel Moellendorf, "Constructing the Law of Peoples," *Pacific Philosophic Quarterly* 77, no. 2 (1996): 135–44; Kok-Chor Tan, "Liberal Toleration in Rawls's Law of Peoples," *Ethics* 108 (January 1998): 283–85.

6. John Rawls, *Political Liberalism* (New York: Columbia University Press, 1993), 49 (unless otherwise noted, in this chapter references to *Political Liberalism* are to the 1993 edition).

7. Ibid., 49–50.

8. Ibid., 54.

9. John Rawls, *Political Liberalism*, pbk. ed. (Cambridge, Mass.: Harvard University Press, 1996), xlvi, 136.

10. Rawls, *Political Liberalism*, 60–61.

11. Rawls, "Law of Peoples," 62–68.

12. Ibid., 53.

13. This evaluation applies to the criticisms in Tesón, *A Philosophy of International Law*; Moellendorf, "Constructing the Law of Peoples"; and Tan, "Liberal Toleration," as well as by others.

14. Rawls, "Law of Peoples," 57.

15. See, for example, Amartya Sen, *Poverty and Famines: An Essay on Entitlement and Deprivation* (Oxford: Oxford University Press, 1981).

16. Rawls, *Political Liberalism*, 53.

17. I am indebted to Thomas Christiano for clarifying this point.

2

TAKING THE HUMAN OUT OF HUMAN RIGHTS

1. RAWLS'S COMMITMENT TO AVOIDING PAROCHIALISM

One of the most valuable features of *The Law of Peoples* is the unflinching acknowledgment of the need to develop a conception of human rights that is not vulnerable to the objection that human rights are parochial—more precisely, that what are called human rights are merely rights suitable for members of liberal societies. It is at least in part because he takes the problem of parochialism so seriously that in order to avoid it he is willing to reduce the list of human rights found in the six major human rights conventions by more than 50 percent.[1] For Rawls parochialism is a grievous deficiency from a liberal perspective because it signals a failure to honor what he takes to be the liberal commitment to tolerance, which in turn requires reciprocity of justification: the principles to which we hold others must be such that they cannot reasonably reject them, at least so far as their comprehensive moral views are themselves not unreasonable.

In this chapter I critically examine Rawls's response to the parochialism objection. I will argue that Rawls's approach can be understood as an attempt to ground a theory of human rights without recourse to a conception of minimal human good and indeed without reliance on the idea that there are any morally fundamental characteristics that all human beings have. In that respect, I shall argue, the most distinctive feature of Rawls's theory is not that he takes the parochialism objection seriously, but that in order to rebut it he develops a theory of human rights in which the idea that these rights are grounded in our humanity is conspicuously absent. I will show that Rawls's reasons for eschewing the idea of humanity are not cogent and that his arguments for shortening the list of human rights are unconvincing.

Rawls's List of Human Rights

Rawls's list of human rights does *not* include the right to freedom from religious discrimination, but rather only the right to freedom from religious persecution, understood as the right to freedom of religious thought and to practice one's religion "without fear." Nor does it include a right to freedom from other forms of discrimination—including systematic, institutionalized, public discrimination—on grounds of race, gender, ethnicity, nationality, or sexual orientation. Beyond the right to subsistence and a wholly unspecified right to personal property, so-called welfare rights of any kind are also absent. So it appears that for Rawls a society in which there is a permanent racial, ethnic, religious, or gender underclass, hovering just above subsistence, systematically excluded from the more desirable economic positions, having grossly inferior property rights, lacking access to education and health care services available to the dominant classes, unable to afford legal counsel and bereft of sophisticated due process protections available to others, would *not* be a society in which those who were thus disadvantaged could complain that their human rights were violated.[2]

No Aid from Kazanistan

It is true that Rawls's brief description of Kazanistan, his hypothetical example of a nonliberal ("hierarchical") decent society, is not so bleak. However, Rawls gives us no reason to believe that a society whose respect for human rights was limited to his truncated list of rights would be as tolerant as Kazanistan. Our understanding of Rawls's conception of human rights must be based on his arguments, not on his very sketchy and misleading example of a nonliberal, but decent society. Perhaps a nonliberal society *could* be as benign as Kazanistan, but that is beside the point.[3] The question is whether the implementation of Rawls's austere conception of human rights would provide adequate protection against egregious discrimination. It would not.[4]

Given that Rawls's attempt to avoid the charge of parochialism appears to lead him to a truncated list of human rights whose implementation is compatible with severe discrimination and oppression, it behooves us to examine critically the arguments by which Rawls arrives at this unsettling destination. Although the text of *The Law of Peoples* is arguably more ambiguous than Rawls's other works,

I believe four mutually compatible lines of argument can be distinguished. The first, the Political Conception Argument, begins with the idea, taken from *Political Liberalism*, that avoiding parochialism requires not relying upon *comprehensive conceptions of morality or the good*.[5] The second, the Associationist Argument, holds that any attempt to ground human rights in a conception of basic *human* interests would be biased against and hence intolerant of what Rawls calls "associative social forms," because this type of society "sees individuals first as members of groups" within society, rather than as having certain interests common to all human beings. The third, the Cooperation Argument, attempts to derive Rawls's lean list of rights from intuitions about what it is for a society to be a form of cooperation as opposed to a command system based on force and about the moral significance of cooperation. The fourth, or Functionalist Argument, tries to derive Rawls's list of human rights from the assumption that the distinctive function of human rights norms is that their violation supplies grounds for interventions across borders.

2. AVOIDING PAROCHIALISM BY AVOIDING COMPREHENSIVE CONCEPTIONS

In the following passage from *The Law of Peoples* Rawls appears to say that unless a theory of human rights avoids reliance on a comprehensive moral conception, it will be parochial and for that reason unacceptable. The implication is that a more expansive list of human rights than his, in particular one that includes rights distinctive of liberal societies, must rely on a comprehensive moral conception.

> [Human] rights do not depend upon any particular comprehensive religious doctrine or philosophical doctrine of human nature. The Law of Peoples does not say, for example, that human beings are moral persons and have equal worth in the eyes of God: or that they have certain moral and intellectual powers that entitle them to these rights. To argue in any of these ways would involve religious and philosophical doctrines that many decent hierarchical peoples might [not unreasonably] reject as liberal or democratic, or as in some way distinctive of Western political tradition and prejudicial to other cultures.[6]

Political versus Comprehensive Conceptions

For Rawls comprehensive and political conceptions differ in scope. In *Political Liberalism*, where the contrast is introduced, we are told that political conceptions are conceived of as applying to only a part of the domain of morality—the political realm of public principles of justice for the regulation of the basic structure of a society—while comprehensive conceptions speak to a wider range of subjects, including "what is of value in human life, and ideals of personal character, as well as ideals of friendship and of familial and associational relationships, and much else that is to inform our conduct, and in the limit to our life as a whole."[7] Political conceptions, in contrast, address individuals only as citizens, not as whole moral persons. Comprehensive conceptions and political conceptions differ epistemically as well: Comprehensive conceptions claim to be true while political conceptions claim only reasonableness.[8]

Given that Rawls sees *The Law of Peoples* as building on *Political Liberalism*, it is hardly surprising that in the former he holds that a theory of human rights must not rely upon any comprehensive moral conception. But in the first passage above he seems to be saying more than this—that to avoid parochialism a theory of human rights cannot include the idea that human rights are grounded in characteristics that all human beings have, such as certain "moral and intellectual powers." So the question arises: Must any theory of human rights that grounds these rights in characteristics that all human beings have rely on a comprehensive moral conception? Alternatively, to be a political conception in the sense required to avoid parochialism must a theory of human rights avoid reference to common human characteristics in its justification of a list of human rights?

Rawls versus the Dominant Philosophical View

It is clear enough that the dominant contemporary philosophical theories of human rights all hold that human rights are grounded in certain common characteristics of human beings. For example, James Nickel, Henry Shue, Amartya Sen, and Martha Nussbaum each ground human rights in common characteristics of human beings—more specifically, in a conception of basic human interests (or of central human capabilities in the cases of Sen and Nussbaum) understood as those interests that must be realized (or those capabilities that an individual must have) if a human being is to have the opportunity to live a *decent* or *minimally* good life.[9] It is also clear that all of these theories are intended to support longer lists of rights than Rawls's.

In grounding more extensive lists of human rights in characteristics common to all human beings these theorists scrupulously avoid at least one key feature of comprehensive conceptions of the good that does seem to run the risk of parochialism: These theories do not purport to apply to all or even most subjects in the domain of morality and they do not rely on anything approaching a full specification of human good. Because they assume that human rights are in some importance sense *minimal moral standards*, all of these theorists hold that the appropriate benchmark is a decent or minimally good human life, not the best human life or a fully good human life. The point is that an account of the conditions for having the opportunity to have a minimally good human life is agnostic as to the question of whether an encompassing theory of morality, one that covers all moral subjects, is even possible. Such theories are simply silent on most of the subjects within the domain of theories of morality; thus they have nothing approaching the scope of comprehensive conceptions. To the extent that their claims are modest in this way, the risk of parochialism is reduced.

Nor is it at all clear that these theories have the epistemic characteristic of comprehensive conceptions, namely an insistence on the truth of the human rights norms they ground. Little or nothing seems to be lost if we interpret them as holding that their claims about the moral significance of basic human interests (or fundamental human capabilities) are justified while remaining agnostic as to whether, or in what sense, such claims are strictly speaking true.

Yet all such theories fail to meet *one* of Rawls's criteria for being political conceptions, even if they satisfy the others, and they are therefore comprehensive conceptions in Rawls's special sense, in spite of their minimalism: There is a (quite limited) sense in which they extend beyond "the political." For even if all of these theories of human rights apply primarily to the basic structure of society, they all also seem to include some human rights norms that apply, under some circumstances, to other areas of human life as well. Given their accounts of the preeminent moral importance of not undercutting human beings' basic interests (or capabilities), all seem to imply that individuals or groups can violate human rights in extra-institutional ways. In addition, they all include characterizations (though minimal ones) of human beings as such, not simply of human beings as *citizens*, viewed from the standpoint of their being subject to political institutions that are to meet standards of justice, and perhaps this too counts as having a scope that exceeds the political.

Suppose that we grant that the dominant contemporary theories are all, strictly speaking, comprehensive, not political conceptions in Rawls's sense. Does it follow from their being comprehensive conceptions in this very special sense that they are parochial and for that reason unacceptable? Why should the mere fact that a theory of human rights has some implications beyond the political realm make it parochial?

Why Comprehensive Conceptions Are Supposed to Be Parochial

To answer this crucial question one must understand why Rawls thinks it is necessary to restrict the inquiry to political conceptions. In *Political Liberalism*, Rawls makes it clear that the point of relying on political conceptions and avoiding comprehensive ones is that doing so is required by a proper acknowledgment of "the fact of reasonable pluralism." In *The Law of Peoples* it seems to be "the fact of not unreasonable pluralism" that underlies the insistence that a conception of human rights be political, not comprehensive. Rawls thinks that the conceptions of the good or of morality that distinguish certain nonliberal societies are "not unreasonable" and that a more expansive list of human rights would express an intolerant attitude toward them. The assumption here is that if someone can "not unreasonably" reject a principle, it is intolerant to impose it on them and violates the requirement of reciprocity of justification.

However, *if* the claims about basic human interests (or capabilities) that a theory relies on to ground a list of human rights are *justified*, then the fact that such theories are not political conceptions in Rawls's sense—the fact that they include elements whose applicability extends somewhat beyond "the political"—seems irrelevant to the question of whether they are parochial. What matters is whether the claims are sufficiently justified; if they are, then it is unreasonable to deny them, and attempting to implement the human rights norms in question may not be parochial or intolerant in the sense of imposing an alien conception on those whose rejection of it is not unreasonable.

Remarkably, Rawls never directly addresses any of the interest-based (or capabilities-based) theories of human rights. He never argues explicitly that any such claims about morally significant common human characteristics ("moral and intellectual powers," etc.) are unjustifiable. Instead, he appears simply to dismiss all such theories because they exemplify *one* of his criteria for being comprehensive, as opposed to political—some of their key concepts apply beyond the political realm. Yet the connection between failing to meet this one criterion and being parochial is tenuous at best.

It is not my aim here to provide a convincing defense of the dominant approach to theorizing about human rights that Rawls dismisses, though I think this can be done. Instead, I simply want to emphasize how intuitively implausible it is to say that the mere fact that a theory of human rights (a) includes norms that in some cases apply to individual actions, not simply to the basic structure of society, and to that extent addresses individuals as human beings, not strictly as citizens of this or that polity, and (b) grounds human rights in characteristics common to all human beings, somehow disqualifies it from serious consideration because any such theory must be parochial and therefore intolerant.

The objection that the dominant contemporary theories of human rights are parochial deserves to be taken seriously; I do not mean to deny that. But whether they are parochial can only be determined by scrutinizing the content of the theories—in particular their claims about what the basic human interests are and their moral significance—and the institutional processes that allow for the ongoing criticism and revision of the norms in question. They cannot be ruled out as parochial simply because they have features (a) and (b).

No doubt Rawls would reply that he provides the needed argument in *Political Liberalism*—that there he has shown that the only proper response to the fact of reasonable pluralism is to develop a political conception of justice. But of course it is precisely the soundness of the central argument of *Political Liberalism* that is in question here. Those who hold that there are justifiable claims about morally significant basic human interests (or capabilities) needn't reject Rawls's claim that tolerance requires refraining from espousing conceptions of justice that others can reasonably (or not unreasonably) reject. Instead they can argue that the claims about human interests (or capabilities) on which they ground a list of human rights are sufficiently justified that they cannot be reasonably rejected. Or, perhaps more plausibly, they can reject Rawls's assumption that it is intolerant to apply a conception of justice to anyone who can reasonably (or not unreasonably) reject it and hold instead that what matters is whether we are sufficiently justified in holding the theory of justice we apply to them and whether the concrete efforts to implement that theory manifest the values that underlie tolerance, including respect for others' convictions and a proper appreciation of our own fallibility.

One reason for preferring the second alternative is an understandable skepticism about the usefulness of the notion of what cannot unreasonably be rejected. The problem, as many critics have noted, is that Rawls says far too little about what counts as reasonableness or the lack thereof. In one sense, we can well imagine cases where, given his systematically distorted belief system, it would not be unreasonable for someone to deny that certain rights are human rights, for example, those that protect women from serious and systematic discrimination. In one sense people who have only known life in an extremely sexist society may "not unreasonably" reject a more expansive list of human rights that includes equal rights for women—*if* what is not unreasonable for an individual to believe can depend upon the character of his or her overall system of beliefs. But even if that is so, it doesn't follow that efforts to secure the rights of women through the power of law in such societies are necessarily intolerant. To show that they are, one would need to do more than merely assert that tolerance requires not imposing on people principles that they can "not unreasonably" reject. If the reason why someone can "not unreasonably" reject a human rights norm is that his conception of morality is seriously distorted by indefensible beliefs about the natural inferiority of women, then it may not be intolerant to impose that norm on him. Surprisingly, Rawls never engages the question of whether meeting minimal epistemic standards is necessary for being entitled to toleration.[10]

To summarize: Rawls's view that if it is to avoid parochialism a theory of human rights must be a political, not a comprehensive conception, is not convincing and therefore does not supply a good reason for dismissing attempts to ground human rights in some set of morally significant characteristics common to all individuals. Interest-based (and capabilities-based) theories, being quite minimalist, need not be "comprehensive" in any sense that entails parochialism. Nor does the Rawlsian principle that it is illegitimate to impose principles on others that they can reasonably (or not unreasonably) reject, provide a cogent reason for assuming that any such theories are parochial and dismissing them out of hand.

3. TOLERANCE TOWARD ASSOCIATIONIST CONCEPTIONS OF INDIVIDUAL GOOD

The key passage for this argument is one in which Rawls says that his list of human rights can be accounted for in two ways: One is to view them "as belonging to a reasonably just liberal political conception of justice...The other is to view them as belonging to an associationist social form...which sees persons first as members of groups..."[11]

Presumably the point of saying that an associationist social form sees persons "first" as members of groups is that in such a society what might be called an individual's *associative* (or *ascriptive*) *identity* is primary, in the sense that there is no more fundamental conception of an individual's good that is not tied to her being a member of this or that group within society. An associationist conception of individual good, then, is one according to which an individual's basic interests cannot be specified without reference to his or her identity as a member of this or that group (corporation, estate, etc.).[12]

Are Appeals to Basic Human Interests Illegitimate?

If this interpretation is correct, Rawls is saying two things in this passage that have momentous import for his conception of human rights. First, he is saying that although the individual's good is conceived in a *nonassociationist* way in *liberal* societies, in that certain basic interests are ascribed to all individuals regardless of their group affiliation or social role, in *nonliberal* societies (or at least some of them, those that are "associationist social forms") an individual's good is *not* understood in this way. Instead, in "associationist social forms" any characterization of the individual's good is irreducibly social, and indeed not just social, but *particularistic* in the sense that the good of an individual cannot even be characterized simply by reference to his or her membership in a particular society, but also must include reference to her particular associative identity within that society.[13] Second, Rawls is saying—or at least implying—that it would be wrong to construct a list of human rights that ignores the fact that the individual's good is conceived in an associationist way in (at least some) nonliberal societies. Any conception of basic *human* interests assumes that it is possible to characterize a set of conditions necessary for *any* human being to have a good human life, and this is inconsistent with the view that what is necessary for a good life for an individual varies depending upon his or her membership in this or that corporation, association, or estate, and upon the role of that group in his or her society. That seems to be the point of his remark that his human rights—as distinct from what he takes to be the inflated conventional list—*can* be conceived of from the associationist standpoint. The idea is that to be legitimate a list of human rights must be accessible to members of associationist social forms, and this means that it cannot ground human rights on any conception of basic human interests, interests that all human beings have. The *point* of the passage seems to be that his list of human rights meets this criterion of accessibility and that this counts in favor of it; otherwise, the passage is mysterious.

According to this interpretation, Rawls is (1) stating that a theory of human rights grounded in a conception of interests that all human beings have would not be acceptable from the standpoint of (some) nonliberal societies, due to their associationist conceptions of individual good, *and* (2) assuming that reliance on a standpoint that is unacceptable to such nonliberal societies is illegitimate.

There are two distinct reasons why Rawls might think that it is illegitimate to ground a list of human rights in a conception of individual good that is not acceptable in societies in which the conception of individual good is associationist. First, he might think that in fact *there are no basic human interests.* In other words, Rawls might believe that Sen, Nussbaum, Nickel, Shue, and others who hold that there are conditions that must be satisfied for any human to have the opportunity for a good life are simply wrong. Instead, there are simply the conditions necessary for a good life for members of a liberal society, on the one hand, and, in the case of nonliberal, associationist societies, the various conditions necessary for a good life for this or that individual, as a member of this or that association, in this or that society, on the other.

On the first interpretation, Rawls is denying that there can be an objectivist conception of human rights, a conception of human rights based on facts about the basic interests of all individuals, because *there are no such facts.* In my judgment, there is no textual evidence in favor of this first interpretation, and the following statement, which follows immediately after the passage cited above about associationist social forms, counts against it: "…The Law of Peoples does not deny these doctrines."[14]

On the second interpretation Rawls is agnostic—or at least noncommittal—as to whether there are certain basic interests common to all individuals. Instead, his claim is that the existence of basic human interests is sufficiently controversial that it would be *intolerant* to construct a list of human rights grounded on these interests. According to the second interpretation, Rawls believes that those who deny that there are basic human interests are not unreasonable and that if they are not unreasonable it is illegitimate to impose upon them a conception of human rights that relies on the assumption that there are basic human interests.

Human Interests, Parochialism, and Intolerance

Are there any basic human interests, understood as conditions that are generally necessary and sufficient for the opportunity to lead a decent or minimally good human life (and hence necessary conditions for a good human life)? Some obvious candidates are the interest in avoiding torture, in physical security, and in not being enslaved.

Notice that what is at stake here is *how* one argues for human rights—whether or not it is legitimate to appeal to basic human interests—not whether Rawls, who on my interpretation claims to eschew any such appeal, includes among the human rights any rights that can be grounded in basic human interests.

My aim here is not to make a conclusive case that there are basic human interests, much less to ground a theory of human rights in them and then show conclusively that such a theory would support a significantly more expansive list of rights than Rawls's. The mainstream human rights theorists noted above all have written sophisticated, closely reasoned volumes to do just that. My objective, rather, is to make clear how much of a departure from the mainstream Rawls's approach is and to demonstrate how unconvincing his reasons for pursuing it are. Consequently, I will focus primarily on how implausible it is to say that grounding human rights in basic human interests is illegitimate if one believes, as the mainstream theorists do, that there are basic human interests.

The key point is that there is nothing *parochial* about grounding human rights in basic human interests if, as seems clear enough, such interests exist. To say that a theory of human rights is parochial is to say that it is based on a partial, or narrow, or unduly circumscribed perspective—that it leaves out something of relevance. A theory of human rights based on interests that are common to all human beings is not based on a parochial conception of human good, if this means a conception of human good that is appropriate only for human beings in this or that particular society. To take the examples of basic human interests noted above, human beings have an interest in being able to avoid torture and violent death and in having enough to eat, regardless of what sort of society they live in. So such a conception of human rights is not parochial; nor, consequently, is it intolerant by virtue of being parochial. It is true that it counts as a "comprehensive conception" in Rawls's peculiar sense because, as I noted earlier, it has implications beyond "the political," even though it relies only on a minimalist conception of the good and does not claim to cover a wide range of subjects in the domain of morality or value. However, as I have argued, that one feature of what Rawls calls comprehensive conceptions alone does not justify the charge of parochialism.

If anything is parochial here, it is to deny that there are basic human interests or capabilities because one is so enmeshed in an "associationist social form" that one cannot conceive of an individual as having any interests or capabilities apart from those ascribed to her in virtue of the particular social identity she has in her own particular society. In other words, if there are basic human interests or capabilities, as it certainly appears there are, then to be limited in one's conception of individual good in the way Rawls attributes to members of associationist social forms is to hold a parochial view, one that fails to look beyond the confines of one's own society and one's particular place in it to recognize something that is common to all human beings. If this kind of parochialism is what causes people in certain societies to reject some of the conventional human rights, then the assumption that their views are "not unreasonable"—and for that reason are entitled to tolerance—is dubious at best.

Furthermore, if the goal is to be tolerant, there are many ways in which this can be achieved in the process of attempting to promulgate and institutionalize a theory of human rights that is grounded in assumptions about basic human interests or capabilities, without abandoning the whole enterprise. Tolerance can be given its due in many aspects of the institutionalized processes of formulating human rights conventions and devising procedures to monitor compliance with their norms. For example, provision can be made, as it is in the current institutionalization of human rights, for ensuring that the various adjudication and compliance monitoring processes through which the content of human rights norms is specified and critically revised over time include inputs from a variety of cultural perspectives, under conditions of accurate information about what sorts of institutional arrangements are needed to protect human beings' basic interests.

If, as I have suggested, what is most distinctive about Rawls's approach to human rights is his rejection of the mainstream assumption that human rights are grounded in basic human interests, then one would expect that his international hypothetical agreement argument for his list of human rights would reflect this fact. I now want to argue that it does. In the next section I show that there is a plausible interpretation of the most controversial feature of Rawls's international hypothetical agreements that also supports my hypothesis that Rawls holds that it is illegitimate to ground a list of human rights on any conception of basic interests all human beings have because doing so is inconsistent with the way peoples with "associationist social forms" conceive of an individual's good.

Rawls's International Hypothetical Agreement

A number of Rawls's critics have taken issue with the hypothetical agreement derivation of Rawlsian human rights.[15] Here I will focus on what I take to be the most obviously problematic feature of the hypothetical contract argument and show that it can be seen as a consequence of Rawls's rejection of the possibility of an account of human rights that grounds them in basic human interests.

Rawls says that both representatives of liberal and of decent nonliberal peoples would agree that all peoples are to respect his shortened list of human rights and that any society that respects these rights is entitled to nonintervention.[16] The crucial point—and the one that has drawn the most critical fire—is that for Rawls the choosers represent peoples, not individuals. Rawls asserts that the representatives of liberal peoples and of nonliberal decent peoples would choose the same principles for an international legal order, including the same list of human rights.[17]

Why Peoples, Not Individuals?

The obvious question, for anyone who takes the international human rights movement seriously, is why the hypothetical agreements that determine the most fundamental principles of the international legal order should only include choosers representing peoples, not individuals. Given that the first modern human rights conventions were in large part a conscious response to the Holocaust—in which millions of individuals were slaughtered by their own government in the name of a people (the German *Volk*)—one would think that the hypothetical international contract should include choosers who represent individuals. (Whether or not there should be a two-stage agreement that includes choices by representatives of groups and by representatives of individuals is another matter, and one that I have explored elsewhere.[18]) The result of not including representatives of individuals is a list of human rights sharply constrained by what is acceptable from the standpoint of nonliberal peoples, whose political cultures do not include the idea that society should be a system of fair cooperation among free and equal individuals.

Rawls believes that the parties must be representatives of peoples, not individuals, if the principles chosen are to remain within the bounds of tolerance. In the only passage in which he responds explicitly to those who criticize his assumption that the parties should be representatives of peoples, not of individuals, he suggests that it would be parochial, and hence intolerant, to conceive of the parties as representing individuals *as liberals conceive them*—as free and equal participants in cooperation:

> Some think that any liberal Law of Peoples, particularly any social contract [*sic*, any social contract theory of?] such law, should begin by first taking up the question of cosmopolitan or global justice for all persons.[19]

Here Rawls is addressing those who say that a law of peoples should be derived from a hypothetical agreement among representatives of individuals, and hence cosmopolitan, so far as cosmopolitanism takes individuals as morally primary. But he then goes on to say something quite different:

> They argue that in such a view all persons are considered to be reasonable and rational and to possess what I have called "the two moral powers"—a capacity for a sense of justice and a capacity for a conception of the good—which are the basis of political equality both in comprehensive liberalism...and in political liberalism. From this starting point they go on to imagine a global original position with a veil of ignorance behind which all parties [representing individuals] are situated...Proceeding this way would straightaway ground human rights in a political (moral) conception of liberal cosmopolitan justice. To proceed in this way, however, takes us back where we were in [section] 7.2 (where I considered and rejected the argument that nonliberal

societies are always properly subject to some form of sanctions), since it amounts to saying that all persons are to have the equal liberal rights of citizens in a constitutional democracy.[20]

On the face of it, this passage contains a major confusion. Rawls is supposed to be rebutting the objection to having the parties represent peoples rather than individuals, but in fact he argues *that if the parties representing individuals are characterized in one particular way*, as having the distinctive interests of persons *as conceived in liberal societies*, then the theory of human rights will confuse human rights with liberal rights—that it will be parochial. In brief, Rawls seems to slip from "including representatives of individuals as liberals conceive them would be parochial and hence intolerant" to "including representatives of individuals (*tout court*) would be parochial and hence intolerant."

But perhaps there is no confusion. Perhaps Rawls is assuming the following thesis: There is no way of conceiving of individuals such that the choice of principles of international law by their representatives in a hypothetical original position would not be biased toward liberal political conceptions. Call this assumption IB, for individualist bias.

Why might Rawls think that IB is true? My hypothesis is that he thinks that if the parties are to be representatives of individuals they must be characterized in ways that would be incompatible with the associationist conceptions of individual good that he believes are found in nonliberal societies and that this is tantamount to a bias in favor of liberal conceptions. In other words, there is no way of characterizing individuals—all individuals, regardless of whether they come from liberal or nonliberal decent societies—so that they could be represented in an original position for the choice of principles of international order, that would not conflict with the way individuals are conceived in associationist social forms. Any characterization that relied on a nonassociationist conception of individual good, any characterization that conceived of individuals' basic interests without reference to their particular associative identities, would be unacceptable from the perspective of (associationist) nonliberal societies—and therefore ruled out by principle IB above. So any attempt to include representatives of individuals in the original position is unacceptable, if one accepts IB.

Charity speaks in favor of attributing IB to Rawls: Unless Rawls subscribes to it, his justification for excluding individuals from the original position is based on an egregious slip from "don't include representatives of individuals as liberals conceive them" to "don't include representatives of individuals." If there are any basic human interests, then appealing to them in the characterization of representatives of individuals in a hypothetical choice situation is *not* the same as conceiving of the representatives in a peculiarly liberal way and hence is not parochial.

If this is Rawls's justification for excluding representatives of individuals from the original position, then his hypothetical agreement argument for the shortened list of human rights relies upon (1) the assumption that there is no defensible conception of basic human interests, interests that can be ascribed to all individuals regardless of what sort of society they live in, or upon (2) the assumption that even if there are basic human interests it is illegitimate to appeal to them in deriving human rights because doing so runs contrary to the way individuals are conceived in (associationist) nonliberal societies. I have already argued that neither of these assumptions is warranted.

4. THE ARGUMENT FROM COOPERATION

The following passage can be read as an attempt to derive Rawls's list of human rights from intuitions about cooperation and its moral significance. "What have come to be called human rights are recognized as necessary conditions of any system of social cooperation. When they are regularly violated, we have command by force, a slave system, and no cooperation of any kind."[21]

In this passage Rawls suggests that a list of human rights can be derived from the idea of *cooperation*. The argument would go like this: (1) Every society that qualifies as a cooperative association is entitled to immunity from intervention. (2) A society is a cooperative association if and only if it is not based (primarily? exclusively?) on force, but rather exemplifies a common good conception of justice. (3) If a society respects the human rights R1, R2, etc. (Rawls's shortened list of human rights) of its members, then it is not based (primarily? exclusively?) on force, but rather exemplifies a common good conception of justice and is therefore a cooperative association. (4) Therefore, if a society respects rights R1, R2, etc. (Rawls's shortened list of human rights), then it is entitled to immunity from intervention. (5) A right is a human right if and only if it is a member of a set of rights such that if a society respects them, that society is entitled to immunity from intervention. (6) Therefore, rights R1, R2, etc. (i.e., Rawls's shortened list of human rights), and only these, are human rights. For Rawls a cooperative association exemplifies a common good conception of justice, and this in turn implies that social relations are rule-governed, that the good of every member of society counts, and that every member is regarded as a moral agent in the sense of being a subject of duties specified by his or her role or position.

Grounding Human Rights in Characteristics of Societies, Not Individuals

What is striking about the Cooperation Argument is that it *appears* to avoid any appeal to a conception of basic human interests or capabilities or to the idea that there are some characteristics that all human beings have that ground human rights. In brief, it seems to be an attempt to ground a list of human rights without recourse to the idea of humanity, the idea that there is something of moral significance that is common to all human beings. Instead, it purports to derive a list of human rights from a view about what characteristics a *society* must have if it is to be decent, or worthy of nonintervention—namely, it must be a cooperative association in Rawls's technical sense.

Perhaps the most obvious difficulty with the Cooperation Argument is premise (1): Merely being a cooperative association in the sense of being a form of human association that is not based exclusively or primarily on force and exemplifies a common good conception of justice is a rather anemic conception of what it takes to be a decent society, or to be entitled to nonintervention. In brief, given Rawls's undemanding criteria for what counts as a cooperative scheme, premise (1) begs the question at issue. Being a cooperative scheme in Rawls's quite minimal sense may well be a *necessary* condition for being a decent society or for being entitled to immunity from intervention, but why should one think it is sufficient? Why should we assume that tolerance rules out any higher standard for immunity from intervention? Recall that a society can exemplify a common good conception of justice—everyone's good, as specified according to that society's conception of the common good, can count—and yet the good of some (e.g., women) can count much less than that of others and this devaluing of their good can be reflected in systematic institutionalized discrimination. Moreover, the societal justifications given for their good counting less, and hence for the discrimination they are subjected to, can rely upon grossly false beliefs about natural differences among types of human individuals.

If Rawls were to respond that cooperation (as he understands it) is an *intuitively plausible* criterion for nonintervention, there is an obvious reply: These intuitions are not widely shared, as the considerable volume of criticisms of Rawls's lean list of human rights attests. If his goal is to produce a conception of human rights that avoids the charge of bias or parochialism, it cannot be one that is based on intuitions that are not widely shared even among liberals. Many liberals would question whether a Rawlsian "decent" society, in which there was systematic, institutionalized discrimination against women or against people of color or members of a minority nationality, can never be subject to justifiable intervention.

Why the Cooperation Argument Violates Rawls's Own Strictures

The Cooperation Argument appears to contradict Rawls's claim that he will not rely upon any premise about the moral equality of persons or upon the idea that all are entitled to certain rights because they possess certain "moral or intellectual powers." Presumably Rawls's claim must be that a society is entitled to toleration only if it is a form of association that exemplifies a common good conception of justice, according to which everyone's good counts, and is therefore not based exclusively or primarily on force when viewed from the standpoint of every member—otherwise he would not say that to qualify as a cooperative association a society must respect the (Rawlsian) human rights of *all* its members. That is, for each member it must be true that society is a cooperative association. But surely to ground a list of human rights on this requirement makes sense only if the well-being and freedom of every individual is of fundamental importance, morally speaking; and this is to rely upon a premise of the moral equality of all persons, though a rather limited one. However, in the passage I cited at the beginning of this inquiry, Rawls explicitly eschews recourse to any notion that "human beings are moral persons." If all human beings are entitled to this rather minimal sort of freedom and well-being, then presumably this must be so by virtue of some characteristics that all humans have—presumably some "moral or intellectual powers" that they all have. Yet Rawls explicitly denies that his conception of human rights is grounded in any such characteristics.

If it is so important that every society be a scheme of cooperation, then surely this must be because of how the difference between being a scheme of cooperation and being a "command system based on force" affects human beings. Otherwise, we must attribute to Rawls the spooky, repugnant, and implausible view that protecting individuals' human rights is only instrumentally important because it guarantees that *societies* will have a certain characteristic, namely, that they will be cooperative schemes. But if what is so important about cooperation is that it serves certain morally important interests—including the interest in freedom—that all human beings have, then the cooperation argument, if sound, tacitly appeals to just the sort of premises about basic human interests and the moral equality of persons Rawls says he avoids. Furthermore, if it is so morally important that all human beings enjoy some minimum of freedom and well-being, then presumably this has implications beyond "the political," in which case Rawls's theory of human rights, like the dominant views he dismisses, counts as a "comprehensive," not a "political" conception.

5. THE FUNCTIONALIST ARGUMENT

This argument proceeds from a very striking assumption Rawls makes about the function of human rights norms: Human rights are those rights whose violation can provide a ground for intervention.[22] In outline, the argument goes like this. (1) Human rights are those rights whose violation can provide a ground for intervention. (2) Any list of human rights more extensive than Rawls's shortened list would include some rights whose violation cannot provide a ground for intervention. (3) Therefore, the list of human rights is not more extensive than Rawls's shortened list.

To assume that human rights have this direct connection with intervention is nothing less than a stipulative redefinition of "human rights," and Rawls gives us no good reason to accept it. Appeals to human rights perform many functions, and providing premises in arguments about the justification for intervention is only one of them and, currently, not the most important. To mention only a few of these other roles, human rights norms serve as standards for evaluating domestic institutions by their own citizens, as norms appealed to by judges in domestic legal systems, as conditions for membership in desirable international organizations (such as membership in NATO or the EU), and as qualifications for receiving loans and credits from organizations such as the World Bank and the International Monetary Fund. Given the valuable role that appeals to human rights have in these varied contexts, we would have to have a weighty reason to accept a stipulative redefinition as radical as Rawls's; we must gain something of considerable value by accepting the stipulative redefinition, something that cannot be gained by less costly alternatives.

The reason for accepting the stipulative redefinition cannot be that unless we restrict the meaning of the term "human rights" in this way, we will have no adequate way of addressing the risk of over-intervention generally or the risk of interventions based on parochial conceptions. There is another strategy for reducing these risks and it is in fact the strategy that is embodied (though imperfectly) in international law and endorsed by most theorists of intervention. A distinction can be made within the more expansive set of human rights, between those whose violation triggers serious consideration of intervention and those that do not. On some versions of this strategy the former includes an even leaner list of rights than Rawls's, effectively taking the question of intervention off the table unless there is genocide or other massive violations of the right to life. The risk of over-intervention and in particular of interventions that are the result of intolerance or parochialism can be further reduced by embedding the decision to intervene in an appropriate institutional framework for collective decision making, one that includes provisions for the representation of points of view from a wide range of societies and cultures.

Redefining "Human Rights" to Curb Human Rights Inflation

Rawls might reply that there is another reason for accepting his stipulative redefinition of "human rights": doing so would curb human rights inflation, the tendency to label everything that justice requires or, worse still, everything that is morally desirable as a human right. Human rights inflation is a problem, but there are less drastic ways to counter it. Furthermore, interest-based or capabilities-based theories are not inherently inflationary. What unites such theories, after all, is clear recognition that human rights are minimal moral standards, anchored in a minimalist conception of human good. A plausible conception of basic human interests (or capabilities) would resist the temptation to expand the notion of a minimally good human life toward that of a good life and would therefore almost certainly deny that some items on conventional lists of human rights belong there. Rawls does nothing to show that this approach to curbing rights inflation will not work. Instead, he simply removes it from consideration on the basis of the four weak arguments examined above, pursues a strategy that severs the idea of human rights from that of the moral significance of our common humanity, attempts to ground human rights in features of societies and their relation to one another, and produces a shortened list of human rights that allows grievous injustices and oppression.

6. CONCLUSION

Many commentators have criticized Rawls's thesis that the list of human rights is much leaner than is usually assumed. In this chapter I have reconstructed from the text of *The Law of Peoples* four distinct Rawlsian arguments to support this thesis. What unifies the four arguments is a determination to avoid any attempt to ground a list of human rights in a conception of basic human interests or fundamental human capabilities or indeed in any morally significant characteristics common to all human beings. In that sense, Rawls's theory of human rights is a radical departure from the dominant philosophical theories and from the widespread idea that human rights are grounded in our common humanity. I have argued that none of the four arguments succeeds, either in supporting Rawls's thesis that his lean list encompasses all human rights or in justifying his dismissal of the dominant philosophical theories and the commonsense idea that human rights are grounded in our common humanity.

Notes

I am grateful to John Tasioulas, Rex Martin, and David Reidy for their insightful comments on earlier drafts of this chapter.

1. James Nickel, *Making Sense of Human Rights*, revised ed. (Baltimore: Johns Hopkins University Press, 2007).

2. John Rawls, *The Law of Peoples* (Cambridge, Mass.: Harvard University Press, 1999), 65.

3. I have argued elsewhere, on social epistemological grounds, that members of nonliberal societies run a greater risk of coming to have and sustaining widespread false beliefs about natural differences among various groups of human beings (men and women, Blacks and Whites, etc.) than liberal societies, other things equal. If this is the case, then even if a nonliberal society that respects Rawls's austere list of human rights avoids serious discrimination and oppression for a time, it may not continue to do so. Rawls does not consider the important question of whether what he calls decent nonliberal societies will remain decent. I would argue that he is unable to do so effectively because his conception of society is static and lacks a social epistemological dimension. Allen Buchanan, "Political Liberalism and Social Epistemology," *Philosophy and Public Affairs*, 32, no. 2 (2004): 95–130.

4. Some defenders of Rawls would argue that the fact that implementation of his lean list of human rights is compatible with egregious discrimination is not a problem because Rawls stipulatively redefines "human rights" in a very narrow way, as those whose violation can ground intervention. Later I take up this interpretation, arguing that such a stipulation comes at a steep moral cost and is quite unnecessary because there are other ways to reduce the risk of over-intervention and human rights inflation.

5. The labels for these lines of argument are mine, not Rawls's.

6. Rawls, *Law of Peoples*, 68.

7. John Rawls, *Political Liberalism* (New York: Columbia University Press, 1993), 13.

8. Ibid., 94.

9. Nickel, *Making Sense of Human Rights*; Martha Nussbaum, *Women and Human Development* (New York: Cambridge University Press, 2000); Amartya Sen, *Development as Freedom* (New York: Knopf, 1999) and *On Ethics and Economics* (New York: Basil Blackwell, 1987); Henry Shue, *Basic Rights: Subsistence, Affluence, and U.S. Foreign Policy*, 2nd edition (Princeton, NJ: Princeton University Press, 1996). See also Allen Buchanan, *Justice, Legitimacy, and Self-determination* (Oxford: Oxford University Press, 2003), ch. 3.

10. I develop this line of criticism in detail in "Justice, Legitimacy, and Human Rights," *The Idea of Political Liberalism: Essays on Rawls*, ed. Victoria Davion and Clark Wolf (Lanham, Md.: Rowman and Littlefield, 2000), 73–89.

11. Rawls, *Law of Peoples*, 68.

12. Ibid.

13. Notice that this particularism is quite consistent with Rawls's claim that decent societies are organized according to a common good conception of justice. The point is that different societies will have different conceptions of what the common good is and that in each such society the content of an individual's good will be specified by reference to that society's conception of the common good.

14. Rawls, *Law of Peoples*, 68.

15. Fernando Tesón, *A Philosophy of International Law* (Boulder, Colo.: Westview Press, 1998), 109–22; Darrel Moellendorf, *Cosmopolitan Justice* (Boulder, Colo.: Westview Press, 2002), 7–29; Kok-Chor Tan, *Toleration, Diversity, and Global Justice* (University Park: Pennsylvania State University Press, 2000), 19–45.

16. Rawls, *Law of Peoples*, 80.

17. Ibid., 68–70.

18. Allen Buchanan, "Rawls's Law of Peoples: Rules for a Vanished Westphalian World," *Ethics*, 110, no. 4 (2000): 697–721.

19. Rawls, *Law of Peoples*, 82.

20. Ibid.

21. Ibid., 68.

22. Ibid., 27, 42, 79.

3

EQUALITY AND HUMAN RIGHTS

1. EGALITARIANISM AND HUMAN RIGHTS: A STRIKING DISCONNECT

A remarkable feature of the robust and nuanced contemporary philosophical literature on egalitarianism is its lack of engagement with the theory and practice of human rights.[1] This disconnect is puzzling because the modern human rights movement is arguably the most salient and powerful manifestation of a commitment to equality in our time.

Perhaps philosophers writing on equality have not articulated the implications of their work for human rights because they have operated within the strictures of a problematic, but largely unquestioned, assumption: that it is possible to develop a political philosophy for the individual state, considered in isolation.[2] This assumption, coupled with the even more dubious belief that human rights are a concern in other parts of the world, but not in liberal constitutional democracies, may explain why philosophical egalitarians have neglected human rights.[3]

Much of the philosophical literature on egalitarianism suffers from a deep ambiguity. On the one hand, the interpretations of equality various theorists put forward can be seen as intended for the domestic case only—as principled specifications of the sort of equality that ought to obtain *among fellow citizens*. On the other hand, they can be seen as accounts of equality *among human beings*, but on the assumption that, at least for the present, the only institution capable of realizing the sort of equality advocated is the state. The latter alternative leaves open the possibility that the theories of domestic equality being offered are, in fact, ideal theories of cosmopolitan egalitarian justice. For the most part, however, the major egalitarian theorists simply expound what they think equality requires, or consists in, without making it clear that equality of citizens may be more robust than equality among persons generally. Nor do they answer, or even ask, the obvious question: if what we owe people generally is significantly less than what we owe our fellow citizens, what is the basis for a commitment to human rights, where the latter are understood as universal standards that are in some meaningful sense egalitarian? Later I will show that whether the minimal egalitarianism of human rights is compatible with a particular philosophical account of egalitarianism will depend crucially upon whether and how the latter distinguishes between the domestic and international cases.

In addition to the fixation on the domestic case considered in isolation, there may be another reason why the philosophical egalitarian literature fails to engage with the theory and practice of human rights. Some contributors to the egalitarianism literature may reject the idea that a moral theory can literally take rights as basic (not grounded in any further moral considerations) and assume that human rights by definition are basic in just that sense. But the conception of human rights I outline later does not assume that they are morally basic in the sense of not being grounded in any further moral considerations.

The lack of engagement between the egalitarianism literature and the human rights literature is mutual. For the most part, international lawyers and others professionally concerned with human rights, to the extent that they have examined the theoretical grounding of human rights at all, have not utilized the rich philosophical literature on egalitarianism.[4]

In this chapter, I begin the task of connection. Section 2 outlines what I call the Modest Objectivist View, a philosophical conception of human rights that, as I have argued elsewhere in more detail, can provide a basis for critically reconstructing the conventional view of human rights.[5] (By the 'conventional view' I mean the dominant contemporary understanding of human rights that is embodied in the major human rights conventions and manifested in the mainstream of the international practice of human rights.[6]) First, I explain how the Modest Objectivist View captures the familiar idea that conventional human rights norms specify a standard that is in some important sense *minimal*—that the egalitarianism of human rights is a *constrained* or *limited egalitarianism.* I also make explicit the nature of the egalitarian assumptions that lie at the core of the Modest Objectivist View and are therefore crucial to justifying the doctrine and practice of human rights that it is designed to support. I then argue that while the Modest Objectivist View provides support for the most distinctive and progressive features of the modern conception of human rights, it also supplies powerful resources for critically evaluating and revising that conception.

In particular, I show that the Modest Objectivist View can help to combat tendencies toward human rights inflation and to avoid parochialism in our understanding of human rights. Section 3 explores challenges to the egalitarian assumptions of the Modest Objectivist View and considers how they can be met. Section 4 examines the question of whether the minimal or constrained egalitarianism of human rights is compatible with the more robust egalitarianism advanced in the contemporary philosophical literature on equality. I conclude that the minimalist egalitarianism of human rights is compatible with more robust egalitarian views, once we understand the distinctive functions of appeals to human rights. Among the most important of these is that human rights norms specify standards of transnational justice, minimal conditions that a just international order would require every state to meet in its treatment of human beings, both domestically and abroad. The thesis that human rights are the substance of transnational justice allows for individual states (or regional organizations such as the European Union) to adopt more robust egalitarian principles of justice for their own institutions and to use them to guide their humanitarian assistance to those who lie beyond their borders.

2. THE MODEST OBJECTIVIST VIEW OF HUMAN RIGHTS

The Equality Assumptions

According to this view, human rights are normative relations (more specifically, claim rights) which, if realized in the case of all persons, would help to ensure that all persons have the opportunity for a decent or minimally good human life.[7] The same point can be put in terms of basic human interests: the various human rights norms specify conditions that protect interests that are constitutive of a decent human life. The concept of basic human interests captures the fact that there is a plurality of conditions that generally must obtain if an individual is to have the opportunity to live a decent human life.

For example, being subjected to torture, or being enslaved, or not being free to practice one's religion, or being subject to arbitrary killing, or the inflicting of serious bodily injury, all tend to undercut the possibility of having a decent human life. The point of saying that there are *rights* against torture, slavery, religious persecution, and a right to physical security is to say more than that we are obligated not to torture, enslave, persecute, kill or maim; it also conveys the crucial idea that these obligations are *owed* to each human being. In that sense, the language of rights, as distinct from that of mere obligations, captures what I have elsewhere called the *subject-centered* character of the human rights discourse.[8]

The relevant distinction here is between having an obligation regarding someone and having an obligation regarding her that is owed to her. One might have obligations regarding some or all human beings, but these would not be owed to them if, for example, the obligations were derived from more fundamental obligations owed to God or to the nation or the community. This subject-centered feature of human rights discourse finds emphatic expression in two of the most important rights documents, the *Universal Declaration of Human Rights* and the *International Covenant on Civil and Political Rights*, whose preambles present the human rights they list as being derived from the 'inherent dignity' of each human being.[9] Below I show that, although the notion that each human being has inherent dignity is valuable for conveying the idea that obligations are subject centered, it is wrong to suggest that the notion of the inherent dignity of the individual is sufficient for deriving a list of human rights.

The point of saying that the rights against torture and so on are *human* rights is to emphasize that the ground of these rights, that by virtue of which they are owed to us, is something that is common to all human beings. According to the Modest Objectivist View, this something is the set of basic human interests, the constituents of a minimally good human life. Therefore, simply to say that human rights are presented in these documents as common standards for all societies to meet, though true, is misleading. The point is that these are standards of a very special sort: they are subject-centered obligations, grounded in characteristics shared by all human beings. The fact that these 'common standards' take the form of *rights*, and, more specifically, *human* rights, is not insignificant.[10]

The Modest Objectivist View does not take human rights to be basic in the sense of being moral axioms. Instead, human rights norms are understood as requiring justification, and the justification appeals to basic human interests, to the idea that these basic interests ought to be protected, to assumptions about what threatens these interests, and to assumptions about what is needed to protect them.

The conventional understanding of human rights is essentially egalitarian in two respects: human rights norms not only assume that there are some characteristics shared by all human beings (the Descriptive Equality Assumption), but also that a proper recognition of the moral significance of these characteristics requires that they be treated in certain ways and that this places significant restrictions on permissible inequalities among them (the Moral Equality Assumption). According to the Modest Objectivist View, the Moral Equality Assumption that grounds the conventional conception of human rights can be formulated as follows: each of us has an obligation to help ensure that every individual has the opportunity to have a minimally decent human life. If it is to ground the commitment to human rights and convey the moral priority that the conventional conception of human rights claims, the Moral Equality Assumption must be understood as a fundamental moral obligation that falls on all individuals, though fulfilling it, as I elaborate below, typically requires appropriate institutions. In many cases, individuals' chief opportunities for acting on this obligation consist in their supporting the relevant institutions.

Standard Threats and Institutional Responses

On the Modest Objectivist View, to move from the very abstract Moral Equality Assumption to a list of human rights, three things are needed. First, we need to disaggregate the concept of a minimally good human life into its components—the basic interests that are common to all human beings, thereby specifying the content of the Descriptive Equality Assumption. Second, we need an empirically accurate understanding of the conditions that typically undercut those interests, thereby depriving individuals of the opportunity to have a minimally decent human life—an evidence-based account of what might be called *standard threats* to human well-being. Earlier I suggested some of the more obvious standard threats (torture, persecution, physical insecurity, and enslavement). To a large extent, the basic human interests can be understood negatively, simply as our interests in avoiding these standard threats. Third, we need an empirically accurate understanding of the collective, and largely institutional, responses that are needed to counter the standard threats.

In some cases, the titles of human rights directly reveal the interest at stake, as is the case with the rights against slavery and against torture. In other cases, the title of the right indicates a condition or institution that, as a matter of fact, protects basic human interests, as is the case with the right to participate in governance.

Voting or otherwise participating in governance may not be a constituent of a minimally good life for all human beings, but there is considerable evidence that various constituents of a minimally good life are typically at risk when those who are governed are not able to participate in governance. Thus it is said that even if the right to democratic governance is not itself a human right, it provides the most reliable protection for human rights.

In many cases, the titles of human rights directly indicate types of institutions that are valuable for countering standard threats to human well-being. This is true, for example, of the right to equal protection under the law. In other cases, particular human rights presuppose, even when they do not explicitly mention, certain institutions as resources for countering certain standard threats. For example, the right to an adequate standard of living is generally thought to presuppose some form of welfare state.

Furthermore, some human rights reflect an awareness that in our world some of the most serious threats to human well-being are institutionally based. Thus, for example, the right to due process under the law is plausibly said to be a human right precisely because in the modern world the power of the state, operating through the legal system, has the potential to do great harm to individuals. To summarize, human rights are institutional in the sense that their formulation recognizes the role of institutions, both in standard threats to human well-being and in countering those threats.[11]

This institutional aspect of human rights makes it clear that at least some, if not all, human rights are not natural rights in the traditional sense: they are not rights that can be ascribed to all human beings, throughout history, independently of the sorts of institutional arrangements under which they live. If human rights were restricted to natural rights in this sense, they would not be as practically useful as they are. Their efficacy depends in part upon their concreteness, upon their ability to provide guidance for how to protect human beings from the actual threats to the opportunity to live a decent life that they now face.[12] To achieve this practicality, they must recognize the importance of institutions, both as threats and as resources for countering threats.

Nor are human rights, according to the Modest Objectivist View, derivable solely from the concept of human nature or grounded solely in our common humanity. This view does assume that there is a set of characteristics common to all human beings that makes possible justified judgments about what undercuts the opportunity for a decent life. But it rejects the notion that human rights can be derived solely from these characteristics, insisting instead on the need for accurate empirical premises about the conditions that tend to undercut the basic human interests and the institutional arrangements that counter those threats.

The Minimalism of Human Rights

There are several respects in which the Modest Objectivist View is rightly called minimalist. First, it does not rely upon any assumptions about what is best for human beings and, indeed, is agnostic as to whether there is one kind of life that is best for all. Second, it does not assume what Rawls calls a comprehensive conception of the good, that is, a systematic scheme of values that integrates all that is valuable in private and public life. Third, according to the Modest Objectivist View, honoring the commitment to human rights does not require anything approaching equality of condition or outcome for all human beings, nor even that all human beings actually have decent lives; instead, it only requires that all have the opportunity for a decent life.

In fact, the Modest Objectivist View does not even require *equality* of opportunity for a decent life strictly speaking. It requires neither that everyone is to have the same probability of achieving a decent life nor that the costs to each of realizing that opportunity must be the same. Instead, what is required is that no one is to face unduly burdensome obstacles to having a decent life, if he or she chooses to try to have such a life. Hence, a more accurate formulation of the Moral Equality Assumption would be as follows: each of us is obligated to help ensure that every individual has the opportunity to have a minimally good life, without facing undue burdens in achieving it.

Here an analogy with a common way of understanding the right to health care is illuminating. It is sometimes said that the right to health care requires that everyone is to have access to a 'decent minimum' or 'adequate level' of care, but that it is overly demanding to require that each should face exactly the same costs (in terms of travel, waiting time, co-payments, and so on) in accessing the care to which all are entitled.[13] Instead, none should face 'undue burdens' in accessing care.

In other words, it is not enough that one be able to access the health-care services in question; one must also be able to do so without excessive costs. Yet it would be either impractical or morally problematic, or both, to require that the costs of securing access be strictly equal across all individuals. Similarly, a proper recognition of the moral worth of all human beings requires that we are each obligated to help ensure that every individual has what might be called a reasonable opportunity for a decent life, not that the probability or the cost of achieving a decent life be strictly equal for all. To require that every person with a particular medical condition have the same probability of gaining treatment for it or that every human being have the same probability of having a decent life would be excessive, if only because this would ignore, or attempt to negate, the role of the individual's choice in determining her opportunities and the costs of realizing them.

Part of the attraction of the Modest Objectivist View is that by including the provision about undue burdens, it avoids being overly demanding in a way that may seem intuitively inappropriate for a conception of human rights. But this comes at a price: how exactly are we to determine what counts as undue burdens? If human rights are to serve as universal standards, it will not do simply to say that what counts as undue burdens will vary from society to society, depending upon what happens to be regarded as undue burdens. In a society in which women suffer great deprivations due to sexist social and economic institutions, what is regarded as undue burdens might be systematically distorted.

Nonetheless, the provision concerning undue burdens should allow for some principled variation. Much will depend upon what assumptions are made concerning the institutional capacity of international institutions to provide resources to poor states to help them meet the requirements of human rights norms. Suppose that this capacity is very low and the most that can be expected is that international institutions will help ensure that each state does the best it can, given its resources, to secure the human rights of all its citizens. Under these circumstances, the threshold for what counts as undue burdens in securing the opportunity to live a minimally good life in the poorest countries may be quite high. For example, it may be reasonable to expect that individuals will have to travel further to secure the basic health care needed to avoid severe limitations on the opportunity to live a decent life due to disability or early death from preventable diseases. Alternatively, if international institutional capacity is much more robust, it may make sense to set higher standards for access to medical care, so that it is expected that the average distance a person has to travel for medical care is less.[14]

Although human rights, as understood in the Modest Objectivist View, are 'minimal' in these three senses, there are two respects in which they are *not* minimal. First, given current realities, realizing the human rights of all persons is a daunting task that would require large expenditures and considerable redistribution of wealth. Second, and more importantly, simply to say, without qualification, that human rights are minimal standards is misleading because it overlooks the *dynamism* implicit in the Modest Objectivist View. As we learn more about the complex relations among various institutions that affect human well-being, it may be necessary to add new rights to the list of human rights. For example, if it becomes clear that liberal constitutional democracy is the only reliable form of government from the standpoint of securing certain especially important human rights, then it may become justifiable to include a right to this type of government among the human rights.

There is a more fundamental way in which human rights could become less minimal over time. If biomedical technologies continue to develop and their widespread use becomes much less costly, our conception of what counts as a decent human life may well become more ambitious. For example, if an inexpensive vaccine became available that would significantly extend the human lifespan, we might come to think of a decent human life as being longer than we do now. Our conception of one standard threat to human well-being, premature death, might change and with it our conception of human rights.[15]

Although the Modest Objectivist View allows this sort of dynamism in our understanding of human rights, it still presents human rights as minimal in one key respect that is relevant to the project of connecting human rights and philosophical egalitarianism: the core idea that each should have a (reasonable) opportunity for a decent life is a considerably less robust notion of equality than that of equality of outcomes, or equality of resources, or equality of welfare, or even equality of opportunity for welfare. Later, I will consider whether such a 'minimalist' conception of human rights could be consistently embraced by a proponent of any of these more robust forms of egalitarianism.

How the Modest Objectivist View Supports the Conventional Conception of Human Rights, but Also Facilitates Criticism of It

The Modest Objectivist View is an attempt to provide a philosophical framework capable of supporting key features of the conventional conception of human rights, while at the same time facilitating its critical evaluation. The first goal, that of supporting the conventional conception, is tentative and provisional. Pursuing it rests on the assumption that overall the modern human rights movement has been a force for progress and that the idea of human rights enjoys intuitive moral plausibility. But this assumption is quite compatible with skepticism about some of the items included in the conventional list of human rights. Nevertheless, it is clear that the Modest Objectivist View can accommodate and help justify some of the most distinctive features of the conventional conception of human rights.

First, the Modest Objectivist View supports the inclusion of 'positive' or welfare rights in the list of human rights. Having a reasonable opportunity for a decent life typically depends not only upon the so-called negative rights (roughly, the civil and political rights), but also upon access to education, to health care, and to an adequate standard of living. Just as important, the Modest Objectivist View straightforwardly eliminates one of the standard objections to including 'positive' rights: once we give up the assumption that human rights are natural rights and therefore 'pre-institutional', the fact that the 'positive' rights presuppose particular types of institutions (such as the welfare state) that have not always existed in human society is entirely irrelevant.

Second, the implicit dynamism of the Modest Objectivist View turns what some have assumed to be a weakness of the conventional conception into a strength. Once we understand the large empirical component of human rights claims (the factual assumptions about the role of institutions in standard threats and in their mitigation) then the fact that the list of human rights has changed over time is not an embarrassment, but instead an indication of the possibility of progress. As we learn more about the complex interrelations among the conditions for a decent human life (and as our evolving institutions present both new threats and new resources for countering them), our conception of human rights should change accordingly.

Third, as I have already noted, the Modest Objectivist View, in making explicit the Moral Equality Assumption, captures both the universality of human rights and the widely held notion that they provide a 'minimal' standard. The Modest Objectivist View shows how human rights can be both essentially egalitarian and yet limited in their demands.

Fourth, the Modest Objectivist View provides a substantive explanation of why the 'common standards' presented in human rights conventions take the form of rights and more specifically of rights that are attributed to all human beings by virtue of their common humanity or 'inherent dignity'; and it does so without making the mistake of assuming that human rights are natural rights, 'pre-institutional', and derivable from the concept of human nature alone. According to the Modest Objectivist View, the obligations implied by human rights norms are owed to individuals by virtue of characteristics they share with other human beings, but not solely in virtue of this, because empirical assumptions are also needed. In brief, the Modest Objectivist View explains the crucial feature of 'subject-centeredness' without collapsing the theory of human rights into natural rights theory.

A Systematic Perspective for Critically Evaluating the Conventional Conception of Human Rights

At the same time, the Modest Objectivist View also supplies a powerful critical perspective on the conventional conception of human rights. Examining all of the rights included in the major conventions in the light of the Modest Objectivist

View is not feasible given the limitations of this chapter. At best, I can indicate how the Modest Objectivist View could be used in a principled explanation of why some of the intuitively problematic items included in some of the conventions are not human rights.

First, the Modest Objectivist View provides principled checks against tendencies toward human rights inflation. Consider, for example, the notorious 'right to periodic holidays with pay' and the right to 'the highest attainable standard of physical and mental health.'[16] These are not plausibly included among the human rights for the simple reason that it is far-fetched to say that their realization is necessary for having the opportunity for a decent human life. By making explicit the minimalist character of the Moral Equality Assumption that grounds human rights, the Modest Objectivist View helps us avoid human rights inflation.

In addition, the Modest Objectivist View's emphasis on empirical assumptions both exposes the parochiality of certain claims that may be made about human rights and provides concrete guidance for how to mitigate the risk of parochiality. This is a significant advantage, because the legitimacy of the human rights enterprise is threatened unless the charge of parochialism can be met.

To say that the conventional conception of human rights is parochial is to imply that it is distorted by a foreshortened or narrow perspective (and that those who espouse it are unaware of these limitations). In its most common form, the claim is that the supposed human rights are, at best, rights that are valuable from a peculiarly western, liberal perspective. It is beyond the scope of this chapter to explore the charge of parochialism in any detail; I have done so elsewhere.[17] Here I will only identify one way in which some items on the conventional list of human rights might be parochial and then sketch how the Modest Objectivist View supplies resources for responding to the objection.

Article 25 of the *International Covenant on Civil and Political Rights* affirms a right to democratic political participation as a human right:

Every citizen shall have the right and the opportunity...

(a) To take part in the conduct of public affairs, either directly or through freely chosen representatives;
(b) To vote and to be elected at genuine periodic elections which shall be by universal and equal suffrage and shall be held by secret ballot.[18]

According to the Modest Objectivist View, whether a right of democratic participation is a human right depends upon whether living in a state in which this right is extended to all citizens is among the conditions that are generally necessary if the individual is to have an opportunity for a decent human life. Recently, some leaders of non-democratic states have claimed that the right of democratic participation is not a human right at all, but merely a right that is suitable for 'western' societies, and that democracy is not consonant with 'Asian values'.[19]

The implication is that societies in which 'Asian values' are predominant can achieve prosperity (that all their members can have the opportunity for a decent life) without democracy.

Amartya Sen and others have provided impressive evidence that democratic governments are less likely to persist in disastrous economic policies than non-democratic ones, because periodic elections tend to make government officials more accountable.[20] In its most general form, this sort of empirically based, instrumental justification for including the right to democratic participation among the human rights would make the case that democracy is needed not only to help secure the right to an adequate standard of living, but other important human rights as well.

To flesh the justification out, it is necessary to show that democracy, understood as including periodic elections under equal and universal suffrage, is the most reliable institutional arrangement for providing the needed accountability, among those that are generally feasible, and when the compatibility of a form of government with other institutions needed to protect human rights is duly taken into account. More specifically, it is necessary to show that (again, when compared with the feasible alternatives) extending the right of political participation to *all*, not just to some, is the best way to achieve the accountability that is of such great instrumental value for securing human rights.

My objective here is not to fill the justification out, but to sketch its outlines in sufficient detail to show its initial plausibility and to emphasize that an appreciation of the empirical character of the justification can help us avoid what might be called parochialism by over-specification. The right to democratic participation, as set out in Article 25, is quite abstract: although periodic elections under universal equal suffrage are required, nothing is said about whether a parliamentary or presidential system is preferable, about the virtues of unicameral versus bicameral legislatures, about the role of judicial review as a constraint on democratically authorized laws, about whether proportional representation is optimal, or, if so, under what conditions, and so on.

Efforts to specify the right to democratic governance along any of these dimensions would raise the issue of parochialism. It is possible that in the future we will possess much better theories of how alternative political arrangements work than we do now and these will yield a further specification of the right to democratic governance, but at this point in time there is considerable risk that further specification would be parochialism—more precisely, a case of thinking that accountability can only be achieved by what is, in fact, only one of several distinct institutional forms capable of achieving accountability. The Modest Objectivist View, with its emphasis on the empirical component in the justification of human rights claims, provides guidance for defending the rather abstract right of democratic governance against the charge of parochialism and at the same time gives us reason to resist the temptation of parochial over-specification.

3. CHALLENGES TO THE EGALITARIAN ASSUMPTIONS OF THE MODEST OBJECTIVIST VIEW

So far, I have emphasized that the justification of human rights norms (according to the Modest Objectivist View) depends importantly upon empirical assumptions about standard threats to minimal human well-being and about the range of alternative institutional arrangements that reliably mitigate those threats. The conventional human rights could also be challenged from a different perspective, however, by rejecting either the Descriptive Equality Assumption or the Moral Equality Assumption.

Descriptive Equality

According to the Descriptive Equality Assumption, all human beings share certain basic interests—there are some conditions that generally must obtain if a human being is to have the opportunity to live a decent life. In spite of other differences among them, human beings, whether male or female, Black or White, and regardless of culture, nationality, and ethnicity have enough in common that it makes sense to ground a set of rights on the notion of a decent human life or a minimally good human existence. In its most modest form, this is simply the claim that however else they may differ (for example, as to what makes them happy), human beings are all vulnerable to certain very serious harms, harms that are so damaging to the individual who suffers them that we are inclined to say that as a result of suffering them her life is of poor quality from the standpoint of her own well-being.

One of the most distinctive and important functions of proclaiming that such and such is a human right is to affirm what I have called 'descriptive equality' in the face of statements or policies that presuppose natural differences among various classes of human beings. For example, until very recently, the right to democratic participation was denied to women everywhere and to Blacks in the United States and in South Africa. Those who tried to justify this deprivation of rights invariably appealed to false empirical claims about natural differences (between men and women or Whites and Blacks). They either assumed that, due to natural differences, the conditions for a decent life for one group of human beings were significantly different from those for another group or, in the case of the most radical racists, failed to see that some individuals were humans.

It seems unlikely that anyone today is likely to challenge (in public) the very notion of human rights by denying that there are any basic interests that all human beings share. For example, no one is likely to deny that all human beings, male and female, have a fundamental interest in physical security and in freedom from torture or enslavement. Controversy, if it exists, is likely to concern other rights, in particular, the right against discrimination on the basis of gender (understood as including the right not to be excluded from various important economic activities).

According to the Modest Objectivist View, every human being ought to have the opportunity for a decent life. Given that those who now enjoy rights against economic discrimination have good reason to value them highly, the burden of empirical evidence is on those who would claim that economic discrimination does not deprive women of the opportunity for a decent life. Someone who advocates dropping the right against discrimination on grounds of gender from the conventional list of human rights would have to argue either, (1) that women, by nature, are not well-suited to certain forms of economic activity for which males are suited, or that (2) being barred from these activities does not adversely affect the well-being of women.

Neither claim is supportable. To the extent that women are allowed equal opportunities to compete with men for economic positions, there is no evidence that they are less able than men. Moreover, even if there were good data to show that they are, on average, less able than men to perform certain jobs, it would be arbitrary to exclude them from these positions, since there are other identifiable groups (for example, individuals with lower levels of quantitative skills, both men and women) who are not barred from competing for jobs that they have less likelihood of getting than some others.

The claim that economic discrimination does not undercut women's opportunity for a decent life is even less plausible. Recent work in development economics supplies a wealth of evidence to show that being excluded from important spheres of economic activity is highly damaging to women (and their children). When women are barred from entry into labor markets and lack access to credit, loans, and other financial tools, they are more likely to be trapped in abusive relations, to be sexually exploited by landlords, and to be malnourished and in poor health generally.[21] So the Modest Objectivist View provides guidance for how to debunk denials of human rights based on bogus empirical claims about natural differences among classes of human beings and also empowers human rights advocates to use good social science to show how the denial of various rights to certain groups in fact undercuts their opportunities for a decent life.

Moral Equality

The Modest Objectivist View's fundamental egalitarian moral assumption is that we are all obligated to help ensure that everyone has the opportunity for a decent life. A fully adequate presentation of the Modest Objectivist View, and hence the use of the Modest Objectivist View to support the conventional conception of human rights, would ultimately include a defense of this assumption. Here I will only note briefly that there are two quite different objections that might be raised against it, but that it appears that neither can be consistently advanced from the perspective of the recent philosophical egalitarian theorists.

The first, more radical objection is simply a denial that any of us owes anything to human beings generally, as opposed to those human beings who are our fellow citizens or others with whom we are in special relationships. Call this the radical particularist or extreme anti-cosmopolitan objection. To my knowledge, none of the major contributors to the philosophical egalitarianism literature holds this view. If I am correct in assuming that none of the contemporary egalitarian theorists is a radical particularist, then this first type of objection to the Modest Objectivist View is irrelevant to our task of determining whether that account of human rights is compatible with contemporary egalitarianism.

A second objection to the Modest Objectivist View's Moral Equality Assumption assumes that we owe something to human beings generally, but denies that this includes helping to ensure that they have the opportunity for a decent life. Instead, it is said that our obligations to other human beings generally (as distinct from special obligations) encompass only those obligations that are the correlatives of the so-called negative rights that constitute libertarian moral theory. Libertarians contend that a proper regard for equality requires only that we refrain from violating persons' rights against being killed, injured, defrauded, or deprived of their property — that treating others as equals only involves refraining from certain injurious acts, not helping to ensure that everyone has the opportunity for a decent life.

For the most part, the mainstream egalitarian literature, like the contemporary practice of human rights, rejects the libertarian, 'negative rights only' view. There are a number of reasons for doing so. Here I will only mention some of them, which I, among others, have developed in more detail elsewhere.[22]

To defend their claim that human rights or a proper regard for equality is limited to not violating certain 'negative rights', including pre-eminently the right to property and rights against physical harm and fraud, libertarians typically pursue either or both of two strategies. The first is simply to claim, on the basis of supposedly authoritative moral intuitions, that the only genuine moral rights are these 'negative rights'. The difficulty with this strategy is that a number of people, including most contemporary philosophical theorists of equality, have quite different intuitions.

If the libertarian attempts to resolve this clash of intuitions by adducing reasons why it is so important to respect the 'negative rights' and only these, she is likely to invoke notions such as the importance of being able to lead one's own life or the value of liberty. However, it is readily seen that if one values individuals having the ability to lead their own lives, one should also recognize the fact that this ability can be undercut by lack of food, lack of education, lack of resources required for representing one's interests effectively in the legal system, and so on, not just by having one's property taken by fraud or theft or being knocked on the head. Moreover, although we can all agree that liberty is valuable, the question is whether our conception of rights should be constrained by exclusive attention to the value of liberty as the absence of physical coercion, as the libertarian assumes. Any appeal to intuitions to support the claim that the only sort of liberty that counts is liberty from physical coercion is a nonstarter: it is because contemporary egalitarians and human rights advocates appreciate other dimensions of liberty as well that they think that more than the so-called negative rights are required. In brief, the libertarian's attempt to appeal to intuitions in order to restrict genuine moral rights to so-called negative rights fails.

The second libertarian strategy is to try to show that recognizing any rights other than 'negative' ones faces insuperable difficulties. More specifically, the claim is that 'positive rights' involve excessive costs, excessive moral demands, or a debilitating vagueness.

However, this attempt to drive a wedge between 'positive' and 'negative' rights is doomed. First, on any reasonable understanding of what it is to take 'negative rights' seriously, a multitude of 'positive' actions must be undertaken; so whatever difficulties afflict 'positive rights' attend 'negative' ones as well. For example, protecting property rights requires courts, police, legal services, the establishment of various authoritative social conventions concerning the marking of boundaries, the transfer of title, and so on. If the right to property is so morally important that it involves extremely strong obligations on my part not to take someone else's property, even when I need to do so for my own survival, then it seems odd to say that all justice requires in this regard is that each of us refrain from taking others' property, and that we have no obligation to work together to develop the institutions needed to provide meaningful protection for property.[23] Moreover, without authoritative social practices and conventions (the establishment and maintenance of which requires positive actions, not just refraining) there will be many cases in which one will simply not know how to refrain from violating someone else's property, in part because one will have no way of telling what is her property. In brief, taking property rights seriously requires shouldering 'positive duties'. But if this is the case, then there is no objection, in principle, to the idea that equality requires the fulfillment of 'positive duties'.

Alternatively, if the libertarian's claim is that a proper regard for equality must be restricted to 'negative obligations' because 'positive obligations' are necessarily open-ended and hence unfeasible to enforce and too costly to fulfill, this is clearly false. First of all, as I have just indicated, meaningful protection of 'negative rights' typically involves a multiplicity of 'positive' actions, not just refraining, and these may be extremely costly (for example, the costs of establishing and maintaining an effective and fair system for the enforcement of property rights). Moreover, the commitment to undertake such 'positive' actions for the sake of 'negative rights' is open-ended, in the sense that there is virtually no limit as to how many resources one could devote to achieving additional increments in the effectiveness and fairness of a system of enforcement, if cost were no object. The point is that properly designed institutions serve to specify otherwise open-ended commitments in the light of trade-offs with other important values, to limit the costs that any individual must bear in the name of fulfilling 'positive duties', and to help ensure that the costs are distributed equitably.

Second, in some cases fulfilling negative duties is more costly than fulfilling positive ones, so it cannot be the case that positive duties are ruled out on grounds of excessive cost. For example, refraining from taking your kidney to save my own life is much more costly to me than contributing a small percentage of my ample income toward support of universal health insurance.

For these and many more reasons, it is implausible to restrict the list of human rights, or the scope of a principle of equality for the domestic sphere, to so-called negative rights. Since my concern here is with the relationship between what I have characterized as the mainstream of recent philosophical literature on equality and the best reconstruction of the conventional conception of human rights, I will not develop such arguments in more detail, but simply bracket the libertarian (or 'negative rights only') challenge to the Modest Objectivist View's Moral Egalitarian Assumption and focus instead on whether it can be accommodated within the major recent philosophical accounts of equality.

4. IS THE MINIMALISM OF HUMAN RIGHTS COMPATIBLE WITH ROBUST EGALITARIANISM?

Ideal versus Non-ideal Theory and Pluralism versus Monism

I have argued that the conventional conception of human rights can best be supported by basing it on what I have called the Modest Objectivist View. The latter includes an egalitarian moral assumption, but one that appears to be more minimal or constrained than the egalitarianism of some prominent philosophical theorists of equality. For example, the views that equality requires equality of welfare for all or equality of opportunity for welfare for all, or equal resources all seem to be more robustly egalitarian than the claim that everyone ought to have the opportunity for a decent life.

However, as I have already hinted, whether any of these robust egalitarian theories is compatible with minimal egalitarianism depends upon the answer to a question that the theories generally leave unanswered, due to their lack of attention to the distinction between domestic and international justice. That question is simply whether the egalitarian principles that the theories articulate and defend are intended only for domestic application or are, at least in principle, globally applicable.

There are, in fact, two distinctions whose neglect complicates the issue of whether contemporary egalitarian theories are compatible with what I have argued is the most plausible reconstruction of the conventional conception of human rights. The first is the distinction between domestic justice and global justice, while the second is between ideal and non-ideal theory.

From the standpoint of ideal theory, the most obvious way to render compatible the Modest Objectivist View's minimal egalitarianism with robust egalitarianism (whether of welfare, resources, or opportunity for welfare) is to construe the latter as principles of justice for a particular kind of state, namely, a liberal democratic one, and the former as a principle of transnational justice. Principles of transnational justice specify the conditions that the international legal order ought to require every state to meet concerning the treatment of those within each state's own borders. What might be called *pluralist ideal egalitarianism* could consistently hold that while robust egalitarian principles may be appropriate for certain kinds of states, but not others, there is a minimal egalitarianism that ought to be realized, as a matter of justice, in all states.

Alternatively, according to *monist ideal egalitarianism*, there is, as a matter of ideal theory, only one fundamental standard of distributive justice. A robust monist egalitarian holds that this standard is something more demanding than the minimal egalitarianism of the Modest Objectivist View—equality of welfare, of opportunity for welfare, or of resources, for example. However, a monist ideal egalitarian can be a pluralist in the domain of non-ideal theory. She might quite reasonably hold that, for the foreseeable future, the most that can be hoped is that robust egalitarian principles can be effectively implemented in some states (those that have more egalitarian political cultures and institutions capable of relatively effective and politically feasible redistribution), but not in all. According to this kind of non-ideal theory, a conception of human rights grounded in the minimal egalitarianism of the Modest Objectivist View is, for now at least, a plausible principle of transnational justice. But the hope is that eventually a more robust international standard will become feasible. According to this view, the distinction between domestic and transnational justice, at least so far as equality is concerned, is not a feature of ideal theory, but rather a concession to current limitations. So both ideal and non-ideal robust egalitarians can accommodate the minimalist egalitarianism of human rights, at least if human rights are understood according to the Modest Objectivist View.

There seem to be only two kinds of egalitarian position that are inconsistent with the Modest Objectivist View's conception of human rights. The first is equality of outcomes. Giving everyone the opportunity to live a decent life will presumably lead to unequal outcomes, because some people will not use their opportunities well.[24] I will not dwell on this inconsistency for two reasons: first, I find the many obvious objections to a requirement of equality of outcomes convincing; second, none of the contributors to the recent philosophical literature on egalitarianism I am addressing advocates equality of outcomes. A more interesting inconsistency is between the Modest Objectivist View and an alleged right of self-determination.

Self-determination and Equality

According to this view, the (moral) right of self-determination of nations (or to use an even vaguer, but less contested term, primary moral communities) trumps demands for cosmopolitan justice, including those of a minimalist egalitarian principle of transnational justice. For the extreme self-determinationist, each primary moral community has the right to determine what its domestic standard of justice shall be and this right takes precedence over any duties such a community has to contribute to the achievement of a standard of transnational justice. According to a more refined (and, in my view, more plausible) version of this view, being a primary moral community is necessary, but not sufficient for having this strong right of self-determination: a primary moral community must also meet certain other normative criteria, for example, it must be democratic, must respect the human rights of its own citizens and others within its borders, must not be aggressive toward others, and so on. According to this view, if there are any primary moral communities that feature principles of distributive justice less egalitarian than the conventional conception of human rights, then the latter cannot legitimately function as a standard of transnational justice. Any attempt to impose human rights on a primary community with a less egalitarian conception of justice would violate the latter's right of self-determination.

Now it might be thought that in practice the proponent of human rights minimalist egalitarianism and the extreme self-determinationist will be indistinguishable, at least for the foreseeable future. The idea here is that at present human rights are interpreted in practice in a rather minimal way such that it is unlikely that they would be at odds with any morally acceptable domestic conception of distributive justice. Whether this is so will depend, however, upon how demanding domestic standards of distributive justice are and how extensive the resources are that states (or primary moral communities) have to try to realize them.

Suppose, for example, that some of the wealthiest states have very demanding domestic distributive standards: they require that every citizen have access to very high levels of education, health care, and so on. Under such circumstances, the domestic pursuit of what might be called equality of abundance may seriously undercut the possibility of achieving even a considerably less ambitious standard of living for all people everywhere, so far as achieving this requires substantial contributions of resources from the wealthiest states. So extreme self-determinationism may be incompatible with the acknowledgment of the minimal egalitarianism of human rights not only as a matter of ideal theory, but, under certain circumstances, in practice as well.

5. CONCLUSIONS

Recent philosophical theories of egalitarianism have generally proceeded as if there were no human rights movement or as if the idea of human rights was not an important expression of the commitment to equality. Human rights lawyers and activists have generally not drawn on recent philosophical egalitarian theories to help ground the conventional conception of human rights or to defend it against those who charge that it is merely a manifestation of parochial, 'western' values. In this chapter, I have outlined a philosophical grounding for the conventional conception of human rights, articulated its descriptive and moral egalitarian assumptions, shown how it provides resources for responding to familiar objections to the conventional conception, and explored its compatibility with the more robust egalitarian principles that distinguish the recent philosophical literature.

My conclusion is that the minimalist egalitarianism of human rights and the more robust egalitarianism of contemporary philosophical views of equality can be reconciled, but that to achieve this reconciliation philosophical theorists of egalitarianism must do something they have hitherto failed to do: place their egalitarian principles within a larger framework that is responsive to concerns about global inequalities and abandon the assumption that one can develop an adequate theory of equality for the domestic case without theorizing about global justice.

Notes

I am grateful to Scott Arnold for his comments on an early version of this chapter and to Gerald Gaus for his comments on the penultimate version.

1. Reference to human rights and to the commitment to human rights as an expression of egalitarianism is largely absent in the influential works on equality such as G.A. Cohen, "On the Currency of Egalitarian Justice," *Ethics* 99 (1989): 906–44; Richard Arneson, "Equality and Equal Opportunity for Welfare," *Philosophical Studies* 56 (1989): 77–93; John Roemer, "Equality of Resources Implies Equality of Welfare," *The Quarterly Journal of Economics* 101 (1986): 751–84. Amartya Sen's view that fundamental human equality requires that all have what he calls central human capabilities has important implications for how we are to understand human rights, but Sen has not attempted to ground the conventional list of human rights in his theory of capabilities or to use that theory to evaluate critically the conventional list. See Amartya K. Sen, *Development as Freedom*, 1st ed. (New York: Knopf, 1999). Martha Nussbaum has been more explicit about the possibility of grounding human rights in a theory of capabilities, but has not pursued this project in any detail and generally has not connected her notion of fundamental equality as treating everyone as an end with the recent philosophical literature on equality. See Martha Nussbaum, *Women and Human Development* (New York: Cambridge University Press, 2000). Ronald Dworkin, one of the most influential contributors to the contemporary debate about equality, has focused chiefly on equality in the context of the single state, rather than in the international human rights context. Dworkin assumes that although equal concern and respect are owed to all of our fellow citizens (at least in a liberal democracy), a weaker equality is appropriate for our relations with noncitizens, including persons in other countries. See Ronald Dworkin, "What Is Equality? Part 1: Equality of Welfare," *Philosophy and Public Affairs* 10 (1981): 185–246 and "What Is Equality? Part 2: Equality of Resources," *Philosophy and Public Affairs* 10 (1981): 283–345. So far he has not developed a theory of human rights, however. References to human rights were absent in John Rawls's work until *The Law of Peoples* (Cambridge, Mass.: Harvard University Press, 1999). However, Rawls's view of human rights in that work is surprisingly anti-egalitarian, insofar as his truncated list of human rights permits serious and systematic, institutionalized inequalities, for example, between men and women. For criticisms of Rawls's view of human rights, see the following: Fernando Tesón, *A Philosophy of International Law* (Boulder, Colo.: Westview Press, 1998), 109–22; James W. Nickel, "Rawls on Human Rights," unpublished paper; Allen Buchanan, "Justice, Legitimacy, and Human Rights," in *The Idea of a Political Liberalism*, ed. Victoria Davion and Clark Wolf (Totowa, N.J. : Rowman & Littlefield, 2000), 73–89; Allen Buchanan, "Towards an Institutional Theory of Human Rights," unpublished paper.

2. Here Amartya Sen is an exception. Yet his work on the 'Equality of what?' question, in which he engages the analytic philosophers writing on equality, does not make explicit

his views on human rights. See Amartya Sen, "Equality of What?" in *The Tanner Lectures on Human Values*, Vol. 1, ed. Sterling McMurrin (Salt Lake City: University of Utah Press, 1980), 195–220. Moreover, his work on international development has not explicitly drawn the implications for human rights of his views on capabilities.

3. The authors of the egalitarian literature of concern in this article are for the most part located in the United Kingdom, Australia, Canada, New Zealand, and the United States.

4. See, for example, Jack Donnelly, *International Human Rights*, 2nd ed. (Boulder, Colo.: Westview Press, 1998); Rhoda Howard-Hassmann, *Human Rights and the Search for Community* (Boulder, Colo.: Westview Press, 1995). Michael Perry recognizes that the justification for human rights norms depends upon a fundamental commitment to equality and argues that this commitment only makes sense from within a religious perspective. Although he rejects all secular philosophical groundings for human rights, he does not engage the philosophical literature on egalitarianism. See Michael Perry, *The Idea of Human Rights* (New York: Oxford University Press, 1998). In Perry's defense, one might note that the philosophical egalitarian literature largely either ignores the fundamental question of why we ought to treat others as equals, focusing instead on an explication of what it is to treat them as equals (the 'equality of what?' question) or simply appeals to intuitions about equality, as with the claim that people should be compensated for disadvantages that they have neither chosen nor deserve.

5. Buchanan, "Towards an Institutional Theory of Human Rights."

6. By the major human rights conventions I mean the *Universal Declaration of Human Rights*, the *International Covenant on Civil and Political Rights*, the *International Covenant on Economic, Social, and Cultural Rights*, the *Convention on Eliminating All Forms of Discrimination Against Women*, and the *Genocide Convention*. For all these documents and other human rights conventions, see Henry J. Steiner and Philip Alston, eds., *International Human Rights In Context: Law, Politics, and Morals*, 2nd ed. (Oxford: Oxford University Press, 2000).

7. It can be argued that some human rights, such as the right to freedom of expression, also include immunities. This point is due to George Rainbolt.

8. Allen Buchanan, "Justice as Reciprocity Versus Subject-centered Justice," *Philosophy and Public Affairs* 19 (1990): 227–52.

9. *Universal Declaration of Human Rights*, 1376, and *International Covenant on Civil and Political* Rights, 1381, both in Steiner and Alston, *International Human Rights In Context*. For indications of the important role of the concept of inherent dignity in the creation of the *Universal Declaration of Human Rights*, see Mary Ann Glendon, *A World Made New* (New York: Random House, 2001), 174–75.

10. A peculiarity of Rawls's theory of human rights is that it renders mysterious both the fact that they are called rights and that they are called human rights. The source of this difficulty is that Rawls attempts to ground a list of human rights without appeal to any notion of basic human interests, relying instead on the idea that human rights are those rights that play an especially important role in the morality of a liberal people's foreign policy and that are acceptable to illiberal decent peoples as well. I have argued that Rawls in fact appeals to one basic human interest, the interest in avoiding enslavement, but arbitrarily excludes appeals to other basic human interests. See Buchanan, "Taking the Human Out of Human Rights."

11. This is not to say that justice is institutional in the sense that principles of justice apply primarily to institutions, and to individuals derivatively via their place in institutional arrangements. Nor is it to say that individuals have rights only by virtue of their being co-participants with us in a common cooperative scheme. Lastly, the Modest Objectivist View does not assume that we have moral obligations to persons, including those that are implied by human rights norms, only to the extent that we interact with them. For a critique of

institutionalist and interactionist conceptions of justice, including those that limit relations of justice to those who share a cooperative scheme, see Allen Buchanan, *Justice, Legitimacy, and Self-determination: Moral Foundations for International Law* (Oxford: Oxford University Press, 2003), 73–117.

12. For a lucid critique of the assumption that human rights are natural rights, see Charles R. Beitz, "Human Rights as a Common Concern," *American Political Science Review* 95 (2001): 269–87; Charles R. Beitz, "Human Rights and the Law of Peoples," in *The Ethics of Assistance: Morality and the Distant Needy*, ed. Deen K. Chaterjee (New York: Cambridge University Press, 2004), 196–98.

13. President's Commission for the Study of Ethical Problems in Medicine and Biomedical and Behavioral Research, *Securing Access to Health Care*, Vol. 1 (Washington, D.C.: President's Commission for the Study of Ethical Problems in Medicine and Biomedical and Behavioral Research, 1983), 42–47; Allen Buchanan, "The Right to a Decent Minimum of Health Care," *Philosophy and Public Affairs* 13 (1984): 55–78.

14. There is another complexity in the notion of undue burdens that I can only indicate here. I would argue that what counts as undue burdens should be determined, in part, on comparative grounds. For example, if the financial and travel burdens that different classes of individuals face in accessing medical care vary greatly, systematically, and in morally arbitrary ways, this could lead to the conclusion that a burden is excessive, even if the same burden would not be if it were distributed more equally.

15. Allen Buchanan, Dan W. Brock, Norman Daniels and Daniel Wikler, *From Chance to Choice: Genetics and Justice* (Cambridge: Cambridge University Press, 2000), 94–98.

16. *Universal Declaration of Human Rights*, Article 24, in Steiner and Alston, *International Human Rights in Context*, 1379; *International Covenant on Economic, Social, and Cultural Rights*, Article 12, in Steiner and Alston, *International Human Rights in Context*, 1398.

17. Buchanan, "Human Rights and the Legitimacy of the International Order" (chapter 4, this volume).

18. Steiner and Alston, *International Human Rights in Context*, 1388.

19. For a valuable collection of essays on the question of 'Asian values', see Joanne R. Bauer and Daniel A. Bell, eds., *The East Asian Challenge to Human Rights* (New York: Cambridge University Press, 1999).

20. Amartya Sen, *Poverty and Famines: An Essay on Entitlement and Deprivation* (New York: Oxford University Press, 1981); Sen, *Development as Freedom*, 51–53.

21. Nussbaum, *Women and Human Development*, 1–4, 24–30; Sen, *Development as Freedom*, 115–16.

22. Allen Buchanan, *Ethics, Efficiency, and the Market* (Totowa, N.J.: Rowman and Allanheld, 1985), 64–86; Buchanan, *Justice, Legitimacy, and Self-determination*, 88–93.

23. I am not assuming here that in all cases being obligated not to X entails being obligated to help prevent others from X-ing. The point, rather, is that, given the best account of why we have the obligation not to do what human rights norms forbid us to do (an account that presents these obligations as the most fundamental obligations we have by basing them on the moral equality of persons), it is implausible to say that we have no significant obligation to help ensure that others do not violate them.

24. I am indebted to Gerald Gaus for this point.

4

HUMAN RIGHTS AND THE LEGITIMACY OF THE INTERNATIONAL ORDER

At the dawn of the modern human-rights era, the role of human rights in the international legal order was rather minimal. The rights listed in the Universal Declaration of Human Rights (UDHR, 1948) were not legally binding; they were largely aspirational. The situation is different today: the international legal order is beginning to take human rights seriously. The Security Council has authorized military interventions to stop massive violations of human rights in Bosnia and Somalia. A permanent International Criminal Court has been established to prosecute persons accused of war crimes, crimes against humanity, and genocide. There is growing acceptance of the idea that conformity to human-rights norms is a necessary condition of the legitimacy of governments and even of states, at least in the context of new states emerging from secession.[1] Taken together, these developments signal the transition from an international legal system whose constitutive, legitimizing aim was peace among states (and before that merely the regulation of war among states) to one that takes the protection of human rights as one of its central goals.

1. A FUNDAMENTAL LEGITIMACY ISSUE

When international legal institutions authorize military interventions, prosecute state leaders for war crimes, or judge states or governments to be illegitimate, they justify such actions by appealing to the special status of certain norms. These norms are thought to be capable of grounding enforcement efforts and legitimacy assessments *because they are human-rights norms*, norms that identify rights that all human individuals have, independently of whether their own governments acknowledge them.[2] Only such universal rights could justify the kinds of restraints on sovereignty and even on the self-determination of democratic peoples that the international legal order now attempts to impose. So when international legal institutions justify their most important and controversial functions by appeals to human rights, the rights they appeal to not only must be justifiable; they must be justifiable as human-rights norms.

For this justification to succeed, it must include a credible response to a perennial challenge to the very idea of human rights: the parochialism objection, according to which *what are called human rights are not really universal in the sense of being rights of all individuals but instead merely reflect (1) an arbitrarily restricted set of moral values; or (2) an arbitrary ranking of certain moral values.* According to this objection, both sorts of arbitrariness are due to cultural bias: supposedly universal values (or rankings of values) are merely the expression of a mistake—the mistake of thinking that what happens to be *valued* from the perspective of some particular culture or type of society is universally *valuable.* A culturally biased view is parochial in the pejorative sense: it suffers from limitations that indicate a failure to appreciate different, equally valid perspectives, a kind of evaluative myopia.

A justification responsive to the parochialism objection is nowhere to be found in the texts of the conventions that list putative human rights. The preambles of these documents content themselves with vague references to the dignity of the individual without saying anything about what dignity is and without sketching the supposed argument from dignity to particular human rights.

Until recently, silence on the question of justification was a virtue. For those who found themselves in a world devastated by World War II and the Holocaust, the urgent priority was to get as much agreement as possible on a set of minimal standards for how states should treat their own peoples, and this appeared to require three things: a highly abstract set of rights, avoidance of potentially divisive debates about their foundations, and assurance that these "rights" were not enforceable against states.

This rationale for avoiding the issue of justification is no longer cogent.[3] The very success of the institutionalization of human rights makes the issue of legitimacy and hence of justification inescapable. The more seriously the international legal system takes the protection of human rights and the more teeth this commitment has, the more problematic the lack of a credible public justification for human-rights norms becomes. Here I make no attempt to provide a full justification for human rights. My focus is on only one important aspect of the problem of justification: providing a plausible answer to the parochialism objection.

The parochialism objection may seem weak in the case of what are sometimes called *basic* human rights, such as those against enslavement, torture, and religious persecution and the rights to subsistence and physical security. These rights, at least, are clearly valuable for people generally, not just for "Westerners" or "liberal-individualists." The objection cannot be met so easily, however. There can be serious disagreements, rooted in different cultural views, about the specific content of even the most basic human rights, about how they ought to be balanced against one another in cases of conflicts of rights, and about what conditions, if any, would have to be satisfied if they were to be permissibly abrogated to avoid a moral catastrophe. The right against cruel and inhumane treatment is an obvious example among many. Does it prohibit corporal punishment in all forms or only some, and if so, which?

The point is that even the most uncontroversial human-rights norms are not self-specifying, nor do they come with their relative weights stamped on their foreheads. The more an intuitively plausible, highly abstract human-rights norm becomes legalized, the more vulnerable it can become to the charge of parochialism, because legalization involves, among other things, greater specificity of content and in some cases the establishment of rules for weighing conflicting rights. If enforcement mechanisms are to be legitimate, the law must be reasonably clear and the legal consequences of actions must be reasonably predictable. But efforts to achieve clarity and predictability create their own problem of legitimacy in the absence of a credible justification. The proper target of the parochialism objection, then, is the modern conception of human rights (MCHR for short), which consists of the norms listed in the major human-rights conventions as they have been interpreted and specified over time through complex institutional processes that encompass not only international courts, treaty bodies, and other international institutions but also national and regional courts so far as they attempt to apply and enforce international human-rights law.[4]

Once it is understood that what requires justification is not simply some very abstract norms that are found in the more important human-rights conventions but the more determinate norms that are required to make the idea of human rights an effective force in the international order, it becomes clear that one popular strategy for answering the parochialism objection is inadequate. Some theorists have tried to respond to the parochialism objection by showing that all of the major religious and/or cultural traditions contain ideas that can be given expression in the language of human rights.[5] Call this the overlapping-consensus approach.

The overlapping-consensus approach is inadequate, both as a reply to the parochialism objection and as a strategy for providing a full justification of human rights. It is hard to see what justificatory force the mere presence of human-rights-friendly ideas within a particular culture should have for those who belong to the culture, if the same culture also contains ideas that are hostile to human rights. Unfortunately, for at least some of the major religious cultural traditions, including Islam, Christianity, and Judaism, there are some ideas that might be expressed in terms of human rights and others that seem to be in opposition to them. Further, even if a particular tradition contained a preponderance of ideas that were consonant with a very abstract formulation of a human-rights norm, it might also contain elements that were quite at odds with the more determinate norms that are increasingly structuring the international order. But if this were the case, how could the existence of the human-rights-friendly elements of the tradition be an adequate justification for human rights?

If the underlying rationale of the overlapping-consensus approach is contractualist, then its inadequacy is all the clearer: the fact that someone could accept (or could not reasonably reject) a certain norm *if she focused only on elements of her moral view that are consonant with it while ignoring elements that repudiate it* does not show that requiring her to comply with the norm is either respectful or tolerant.

Similarly, establishing that the idea of human rights can be seen as an expression of *some* of the values of a particular religious or cultural tradition would not rebut the charge that human rights are parochial. Human rights might be consonant with some values in a particular religious or cultural tradition, but if they were in conflict with other values in that tradition or if they reflected a ranking of values that was clearly repudiated by important elements of that tradition, they could still be parochial. Those who make the charge of parochialism hold that human-rights norms are parochial precisely because they seem systematically to ignore some of the values or rankings of values that are present in a number of traditions. If human-rights norms represent an arbitrary selection of values that is rooted in a cultural bias that finds in other traditions only what it already values and ignores the rest, that is, indeed, a kind of parochialism. So the existence of human-rights-friendly ideas or values in wide range of religious or cultural traditions does not rebut the parochialism objection.

The relationship between parochialism and cultural acceptability warrants further comment. It is simply a misunderstanding of the concept of the parochial to think that if a norm is not acceptable from the standpoint of some cultures, then it is parochial. To be guilty of parochialism is to have a view that is limited by a narrow perception or partial understanding and to be unaware of the fact that one's view is thus limited. Consider the case of cultural views that foster gender discrimination. The claim that there is a human right against gender discrimination may be rejected by people whose beliefs about natural differences between men and women are distorted by a parochial social experience, the kind of experience that is generated by systematic discrimination against women. Where there is systematic discrimination, women will not have the opportunity to show that they are as rational as men. In these circumstances, a claim about the existence of a universal right against gender discrimination may not be universally acceptable precisely *because those who reject it have parochial views*. To elaborate: a person growing up in a deeply sexist culture who has uncritically imbibed false factual beliefs about natural differences between men and women may be unable—given those beliefs—to accept a norm against gender discrimination. Parochialism can be the cause of lack of universal acceptability, but lack of universal acceptability does not imply parochialism.

The results of the argument so far can be summarized. Some who have attempted to rebut the charge of parochialism have tried to show that human rights are acceptable to all major cultures in the sense that in all such cultures there are some ideas or values in the culture that can be expressed in terms of human rights. But cultural acceptability in this very weak sense does not refute the charge of parochialism. If human rights are consonant with some ideas or values in a culture but at odds with others, the dissonance could be the result of the human rights in question expressing parochial values. Nor does limiting the imposition of human-rights norms to those that enjoy cultural acceptability in the weak sense demonstrate tolerance or respect; it may involve focusing only on the areas of consonance and arbitrarily ignoring those where there is dissonance. Finally, lack of cultural acceptability, far from implying parochialism, may be the result of it; human rights may be unacceptable from the standpoint of a particular culture because that culture includes values that are based on beliefs or social experience that is parochial in the pejorative sense. So the idea of cultural acceptability seems incapable of showing either that human rights are parochial or that they are not.

A New Way of Framing the Issue

At least among political philosophers, there seems to be a growing conviction that a justification of human rights is needed to answer the parochialism objection and to resolve conflicts among rights. While agreeing that a legitimate human-rights-informed international legal order must rest on a sound philosophical conception of human rights, I show here that this is not sufficient, because the justification of human rights is in part an *institutional* matter. I argue that on a proper understanding of what human rights are, there is a risk that the specification of various rights may be distorted by parochialism but that this risk can be reduced if the institutions through which human rights norms are articulated have certain epistemic virtues. I show that the justification of human rights, properly understood, is a dynamic *process* in which a provisional philosophical conception of human rights both guides and is fleshed out by public processes of practical reasoning structured by legal institutions.

My conclusion is that whether the modern conception of human rights (henceforth the MCHR) can answer the charge of parochialism depends not only upon the content of human-rights norms as set out in the major conventions and the arguments philosophers can marshal to justify them but also upon the epistemic virtues of the institutions through which the norms are specified, contested, and revised over time. My more fundamental aim is to reframe the issue of the justification of human rights. If my analysis is correct, neither those who doubt that human-rights norms are justified nor those who have attempted to justify them have understood the nature of the task of justification.

2. SORTING OUT PAROCHIALISM COMPLAINTS

The parochialism objection takes many forms. What they all have in common is the charge that human rights are expressions of either an arbitrarily limited set of values or an arbitrary ranking of values. In what follows I sort out various forms of the objection and critically evaluate them.

Is the Concept of Rights Itself Parochial?

It is sometimes said that the very notion of rights is parochial because some cultures either do not contain it at all or do not give it the moral preeminence that the MCHR accords it.[6] We have already seen why this particular form of the claim that the idea rights is parochial is mistaken: from the fact that a moral norm or a concept is not found in a particular culture, it does not follow that it is parochial. On the contrary, as the case of the concept of a right against gender discrimination indicates, the best explanation of why a concept is absent in a particular culture may be that the culture contains parochial views.

To show that the concept of a right is parochial, then, it is not enough to point out that this concept is not present in some societies or cultures.

Establishing even that much would be difficult, however. The concept of rights appears to have penetrated into every society. Even if it were true that this concept initially emerged only in Western societies (itself a contestable claim), it is now accessible to people the world over. Indeed, people in whose cultures the concept of a right may not be indigenous nonetheless have found it to be extremely valuable for protecting their vital interests.[7]

The real issue is not whether the concept of a right is accessible in all cultures but rather whether it reflects an arbitrarily narrow set of values or rankings of values due to cultural biases. Whether a particular concept is parochial may depend upon what its function is supposed to be; the fact that a concept does not reflect the full range of moral values may be no indication of parochialism if the narrowing of normative focus is appropriate, given the use to which the concept is to be put. Asking whether the concept of a right is parochial may not be precisely the right question to ask; instead, we should ask whether the use to which the concept is put in the MCHR involves parochialism.

The concept of a right has certain characteristics that make it peculiarly well suited to expressing the notion of the inherent dignity of human beings, a notion that has played a prominent role in the modern human-rights movements from its beginning and which is explicitly invoked in some of the major human-rights conventions.[8] The concept of a right, at least that of a claim-right (in Hohfeldian terms), conveys not only the idea of obligation but also that of the right-holder being entitled to be treated in certain ways. Because the concept of a right allows us to distinguish between merely having an obligation *toward or regarding* an individual and the obligation being *owed to her*, it can effectively convey the idea that individuals have inherent dignity—an idea that, as I note above, finds forceful expression in the preambles of major human-rights conventions.[9] The notion of dignity implies that individuals have a moral status on their own account independent of their worth to others or their contribution to social utility and even independent of whether God commands us to act toward them in certain ways. So if the aim is not only to list important obligations regarding all individuals but also to make it clear that they are owed to individuals on their own account, then recourse to the language of rights is highly appropriate.

Given that the concept of a right has this advantage and in addition is both accessible to and valuable for individuals across a wide range of cultures, it is not parochial to employ it in the articulation of the most fundamental standards for how individuals should be treated on their own account. The reasons just stated for expressing the notion of human dignity in terms of rights are reflective and well considered and they can acknowledge that other moral concepts have a valuable role to play in other contexts; there is no reason so far to think that they evidence a parochial outlook.

Of course, the domain of rights is only one part of morality, and in some of the most valuable forms of interaction among human beings, the concept of a right typically is not nor should be invoked. This does not show that the conventional conception of human rights is parochial, however, because from the beginning the MCHR has acknowledged that human rights are not coextensive with morality but play a more limited role.[10]

Parochial Inputs versus Parochial Outputs

The familiar complaint that the rights included in the MCHR are reflections of peculiarly Western liberal values suggests that the concepts and norms that are employed in the major human-rights conventions were introduced by people who uncritically internalized these supposedly parochial values. There is much evidence, however, that the actual processes by which the major human-rights conventions were created were not, in fact, so culturally or ideologically one-sided nor so unreflective.

Mary Ann Glendon documents that credible efforts were made to reduce the risk of what might be called input bias in the drafting of the UDHR by the initial UN Human Rights Commission. First, there was an extensive inquiry to inform the Human Rights Commission of the full range of existing bills of rights and other relevant constitutional provisions from around the world.[11] Second, a multicultural UN "Philosophers Committee" was convened to address the question of whether or to what extent it was possible for the UDHR itself to articulate the moral, religious, or philosophical foundations of the rights it was to list.[12] Third, the composition of the Human Rights Commission itself was remarkably inclusive.[13] Two of its most forceful members were non-Europeans, ably representing Chinese and Arab-Muslim philosophical and religious traditions, respectively. Two other especially articulate and assertive members were a woman from India, who pressed the issue of women's rights, and a representative from the Philippines, who voiced concerns of colonized peoples. Fourth, the draft document that the Commission eventually produced was approved by the UN General Assembly, which then represented states from every geographical area and most major cultural traditions in the world, with no negative votes and only eight abstentions (including Saudi Arabia because of its rejection of equal rights for women and the U.S.S.R. because it viewed the very idea of human rights as an unacceptable constraint on state power).[14]

As UN membership expanded—chiefly through a process of decolonization mobilized in part by the discourse of human rights—the institutionalized procedures within which the original human-rights conventions were interpreted, as well as those through which new conventions were created, became increasingly inclusive and to that extent less prone to parochialism. This institutionalized commitment to inclusiveness has been consistently reflected in administrative rules and procedures governing the composition of judicial and quasi-judicial bodies tasked with monitoring compliance with human-rights conventions as well as in the composition of bodies to draft new conventions.[15]

None of this is to suggest that the MCHR is free of parochial distortions. The point is that from the beginning, the design of the human-rights *institutional framework* has included significant provisions for reducing the risks of parochialism. In addition, as human-rights nongovernmental organizations (NGOs) have come to play a larger role in the processes that specify the content of human-rights norms for purposes of monitoring compliance, the deficiencies of the original state-centered system have been ameliorated to some extent. One of the key functions of such organizations is to help insure a more inclusive representation of interests by giving voice to the concerns of the disempowered. Greater inclusiveness is one obvious way to avoid or at least minimize the risk of parochialism.

Whether a conception of human rights is parochial, then, can depend in part upon the institutions through which it is articulated. Even if a conception of human rights is damagingly parochial in its origins, this defect can be ameliorated over time through the working of properly designed institutions. Here there is a clear analogy with the evolution of constitutional rights in domestic systems. The individual rights added to the U.S. Constitution were at first interpreted as having quite narrow application—only to white men—but through complex legal and political processes that spanned two centuries, the domain of right-holders was expanded to include women and people of color and more recently people with disabilities. Two factors made this transformation possible: (1) the conceptual instability of attempts to restrict rights said to be grounded in very general human characteristics, such as rationality, to only a subclass of people; and (2) a legal system that empowered people to expose this inconsistency and that provided resources for helping to translate the conceptual shift toward greater inclusiveness into institutional reality.

This U.S. constitutional example illustrates two points that are of crucial significance for the task of justifying human rights. The first is that a parochial conception of rights can be replaced over time with one that is not parochial and that institutions can play a critical role in this transformation. The second is that we should not assume that legal processes are merely mechanisms for translating independently justified moral rights into legal ones; they can constitute modes of public practical reasoning that contribute to our understanding of moral rights and to their justification.

The question at this point in my argument is whether, in spite of impressive institutional efforts to avoid parochialism in "inputs," the "outputs" of the institutional processes through which human rights norms are interpreted and applied—the actual content of the rights as they are *now* understood in international human-rights practice—is damagingly parochial. To begin to answer this question it is first necessary to examine the different ways in which the *content* of human-rights norms could be said to be parochial.

The Excessive-individualism Objection

Some complain that the MCHR is too individualistic, that it reflects and helps perpetuate the distorted liberal conception of human beings as egoistic, atomistic beings.[16] The liberal conception of human beings is said to be parochial either because it excludes certain important values, including, preeminently, the goods of community, or because even when it does not exclude such values entirely, it ranks them too low compared with individualistic values.

There are two distinct lines of response to this version of the parochialism objection. The first focuses on the character of human rights as they were *initially* conceived in the first decades of the modern human-rights era, in the three documents that together comprise what is sometimes called the International Bill of Rights: the UDHR, the International Covenant on Civil and Political Rights (ICCPR), and the International Covenant on Social, Cultural, and Economic Rights (ICESCR). The point I make in this regard is that even though the majority of the rights in these documents are individual in the trivial sense that they are attributed to individuals, this does not show that they are excessively individualistic, because they are of great value for protecting the life of communities and to that extent reflect a clear recognition of the social nature of human beings.

The second line of response focuses on the *development* of the MCHR as it has occurred within the changing social, political, and institutional context of the decades following the drafting of the major documents. Here, I argue that over time a more "community-friendly" conception of human rights has emerged.

How Rights Ascribed to Individuals Protect Communities

Both the UDHR and the ICCPR contain the civil and political rights that are associated with liberalism, and liberalism, at least in some of its forms, can be excessively individualistic. Nevertheless, these rights provide powerful protections for communities. This is most obviously true of the rights of freedom of association, thought, expression, and religion. It is equally true of the rights of equal treatment and due process under the law, because these rights, too, make it more difficult for those who control the state to use its power to harm national, ethnic, or religious minorities.[17] Political-participation rights, even when ascribed exclusively to individuals, protect communitarian values as well because they make it harder for government to harm minorities.

The effectiveness of civil and political rights in protecting communities is significantly enhanced by the addition of social, economic, and cultural human rights, both in the UDHR and, in greater detail, in the ICESCR. In the UDHR these include rights to work and to an adequate standard of living (Articles 22 and 25) and the right to participate freely in the cultural life of the community (Article 27). The UDHR also includes specific rights designed to support two types of community that play a vital role in human life in our world: the right of every person to a nationality and the right against being arbitrarily deprived of one's nationality or denied the right to change one's nationality (Article 15, 1 and 2); and the right to "found a family" (Article 16, 1).

How Human Rights Have Become More Community-friendly

Further, it is simply not the case that the conventional conception of human rights is individualistic in the sense of ascribing rights only to individuals.[18] Both the ICCPR and the ICESCR assert a "right of self-determination of peoples,"[19] without any suggestion that this right is reducible to the rights of individuals who make up peoples. Further, the Genocide Convention (1948), generally regarded as a cornerstone of international human-rights law, is an explicit and forceful assertion of the value of community insofar as it recognizes as a distinct international crime various acts that are intended to destroy groups.

Finally, two other developments make even less cogent the claim that the conventional conception of human rights is excessively individualistic. The first is the emergence in international customary law of norms recognizing the rights of indigenous peoples, understood as including some rights that are ascribed to groups, not individuals.[20] The second is the tendency to interpret some of the human rights ascribed to individuals in the International Bill of Rights in a more communitarian fashion. For example, in the Lubicon Lake Band case, the International Human Rights Committee interpreted the right of the individual to enjoy culture (Article 27 of the International Covenant on Civil and Political Rights) as supporting the protection of collective land rights.[21]

Here it might be objected that the recognition of the right of self-determination, the Genocide Convention, and emerging customary norms recognizing collective rights of indigenous peoples do not fall under the heading of human rights properly speaking, because human rights by definition are rights of individuals. The latter claim is vigorously contested by a number of international legal scholars.[22] Be that as it may, whether an international legal order that takes human rights seriously is thereby excessively individualistic can only be determined by evaluating the *overall* institutional framework in which the rights ascribed to individuals are located. Even if the foregoing international legal "group rights" are not included in the human rights properly speaking, they nevertheless provide some corrective to whatever tendencies to excessive individualism might exist if human rights ascribed to individuals functioned in isolation.

A worry persists, however. The right of self-determination in international law applies only to populations subject to colonial rule or to military occupation.[23] As such, it fails to address the concerns of indigenous peoples and national minorities embedded within states. The Genocide Convention covers only the most extreme cases of oppression against groups, while existing customary norms regarding indigenous peoples' rights are arguably inadequate for those groups and are of dubious applicability to the plight of national minorities.

Here a distinction ought to be made between two questions: (1) is the existing normative structure of international law adequate for addressing the valid concerns of groups? and (2) is the MCHR excessively individualistic? Above I provide the outlines of an argument to show that the answer to the second question is negative, but this is quite compatible with the answer to the first question being negative as well. The chief reason for a negative answer to the first question is that current international law does not adequately address all of the valid concerns of indigenous peoples and national minorities. But from this it does not follow that the MCHR is excessively individualistic. A more accurate description of the current state of affairs is that the existing normative structure for the international legal order is incomplete, *not* that human-rights law is defective because it does not supply the whole normative structure that is needed.

The situation would be quite different if the current human-rights law or practice could be shown to be somehow thwarting the development of a more complete normative structure that would do justice to the claims of indigenous peoples and national minorities or if it could be shown that human rights, as now conceived, are conceptually incompatible with due recognition of group rights.[24] Neither of these hypotheses seems plausible, however, and to my knowledge, no one has made the case for them. On the contrary, better protection of the human rights of members of oppressed groups is generally a precondition of the effective exercise of group rights. So even if an international legal order that takes human rights seriously does not *thereby* provide adequate protection for groups, it does *not* follow that human rights themselves are excessively individualistic or that efforts to enforce human rights are illegitimate. The fact that human rights do not by themselves adequately protect all the interests that ought to receive protection in the international legal order does not imply that they represent a parochial moral outlook.

The Biased Abstractness Objection

A second version of the parochialism objection, like the first, takes its inspiration from Marx and is voiced in some contemporary feminist critiques as well.[25] The charge is that rights generally, or at least some human rights, perniciously abstract from crucial class or gender differences among human beings in ways that undercut their value for the oppressed. This abstractness is seen as a kind of parochialism, because the rights in question are supposedly modeled on and only responsive to the peculiar, limited experience of males, or of property-owning males in capitalist societies. The idea here is that human rights are parochial because they express a set of values that are limited because they are rooted in a limited kind of human experience.

The first response to this version of the parochialism objection is to acknowledge frankly that any conception of rights possessed by all humans is necessarily abstract, and that this abstractness inevitably results in a failure to address fully the concerns of groups or individuals with special needs. The reply then goes on to note that a world in which human rights are taken seriously is better, from the standpoint of the most vulnerable, than one in which scruples about abstractness result in the rejection of the human rights project.[26] Further, abstractness has benefits as well as costs: It allows for a degree of diversity in the specification and application of human rights norms, in order to take into account differences among societies.

The second response is institutional. International institutions have served as venues for the development of specialized human-rights conventions to supplement the highly abstract major conventions. The Convention on the Elimination of All Forms of Discrimination Against Women,[27] the Convention on the Rights of the Child,[28] and the Convention on the Rights of All Migrant Workers and Members of Their Families[29] were created to address the special needs and vulnerabilities of these groups. The more recent ratification of the Convention on the Rights of Persons with Disabilities is another case in point.[30] Whether such specialized conventions can be improved and supplemented is a complex question warranting more attention than I can give it here, but the point is that they are direct and impressive responses to the worry about biased abstraction.

Excessive Emphasis on Autonomy?

Some complain that the MCHR reflects an overestimation of the value of individual autonomy, that it arbitrarily privileges autonomy over other values, thereby expressing cultural bias. To determine whether this version of the parochialism objection is cogent, it is necessary to do two things. First, we must determine both whether there are in fact some rights in the MCHR whose justification depends upon a culturally biased overestimation of the value of autonomy *and* how central these rights are to the MCHR. Second, we must ascertain whether the institutional framework within which the MCHR is articulated has adequate resources for detecting and correcting whatever bias exists in favor of autonomy.

It is clearly beyond the scope of this chapter to undertake a systematic evaluation of all the more than two dozen rights in the major human-rights documents in order to determine whether they exhibit a bias toward autonomy. Instead, my strategy is to focus on the rights that are the most likely candidates for being biased in this way. These include (1) the right to freedom from discrimination (in economic activity and political participation) on grounds of gender or race; (2) the right to freedom of association; (3) the right to freedom of religion, thought, conscience, and expression; (4) the right to freedom in the choice of an occupation; and (5) the right to consensual marriage and to found a family. These rights might be thought to reflect an undue emphasis on individual autonomy at the expense of communal values of the sort sometimes associated with "traditional societies."

The first thing to notice is that each of these rights can be justified by appeal to its value in protecting values *other than autonomy*. For example, as my consideration of the excessive-individualism objection suggests, to justify inclusion of the right against discrimination on grounds of gender or race and the right of freedom of religion, conscience, and expression, it is *not* necessary to assume that a high degree of autonomy is a necessary condition for a decent human life. These rights provide valuable protections from much more tangible harms than diminution of autonomy by shielding individuals and groups against persecution, marginalization, and other threats to important basic human interests, including the interest in physical security and in achieving an adequate standard of living. Similarly, to make a strong case for the right to political participation as a human right, one need not show that political participation is itself an important, much less preeminent, form of autonomy or that if it is, this form of autonomy is in itself a constituent of a decent or dignified life for humans generally. Instead, one can argue that political-participation rights help ensure the political accountability upon which the protection of other human rights, including those that protect communal goods, generally depends. So from the fact that certain rights in the MCHR promote individual autonomy or would be especially attractive to those who value autonomy highly, it does not follow that they reflect a bias in favor of autonomy.

Second, like all other human rights in the major conventions, these autonomy-promoting rights are so abstract that it is difficult to argue that they exhibit an inflated valorization of autonomy. Efforts to articulate and implement the MCHR have generally proceeded on the assumption that a degree of abstractness is necessary for universality and that specification and implementation can and should vary, to some extent, across different social contexts and cultures.[31] So whether a particular right exhibits a bias toward autonomy cannot be determined in the abstract. The question is whether the complex web of international, national, and regional institutions through which sufficient specification for implementation is achieved promotes a bias toward autonomy and whether it includes adequate resources for detecting and correcting such bias. To the extent that this complex web of institutions includes provisions for increasing inclusiveness and is responsive to voices that contest the importance of autonomy relative to other values in securing the conditions for a decent human life, the problem of autonomy bias looks both less serious and more tractable. My aim here is not to refute the autonomy-bias version of the parochialism objection conclusively but only to use a consideration of it to make a more general methodological point: whether the MCHR is parochial cannot be determined without an examination of its institutionalization, because "institutionalization" here means much more than giving legal form to antecedently specified and justified norms.

The False Universality or Institutional Relativity Objection

Even if the MCHR is not excessively individualistic, has sufficient conceptual and institutional resources for avoiding biased abstractness, and is not guilty of giving too much weight to autonomy, it might still be parochial in the sense that its validity is restricted to conditions in which certain kinds of institutions exist. The argument would go like this:

(1) Human rights are by definition rights that apply to all persons regardless of the sort of society they live in; in that sense human rights are preinstitutional.
(2) But many putative human rights presuppose certain types of institutions, such as the welfare state (in the case of social and economic rights) or a fairly developed legal system (as in the case of various due-process rights)—institutions that have not always existed in human societies.
(3) (Therefore) many putative human rights do not apply to all persons, regardless of the sort of society they live in.
(4) (Therefore) many putative human rights are not human rights. (Rawls raises this objection in *The Law of Peoples* and suggests that a much leaner list of human rights can avoid it.)[32]

Mistaking the rights that human beings have under current conditions for the rights of human beings as such would be a kind of parochialism. However, this objection confuses the MCHR with the traditional conception of natural rights.[33] Premise 1 need not be accepted by a proponent of the MCHR, and there is considerable evidence that it was not held by those who helped create the first major human-rights documents.[34] Although natural rights have sometimes been conceived as applicable to all persons regardless of the kind of society they live in, human rights typically are not and need not be understood in this way. In the mainstream of contemporary theorizing about human rights, they are conceived as rights that individuals have in the kind of social world in which human beings now find themselves. In the next section I explore a philosophical underpinning for the conventional human rights, a version of the interest-based approach that I call the modest objectivist view (MOV), which makes sense of the idea that human rights are grounded in our common humanity without assuming that they are natural rights in the sense of being preinstitutional and derivable *solely* from our humanity.

The core idea of the MOV is that human rights provide protections of basic human interests against standard threats to those interests. The character of the standard threats and what serves as adequate protections against them both reflect the nature of the kind of social world in which human beings now find themselves. If human rights accurately reflect the conditions under which human beings now live, then the fact that those conditions did not always obtain does nothing whatsoever to show that human rights are parochial.

The Need for a Philosophical Conception of Human Rights

So far I have shown that the MCHR, as it is institutionally embodied, has considerable resources for responding to the parochialism objection. However, worries about parochialism will no doubt persist in the absence of a satisfactory philosophical account of human rights that goes beyond the evocative but obscure idea that they are grounded in the inherent dignity of persons. I now outline an account that appears to be capable of doing this. For reasons that will become clear as I proceed, this outline is not intended as a full justification of human rights. Instead, it is an attempt to begin the process of justification in a way that is responsive to the parochialism objection.

3. THE MODEST OBJECTIVIST VIEW OF HUMAN RIGHTS

Moral and Factual Assumptions

According to the MOV, assertions about human rights rest on three assumptions:

(1) Every person counts equally in some morally fundamental sense, and this basic equality of moral worth grounds an entitlement to conditions needed to secure the opportunity to live a decent or dignified life (the equal regard assumption).[35]

(2) Certain things can be done to human beings or certain deprivations they can suffer that generally undercut the opportunity for their living a decent life (the standard threat assumption).[36]
(3) Feasible and morally acceptable social institutions and practices can significantly reduce these standard threats (the institutional response assumption).[37]

Assumption 1 is one way of capturing the idea that the obligations in question are owed to individuals on their own account, and to that extent it is consonant with the idea that human rights are grounded in the inherent dignity of human beings. Assumptions 2 and 3 make it clear that this view of human rights has a substantial *empirical* component and that a list of human rights cannot be derived from a concept of human nature alone. More precisely, the MOV implies that sound justifications for assertions about the existence of human rights will rely significantly on factual premises, both about standard threats to basic human interests and about how these threats can be countered. According to the MOV, human rights are bundles of normative relations, primarily entitlements and duties.[38] When these normative relations are realized—when human rights are respected—human beings enjoy powerful protections against the standard threats to their basic interests, the constituents of a decent human life.[39]

Basic Human Interests

The modesty of the MOV's conception of basic human interests is perhaps most apparent when it is formulated in a negative fashion; the idea is that we can make justified judgments about what sorts of actions and policies generally undercut human beings' opportunities to live a decent or dignified human life. Given human history, there is quite a lot of reliable information about what makes for human misery and degradation.[40]

For example, we know that being tortured or enslaved or lacking physical security generally undercuts the opportunity to live a decent, dignified life.[41] We also know that because they possess cognitive and emotional capacities that other animals seem to lack, human beings can suffer intensely when they are humiliated, that certain forms of punishment and the more serious types of discrimination are humiliating, and that severe humiliation has severe effects on our psychological well-being as well as being an assault on dignity in its own right. We know, too, that when individuals do not enjoy rights of due process, they are especially vulnerable to being harmed by the state, that women and racial and ethnic minorities are liable to serious harms where rights against discrimination are not respected, and that when free speech is not protected, government is more likely to persist in acting in injurious ways.

The Equal Regard Assumption

To my knowledge, those who say the MCHR is parochial do *not* reject the assumption that all human beings ought to have the opportunity for a decent life. To claim that equal regard in this sense is a parochial moral notion would be an especially poor strategy for those who tend to assume that broad if not universal acceptability is a necessary condition for the legitimacy of a conception of human rights. For whether it is a cause or an effect of the modern human rights movement, the belief that everyone ought to have the opportunity for a decent life appears to be the focus of a rather broad "overlapping consensus," if anything is. Instead, it appears that those who say that the MCHR is parochial are best understood to be implicitly rejecting either the conception of a decent human life that is presupposed by human-rights norms or the factual assumptions about what the standard threats to basic human interests are or about what the standard threats to those interests are.

I indicate above why I think the complaint that the underlying conception of a decent human life is parochial looks much less plausible once we recognize that human rights norms acknowledge the deeply social character of a decent human life and that individual autonomy is not the only value served by the protection of human rights. I also argue that the institutional processes within which human-rights norms are articulated include substantial provisions for reducing the threat of parochialism by ensuring an inclusive representation of interests and moral points of view. So I will now concentrate on the question of whether it is credible to say that the *factual* presuppositions of human rights norms are parochial.

The Real Risks of Parochialism

There are three ways in which a conception of human rights grounded in the MOV could be parochial as a result of having false factual presuppositions:

(1) A conception of human rights would be parochial if it were based on an unduly narrow understanding of the conditions that typically undercut a human being's opportunities for a decent life. For example, it might include only civil and political rights, omitting key economic rights and the rights to basic education and health care, due to a failure to appreciate the fact that without these latter rights, people may be unable to exercise their civil and political rights effectively. To the extent that such a restricted understanding of the threats to human well-being is rooted in a particular class perspective and sustained by a limited social experience that either does not include acquaintance with poverty or encourages

the illusion that poverty can always be overcome by hard work, it could properly be called parochial. Some conceptions of natural rights may have been parochial in precisely this way, but the MCHR is not. It includes economic, social, and cultural rights.

(2) A conception of human rights would be parochial if it were based on an unduly restricted view about which institutional arrangements can effectively counter a particular standard threat to basic human interests. For example, someone who is acquainted with only the Anglo-Saxon legal systems and ignorant of the sorts of systems found in most European countries might falsely assume that adequate due-process protections require trial by jury in all criminal cases. The MCHR is not guilty of this sort of parochialism. It recognizes that due-process rights can be realized in a plurality of institutional arrangements.[42]

(3) A conception of human rights would be parochial if it incorporated a one-sided understanding of the effects on basic human interests of the enforcement of some of the rights it encompasses. For example, the MCHR encompasses economic liberties, including the right to property as an individual.[43] To justify the inclusion of such economic liberties in a list of human rights, it is not enough to show that they can serve to protect basic human interests. One must also consider whether the exercise of these rights under certain conditions can have a negative impact on basic human interests, or at least the basic human interests of some people, such as those who lack effective property rights in land in a predominantly agricultural society or those who lack access to the sort of education needed to operate effectively in the marketplace.[44] A conception of human rights would be parochial if it failed to reflect a proper appreciation of the fact that a given right can have negative as well as positive impacts on human interests.

It would be difficult to argue, however, that the MCHR is seriously flawed in this way. After all, the UDHR and various human rights treaties include economic, social, and cultural (claim-) *rights*, as well as economic liberties. One could argue that the protection of economic liberties has been more zealously pursued than the protection of economic, social, and cultural rights and that this is unjust; but from that it does not follow that the inclusion of economic liberties in the list of human rights exhibits a parochial understanding of the conditions needed to protect basic human interests or is in any way erroneous.[45]

We can now take stock of the argument up to this point. From the perspective of the MOV, whether a conception of human rights is parochial depends importantly on the accuracy of its *factual* presuppositions about what threatens basic human interests and about which combinations of rights and institutions provide effective protections against those threats. This focus on the crucial role of factual premises in the justification of human rights is a consequence of the MOV's rejection of the view that human rights are natural rights, that is, timeless and preinstitutional.

Once we appreciate the importance of factual premises, it becomes clear that the task of specifying human-rights norms is *ongoing*: as conditions change, new threats to basic interests may present themselves and new institutional arrangements for countering them may be needed. This means that the institutions that formulate, interpret, and apply human rights norms must be able to identify and take into account changing factual information and do so in a way that makes credible the claim that the norms they produce are not parochial.

So the capacity for making explicit and critically revising the factual presuppositions of claims about human rights is one important *epistemic virtue* that human rights institutions must have if there is to be a convincing reply to the parochialism objection. At this juncture we move to the terrain of social epistemology, which, I shall argue, has been curiously neglected by human-rights theorists.

4. THE NEED FOR A SOCIAL EPISTEMOLOGY OF HUMAN RIGHTS

Social epistemology, as I understand it here, is a normative, not a purely descriptive enterprise; it is the comparative evaluation of alternative institutional arrangements according to their tendency to foster true or justified beliefs. The guiding premise of the enterprise of developing a social epistemology is the anti-Cartesian insight that knowledge—and justification—are to a great extent social achievements.

The institutions that specify and apply human rights norms, as well as those that formulate new norms in specialized conventions, have important epistemic functions. They include mechanisms for accessing relevant empirical information by drawing on various "epistemic communities,"[46] including experts from NGOs and academic researchers. Such testimony has been conspicuous in proceedings of the European Court of Human Rights in a wide range of cases where violations of individuals' rights have been alleged. To take only one example of many, in Salah v. Netherlands (2006), an individual alleged that his right against inhumane treatment had been violated by the conditions of a maximum security prison in which he was held. The Court agreed, relying heavily on a 2003 study by the Free University of Amsterdam, according to which prison conditions caused damage to inmates' cognitive functions, increased rates of depression, and involved humiliation.

Other instances of the epistemic functions of human-rights institutions are not hard to find. Earlier I noted that the abstract rights of the UDHR, ICCPR, and ICESCR have been supplemented in specialized conventions with more determinate rights for women, children, and others who have special needs and vulnerabilities. The content of these new norms depends on factual assumptions about the character of these special needs and vulnerabilities. The bodies that formulate specialized institutions have developed procedures for gathering relevant factual information and have also provided forums for contesting claims about the validity of various factual claims.[47]

Whether international human-rights norms are justifiable and whether the actions of international institutions that appeal to these norms are legitimate depends in part, then, on the reliability of such institutionalized fact-finding mechanisms. To the extent that we can come to know which sorts of institutional arrangements are more epistemically reliable, we can reduce the risks of parochialism and thereby address the concerns about legitimacy that they raise.

In some cases, making sure that the content of human-rights norms is informed by reliable factual information may require the creation of new knowledge, for example, about the comparative effectiveness of alternative due-process mechanisms or about which social and economic rights must be realized if political participation is to be meaningful. In others, it will require more effective dissemination of knowledge that is already available or organized attempts to correct misinformation, for example, about natural differences between men and women, about the supposed fertility-enhancing effects of female genital cutting, or about whether certain ways of treating prisoners are deeply humiliating, given their culture.

Other important epistemic institutional virtues, beyond the ability to identify and properly utilize factual information relevant to ascertaining standard threats to basic interests and reliable ways of reducing those threats, can be described abstractly but are perhaps even more difficult to characterize in concrete terms capable of guiding institutional design. At least this much can be said, however: institutions that contribute to the articulation of human-rights norms ought to provide venues for deliberation in which the authority of good reasons is recognized, in which credible efforts are made to reduce the risk that strategic bargaining or raw power will displace rational deliberation, in which principled contestation of alternative views is encouraged, in which no points of view are excluded on the basis of prejudicial attitudes toward those who voice them, and in which conclusions about human rights are consonant with the foundational idea that these are moral rights that all human beings (now) have, independent of whether they are legally recognized by any legal system. Such arrangements could significantly reduce the risk that the underlying conception of a decent life would be subject to serious distortions of parochialism.

Principled, Authoritative Specification of Rights

Institutions can perform another more subtle but equally crucial epistemic function: they can help states, nonstate private and public groups, and individuals come to know what respect for human rights requires by authoritatively specifying the interpretation of a particular human right when there is a plurality of reasonable interpretations.[48] An analogy with the state's role in specifying property rights is helpful here. Justice requires respect for property rights. A conception of justice narrows the range of acceptable alternative property-rights systems but it does not pick out one arrangement as uniquely correct. Under these conditions, individuals cannot know what justice requires of them regarding property rights, until some legitimate governance institution creates a normative coordination point by authoritatively specifying one arrangement from among the acceptable alternatives.

The selection of such a normative coordination point, unlike the decision to drive on the right, is not morally arbitrary. The institution in question must provide public reasons of the right sort through the right sorts of processes. The public reasoning process must be morally coherent—in particular it must be consonant with the equal regard for individuals that grounds the idea of human rights—and it must be informed by reliable, relevant, factual information.

The need for principled, authoritative specification of norms to achieve normative coordination points is one of the principal reasons for the effort to move from highly abstract moral human-rights norms to international legal human-rights norms.[49] Calling this institutional function mere "legalization" underestimates both its importance and its epistemic character. Legal processes do not achieve normative coordination by flipping a coin; they do it by complex modes of practical reasoning in which both moral values and responsible fact-finding play a prominent role.

The argument so far can now be summarized. The legitimacy of an international order grounded in the commitment to human rights depends in part upon whether there is a credible public justification for human-rights norms. A credible public justification requires a response to the parochialism objection, the charge that what are called human rights reflect an arbitrarily restricted set of moral values or an arbitrary ranking of values due to cultural biases. Properly designed institutions can reduce the risk of parochialism in the articulation of human rights norms and thereby contribute to establishing the legitimacy of an international legal order that is centrally committed to the protection of human rights, in at least the following ways:

(1) They can access and utilize reliable factual information crucial for the justification and/or specification of human rights norms.
(2) They can achieve a more inclusive representation of interests and viewpoints than is likely to be available at the domestic level and to that extent can mitigate the risk of culturally biased understandings of basic human interests, of what threatens them, and of what institutional arrangements are needed to counter the threats.
(3) They can help us know what our obligations are regarding human rights by providing principled, authoritative specifications of human rights when there is a range of reasonable alternative specifications.

It is important to emphasize that I am not unwittingly sliding from moral human rights to legal human rights. I am saying that institutional processes that articulate international legal rights can play a valuable role—and I venture to say an indispensable role—in fleshing out the justification and specification of moral human rights. The point is that the process of "legalizing" moral rights does not leave our understanding of moral rights unaffected; it contributes to both the specification and the justification of those moral rights. Once it is admitted that justified moral belief, like justified belief generally, is in significant part a social achievement in which institutions play an important role, this claim looks less radical than it may at first appear to be.

Institutions and the Parochialism Problem

I note above that the refusal to acknowledge that there is a human right against gender-based discrimination can be the expression of a parochial point of view. People can come to have and to sustain false beliefs about women's capacities for rationality because they are told that women are inferior in this regard by their parents, clergymen, and teachers and because the sexist institutions within which they live shape their experience in such a way as to seem to confirm these beliefs. In brief, sexist institutions can promote a parochial conception of human rights, one that indefensibly limits certain human rights to men. From a social epistemology perspective, the obvious question to ask at this point is this: Under what social conditions is such a parochial conception of human rights likely to be prevalent and sustainable? A plausible answer is: other things being equal, under conditions in which the human rights of women are systematically violated.

Whether people have access to experience in which the capabilities of women can be appreciated will depend upon the character of the institutions that shape their experiences and the beliefs in light of which they interpret their experiences. If those institutions uphold equal educational rights and equal opportunity for economic advancement for women and the right to participate in governance, then false beliefs about the natural inferiority of women will be harder to sustain and promulgate because people's experiences of women will be more likely to exhibit the true capacities of women.[50] So implementation of certain human-rights norms—preeminently those that prohibit discrimination and protect the free exchange of information and opinions but also those that protect economic liberties and social rights for all—can help create social conditions that reduce the risk of parochialism in how human rights are conceived.

There is another, less obvious way in which the protection of human rights reduces the risk of parochialism in how we conceive of human rights: where human rights are protected, people are more likely to have the physical and economic security and the freedom to conduct sound social-scientific research relevant to the specification and justification of human-rights norms and to disseminate the results of their inquiries to others, including those who will play important roles in the institutions that articulate human rights. Once we understand that the justification of human rights is an ongoing process in which institutions play an important role, there is nothing paradoxical about the claim that the protection of human rights can help guard against parochial understandings of which rights are human rights. This is simply another illustration of my general theme: the character of institutions can either exacerbate or reduce the risk of having a parochial conception of human rights.

5. IS THE SOCIAL-EPISTEMOLOGY APPROACH VICIOUSLY CIRCULAR?

So far I have argued for three conclusions:

(1) The more central the protection of human rights becomes in international law, the more the lack of a credible public justification for human-rights norms calls into question the legitimacy of the international legal system.
(2) One key element of a credible public justification is a plausible answer to the parochialism objection—the charge that human rights reflect an arbitrarily restricted set of values or an arbitrary ranking of values due to cultural biases.
(3) A plausible answer to the parochialism objection must show that the institutions that articulate legal human-rights norms have certain epistemic virtues.

I now want to state a potentially lethal objection to my third conclusion and then show how rebutting it helps to explain the complex relationship between philosophical argumentation and institutionally embedded practical reasoning in the justification of human-rights norms.

In order to determine whether the complex web of international, regional, and national institutions that articulate human-rights norms has the epistemic virtues needed for the publicly credible specification and justification of these norms, it is not enough to have an accurate description of what might be called the *general* epistemic virtues of these institutions—their arrangements for inclusiveness of diverse perspectives, for facilitating principled deliberation, for accessing reliable empirical information, for correcting false beliefs, and so on. Merely knowing that these institutions include processes that are *generally* conducive to specifying and justifying norms, though necessary, is not sufficient; they must have what it takes for the task of justifying and specifying *human-rights norms*. In other words, their epistemic adequacy depends in part upon the particular character of the norms they are supposed to articulate. Thus we need further assurance if we are to conclude that their "norm outputs" are likely to be credible candidates for being specifications of *human-rights norms*.

Yet to determine whether existing institutions are adequate for contributing to the task of justifying and specifying human-rights norms as such, it seems that we must *already* have at hand a conception of human rights. Furthermore, it must be possible to articulate this conception of human rights *independent* of a description of the "norm outputs" of the institutions if it is to provide a standard by which to evaluate the institutions' specific moral-epistemic virtues.

But if this is so, then this seems viciously circular. How can an appeal to the epistemic virtues of the institutions that articulate human-rights norms help to establish the credibility of claims about human rights and hence the appropriateness of giving the promotion of human rights a prominent role in the international legal order if we must *already* be able to identify valid human-rights norms in order to assess the specific epistemic virtues of those institutions?[51]

There is no problem of vicious circularity if the process of specifying and justifying human-rights norms is understood to be a matter of ongoing mutual adjustment between our *provisional core conception of human rights*, our standards for the epistemic performance of the institutions that articulate human-rights norms, and our judgments about the existence and content of particular human rights. The core conception of human rights we bring to this complex institutional process must be (1) rich enough to ground a provisional list of human rights and to guide the design of institutions for further specifying their content in ways that are suitable for legal implementation; and (2) of sufficient initial moral credibility to justify the creation of such institutions.

My surmise is that some version of the MOV satisfies these two conditions for a provisional core conception of human rights. The MOV's idea of generally effective protections against standard threats to basic human interests provides guidance for constructing a provisional list of human rights and for the initial design of institutions for articulating human rights. More precisely, the MOV makes it clear that these institutions must be designed so as to mitigate the risks of parochial specifications of the rights in question by utilizing reliable factual information about standard threats and adequate protections against them and by facilitating the inclusion of diverse cultural perspectives on what count as basic human interests in the deliberative processes by which norm specification occurs. The MOV also has considerable initial moral plausibility because it provides a coherent, attractive interpretation of the idea of equal moral regard, namely, the notion that the basic interests of all people deserve serious protections. It appears, then, that we already have a provisional, initially credible core conception of human rights that can get us started on an account of what sort of features institutions must have if they are to contribute to the credible specification and justification of human-rights norms.

If, after carefully examining the relevant institutions and implementing appropriate reforms to remedy their defects, we were to gain greater confidence in their epistemic virtues, we might revise our initial understanding of the *content* of a particular human-rights norm. More radically, the deliberative processes that occur in these institutions may lead us to modify our current *list* of human rights, either by addition or (in my opinion, more likely) by subtraction. So the fact that we need a provisional substantive conception of human rights in order to be able to make an initial assessment of the epistemic adequacy of the institutions that articulate human-rights norms is *not* inconsistent with the claim that such institutions can contribute to the credible specification and justification of those same norms.

If we were to gain sufficient confidence in the epistemic virtues of the institutions that articulate human-rights norms, we might eventually come to have reason to revise the core conception itself. Whether this is likely to happen will depend, inter alia, on how contentful we take the core conception to be. Suppose, for purposes of illustration, that the core concept's understanding of basic interests is limited to a few very abstractly characterized interests—for example, the interests in physical security, in having access to resources sufficient for subsistence, and in avoiding the most dire restrictions on personal liberty, such as slavery. Each of these interests is, on the one hand, so obviously generally important for a decent or dignified human life and, on the other hand, so highly abstract that it is unlikely we will come to doubt that they are an important part of what grounds claims about particular human-rights norms. Instead, it is much more likely that what will change is our understanding of what particular rights must be realized in order to protect these basic interests.

To take the MOV as our provisional starting point is *not* to assume that it can provide by itself a fully adequate justification and specification of human-rights norms. Instead, the idea is to use the core conception to make a *provisional* assessment of the plausibility of the lists of human rights that are contained in the major international human-rights treaties. Once this is accomplished, we can then begin to make provisional assessments of the epistemic adequacy of existing institutions in their role of specifying and supplementing these rights without any vicious circularity—so long as we take seriously the possibility that the workings of these institutions may in turn require revisions in our initial conception of human-rights norms and even in the core conception itself.

Vicious circularity is avoided, then, if two conditions are satisfied:

(1) We have a provisional core conception of human rights that is both morally plausible and sufficiently contentful to guide the formulation of a list of rights and an initial evaluation of the epistemic adequacy of the relevant institutions.
(2) We have reasons to be confident in the epistemic virtues of these institutions, reasons that are independent of the congruence between their specification of human-rights norms and our initial core conception of human rights.

I argue above that some version of the MOV will satisfy condition 1. With respect to condition 2, what sort of epistemic virtues might we reasonably expect the institutions that articulate human-rights norms to have, given provisional acceptance of the MOV? At the very least, they should have provisions for accessing reliable factual information and correcting errors regarding the facts when they make them, given how crucial reliable factual information is to the justification and specification of human rights according to our core conception of human rights, the MOV. As I argue above, relevant factual information here includes information about what the standard threats to basic human interests (as these interests are provisionally characterized in the core conception) are and what combinations of rights and institutional arrangements to implement them are generally needed to counter those threats.

The crucial point is that whether the institutions have this epistemic virtue can be assessed independently *without* assuming that the particular conception of human-rights norms we are now operating with is the correct one. What matters is whether the institutions have what it takes to produce or access reliable factual information *of the sort* that is likely to be relevant for specifying and justifying claims about human rights from the perspective of *something like* our provisional core conception of human rights.

6. CONCLUSION

Human rights play an increasingly central role in the international legal order. Without a publicly credible justification for human rights, the legitimacy of such a legal order is dubious. A necessary condition for such a justification is a convincing response to the parochialism objection—the charge that human rights reflect a set of moral values or a ranking of moral values that is culturally biased.

Both those who have advanced the parochialism objection and those who attempt to meet it proceed as if the answer to whether human rights are parochial can be determined in a purely discursive manner—by inspecting the textual meaning of putative human-rights norms and evaluating the quality of philosophical arguments that can be given in support of them.[52] They fail to consider the possibility that whether the modern conception of human rights is parochial depends *in part* on the epistemic virtues of the institutions within which human-rights norms are articulated, contested, specified, supplemented, and revised over time.[53]

In contrast, my strategy has been to conceive of the modern conception of human rights as institutionally embodied rather than as a list of abstract norms to be supported or debunked by free-floating philosophical argumentation. I argue that whether human rights as they actually function in the international legal order can escape the objection of parochialism depends in part upon whether the institutions within which they are articulated possess the epistemic virtues that are relevant to the task of justification, given what I take to be the most plausible core philosophical conception of human rights currently available. I show that these institutions *already* include a variety of measures for reducing the risk of parochialism. In effect, international human-rights institutions have recognized the relevance of social epistemology to the justification of human rights and, by implication, to the legitimacy of a human-rights-based international legal order, even if philosophical theorists of human rights have not.

I conclude that whether an international legal order that takes human rights seriously is legitimate does not depend upon whether attempts to formulate human-rights norms are at risk for being parochial (they clearly are) or whether such formulations have been tainted by parochialism (they almost certainly have been). The issue, rather, is whether the risks of parochialism can be reduced to tolerable levels by feasible institutional arrangements for helping to ensure that the beliefs upon which the justification and specification of human-rights norms depend are sufficiently reliable to make efforts to secure compliance with these norms legitimate. To answer that question requires a careful examination of the epistemic virtues and deficiencies of the complex web of international, regional, and national institutions that articulate international legal human-rights norms in the light of a plausible provisional philosophical conception of human rights.

The bad news, for those who view the increasing role of human rights in the international legal order as progress, is that absent such an inquiry, there can be no fully satisfying reply to the parochialism objection—and that, therefore, the legitimacy of the international legal order will remain deeply questionable. The good news is that until the epistemic virtues of the institutions that articulate human rights are more thoroughly evaluated, the objection that the modern conception of human rights is parochial cannot be conclusive.[54]

Notes

1. Allen Buchanan, "Recognitional Legitimacy and the State System," *Philosophy and Public Affairs* 28 (1999): 46–78.

2. Saying that all human beings have human rights does not commit one to the view that human rights are natural rights in the traditional sense, where this means preinstitutional moral rights that human beings have regardless of the social conditions under which they exist and hence that are timeless. The claim is that human rights are universal in a less robust sense: they apply to all existing human beings (and to all human beings in the foreseeable future), barring deep changes in the kinds of social relations and institutions human beings now live within, the existence of the state, etc. See Charles R. Beitz, "What Human Rights Mean," *Daedelus* 132 (2003): 36–46.

3. Charles Beitz, among others, makes this point. He states that a "justifying theory" of human rights is needed. I argue that this is an incomplete diagnosis of the problem. I show below that the response to the "justification deficit" must in significant part be institutional. Ibid., 37.

4. Charles Beitz rightly emphasizes that what I call the modern conception—the conception embodied in the actual law and politics of human rights—should be the focus of attempts to provide philosophical accounts of human rights and that philosophers should not begin their analyses by assuming that the proper conception of human rights is the idea of natural human rights familiar in liberal political philosophy. See Charles R. Beitz,

"Human Rights as a Common Concern," *American Political Science Review* 95 (2001): 276–77; Charles R. Beitz, "Human Rights and the Law of Peoples," in *The Ethics of Assistance: Morality and the Distant Needy*, ed. Deen K. Chatterjee (Cambridge: Cambridge University Press, 2004), 196–98.

5. Joshua Cohen, "Minimalism about Human Rights: The Most We Can Hope For?" *Journal of Political Philosophy* 12 (2004): 190–213.

6. David B. Wong, "Rights and Community in Confucianism," in *Confucian Ethics: A Comparative Study of Self, Autonomy and Community*, ed. Kwong-loi Shun and David B. Wong (Cambridge: Cambridge University Press, 2004).

7. To take only one example, irrespective of whether the idea of human rights is found in "Chinese (or Asian) culture," the prodemocracy activists who were gunned down in Tiananmen Square did not hesitate to frame their demands in the language of human rights.

8. See Article I of the Universal Declaration of Human Rights, in *International Law: Selected Documents*, ed. Barry E. Carter and Phillip R. Trimble (Boston: Little, Brown, 1994), 381, which states that "All human beings are born free and equal in dignity." See also the Preamble to the International Covenant on Civil and Political Rights, 387, which states that the rights it lists "derive from the inherent dignity of the human person"; and the Preamble to the International Covenant on Economic, Social, and Cultural Rights, 410, which recognizes "the inherent dignity . . . of all members of the human family . . . [as] the foundation of freedom, justice and peace." For a discussion of the centrality of the idea of the inherent dignity of each human being in the development of the Universal Declaration of Human Rights, see Mary Ann Glendon, *A World Made New* (New York: Random House, 2001), 144–46, esp. 173–75. In some instances, the justification for ascribing a right to individuals appeals to the interests of other persons, not just those of the individual to whom the rights is ascribed, as may be the case with the right of free speech. Nevertheless, it is the interests of persons understood as morally considerable in their own right, not the will of God or the promotion of the maximal aggregate good, that is said to ground the right.

9. For example, consider the International Covenant on Civil and Political Rights (ICCPR) Preamble: "Recognizing that these rights derive from the inherent dignity of the human person"; the International Covenant on Economic, Social and Cultural Rights (ICESCR) Preamble: "Recognizing that these rights derive from the inherent dignity of the human person"; the Convention on the Elimination of All Forms of Discrimination Against Women (CEDAW) Preamble: "Noting that the Charter of the United Nations Reaffirms faith in fundamental human rights, in the dignity and worth of the human person and in the equal rights of men and women," Carter and Trimble, *International Law*.

10. James Nickel, *Making Sense of Human Rights*, 2nd ed. (Malden, Mass.: Blackwell, 2007).

11. Glendon, *World Made New*, 56–38.

12. Ibid., 51, 73–78.

13. Ibid., 32–33, 44, and 35–51 generally.

14. Ibid., 169–71 for voting results.

15. See, e.g., Article 31, International Convention on Civil and Political Rights: "1. The Committee may not include more than one national of the same state. 2. In the election of the Committee, consideration shall be given to equitable geographical distribution of membership and to the representation of different forms of civilization and of the principal legal systems"; Carter and Trimble, *International Law*, 383. The same provision for inclusiveness occurs in Article 17 of the Convention on the Elimination of All Forms of Discrimination Against Women, *id.* at 432. In addition to the ICCPR, CERD, CAT, CRC, and CEDAW require states to nominate only their nationals; in elections to the treaty bodies,

"equitable geographic distribution" must be considered. Some of the treaty texts urge "representation of the different forms of civilization and...the principle legal systems"; see also Article 31 (2) of ICCPR; Article 8(1) of CERD; and article 17(1) of CEDAW.

16. See Allen Buchanan, "Assessing the Communitarian Critique of Liberalism," *Ethics* 99 (1989): 852–82.

17. Articles 8–11 of the Universal Declaration of Human Rights establish that victims of rights violations should have access to effective remedies; that individuals have a right to be protected from "arbitrary arrest, detention of exile"; that persons charged with a crime have the right to a fair hearing; and that persons will be presumed innocent and shall not be subject to ex post facto laws. See Carter and Trimble, *International Law*, 382.

18. Nickel, *Making Sense*, 163–66, also emphasizes that human rights have become less individualistic or more community-friendly.

19. International Covenant on Civil and Political Rights, Part I, Article 1, in Carter and Trimble, *International Law*, 411.

20. S. James Anaya, *Indigenous Peoples in International Law* (New York: Oxford University Press, 1996), 42, 97–125.

21. *Lubicon Lake Band v. Canada*, Communication No. 167/1984 (1990), U.N. Doc. A/45/40, Supp. No. 40 (1990), at 1.

22. See Anaya, *Indigenous Peoples*; and Cindy Holder and Jeff Corntassel, "Indigenous Peoples and Multicultural Citizenship: Bridging Collective and Individual Rights," *Human Rights Quarterly* 24 (2002): 126–51.

23. Antonio Cassese, *International Law*, 2nd ed. (New York: Oxford University Press, 2005), 61.

24. For an effort to sketch the outlines of a normative structure for international law that includes both human rights and rights of national minorities and indigenous peoples, see Allen Buchanan, *Justice, Legitimacy, and Self-determination: Moral Foundations for International Law*, part 3 (New York: Oxford University Press, 2003).

25. See, e.g., Nancy J. Hirschmann, *The Subject of Liberty: Toward a Feminist Theory of Freedom* (Princeton, N.J.: Princeton University Press, 2003), 161–68; and Wendy Brown, *States of Injury: Power and Freedom in Late Modernity* (Princeton, N.J.: Princeton University Press, 1995).

26. For an influential and illuminating view that recognizes the special needs of women but does not reject the conventional human rights as parochial, see Martha Nussbaum, *Women and Human Development: The Capabilities Approach* (New York: Cambridge University Press, 2000).

27. Convention on the Elimination of All Forms of Discrimination Against Women, in Carter and Trimble, *International Law*, 432–43. The preamble to the declaration emphasizes that while the Charter of the United Nations and the Universal Declaration on Human Rights both affirm the equal rights of men and women, there remain inequities between men and women and special attention is needed to ensure that women do not suffer unduly the effects of poverty or the burdens of child rearing.

28. Convention on the Rights of the Child, in ibid., 455–63.

29. Convention on the Protection of the Rights of All Migrant Workers and Members of Their Families, available at http://www.unhchr.ch/html/menu3/b/m_mwctoc.htm.

30. Convention on the Rights of Persons with Disabilities, available at http://www.un.org/disabilities/convention/conventionfull.shtml.

31. Kristen Hessler, "Resolving Interpretive Conflicts in International Human Rights Law," *Journal of Political Philosophy* 13 (2005): 29–52.

32. John Rawls, *The Law of Peoples* (Cambridge, Mass.: Harvard University Press, 1999).

33. See Beitz, "Human Rights as a Common Concern," 276–77. Beitz overgeneralizes when he says that "philosophers" confuse human rights with natural rights. For example, James Nickel exposed this confusion twenty years ago and went on to develop a conception of human rights that is very similar to the one that Beitz proposes in his 2003 article. Henry Shue, John Tasioulas, Martha Nussbaum, Amartya Sen, Allen Buchanan, and perhaps most other contemporary philosophical theorists of human rights reject the identification of human rights with natural rights, as the latter are understood by Beitz.

34. See Glendon, *World Made New*, at 68–70, 115–17 passim.

35. See David Held, "Law of States, Law of Peoples: Three Models of Sovereignty," *Legal Theory* 8 (2002): 24; Amartya Sen, "Equality of What?" in *I Tanner Lectures on Human Values* (Salt Lake City: University of Utah Press, 1980); and Martha Nussbaum, *Women and Human Development*; for very similar formulations of the idea of the fundamental equality of persons. On my view the fundamental equality assumption has an important implication for just institutions: we are all obligated to help ensure that all persons have access to institutions that protect their basic human rights, the latter being those rights that are especially important for having the opportunity to live a decent life. Buchanan, *Justice, Legitimacy, and Self-determination*, ch. 2.

36. See Henry Shue, *Basic Rights: Subsistence, Affluence, and U.S. Foreign Policy*, 2nd ed. (Princeton, N.J.: Princeton University Press, 1996), 5–34.

37. See Thomas M. Scanlon, "Human Rights as a Neutral Concern," in Peter G. Brown and Douglas MacLean, eds., *Human Rights and U.S. Foreign Policy: Principles and Applications* (Lexington, Mass.: Lexington Books, 1979), 83–92; Nickel, *Making Sense*, at 3, 59–67.

38. Some human rights, such as the right to freedom of expression, may also be understood as including immunities. This point is due to George Rainbolt. In some cases human rights can be said to entail determinate duties (e.g., the right against torture entails duties not to torture incumbent on all), but they can also ground the imposition of duties; how determinate the latter are will depend upon a complex set of factors, including existing institutional capacities. In an excellent essay entitled "The Moral Reality of Rights," John Tasioulas persuasively argues that human rights ground the imposition of duties (because of the moral importance of the interests they protect) and that this is compatible with something being a human right even if at present there is no determinate assignment of duties. I agree with this part of Tasioulas's analysis, but instead of arguing from the moral importance of interests to human rights, I frame the MOV in such a way as to make explicit a premise that includes the idea of equal regard for persons, because I think that merely to refer to the moral importance of interests, as Tasioulias does, fails to emphasize that the interests in question are of such moral importance because the are the interests of person. John Tasioulas, "The Moral Reality of Human Rights," in Thomas Pogge, ed., *Freedom from Poverty as a Human Right: Who Owes What to the Very Poor?* (Oxford: Oxford University Press, 2007), 75–101.

39. Shue, *Basic Rights*. For his discussion of "standard threats," see 29–34.

40. This is not to say that our beliefs about what undercuts the opportunity for a decent life are infallible or that what counts as a decent life is uncontestable or uncontested. Later I will suggest that such judgments can be distorted by parochialism or other forms of bias. But I will also show that properly designed institutions can reduce such distortions and offer legitimate venues for contestation.

41. See John Conroy, *Unspeakable Acts, Ordinary People: The Dynamics of Torture* (New York: Knopf, 2000), at 169–83 for a discussion of the debilitating psychological effects of torture.

42. The International Covenant on Civil and Political Rights, Article 14, accords each individual a right to "a fair and public hearing by a competent and impartial tribunal established by law" but does not require trial by jury.

43. Universal Declaration of Human Rights, Article 17, in Carter and Trimble, *International Law*, 383.

44. This point is due to James Nickel.

45. As James Nickel has noted, the protection of economic liberties, including the right to individual property—though in no way sufficient in itself—is often of great importance for the welfare of some of the world's worst off people. Nickel, *Making Sense*, 123–25, 133–34.

46. Peter M. Haas defines an epistemic community as "a network of professionals with recognized expertise and competence in a particular domain and an authoritative claim to policy-relevant knowledge within that domain or issue-area" in his introduction to a special issue of *International Organization* (1992; vol. 46). See Peter M. Haas, "Introduction: Epistemic Communities and International Policy Coordination," 1–35. See also Haas, *Saving the Mediterranean: The Politics of International Environmental Cooperation* (New York: Columbia University Press, 1990).

47. The United Nations Decade for Women, 1976–1985, involved a major shift in international thought regarding women. The new consensus was that development was not possible without the full participation of women. United Nations statistics dramatized the fact that women's rights are an important factor in the well-being of all people, seen, for example, in the connection between declines in infant mortality and the mother's level of education. The Programme for the Decade for Women, adopted by the Commission on the Status of Women (CSW), called for a number of studies in specific areas, for example, comparative studies on different aspects of civil and family law. This period of information-gathering regarding women is recognized for its important legal achievements, in particular the 1979 Convention on the Elimination of All Forms of Discrimination Against Women. The drafting of this convention took several years, the draft document was widely circulated for comment, and the responses were numerous. Today, this convention is monitored by the Committee on the Elimination of Discrimination Against Women (CEDAW). It is recognized that the most glaring omission in the work of the committee is the lack of information from NGOs. As Roberta Jacobson notes, "A spin-off effect of NGO participation could be government reports which are prepared more carefully and comprehensively since detailed information from other sources may be available to Committee members." See Roberta Jacobson, "The Discrimination Against Women Committee," in Philip Alston, ed., *The United Nations and Human Rights: A Critical Appraisal* (New York: Oxford University Press, 1992), 466. For more information on the campaign to promote and protect the rights of women, see United Nations Department of Public Information, *United Nations and the Advancement of Women, 1945–1996* (New York: UN Department of Public Information, 1995).

48. In his comments on an earlier draft of this chapter, John Tasioulas calls this an "executive function" of such institutions, but I think it is accurate to describe it as an epistemic function as well.

49. For a sophisticated and systematic analysis of the role of law generally in achieving normative coordination through specification under conditions of persisting reasonable disagreement, see Samantha Besson, *The Morality of Conflict* (Portland, Ore.: Hart, 2005).

50. Allen Buchanan, "Political Liberalism and Social Epistemology," *Philosophy and Public Affairs* 32 (2004): 95–130; and "Social Moral Epistemology," *Social Philosophy and Policy* 19 (2002): 126–52.

51. I am indebted to Andrew Altman for calling this objection to my attention and for indicating the general outlines of a response to it.

52. A prominent example of the purely discursive, noninstitutional approach to the problem of justification is the valuable work of James Griffin on human rights, culminating in *On Human Rights* (Oxford: Oxford University Press, 2008).

53. Amartya Sen may be a partial exception to this generalization. In a recent essay on human rights he suggests that valid human-rights norms are those that survive discussion and contestation, but he does not consider the role of institutions in this regard, nor does he appreciate the relevance of social moral epistemology. Amartya Sen, "Elements of a Theory of Human Rights," *Philosophy and Public Affairs* 32 (2004): 315–56.

54. I am grateful to Stephen Ratner, Monica Hlavac, Russell Powell, and two anonymous reviewers for their helpful comments on earlier versions of this chapter.

PART II

LEGITIMACY

5

THE LEGITIMACY OF GLOBAL GOVERNANCE INSTITUTIONS

With Robert O. Keohane

"Legitimacy" has both a normative and a sociological meaning. To say that an institution is legitimate in the normative sense is to assert that it has *the right to rule*—where ruling includes promulgating rules and attempting to secure compliance with them by attaching costs to non-compliance and/or benefits to compliance. An institution is legitimate in the sociological sense when it is widely *believed* to have the right to rule.[1] When people disagree over whether the WTO is legitimate, their disagreements are typically normative. They are not disagreeing about whether they or others *believe* that this institution has the right to rule; they are disagreeing about whether it *has* the right to rule.[2] This chapter addresses the normative dimension of recent legitimacy discussions.

We articulate a global public standard for the normative legitimacy of global governance institutions. This standard can provide the basis for principled criticism of global governance institutions and guide reform efforts in circumstances in which people disagree deeply about the demands of global justice and the role that global governance institutions should play in meeting them. We stake out a middle ground between an increasingly discredited conception of legitimacy that conflates legitimacy with international legality understood as state consent, on the one hand, and the unrealistic view that legitimacy for these institutions requires the same democratic standards that are now applied to states, on the other.

Our approach to the problem of legitimacy integrates conceptual analysis and moral reasoning with an appreciation of the fact that global governance institutions are novel, still evolving, and characterized by reasonable disagreement about what their proper goals are and what standards of justice they should meet. Because both standards and institutions are subject to change as a result of further reflection and action, we do not claim to *discover* timeless necessary and sufficient conditions for legitimacy. Instead, we offer a principled *proposal* for how the legitimacy of these institutions ought to be assessed—for the time being. Essential to our account is the idea that to be legitimate a global governance institution must possess certain *epistemic* virtues that facilitate the ongoing critical revision of its goals, through interaction with agents and organizations outside the institution. A principled global public standard of legitimacy can help citizens committed to democratic principles to distinguish legitimate institutions from illegitimate ones and to achieve a reasonable congruence in their legitimacy assessments. Were such a standard widely accepted, it could bolster public support for valuable global governance institutions that either satisfy the standard or at least make credible efforts to do so.

"Global governance institutions" covers a diversity of multilateral entities, including the World Trade Organization (WTO), the International Monetary Fund (IMF), various environmental institutions, such as the climate change regime built around the Kyoto Protocol, judges' and regulators' networks, the UN Security Council, and the new International Criminal Court (ICC).[3] These institutions are like governments in that they issue rules and publicly attach significant consequences to compliance or failure to comply with them—and claim the authority to do so. Nonetheless, they do not attempt to perform anything approaching a full range of governmental functions. These institutions do not seek, as governments do, to monopolize the legitimate use of violence within a permanently specified territory, and their design and major actions require the consent of states.

Determining whether global governance institutions are legitimate—and whether they are widely perceived to be so—is an urgent matter. Global governance institutions can promote international cooperation and also help to construct regulatory frameworks that limit abuses by nonstate actors (from corporations to narcotraffickers and terrorists) who exploit transnational mobility. At the same time, however, they constrain the choices facing societies, sometimes limit the exercise of sovereignty by democratic states, and impose burdens as well as confer benefits. For example, states must belong to the WTO in order to participate effectively in the world economy, yet WTO membership requires accepting a large number of quite intrusive rules, authoritatively applied by its dispute settlement system. Furthermore, individuals can be adversely affected by global rules—for example, by the blacklists maintained by the Security Council's Sanctions Committee[4] or the WTO's policies on intellectual property in "essential medicines." If these institutions lack legitimacy, then their claims to authority are unfounded and they are not entitled to our support.

Judgments about institutional legitimacy have distinctive practical implications. Generally speaking, if an institution is legitimate, then this legitimacy should shape the character of both our responses to the claims it makes on us and the form that our criticisms of it take. We should support or at least refrain from interfering with legitimate institutions. Further, agents of legitimate institutions deserve a kind of impersonal respect, even when we voice serious criticisms of them. Judging an institution to be legitimate, if flawed, focuses critical discourse by signaling that the appropriate objective is to reform it, rather than to reject it outright.

It is important not only that global governance institutions be legitimate, but that they are perceived to be legitimate. The perception of legitimacy matters, because, in a democratic era, multilateral institutions will only thrive if they are viewed as legitimate by democratic publics. If one is unclear about the appropriate standards of legitimacy or if unrealistically demanding standards are assumed, then public support for global governance institutions may be undermined and their effectiveness in providing valuable goods may be impaired.

ASSESSING LEGITIMACY

The Social Function of Legitimacy Assessments

Global governance institutions are valuable because they create norms and information that enable member states and other actors to coordinate their behavior in mutually beneficial ways.[5] They can reduce transaction costs, create opportunities for states and other actors to demonstrate credibility, thereby overcoming commitment problems, and provide public goods, including rule-based, peaceful resolutions of conflicts.[6] An institution's ability to perform these valuable functions, however, may depend on whether those to whom it addresses its rules regard them as binding and whether others within the institution's domain of operation support or at least do not interfere with its functioning. It is not enough that the relevant actors agree that *some* institution is needed; they must agree that *this* institution is worthy of support. So, for institutions to perform their valuable coordinating functions, a higher-order coordination problem must be solved.[7]

Once an institution is in place, ongoing support for it and compliance with its rules are sometimes simply a matter of self-interest from the perspective of states, assuming that the institution actually achieves coordination or other benefits that all or at least the more powerful actors regard as valuable.[8] Similarly, once the rule of the road has been established and penalties for violating it are in place, most people will find compliance with it to be rational from a purely self-interested point of view. In the latter case, no question of legitimacy arises, because the sole function of the institution is coordination and the choice of the particular coordination point raises no issues on which people are likely to disagree. Global governance institutions are not pure coordination devices in the way in which the rule of the road is, however. Even though all may agree that some institution or other is needed in a specific domain (the regulation of global trade, for example), and all may agree that any of several particular institutions is better than the noninstitutional alternative, different parties, depending upon their differing interests and moral perspectives, will find some feasible institutions more attractive than others. The fact that all acknowledge that it is in their interest to achieve coordinated support for some institution or other may not be sufficient to assure adequate support for any particular institution.

The concept of legitimacy allows various actors to coordinate their support for particular institutions by appealing to their common capacity to be moved by *moral reasons*, as distinct from purely strategic or exclusively self-interested reasons. If legitimacy judgments are to perform this coordinating function, however, actors must not insist that only institutions that are *optimal* from the standpoint of their own moral views are acceptable, since this would preclude coordinated support in the face of diverging normative views. More specifically, actors must not assume that an institution is worthy of support only if it is *fully just*. We thus need a standard of legitimacy that is both accessible from a diversity of moral standpoints and less demanding than a standard of justice. Such a standard must appeal to various actors' capacities to be moved by moral reasons, but without presupposing more moral agreement than exists.

Legitimacy and Self-interest

It is one thing to say that an institution promotes one's interests and another to say that it is legitimate. As Andrew Hurrell points out, the rule-following that results from a sense of legitimacy is "distinguishable from purely self-interested or instrumental behaviour on the one hand, and from straightforward imposed or coercive rule on the other."[9] Sometimes self-interest may speak in favor of treating an institution's rules as binding; that is, it can be in one's interest to take the fact that an institution issues a rule as a weighty reason for complying with it, independently of a positive assessment of the content of particular rules. This would be the case if one is likely to do better, from the standpoint of one's own interest, by taking the rules as binding than one would by evaluating each particular rule as to how complying with it would affect one's interests. Yet clearly it makes sense to ask whether an institution that promotes one's interests is legitimate. So legitimacy, understood as the right to rule, is a moral notion that cannot be reduced to rational self-interest. To say that an institution is legitimate implies that it has the right to rule even if it does not act in accordance with the rational self-interest of everyone who is subject to its rule.

There are advantages in achieving coordinated support for institutions on the basis of moral reasons, rather than exclusively on the basis of purely self-interested ones. First, the appeal to moral reasons is instrumentally valuable in securing the benefits that only institutions can provide because, as a matter of psychological fact, moral reasons matter when we try to determine what practical attitudes should be taken toward particular institutional arrangements. For example, we care not only about whether an environmental regulation regime reduces air pollutants and thereby produces benefits for all, but also whether it fairly distributes the costs of the benefits it provides. Given that there is widespread disagreement as to which institutional arrangement would be optimal, we need to find a shared evaluative perspective that makes it possible for us to achieve the coordinated support required for effective institutions without requiring us to disregard our most basic moral commitments. Second, and perhaps most important, if our support for an institution is based on reasons other than self-interest or the fear of coercion, it may be more stable. What is in our self-interest may change as circumstances change and the threat of coercion may not always be credible, and moral commitments can preserve support for valuable institutions in such circumstances.

For questions of legitimacy to arise there must be considerable moral disagreement about how institutions should be designed. Yet for agreement about legitimacy to be reached, there must be sufficient agreement on the sorts of moral considerations that are relevant for evaluating alternative institutional designs. The practice of making legitimacy judgments is grounded in a complex belief—namely, that while it is true that institutions ought to meet standards more demanding than mere mutual benefit (relative to some relevant noninstitutional alternative), they can be worthy of our support even if they do not maximally serve our interests and even if they do not measure up to our highest moral standards.[10]

Legitimacy requires not only that institutional agents are justified in carrying out their roles, but also that those to whom institutional rules are addressed have content-independent reasons to comply with them, and that those within the domain of the institution's operations have content-independent reasons to support the institution or at least to not interfere with its functioning.[11] One has a content-independent reason to comply with a rule if and only if one has a reason to comply regardless of any positive assessment of the content of that rule. For example, I have a content-independent reason to comply with the rules of a club to which I belong if I have agreed to follow them and this reason is independent of whether I judge any particular rule to be a good or useful one. If I acknowledge an institution as having authority, I thereby acknowledge that there are content-independent reasons to comply with its rules or at least to not interfere with their operation. Legitimacy disputes concern not merely what institutional agents are morally permitted to do but also whether those to whom the institution addresses its rules should regard it as having authority.

The debate about the legitimacy of global governance institutions engages both the perspective of states and that of individuals. Indeed, as recent mass protests against the WTO suggest, politically mobilized individuals can adversely affect the functioning of global governance institutions, both directly, by disrupting key meetings, and indirectly, by imposing political costs on their governments for their support of institutional policies. Legitimacy in the case of global governance institutions, then, is the right to rule, understood to mean both that institutional agents are morally justified in making rules and attempting to secure compliance with them and that people subject to those rules have moral, content-independent reasons to follow them and/or to not interfere with others' compliance with them.

If it becomes widely believed that an institution does not measure up to standards of legitimacy, then the result may be a lack of coordination, at least until the institution changes to conform to the standards or a new institution that better conforms to them replaces it. Thus, it would be misleading to say simply that the function of legitimacy judgments is to achieve coordinated support for institutions; rather, their function is to make possible coordinated support based on moral reasons, while at the same time supplying a critical but realistic minimal moral standard by which to determine whether institutions are *worthy* of support.

Justice and Legitimacy

The foregoing account of the social function of legitimacy assessments helps clarify the relationship between justice and legitimacy. Collapsing legitimacy into justice undermines the valuable social function of legitimacy assessments. There are two reasons not to insist that only just institutions have the right to rule. First, there is sufficient disagreement on what justice requires that such a standard for legitimacy would thwart the eminently reasonable goal of securing coordinated support for valuable institutions on the basis of moral reasons. Second, even if we all agreed on what justice requires, withholding support from institutions because they fail to meet the demands of justice would be self-defeating from the standpoint of justice itself, because progress toward justice requires effective institutions. To mistake legitimacy for justice is to make the best the enemy of the good.

COMPETING STANDARDS OF LEGITIMACY

Having explicated our *conception* of legitimacy, we now explore *standards* of legitimacy: the conditions an institution must satisfy in order to have the right to rule. In this section we articulate three candidates for the appropriate standard of legitimacy—state consent, consent by democratic states, and global democracy—and argue that each is inadequate.

State Consent

The first view is relatively simple. Global governance institutions are legitimate if (and only if) they are created through state consent. In this conception, legitimacy is simply a matter of legality. Legally constituted institutions, created by states according to the recognized procedures of public international law and consistent with it, are ipso facto legitimate or at the very least enjoy a strong presumption of legitimacy.[12] Call this the International Legal Pedigree View (the Pedigree View, for short). A more sophisticated version of the Pedigree View would require the periodic reaffirmation of state consent, on the grounds that states have a legitimate interest in determining whether these institutions are performing as they are supposed to.[13]

The Pedigree View fails because it is hard to see how state consent could render global governance institutions legitimate, given that many states are nondemocratic and systematically violate the human rights of their citizens and are for that reason themselves illegitimate. State consent in these cases cannot transfer legitimacy for the simple reason that there is no legitimacy to transfer. To assert that state consent, regardless of the character of the state, is sufficient for the legitimacy of global governance institutions is to regress to a conception of international order that fails to impose even the most minimal normative requirements on states. Indeed, once we abandon that deeply defective conception of international order, it is hard to see why state consent is even a *necessary* condition for legitimacy.

It might be argued, however, that even though the consent of illegitimate states cannot itself make global governance institutions legitimate, there is an important instrumental justification for treating state consent as a necessary condition for their legitimacy: doing so provides a check on the tendency of stronger states to exploit weak ones. In other words, persisting in the fiction that all states—irrespective of whether they respect the basic rights of their own citizens—are moral agents worthy of respect serves an important value. This conception of the state, however, is not a fiction that those who take human rights seriously can consistently accept.

The proponent of state consent might reply as follows: "My proposal is not that we should return to the pernicious fiction of the Morality of States. Instead, it is that we should agree, for good cosmopolitan reasons, to regard a global governance institution as legitimate only if it enjoys the consent of all states." Withholding legitimacy from global governance institutions, no matter how valuable they are, simply because not all states consent to them, however, would purport to protect weaker states at the expense of giving a legitimacy veto to tyrannies. The price is too high. Weak states are in a numerical majority in multilateral institutions. Generally speaking, they are less threatened by the dominance of powerful states within the institutions than they are by the actions of such powerful states acting outside of institutional constraints.

The Consent of Democratic States

The idea that state consent confers legitimacy is much more plausible when restricted to democratic states. On reflection, however, the mere fact of state consent, even when the state in question is democratic and satisfies whatever other conditions are appropriate for state legitimacy, is not sufficient for the legitimacy of global governance institutions.

From the standpoint of a particular weak democratic state, participation in global governance institutions such as the WTO is hardly voluntary, since the state would suffer serious costs by not participating. Yet "substantial" voluntariness is generally thought to be a necessary condition for consent to play a legitimating role.[14] Of course, there may be reasonable disagreements over what counts as substantial voluntariness, but the vulnerability of individual weak states is serious enough to undercut the view that the consent of democratic states is by itself sufficient for legitimacy.

There is another reason why the consent of democratic states is not sufficient for the legitimacy of global governance institutions: the problem of reconciling democratic values with unavoidable "bureaucratic discretion" that plagues democratic theory at the domestic level looms even larger in the global case. The problem is that for a modern state to function, much of what state agents do will not be subject to democratic decisions, and saying that the public has consented in some highly general way to whatever it is that state agents do is clearly inadequate. The difficulty is not in identifying chains of delegation stretching from the individual citizen to state agents, but rather that at some point the impact of the popular will on how political power is used becomes so attenuated as to be merely nominal. Given how problematic democratic authorization is in the modern state and given that global governance institutions require lengthening the chain of delegation, democratic state consent is not sufficient for legitimacy.

Still, the consent of democratic states may appear to be necessary, if not sufficient, for the legitimacy of global governance institutions. Indeed, it seems obvious that for such an institution to attempt to impose its rules on democratic states without their consent would violate the right of self-determination of the people of those states. Matters are not so simple, however. A democratic people's right of self-determination is not absolute. If the majority persecutes a minority, the fact that it does so through democratic processes does not render the state in question immune to sanctions or even to intervention. One might accommodate this fact by stipulating that a necessary condition for the legitimacy of global governance institutions is that they enjoy the consent of states that are democratic *and* that do a credible job of respecting the rights of all their citizens.

This does not mean that *all* such states must consent. A few such states may willfully seek to isolate themselves from global governance (Switzerland only joined the UN in 2002). Furthermore, democratic states may engage in wars that are unnecessary and unjust, and resist pressures from international institutions to desist. It would hardly delegitimize a global governance institution established to constrain unjust warfare that it was opposed by a democratic state that was waging an unjust war. A more reasonable position would be that there is a *strong presumption* that global governance institutions are illegitimate unless they enjoy the ongoing consent of democratic states. Let us say, then, that ongoing consent by rights-respecting democratic states constitutes *the democratic channel* of accountability.[15]

However valuable the democratic channel of accountability is, it is not sufficient. First, as already noted, the problem of bureaucratic discretion that attenuates the power of majoritarian processes at the domestic level seems even more serious in the case of global bureaucracies. Second, not all the people who are affected by global governance institutions are citizens of democratic states, so even if the ongoing consent of democratic states fosters accountability, it may not foster accountability to *them*. If—as is the case at present—democratic states tend to be richer and hence more powerful than nondemocratic ones, then the requirement of ongoing consent by democratic states may actually foster a type of accountability that is detrimental to the interests of the world's worst-off people. From the standpoint of any broadly cosmopolitan moral theory, this is a deep flaw of domestic democracies as ordinarily conceived: government is supposed to be responsive to the interests and preferences of the "sovereign people"—*the people whose government it is*—not all people or even all people whose legitimate interests will be seriously affected by the government's actions.[16] For these reasons, the consent of democratic states seems insufficient. The idea that the legitimacy of global governance institutions requires democracy on a grander scale may seem plausible.

Global Democracy

Because democracy is now widely thought to be the gold standard for legitimacy in the case of the state, it may seem obvious that global governance institutions are legitimate if and only if they are democratic. And since these institutions increasingly affect the welfare of people everywhere, surely this must mean that they ought to be democratic in the sense of giving everyone an equal say in how they operate. Call this the Global Democracy View.

The most obvious difficulty with this view is that the social and political conditions for democracy are not met at the global level and there is no reason to think that they will be in the foreseeable future. At present there is no global political structure that could provide the basis for democratic control over global governance institutions, even if one assumes that democracy requires little direct participation by individuals. Any attempt to create such a structure in the form of a global democratic federation that relies on existing states as federal units would lack legitimacy, and hence could not confer legitimacy on global governance institutions, because, as has already been noted, many states are themselves undemocratic or lack other qualities necessary for state legitimacy. Furthermore, there is at present no global public—no worldwide political community constituted by a broad consensus recognizing a common domain as the proper subject of global collective decision-making and habitually communicating with one another about public issues. Nor is there consensus on a normative framework within which to deliberate together about a global common interest. Indeed, there is not even a global consensus that some form of global government, much less a global democracy, is needed or appropriate. Finally, once it is understood that it is *liberal* democracy, democracy that protects individual and minority rights, that is desirable, the Global Democracy View seems even more unfeasible. Democracy worth aspiring to is more than elections; it includes a complex web of institutions, including a free press and media, an active civil society, and institutions to check abuses of power by administrative agencies and elected officials.

Global governance institutions provide benefits that cannot be provided by states and, as we have argued, securing those benefits may depend upon these institutions being regarded as legitimate. The value of global governance institutions, therefore, warrants being more critical about the assumption that they must be democratic *on the domestic model* and more willing to explore an alternative conception of their legitimacy. In the next section we take up this task.

A COMPLEX STANDARD OF LEGITIMACY

Desiderata for a Standard of Legitimacy

Our discussion of the social function of legitimacy assessments and our critique of the three dominant views on the standard of legitimacy for global governance institutions (state consent, democratic state consent, and global democracy) suggest that a standard of legitimacy for such institutions should have the following characteristics:

1. It must provide a reasonable public basis for coordinated support for the institutions in question, on the basis of moral reasons that are widely accessible in spite of the persistence of significant moral disagreement—in particular, about the requirements of justice.
2. It must not confuse legitimacy with justice but nonetheless must not allow that extremely unjust institutions are legitimate.
3. It must take the ongoing consent of democratic states as a presumptive necessary condition, though not a sufficient condition, for legitimacy.
4. Although the standard should not make authorization by a global democracy a necessary condition of legitimacy, it should nonetheless *promote* the key values that underlie demands for democracy.

5. It must properly reflect the dynamic character of global governance institutions: the fact that not only the means they employ, but even their goals, may and ought to change over time.
6. It must address the two problems we encountered earlier: the problem of bureaucratic discretion and the tendency of democratic states to disregard the legitimate interests of foreigners.

The standard of legitimacy must therefore incorporate mechanisms for accountability that are both more robust and more inclusive than that provided by the consent of democratic states.

Moral Disagreement and Uncertainty

The first desideratum of a standard of legitimacy is complex and warrants further explication and emphasis. We have noted that a central feature of the circumstances of legitimacy is the persistence of disagreement about, first, what the proper goals of the institution are (given the limitations imposed by state sovereignty properly conceived), second, what global justice requires, and third, what role if any the institution should play in the pursuit of global justice. Moral disagreement is not unique to global governance institutions, but extends also to the appropriate role of the state.

There are two circumstances in the case of global governance institutions, however, that exacerbate the problem of moral disagreement. First, in the case of the state, democratic processes, at least ideally, provide a way of accommodating these disagreements, by providing a public process that assures every citizen that she is being treated as an equal, through the electoral process, while, as we have seen, democracy is unavailable at the global level. Second, although there is a widespread perception, at least among cosmopolitans broadly speaking, that there is serious global injustice and that the effective pursuit of global justice requires a significant role for global institutions, it is not possible at present to provide a principled specification of the division of institutional labor for pursuing global justice. In part the problem is that there is no unified system of global institutions within which a fair and effective allocation of institutional responsibilities for justice can be devised. How responsibilities for justice ought to be allocated among global institutions and between states and global institutions depends chiefly on the answers to two questions: What are the proper responsibilities of states in the pursuit of global justice, taking into account the proper scope of state sovereignty (because this will determine how extensive the role of global institutions should be), and what are the capabilities of various global institutions for contributing to the pursuit of global justice? But neither of these questions can be answered satisfactorily at present, in part because global governance institutions are so new and in part because people have only recently begun to think seriously about achieving justice on a global scale. So the difficulty is not just that there is considerable moral disagreement about the proper goals of global governance institutions and about the role these institutions should play in the pursuit of global justice; there is also moral *uncertainty*.[17] A plausible standard of legitimacy for global governance institutions must somehow accommodate *the facts of moral disagreement and uncertainty.*

Three Substantive Criteria

We begin with a set of institutional attributes that have considerable intuitive appeal: minimal moral acceptability, comparative benefit, and institutional integrity.

Minimal Moral Acceptability. Global governance institutions, like institutions generally, must not persist in committing serious injustices. If they do so, they are not entitled to our support. On our view, the primary instance of a serious injustice is the violation of human rights. We also believe that the most plausible conception of human rights is what might be called the basic human interest conception. This conception, which we can only sketch in broad outlines here, builds on Joseph Raz's insight that rights generally are normative relations (in particular, duties and entitlements), which, if realized, provide important protections for interests.[18] On this view, to justify the claim that R is a right, one must identify an interest, support the claim that the interest is of sufficient moral importance to ground duties, explain why the duties are owed to the right holders, and make the case that if the normative relations in question are satisfied, significant protection for the interest will be achieved. Certain rights are properly called human rights because the duties they entail provide especially important protections for basic human interests, given the standard threats to those interests in our world.

What the standard threats are can change over time. For example, when human societies create legal systems and police and courts to enforce laws, they also create new opportunities for damaging basic human interests. For this reason, the content of particular human rights, and even which rights are included among the human rights, may also change, even though the basic interests that ground them do not. For example, all human beings, regardless of where or when they exist, have a basic interest in physical security, but in a society with a legal system backed by the coercive power of the state, adequate protection of this interest requires rights of due process and equal protection under the law.

There is disagreement among basic interest theorists of human rights as to exactly what the list of human rights includes and how the content of particular rights is to be filled out. There is agreement, however, that the list includes the rights to physical security, to liberty (understood as at least encompassing freedom from slavery, servitude, and forced occupations), and the right to subsistence. Assuming that this is so, we can at least say this much: global governance institutions (like institutions generally) are legitimate only if they do not persist in violations of the least controversial human rights. This is a rather minimal moral requirement for legitimacy. Yet in view of the normative disagreement and uncertainty that characterize our attitudes toward these institutions, it might be hard at present to justify a more extensive set of rights that all such institutions are bound to respect. It would certainly be desirable to develop a more meaningful consensus on stronger human rights standards. What this suggests is that we should require global governance institutions to respect minimal human rights, but also expect them to meet higher standards as we gain greater clarity about the scope of human rights.

For many global governance institutions, it is proper to expect that they should *respect* human rights, but not that they should play a major role in *promoting* human rights. Nonetheless, a theory of legitimacy cannot ignore the fact that in some cases the dispute over whether a global governance institution is legitimate is in large part a disagreement over whether it is worthy of support if it does not actively promote human rights. A proposal for a standard of legitimacy for global governance institutions must take into account the fact that some of these institutions play a more direct and substantial role in securing human rights than others.

When we see the injustices of our world and appreciate that ameliorating them requires institutional actions, we are quick to attribute obligations to institutions and then criticize them for failing to fulfill those obligations. It is one thing to say that it would be a good thing if a particular global governance institution took on certain functions that would promote human rights, however, and quite another to say that it has a duty to do so *and* that this duty is of such importance that failure to discharge it makes the institution illegitimate. There are two mistakes to be avoided here. The first is "duty dumping," that is, arbitrarily assuming that some particular institution has a duty simply because it has the resources to fulfill it and no other actor is doing so.[19] Duty dumping not only makes unsupported attributions of institutional responsibility; it also distracts attention from the difficult task of determining what a fair distribution of the burdens—among individuals and institutions—for protecting the human rights in question would be. The second error derives from the first: if one uncritically assumes that the institution has a duty to provide X and also assumes that X is a central matter of justice (as is the case with human rights), then one may conclude that the institution's failure to provide X is such a serious injustice as to rob the institution of legitimacy. But the fact that an institution could provide X and the fact that X is a human right does not imply that in refraining from providing X the institution commits a serious injustice. That conclusion would only follow if it were established that the institution has a duty of justice to provide X. Merely pointing out that the institution could provide X—or even showing that it is the only existing institution that can do so—is not sufficient to show that it has a duty of justice or any duty at all to provide X.

We seem to be in a quandary. Contemporary institutions have to operate in an environment of moral disagreement and uncertainty, which limits the demands we can reasonably place on them to respect or protect particular human rights.

Furthermore, to be sufficiently general, an account of legitimacy must avoid moral requirements that only apply to some global governance institutions. These considerations suggest the appropriateness of something like the minimal moral acceptability requirement, understood as refraining from violations of the least controversial human rights. On the other hand, the standard of legitimacy should somehow reflect the fact that part of what is at issue in disputes over the legitimacy of some of these institutions is whether they should satisfy more robust demands of justice. In other words, the standard should acknowledge the fact that where the issue of legitimacy is most urgent, there is likely to be deep moral disagreement and uncertainty.

In our view, the way out of this impasse is to build the conditions needed for principled, informed deliberation about moral issues *into the standard of legitimacy itself*. The standard of legitimacy should require minimal moral acceptability, but should also accommodate and even encourage the possibility of developing more determinate and demanding requirements of justice for at least some of these institutions, as a principled basis for an institutional division of labor regarding justice emerges.

Comparative Benefit. This second substantive condition for legitimacy is relatively straightforward. The justification for having global governance institutions is primarily if not exclusively instrumental. The basic reason for states or other addressees of institutional rules to take them as binding and for individuals generally to support or at least to not interfere with the operation of these institutions is that they provide benefits that cannot otherwise be obtained. If an institution cannot effectively perform the functions invoked to justify its existence, then this insufficiency undermines its claim to the right to rule.

"Benefit" here is comparative. The legitimacy of an institution is called into question if there is an institutional alternative, providing significantly greater benefits, that is feasible, accessible without excessive transition costs, and meets the minimal moral acceptability criterion. The most difficult issues, as discussed below, concern trade-offs between comparative benefit and our other criteria. Legitimacy is not to be confused with *optimal* efficacy and efficiency. The other values that we discuss are also important in their own right; and in any case, institutional stability is a virtue. Nevertheless, if an institution steadfastly remains instrumentally suboptimal when it could take steps to become significantly more efficient or effective, this could impugn its legitimacy in an indirect way: it would indicate that those in charge of the institution were either grossly incompetent or not seriously committed to providing the benefits that were invoked to justify the creation of the institution in the first place. For instance, as of the beginning of 2006 the United Nations faced the issue of reconstituting a Human Rights Commission that had been discredited by the membership of states that notoriously abuse human rights, with Libya serving as chair in 2003.[20]

Institutional Integrity. If an institution exhibits a pattern of egregious disparity between its actual performance, on the one hand, and its self-proclaimed procedures or major goals, on the other, its legitimacy is seriously called into question. The United Nations Oil-for-Food scandal is a case in point. The Oil-for-Food Program was devised to enable Iraqi oil to be sold, under strict controls, to pay for food imports under the UN-mandated sanctions of the 1990s. The purpose was both to prevent malnutrition in Iraq and to counter Iraqi propaganda holding the United Nations responsible for the deaths of hundreds of thousands of Iraqi children, without relieving the pressure on Saddam Hussein's regime to get rid of its supposed weapons of mass destruction. Yet it led to a great deal of corruption. Oil-for-Food became a huge program, permitting the government of Iraq to sell \$64.2 billion of oil to 248 companies, and enabling 3,614 companies to sell \$34.5 billion of humanitarian goods to Iraq. Yet more than half of the companies involved paid illegal surcharges or kickbacks to Saddam and his cronies, resulting in large profits for corporations and pecuniary benefits for some program administrators, including at least one high-level UN official.[21] The most damning charge is that neither the Security Council oversight bodies nor the Office of the Secretary-General followed the UN's prescribed procedures for accountability. At least when viewed in the light of the historical record of other, perhaps less egregious failures of accountability in the use of resources on the part of the UN, these findings have raised questions about the legitimacy of the Security Council and the secretariat.

It also appears that an institution should be presumed to be illegitimate if its practices or procedures predictably undermine the pursuit of the very goals in terms of which it justifies its existence. Thus, for example, if the fundamental character of the Security Council's decision-making process renders that institution incapable of successfully pursuing what it now acknowledges as one of its chief goals—stopping large-scale violations of basic human rights—this impugns its legitimacy. To take another example, Randall Stone has shown that the IMF during the 1990s inconsistently applied its own standards with respect to its lending, systematically relaxing enforcement on countries that had rich and powerful patrons.[22] Similarly, if the WTO claims to provide the benefits of trade liberalization to *all* of its members, but consistently develops policies that exclude its weaker members from the benefits of liberalization, this undermines its claim to legitimacy. If an institution fails to satisfy the integrity criterion, we have reason to believe that key institutional agents are either untrustworthy or grossly incompetent, that the institution lacks correctives for these deficiencies, and that the institution is therefore unlikely to be effective in providing the goods that would give it a claim to our support.

Integrity and comparative benefit are related but distinct. If there are major discrepancies between an institution's behavior and its prescribed procedures and professed goals, then we can have little confidence that it will succeed in delivering the benefits it is supposed to provide. Integrity, however, is a more forward-looking, dynamic virtue than comparative benefit, which measures benefit solely in terms of the current situation. If an institution satisfies the criterion of integrity, there is reason to be confident that institutional actors will not only deliver the benefits that are now taken to constitute the proper goals of institutional activity, but also that they will be able to maintain the institution's effectiveness if its goals change.

Epistemic Aspects of Legitimacy

Minimal moral acceptability, comparative benefit, and institutional integrity are plausible presumptive substantive requirements for the legitimacy of global governance institutions. It would be excessive to claim that they are necessary conditions *simpliciter*, because there might be extraordinary circumstances in which an institution would fail to satisfy one or two of them, yet still reasonably be regarded as legitimate. This might be the case if there were no feasible and accessible alternative institutional arrangement, if the noninstitutional alternative were sufficiently grim, and if there was reason to believe that the institution had the resources and the political will to correct the deficiency. How much we expect of an institution should depend, inter alia, upon how valuable the benefits it provides are and whether there are acceptable, feasible alternatives to it. For example, we might be warranted in regarding an institution as legitimate even though it lacked integrity, if it were nonetheless providing important protections for basic human rights and the alternatives to relying on it were even less acceptable. In contrast, the fact that an institution is effective in incrementally liberalizing trade would not be sufficient to rebut the presumption that it is illegitimate because it abuses human rights.[23]

Our three substantive conditions are best thought of as what Rawls calls "counting principles": the more of them an institution satisfies, and the higher the degree to which it satisfies them, the stronger its claim to legitimacy.[24]

There are two limitations on the applicability of these three criteria, however. The first is *the problem of factual knowledge*: being able to make reasonable judgments about whether an institution satisfies any of the three substantive conditions requires considerable information about the workings of the institution and their effects in a number of domains, as well as about the likely effects of feasible alternatives. Some institutions may not only fail to supply the needed information, however; they may, whether deliberately or otherwise, make such information either impossible for outsiders to obtain or make obtaining it prohibitively costly. Even if the institution does not try to limit access to the relevant information, it may not be accessible, in suitably integrated, understandable form.

The second difficulty with taking the three substantive conditions as jointly sufficient for legitimacy is *the problem of moral disagreement and uncertainty* noted earlier. Even if there is sufficient agreement on what counts as the violation of basic human rights, there are ongoing disputes about whether some global governance institutions should meet higher moral standards. As emphasized above, there is not only disagreement but also uncertainty as to the role that some of these institutions should play in the pursuit of global justice, chiefly because we do not have a coherent idea of what the institutional division of labor for achieving global justice would look like.

Furthermore, merely requiring that global governance institutions not violate basic human rights is unresponsive to the familiar complaint that rich countries unfairly dominate them, and that even if they provide benefits to all, the richer members receive unjustifiably greater benefits. Although all parties may agree that fairness matters, however, there are likely to be disagreements about what fairness would consist of, disputes about whether fairness would suffice or whether equality is required, and about how equality is to be understood and even over what is to be made equal (welfare, opportunities, resources, and so on). So, quite apart from the issue of what positive role, if any, these institutions should play in the pursuit of global justice, there is disagreement about what standards of fairness they should meet internally. There is also likely to be disagreement about how unfair an institution must be to lack legitimacy. A proposal for a public global standard of legitimacy must not gloss over these disagreements.

In the following sections we argue that the proper response to both the problem of factual knowledge and the problem of moral disagreement and uncertainty is to focus on what might be called the *epistemic-deliberative* quality of the institution, the extent to which the institution provides reliable information needed for grappling with normative disagreement and uncertainty concerning its proper functions. To lay the groundwork for that argument we begin by considering two items that are often assumed to be obvious requirements for the legitimacy of global governance institutions: accountability and transparency.

Accountability. Critics of global governance institutions often complain that they lack accountability. To understand the strengths and limitations of accountability as a gauge of legitimacy, we start with a skeletal but serviceable analysis of accountability. Accountability includes three elements: first, standards that those who are held accountable are expected to meet; second, information available to accountability holders, who can then apply the standards in question to the performance of those who are held to account; and third, the ability of these accountability holders to impose sanctions—to attach costs to the failure to meet the standards. The need for information about whether the institution is meeting the standards accountability holders apply means that a degree of transparency regarding the institution's operations is essential to any form of accountability.

It is misleading to say that global governance institutions are illegitimate because they lack accountability and to suggest that the key to making them legitimate is to make them accountable. Most global governance institutions, including those whose legitimacy is most strenuously denied, include mechanisms for accountability.[25] The problem is that existing patterns of accountability are morally inadequate. For example, the World Bank has traditionally exhibited a high degree of accountability, but it has been accountability to the biggest donor countries, and the Bank therefore has to act in conformity with their interests, at least insofar as they agree. This kind of accountability does not ensure meaningful participation by those affected by rules or due consideration of their legitimate interests.[26] A high degree of accountability in this case may serve to perpetuate the defects of the institution.

So accountability per se is not sufficient; it must be the right sort of accountability. At the very least, this means that there must be effective provisions in the structure of the institution to hold institutional agents accountable for acting in ways that ensure satisfaction of the minimal moral acceptability and comparative benefit conditions. But accountability understood in this narrow way is not sufficiently *dynamic* to serve as an assurance of the legitimacy of global governance institutions, given that in some cases there is serious disagreement about what the goals of the institution should be and, more specifically, about what role if any the institution should play in the pursuit of global justice. The point is that what the *terms of accountability* ought to be—what standards of accountability ought to be employed, who the accountability holders should be, and whose interests the accountability holders should represent—cannot be definitively ascertained without knowing what role, if any, the institution should play in the pursuit of global justice.

Therefore, what might be called narrow accountability—accountability without provision for contestation of the terms of accountability—is insufficient for legitimacy, given the facts of moral disagreement and uncertainty. Because what constitutes appropriate accountability is itself subject to reasonable dispute, the legitimacy of global governance institutions depends in part upon whether they operate in such a way as to facilitate principled, factually informed deliberation about the terms of accountability. There must be provisions for revising existing standards of accountability and current conceptions of who the proper accountability holders are and whose interests they should represent.

Transparency. Achieving transparency is often touted as the proper response to worries about the legitimacy of global governance institutions.[27] But transparency by itself is inadequate. First, if transparency means merely the *availability* of accurate information about how the institution works, it is insufficient even for narrow accountability—that is, for ensuring that the institution is accurately evaluated in accordance with the current terms of accountability. If information about how the institution operates is to serve the end of narrow accountability, it must be (a) accessible at reasonable cost, (b) properly integrated and interpreted, and (c) directed to the accountability holders. Furthermore, (d) the accountability holders must be adequately motivated to use it properly in evaluating the performance of the relevant institutional agents. Second, if, as we have suggested, the capacity for critically revising the terms of accountability is necessary for legitimacy, information about how the institution works must be available not only to those who are presently designated as accountability holders, but also to those who may contest the terms of accountability.

Broad transparency is needed for critical revisability of the terms of accountability. Both institutional practices and the moral principles that shape the terms of accountability must be revisable in the light of critical reflection and discussion.[28] Under conditions of broad transparency, information produced initially to enable institutionally designated accountability holders to assess officials' performance may be appropriated by agents *external* to the institution, such as non-governmental organizations (NGOs) and other actors in transnational civil society, and used to support more fundamental criticisms, not only of the institution's processes and structures, but even of its most fundamental goals and its role in the pursuit of global justice.

One especially important dimension of broad transparency is *responsibility for public justification*.[29] Institutional actors must offer public justifications of at least the more controversial and consequential institutional policies and must facilitate timely critical responses to them. Potential critics must be in a position to determine whether the public justifications are cogent, whether they are consistent with the current terms of accountability, and whether, if taken seriously, these justifications call for revision of the current terms of responsibility. To help ensure this dimension of broad transparency, it may be worthwhile to draw on, while adapting, the notice and comment procedures of administrative law at the domestic level.[30]

Earlier we noted that although comparative benefit, minimal moral acceptability, and integrity are reasonable presumptive necessary conditions for legitimacy, it may be difficult for those outside the institution to determine whether these conditions are satisfied. We suggest that broad transparency can serve as a proxy for satisfaction of the minimal moral acceptability, comparative benefit, and integrity criteria. For example, it may be easier for outsiders to discover that an institution is not responding to demands for information relevant to determining whether it is violating its own prescribed procedures, than to determine whether in fact it is violating them. Similarly, it may be very difficult to determine whether an institution is comparatively effective in solving certain global problems, but much easier to tell whether it generates—or systematically restricts access to—the information outsiders would need to evaluate its effectiveness. If an institution persistently fails to cooperate in making available to outsiders the information that would be needed to determine whether the three presumptive necessary conditions are satisfied, that by itself creates a presumption that it is illegitimate.

Legitimate global governance institutions should possess three epistemic virtues. First, because their chief function is to achieve coordination, they must generate and properly direct reliable information about coordination points; otherwise they will not satisfy the condition of comparative benefit. Second, because accountability is required to determine whether they are in fact performing their current coordinating functions efficiently and effectively requires narrow transparency, they must at least be transparent in the narrow sense. They must also have effective provisions for integrating and interpreting the information current accountability holders need and for directing it to them. Third, and most demanding, they must have the capacity for *revising the terms of accountability*, and this requires broad transparency: institutions must facilitate positive information externalities to permit inclusive, informed contestation of their current terms of accountability. There must be provision for ongoing deliberation about what global justice requires and how the institution in question fits into a division of institutional responsibilities for achieving it.

Overcoming Informational Asymmetries

A fundamental problem of institutional accountability is that insiders generally have better information about the institution than outsiders. Outsiders can determine whether institutions enjoy the consent of states, and whether states are democratic; but it may be very difficult for them to reach well-informed conclusions about the minimal moral acceptability, comparative benefit, and integrity conditions. Our emphasis on epistemic institutional virtues is well suited to illuminate these problems of asymmetrical information.

First, if institutional agents persist in failing to provide public justifications for their policies and withhold other information critical to the evaluation of institutional performance, we have good reason to believe the institution is not satisfying the substantive criteria for legitimacy.[31] Second, there may be an asymmetry of knowledge in the other direction as well, and this can have beneficial consequences for institutional accountability. Consider issue areas such as human rights and the environment, which are richly populated with independent NGOs that seek to monitor and criticize national governments and global governance institutions and to suggest policy alternatives. Suppose that in these domains there is a division of labor among external epistemic actors. Some individuals and groups seek information about certain types of issues, while others focus on other aspects, each drawing on distinct but in some cases overlapping groups of experts. Still others specialize in integrating and interpreting information gathered by other external epistemic actors.

The fact that the information held by external epistemic actors is dispersed will make it difficult for institutional agents to know what is known about their behavior or to predict when potentially damaging information may be integrated and interpreted in ways that make it politically potent. The institutional agents' awareness of this asymmetry will provide incentives for avoiding behavior for which they may be criticized. A condition of *productive uncertainty* will exist: although institutional agents will know that external epistemic actors do not possess the full range of knowledge that they do, they will know that there are many individuals and organizations gathering information about the institution. Further, they will know that some of the information that external epistemic actors have access to can serve as a reliable proxy for information they cannot access. Finally, they will also know that potentially damaging information that is currently harmless because it is dispersed among many external epistemic agents may at any time be integrated and interpreted in such a way as to make it politically effective, but they will not be able to predict when this will occur. Under these conditions, institutional agents will have significant incentives to refrain from behavior that will attract damning criticism, despite the fundamental asymmetry of knowledge between insiders and outsiders.

This is not to say that the effects of transparency will always be benign. Indeed, under some circumstances transparency can have malign effects. As David Stasavage points out, "open-door bargaining...encourages representatives to posture by adopting overly aggressive bargaining positions that increase the risks of breakdown in negotiations."[32] When issues combine highly charged symbolic elements with the need for incentives, conflicts between transparency and efficiency may be severe. Our claim is not that outcomes are necessarily better the more transparent institutions are. Rather, it is that the dispersal of information among a plurality of external epistemic actors provides some counterbalance to informational asymmetries favoring insiders. There should be a very strong but rebuttable presumption of transparency, because the ills of too much transparency can be corrected by deeper, more sophisticated public discussion, whereas there can be no democratic response to secret action by bureaucracies not accountable to the public.

Furthermore, if national legislatures are to retain their relevance—if what we have called the democratic accountability channel is to be effective—they must be able to review the policies of global governance institutions.[33] For legislatures to have information essential to performing these functions, they need a flow of information from transnational civil society. Monitoring is best done pluralistically by transnational civil society, whereas the sanctions aspects of accountability are more effectively carried out by legislatures. With respect both to the monitoring and sanctioning functions, broad transparency is conducive to the principled revisability of institutions and to their improvement through increasingly inclusive criticism and more deeply probing discussion over time.

Institutional agents generally have incentives to prevent outsiders from getting information that may eventually be interpreted and integrated in damaging ways and to deprive outsiders of information that can serve as a reliable proxy to assess institutional legitimacy. The very reasons that make the epistemic virtues valuable from the standpoint of assessing institutional legitimacy may therefore tempt institutional agents to ensure that their institutions do not exemplify these virtues. But institutional agents are also aware that it is important for their institutions to be widely regarded as legitimate. Outsiders deprived of access to information are likely to react as does the prospective buyer of a used car who is prevented from taking it to an independent mechanic. They will discount the claims of the insiders and may conclude that the institution is illegitimate. So if there is a broad consensus among outsiders that institutions are not legitimate unless they exemplify the epistemic virtues, institutional agents will have a weighty reason to ensure that their institutions do so.

Contestation and Revisability: Links to External Actors and Institutions

We have argued that the legitimacy of global governance institutions depends upon whether there is ongoing, informed, principled contestation of their goals and terms of accountability. This process of contestation and revision depends upon activities of actors outside the institution. It is not enough for the institutions to make information available. Other agents, whose interests and commitments do not coincide too closely with those of the institution, must provide a check on the reliability of the information, integrate it, and make it available in understandable, usable form, to all who have a legitimate interest in the operations of the institution. Such activities can produce positive feedback, in which appeal to standards of legitimacy by the external epistemic actors not only increases compliance with existing standards but also leads to improvements in the quality of these standards themselves. For these reasons, in the absence of global democracy, and given the limitations of the democratic channel described earlier, legitimacy depends crucially upon not only the epistemic virtues of the institution itself but also on the activities of *external epistemic actors*. Effective linkage between the institution and external epistemic actors constitutes what might be called the *transnational civil society channel of accountability*.

The needed external epistemic actors, if they are effective, will themselves be institutionally organized.[34] Institutional legitimacy, then, is not simply a function of the institution's characteristics; it also depends upon the broader institutional environment in which the particular institution exists. To borrow a biological metaphor, ours is an ecological conception of legitimacy.

All three elements of our complex standard of legitimacy are now in place. First, global governance institutions should enjoy the ongoing consent of democratic states. That is, the democratic accountability channel must function reasonably well. Second, these institutions should satisfy the substantive criteria of minimal moral acceptability, comparative benefit, and institutional integrity. Third, they should possess the epistemic virtues needed to make credible judgments about whether the three substantive criteria are satisfied and to achieve the ongoing contestation and critical revision of their goals, their terms of accountability, and ultimately their role in a division of labor for the pursuit of global justice, through their interaction with effective external epistemic agents.

The Complex Standard frames the legitimacy of global governance institutions as both dynamic and relational. Its emphasis on the conditions for ongoing contestation and critical revision of the most basic features of the institutions captures the exceptional moral disagreement and uncertainty that characterize the circumstances of legitimacy for this type of institution. While acknowledging the facts of moral disagreement and uncertainty, the Complex Standard includes provisions for developing more robust moral requirements for institutions over time. The Complex Standard also makes it clear that whether the institution is legitimate does not depend solely upon its own characteristics, but also upon the epistemic-deliberative relationships between the institution and epistemic actors outside it.

A Place for Democratic Values in the Absence of Global Democracy

Earlier we argued that it is a mistake to hold global governance institutions to the standard of democratic legitimacy that is now widely applied to states. We now want to suggest that when the Complex Standard of legitimacy we propose is satisfied, important democratic values will be served. For purposes of the present discussion we will assume, rather than argue, that among the most important democratic values are the following: first, equal regard for the fundamental interests of all persons; second, decision-making about the public order through principled, collective deliberation; and third, mutual respect for persons as beings who are guided by reasons.

If the Complex Standard of legitimacy we propose is satisfied, all three of these values will be served. To the extent that connections between the institutions and external epistemic actors provide access to information that is not restricted to certain groups but available globally, it becomes harder for institutions to continue to exclude consideration of the interests of certain groups, and we move closer toward the ideal of equal regard for the fundamental interests of all. Furthermore, by making information available globally, networks of external epistemic actors are in effect addressing all people as individuals for whom moral reasons, not just the threat of coercion, determine whether they regard an institution's rules as authoritative. Finally, if the Complex Standard of legitimacy is satisfied, every feature of the institution becomes a potential object of principled, informed, collective deliberation, and eligibility for participation in deliberation will not be restricted by institutional interests.[35]

Consistency with Democratic Sovereignty

One source of doubts about the legitimacy of global governance institutions is the worry that they are incompatible with democratic sovereignty. Our analysis shows why and how global governance *should* constrain democratic sovereignty. The standard of legitimacy we propose is designed inter alia to help global governance institutions correct for the tendency of democratic governments to disregard the interests and preferences of those outside their own publics. It does this chiefly in two ways. First, the emphasis on the role of external institutional epistemic actors in achieving broad accountability helps to ensure more inclusive representation of interests and preferences over time. Second, the requirement of minimal moral acceptability, understood as nonviolation of basic human rights, provides an important protection for the most vulnerable: if this condition is met, democratic publics cannot ignore the most serious "negative externalities" of their policy choices. Global governance institutions that satisfy our standard of legitimacy should not be viewed as undermining democratic sovereignty, but rather as enabling democracies to function justly.

A legitimate global order will include human rights institutions that promote the conditions for the proper functioning of democracy (the right to basic education, the right to freedom of expression and association, and so on) in countries that are democratizing and help sustain these conditions in countries that already have democratic institutions. Critics of global governance institutions that claim they are illegitimate because they constrain democratic sovereignty either beg the question by assuming that the "will of the people" should not be constrained so as to take into account the interests of those outside their polity or they underestimate the extent to which democracy depends upon global governance institutions.

Having articulated the Complex Standard, and indicated how it reflects several key democratic values, we can now show, briefly, how it satisfies the desiderata for a standard of legitimacy we set out earlier.

1. The Complex Standard provides a reasonable basis for coordinated support of institutions that meet the standard, support based on moral reasons that are widely accessible in the circumstances under which legitimacy is an issue. To serve the social function of legitimacy assessments, the Complex Standard only requires a consensus on the importance of not violating the most widely recognized human rights, broad agreement that comparative benefit and integrity are also presumptive necessary conditions of legitimacy, and a commitment to inclusive, informed deliberation directed toward resolving or at least reducing the moral disagreement and uncertainty that characterize our practical attitudes toward these institutions. In other words, the Complex Standard steers a middle course between requiring more moral agreement than is available in the circumstances of legitimacy and abandoning the attempt to construct a more robust, shared moral perspective from which to evaluate global governance institutions. In particular, the Complex Standard acknowledges that the role that these institutions ought to play in a more just world order is both deeply contested and probably not knowable at present.
2. In requiring only minimal moral acceptability at present, the Complex Standard acknowledges that legitimacy does not require justice, but at the same time affirms the intuition that extreme injustice, understood as violation of the most widely recognized human rights, robs an institution of legitimacy.
3. The Complex Standard takes the ongoing consent of democratic states to be a presumptive necessity, though not a sufficient condition for legitimacy.

4. The Complex Standard rejects the assumption that global governance institutions cannot be legitimate unless there is global democracy, but at the same time promotes some of the key democratic values, including informed, public deliberation conducted on the assumption that every individual has standing to participate and the requirement that key institutional policies must be publicly justified.
5. The Complex Standard reflects a proper appreciation of the dynamic, experimental character of global governance institutions and of the fact that not only the means they employ but even the goals they pursue may and probably should change over time.
6. The Complex Standard's requirement of a functioning transnational civil society channel of accountability—an array of overlapping networks of external epistemic actors—helps to compensate for the limitations of accountability through democratic state consent.

The central argument of this chapter can now be summarized. The Complex Standard provides a reasonable basis for agreement in legitimacy assessments of global governance institutions. When the comparative benefit condition is satisfied, the institution provides goods that are not readily obtainable without it. These goods, however, can be reliably provided only if coordination is achieved, and achieving coordination without excessive costs requires that the relevant agents regard the institution's rules as presumptively binding—that is, that they take the fact that the rule is issued by the institution as a content-independent reason for compliance. The instrumental value of institutions that satisfy the comparative benefit condition also gives individuals generally a content-independent reason not to interfere with the functioning of the institutions. Satisfaction of the minimal moral acceptability condition rules out the more serious moral objections that might otherwise undercut the instrumental reasons for supporting the institution. Satisfaction of the other conditions of the Complex Standard, taken together, provides moral reasons to support or at least not interfere with the institution. Among the most important of these reasons is that the institution has epistemic virtues that facilitate the development of more demanding standards and the progressive improvement of the institution itself. Thus, when a global governance institution meets the demands of the Complex Standard, there is justification for saying that it has the right to rule, not merely that it is beneficial.

CONCLUSION

We have offered a *proposal* for a public standard of legitimacy for global governance institutions. These institutions supply important benefits that neither states nor traditional treaty-based relationships among states can provide, but they are quite new, often fragile, and still evolving. Politically mobilized challenges to the legitimacy of these institutions jeopardize the support they need to function effectively, in spite of the fact that these challenges are typically unprincipled and possibly grounded in unrealistic demands that confuse justice with legitimacy. A principled global public standard of legitimacy could facilitate more responsible criticism while at the same time providing guidance for improvement, through a process of institutionalized, collective learning, both about what it is reasonable to expect from global governance institutions and about how to achieve it. Our hope is that the proposal offered here serves these purposes.

Notes

The authors are grateful to Sahar Akhtar, Christian Barry, Thomas Christiano, Michael Doyle, Nicole Hassoun, Andrew Hurrell, Nan Keohane, Avery Kolers, Joseph S. Nye, John Tasioulas, and two anonymous referees for their helpful comments on earlier versions of this chapter, and to William Alford, Ryan Goodman, and Gerald L. Neuman for valuable criticisms and suggestions when such a version was presented at Harvard Law School, November 3, 2005. We are particularly grateful to comments by Charles Beitz and a number of other colleagues made at a workshop on the normative and empirical evaluation of global governance, Princeton University, February 17–18, 2006. Further useful comments were made at the conference on "Legitimacy and International Law" at the Max Planck Institute for Comparative Public Law and International Law, Heidelberg, Germany, June 13–14, 2006.

1. A thorough review of the sociological literature on organizational legitimacy can be found in Mark C. Suchman, "Managing Legitimacy: Strategic and Institutional Approaches," *Academy of Management Review* 20, no. 3 (1995): 571–610.

2. For an excellent discussion of the inadequacy of existing standards of legitimacy for global governance institutions, see Daniel Bodansky, "The Legitimacy of International Governance: A Coming Challenge for International Environmental Law?" *American Journal of International Law* 93, no. 3 (1999): 596–624. For an impressive earlier book on the subject, see Thomas Franck, *The Power of Legitimacy Among Nations* (New York: Oxford University Press, 1990). Franck's account focuses on the legitimacy of rules more than institutions and in our judgment does not distinguish clearly enough between the normative and sociological senses of legitimacy.

3. A large and growing literature exists on global governance. See, for example, Aseem Prakash and Jeffrey A. Hart, eds., *Globalization and Governance* (London: Routledge, 1999); Joseph S. Nye and John D. Donahue, eds., *Governance in a Globalizing World* (Washington: Brookings Institution Press, 2000); and David Held and Anthony McGrew, eds., *Governing Globalization* (London: Polity Press, 2002).

4. Erika de Wet, "The Security Council as Legislator/Executive in Its Fight against Terrorism and against Proliferation of Weapons of Mass Destruction: The Question of Legitimacy" (presentation at the conference "Legitimacy and International Law," Max Planck Institute for Comparative Public Law and International Law, Heidelberg, Germany, June 14, 2006).

5. The emphasis here on the coordinating function should not be misunderstood: global governance institutions do not merely coordinate state actions in order to satisfy *preexisting* state preferences. As our analysis will make clear, they can also help shape state preferences and lead to the development of new norms and institutional goals.

6. Robert O. Keohane, *After Hegemony: Cooperation and Discord in the World Political Economy* (Princeton: Princeton University Press, 1984 [20th anniversary edition, 2005]).

7. James D. Fearon, "Bargaining, Enforcement, and International Cooperation," *International Organization* 52, no. 2 (Spring 1998): 269–306.

8. This is a major theme of Russell Hardin, *Liberalism, Constitutionalism, and Democracy* (Oxford: Oxford University Press, 1999).

9. Andrew Hurrell, "Legitimacy and the Use of Force: Can the Circle Be Squared?" *Review of International Studies* 31, supp. S1 (2005): 16.

10. Legitimacy can also be seen as providing a "focal point" that helps strategic actors select one equilibrium solution among others. For the classic discussion of focal points, see Thomas C. Schelling, *The Strategy of Conflict* (Cambridge: Harvard University Press, 1960), ch. 3. For a critique of theories of cooperation on the basis of focal point theory, and an application to the European Union, see Geoffrey Garrett and Barry Weingast, "Ideas, Interests, and Institutions: Constructing the European Community's Internal Market," in Judith Goldstein and Robert O. Keohane, eds., *Ideas and Foreign Policy: Beliefs, Institutions and Political Change* (Ithaca: Cornell University Press, 1993), esp. 178–85.

11. Most contemporary analytic philosophical literature on legitimacy tends to focus exclusively on the legitimacy of the *state* and typically assumes a very strong understanding of legitimacy. In particular, it is assumed that legitimacy entails (1) a content-independent moral *obligation* to comply with all institutional rules (not just content-independent moral reasons to comply and/or a content-independent moral obligation to not interfere with others' compliance), (2) being justified in using *coercion* to secure compliance with rules, and (3) being justified in *using coercion to exclude* other actors from operating in the institution's domain. (See, for example, Christopher Heath Wellman and A. John Simmons, *Is There a Duty to Obey the Law? For and Against* [Cambridge: Cambridge University Press, 2005]). It is far from obvious, however, that this very strong conception is even the only conception of legitimacy appropriate for the state, given what is sometimes referred to as the "unbundling" of sovereignty into various types of decentralized states and the existence of the European Union. Be that as it may, this state-centered conception is too strong for global governance institutions, which generally do not wield coercive power or claim such strong authority. For a more detailed development of this point, see Allen Buchanan, "The Legitimacy of International Law," in Samantha Besson and John Tasioulas, eds., *The Philosophy of International Law* (Oxford: Oxford University Press, forthcoming).

12. This view was forcefully expressed by Professor Yoram Dinstein of Tel Aviv University, in comments on a draft of this chapter.

13. For a more detailed discussion, see Allen Buchanan, *Justice, Legitimacy and Self-determination: Moral Foundations for International Law* (Oxford: Oxford University Press, 2003), esp. ch. 5.

14. For a perceptive discussion of how consent to new international trade rules in the Uruguay Round (1986–94) was merely nominal, since the alternatives for poor countries were so unattractive, see Richard H. Steinberg, "In the Shadow of Law or Power? Consensus-based Bargaining and Outcomes in the GATT/WTO," *International Organization* 56, no. 2 (2002): 339–74.

15. How the requirement of ongoing consent should be operationalized is a complex question we need not try to answer here; one possibility would be that the treaties creating the institution would have to be periodically reaffirmed.

16. Buchanan, "Legitimacy of International Law."

17. For a valuable discussion that employs a different conception of normative uncertainty, see Monica Hlavac, "A Developmental Approach to the Legitimacy of Global Governance Institutions" (unpublished paper).

18. See Joseph Raz, *The Morality of Freedom* (New York: Oxford University Press, 1986), n. 17.

19. Allen Buchanan and Matthew DeCamp, "Responsibility for Global Health," *Transnational Medicine* 27, no. 1 (2006): 95–114.

20. In March 2005, Secretary-General Kofi Annan called for the replacement of the Commission on Human Rights (fifty-three members elected from slates put forward by regional groups) with a smaller Human Rights Council elected by a two-thirds vote of members of the General Assembly (see his report "In Larger Freedom," A/59/2005, para. 183).

21. For the report of the Independent Inquiry Committee into the United Nations Oil-for-Food Program (the Volcker Committee), dated October 27, 2005, see www.iic-offp.org/story27oct05.htm.

22. Randall W. Stone, "The Political Economy of IMF Lending in Africa," *American Political Science Review* 98, no. 4 (2004): 577–91. See also Randall W. Stone, *Lending Credibility: The International Monetary Fund and the Post-Communist Transition* (Princeton: Princeton University Press, 2002).

23. We are indebted to Andrew Hurrell for this example.

24. John Rawls, *A Theory of Justice* (Cambridge: Harvard University Press, 1971).

25. Ruth W. Grant and Robert O. Keohane, "Accountability and Abuses of Power in World Politics," *American Political Science Review* 99, no. 1 (2005): 29–44. See also Robert O. Keohane and Joseph S. Nye, "Redefining Accountability for Global Governance," in Miles Kahler and David A. Lake, eds., *Governance in a Global Economy: Political Authority in Transition* (Princeton: Princeton University Press, 2003), 386–411.

26. For a discussion, see Ngaire Woods, "Holding Intergovernmental Institutions to Account," *Ethics and International Affairs* 17, no. 1 (2003): 69–80.

27. Ann Florini, *The Coming Democracy* (Washington, D.C.: Island Press, 2003).

28. For a discussion of the role of critical revisability in practical reasoning, with parallels to theoretical reasoning, see Allen Buchanan, "Revisability and Rational Choice," *Canadian Journal of Philosophy* 5, no. 3 (1975): 395–408.

29. For an illuminating account of the legitimacy of health care institutions that emphasizes responsibility for justifications, see Norman Daniels and James Sabin, "Limits to Health Care: Fair Procedures, Democratic Deliberation, and the Legitimacy Problem for Insurers," *Philosophy and Public Affairs* 26, no. 4 (1997): 303–50.

30. See Richard B. Stewart, "Administrative Law in the Twenty-first Century," *New York University Law Review* 78, no. 2 (2003): 437–60; and Benedict Kingsbury, Nikon Kirsch, and Richard B. Stewart, "The Emergence of Global Administrative Law," *Law and Contemporary Problems* 68, nos. 3 and 4 (2005). See also Daniel Esty, "Toward Good Global Governance: The Role of Administrative Law" (paper presented at a conference on global administrative law, New York University, April 21–23, 2005). See also John Wickham, "Toward a Green Multilateral Investment Framework: NAFTA and the Search for Models," *Georgetown International Environmental Law Review* 12, no. 3 (2000): 617–46; James Salzman, "Labor Rights, Globalization, and Institutions: The Role and Influence of the Organization for Economic Cooperation and Development," *Michigan Journal of International Law* 21, no. 4 (2000): 769–848; and OECD, *Getting to Grips with Globalization: The OECD in a Changing World* (Paris: OECD Publications, 2004).

31. The analogy in the economics of information is to the market for used cars. A potential buyer of a used car would be justified in inferring poor quality if the seller were unwilling to

let him have the car thoroughly examined by a competent mechanic. See George A. Akerlof, "The Market for Lemons: Quality Uncertainty and the Market Mechanism," *Quarterly Journal of Economics* 84, no. 3 (1970): 488–500.

32. David Stasavage, "Open-door or Closed-door? Transparency in Domestic and International Bargaining," *International Organization* 58, no. 4 (2004): 667–704.

33. On the role of legislatures with respect to the legitimacy of an international legal order, see Rudiger Wolfrum, "Legitimacy in International Law: Some Introductory Considerations" (paper prepared for the conference "Legitimacy in International Law" at the Max Planck Institute for Comparative Public Law and International Law, Heidelberg, Germany, June 13–14, 2006).

34. We use the term "external epistemic actor" here broadly, to include individuals and groups outside the institution in question who gain knowledge about the institution, interpret and integrate such knowledge, and exchange it with others, in ways that are intended to influence institutional behavior, whether directly or indirectly (through the mediation of the activities of other individuals and groups).

35. On our view, the legitimacy of global governance institutions, at present at least, does not require participation in the critical evaluation of institutional goals and policies by all who are affected by them; but if the standard of legitimacy we recommend were accepted, opportunities for participation would expand.

6

THE LEGITIMACY OF INTERNATIONAL LAW

1. THE CONCEPT OF LEGITIMACY AS APPLIED TO INTERNATIONAL LAW AND INSTITUTIONS

The Primacy of Institutional Legitimacy

Although writers on international law and international relations frequently fail to make the distinction, 'legitimate' has both a sociological and a normative meaning.[1] An institution that attempts to rule (govern) is legitimate in the normative sense if and only if it has *the right to rule.* Rival theories of legitimacy differ on what the right to rule is and on what conditions must be satisfied for an institution to have the right to rule. Calling an institution legitimate in the sociological sense is a misleading way of saying that it is widely *believed to have the right to rule.* Here I will focus on the normative sense of 'legitimacy'.

Both laws and legal institutions are said to be legitimate or illegitimate, but institutional legitimacy is primary insofar as the legitimacy of particular laws or of a corpus of law depends on the legitimacy of the institutions that make, interpret, and apply the laws (although legitimate institutions may sometimes produce illegitimate laws). Accordingly, international laws are legitimate only if the institutions that make them are legitimate. Let us call international law-making institutions ILIs. By an institution here is meant (roughly) a persisting pattern of organized, rule-governed, coordinated behavior. Using this broad sense of 'institution', we can say there are three types of ILIs: the institution of treaty-making, the institution of customary international law, and global governance institutions, which includes a diversity of entities such as the WTO, the UN Security Council, environmental regimes such as that established by the Kyoto Accords, and various judicial and regulatory 'government networks' composed of officials from several states. Global governance institutions, though created and sustained through treaties made by states, are increasingly taking on law-making functions.

At present there is nothing approaching an adequate theory of legitimacy for international law. Before much headway can be made on this task, several questions must be answered. (1) what is the distinctive character and point of legitimacy judgments and how do they differ from other evaluations of institutions? (2) What concept or conceptions of legitimacy are relevant to international law and what standards of legitimacy ought ILIs meet, assuming that a particular concept of legitimacy is relevant? (Is there one concept of legitimacy and one set of standards for legitimacy that applies to all ILIs?). (3) What are the chief challenges to the legitimacy of international law? (What features of ILIs call their legitimacy into question?). (4) What is at stake in assessments of the legitimacy of international law—more specifically, why does the legitimacy of ILIs matter and to whom? (5) What conditions should a theory of legitimacy for international law satisfy? (6) What are some of the main rival approaches to theorizing the legitimacy of international law and which seem most promising, given an account of the conditions such theories should satisfy? The aim of this chapter is to answer these six questions.

The Nature of Legitimacy Assessments

Assertions about the legitimacy or illegitimacy of institutions (as opposed to reports about people's beliefs about their legitimacy) are moral evaluations, not statements of legal fact.[2] The issue is whether ILIs have the *moral* right to rule and what does the right to rule entail.

Just as legitimacy judgments cannot be reduced to statements of legal fact, they are also not reducible to statements to the effect that noncompliance with the institution's rules will elicit coercion or that compliance with the rules is advantageous. An institution can be effective in coercively enforcing rules and yet not be legitimate; indeed, in the case of the state it has been precisely its success in coercing that has most urgently raised the question of its legitimacy. Similarly, an institution might be advantageous—even advantageous to all whom it attempts to govern—and yet it might still be illegitimate, for example, if it came about through usurpation.

The moral evaluation that institutional legitimacy judgments express is also different from that of justice. Although extreme and persisting injustices can render an institution illegitimate, legitimacy is a less-demanding standard than justice in the sense that an institution can be legitimate though not fully just.[3] Different parties' legitimacy assessments of a particular institution can agree, even if they have serious disagreements about what justice requires. Thus, legitimacy judgments can facilitate *morally based coordinated support*—or *criticism*—of institutions even where consensus on justice is lacking. The current concern about the legitimacy of international law may be due in part to the widespread belief that present disagreements about justice—especially global distributive justice—are not likely soon to be resolved.

Achieving morally based coordination can be of great practical importance when two conditions are satisfied. The first, which I have already suggested, is that there is serious disagreement about justice but considerable consensus that institutions ought to satisfy some moral requirements—a widespread belief that merely being able to enforce their rules and being advantageous relative to the noninstitutional alternative are not sufficient. The second is that the distinctive benefits that an institution creates are most reliably secured if, in addition to the fear of coercion and the expectation of advantage relative to the noninstitutional alternative, there are *moral* reasons to support the functioning of the institution. Moral reason-based support can enable an institution to function successfully when there are lapses in its ability to coerce and during periods when there is reason for some to doubt that it is indeed advantageous for all relative to the noninstitutional alternative. Moral reason-based support can reduce the costs of achieving compliance, which might be prohibitively high if the threat of coercion were the only reason for compliance.

Stronger and Weaker Senses of 'The Right to Rule'

There are stronger and weaker senses of 'the right to rule', although prominent accounts of legitimacy often assume that only one of these senses is of central importance for political philosophy. What might be called the dominant philosophical view (DPV for short) of *state* legitimacy employs a very strong understanding of the right to rule, as including six elements: (a) the institution's agents are morally justified in engaging in governance functions, including issuing rules and attaching costs and benefits to various agents to facilitate compliance with them (the justified governance condition); (b) the institution's agents are morally justified in using coercion to secure compliance with the institution's rules (the justified coercion condition); (c) only the institution's agents are morally justified in engaging in governance functions in the domain of action in question, (the exclusive justification condition); (d) the institution's agents are morally justified in using coercion to prevent others from attempting to engage in governance activities in its domain (the coercive exclusion condition); and (e) those whom the institution attempts to govern have a content-independent moral obligation to comply with (all) the rules the institution imposes (the content-independent moral obligation condition).[4] A content-independent obligation to comply with a rule is an obligation that exists independently of any assessment of the rule itself. In all legal systems, those to whom the rules are addressed typically have content-*dependent* moral obligations to comply with some of the rules: for example, if the law prohibits murder, one has a moral obligation to comply with this law because it is simply the legal expression of a valid moral rule. Since (e) presumably implies (f), a similar obligation *not to interfere* with the institution's efforts to secure compliance with its rules, there are in fact six elements of legitimacy on this account. Because the DPV was developed with the case of the state in mind, it emphasizes the right to coerce.

The DPV's conception of the right to rule is extraordinarily strong, both with regard to what counts as *ruling* (i.e., governance) and with regard to what counts as having a *right* to rule. It assumes that legitimacy not only involves justified governance (ruling) of some sort (element (a)), but *also* justified coercive governance (element (b), *and* the exclusive right to use coercion to secure compliance with rules (element (c)), *and* the right to use coercion to exclude others from engaging in governance activities in its domain (element (d)). However, there is no reason to assume that only institutions that govern (rule) in this very strong sense can be said to be legitimate or illegitimate, that is, can have the right to rule or lack it. Indeed, there are many institutions, including all existing international institutions, that do not rule in this robust way and do not even claim to do so. It is *more* plausible to say that the very strong notion of governance encompassed by the dominant philosophical conception of legitimacy is pertinent if we are focusing only on the legitimacy of one peculiar kind of institution, namely, the state.[5]

A better way of understanding 'being morally justified in governing' element of legitimacy is as follows: 'being morally justified in issuing rules and seeking to secure compliance with them through attaching costs to noncompliance and/or benefits to compliance'. This characterization covers coercion but is not limited to it and can therefore serve as an element in a concept of legitimacy that is applicable to institutions that do not rule coercively, including most ILIs.

The DPV rightly emphasizes that legitimacy, as the term is often used, includes more than being justified in governing if this means merely having the liberty-right to govern.[6] A can have the liberty-right to do X and it can nonetheless be true that no one has any duty or even any reason not to interfere with A doing X. Merely being justified in governing in this sense is arguably insufficient for what might be called the focal sense of 'legitimacy' because it fails to encompass the distinctive *relational* aspect of legitimacy.[7] More specifically, the mere liberty-right to govern omits the crucial idea that the rules of a legitimate institution *have a privileged status vis a vis our reasons for acting and that their having this privileged status is not dependent on their content.* At least in what might be called the focal sense of the term, legitimacy involves not only the liberty-right to govern but also *a content-independent requirement of practical support for (or at least noninterference with) the institution's efforts to govern.*[8]

The DPV's very robust requirement of a content-independent *moral obligation* to comply with rules is not needed to capture the idea of a requirement of content-independent practical support and hence is not necessary for legitimacy in the focal, relational sense. The weaker combination of a content-independent moral obligation or substantial content independent reason not to interfere, along with substantial content-independent *moral reasons* to comply—where these reasons may fall short of grounding an obligation—does the job. Therefore, it is not the case that a proper recognition of the distinction between merely being justified in governing and being legitimate requires anything as strong as DPV's conception of legitimacy. One can acknowledge that legitimacy as the right to rule involves more than being justified in ruling without assuming that it entails something as strong as a content-independent moral obligation to comply.

The DPV's understanding of what counts as *rule* (i.e., governance) is as unduly strong as its understanding of the right to rule. Many international legal institutions do not claim an *exclusive* right to rule, yet it makes perfectly good sense to ask whether they are legitimate (in a relational sense). For example, the World Trade Organization (WTO) does not claim that it alone is justified in engaging in multilateral efforts to promote the liberalization of trade; it recognizes the legitimacy of regional trade regimes that promote liberalization. Similarly, the International Criminal Court (ICC) does not claim to be the only tribunal that may justifiably prosecute the international crimes specified in its statute; it allows for both prosecution of individuals by their own states and the exercise of 'universal jurisdiction' by states over foreign individuals. Second, even when international legal institutions claim the exclusive right to govern in a certain domain, they do not always, or even typically, also claim the right to use coercion to exclude others from attempting to engage in governance functions. Third, 'rule' in the DPV's understanding of the right to rule means governance in the peculiarly strong sense in which *states* (sometimes) govern: seeking to ensure compliance with rules through *coercion*, understood as a credible threat of the use of physical force against non-compliers. Although most international legal institutions do not govern, or attempt to govern, or even claim the right to govern, in this very strong sense, it nevertheless makes sense to ask whether these institutions are legitimate, where legitimacy is understood as relational, as implying more than being morally justified in governing.

My proposal, then, is to proceed on the assumption that for ILIs legitimacy as the right to rule includes two main elements: (1) the institution must be morally justified in attempting to govern (must have the moral liberty-right or permission to try to govern) in the sense of issuing rules (that prescribe duties for various actors) and attempting to secure compliance with them by imposing costs for noncompliance and/or benefits for compliance and (2) those toward whom the rules are directed (chiefly, though not exclusively states) have substantial, content-independent moral reasons for compliance and others (including citizens of states) have substantial content-independent moral reasons for supporting the institution's efforts to secure compliance with its directives or at least have substantial, content-independent moral reasons not to interfere with those efforts.

This formulation has several advantages. First, it acknowledges the fact that most ILIs, like international institutions generally, do not employ coercion to secure compliance with their rules, and do not claim the right to do so. Thus it avoids the error of simply applying to ILIs the very strong conception of legitimacy that may be appropriate for the state. Second, it allows for the fact that there is variation among ILIs as to whether they attempt to achieve or claim exclusive authority over the domain in which they operate. Third, the second conjunct of (2) it recognizes that the legitimacy of ILIs can reasonably be of concern to actors other than states, some of whom may not be subjects of duties the institution attempts to impose.

This understanding of legitimacy seems superior to the Razian conception of authority that John Tasioulas advances, according to which A has the right to rule over B if and only if B's complying with A's rules enables B to do better than B would do were she to act directly on reasons that independently apply to her. The difficulty with the Razian notion is that the mere fact that others would do better were they to obey one does not justify one's attempting to rule over them. So an entity could have authority in the Razian sense but not be justified in attempting to secure compliance with the norms it promulgates. Yet whatever else having the right to rule entails, it surely includes being justified in attempting to rule.

The Chief Challenges to the Legitimacy of International Law

Challenges fall mainly under the following five headings. First, there is a challenge from the perspective of states: it is frequently said that particular ILIs, like the UN Security Council or the WTO, or even the entire international legal order, are unfairly controlled by a handful of powerful states, thereby unfairly disadvantaging weaker ones. Whether it is supposed to be a claim about injustice or about legitimacy is often unclear. It could be both, of course—the idea being that from the perspective fairness to states, this or that ILI or the current international legal order as a whole, is so unjust as to be illegitimate. Some who advance this charge assume that the remedy is state-majoritarian democracy: ILIs should operate according to procedures that assure an equal voice for all states.

A second, quite different challenge to the legitimacy of ILIs is that they are unfair to individuals and/or nonstate groups, such as indigenous peoples or that they fail to take the legitimate interests of non-state individuals or groups seriously enough and often operate so as to threaten their welfare. On this view, the unfairness of ILIs regarding states is of concern only so far as it results in unfairness to nonstate individuals or groups or threats to their welfare. Some versions of this challenge assume that some kind of global democracy is required if ILIs are to be legitimate.[9]

The third legitimacy-challenge focuses on the whether ILIs credibly do the jobs they are supposed to do or act in accordance with the goals and procedures to which they publicly commit. For example, some have argued that the failure of the Security Council to authorize armed intervention to stop genocides or other forms of mass murder have been so egregious as to undermine the legitimacy of the Council. An institution may also be deemed illegitimate if it is deeply and persistently corrupt. Some have concluded that the massive corruption of the Iraq Oil For Food program, when considered in the light of a long history of corruption or at least poor management in many other cases, impugns the legitimacy of the UN Secretariat, which was in charge of the program.

The fourth challenge to the legitimacy of ILIs alleges that all or some of them usurp the proper authority of states or, on one variant of the view, of democracies. There are two different ways of understanding this challenge. On the first, less radical variant, the charge is that *as a matter of fact* some ILIs have so seriously encroached on the proper domain of authority of the state (or democratic states) as to render themselves illegitimate, but there is no claim that international law and sovereignty or the sovereignty of democracies are *in principle* incompatible. On the second, more radical variant, the charge is that the supremacy of international law is incompatible in principle with sovereignty or with democratic constitutional sovereignty. According to the second interpretation, ILIs, so far as they claim supremacy for their norms, are *necessarily* illegitimate, at least vis a vis constitutional democracies, because by definition the supreme law in a constitutional democracy is determined by its own constitution.

It appears, however, that there is no problem of incompatibility in principle. If democracies can subject themselves to international laws by following processes that accord with their own constitutional principles, there is no bar to saying both that they are bound by those laws and that the constitution is the supreme law of the land. One way of accomplishing this is to create a new constitution or amend an old one so that it recognizes the supremacy of international law, or of some types of international law, such as human rights law. Moroever, if a democratic state ratifies a treaty and incorporates the relevant laws into its domestic legal system through a process that satisfies constitutional requirements, then presumably it will be true to say that the state has a substantial content-independent moral reason to comply and that the citizens of the democracy have a substantial content-independent reason to support their state's compliance—namely, because the law in question became the law of the land through a constitutionally sanctioned process. If the worry is only that international law is being incorporated in ways that violate the democracy's constitution and proper constitutional processes for incorporation are available, then the objection is not that constitutional democracy and the supremacy of international law are *in principle* incompatible.

The fifth and final challenge to the legitimacy of international law is that ILIs are not themselves democratic. *If* 'democracy' here means what it does in the case of the state, namely, that those who make the law must be accountable, through periodic electoral processes in which individuals have an equal vote, most theorists agree that democracy (in this 'individual-majoritarian sense) at the global level is not presently feasible or likely to become so in the foreseeable future. Instead of concluding from this that ILIs cannot be legitimate, some argue that they can be, so long as they exemplify the same basic *democratic values* (or principles) that mandate individual-majoritarian democracy in the case of the state. Whether the current democracy deficit is sufficiently serious to deprive the existing international order of legitimacy is a further question, and one which in my judgment has not been adequately addressed.

Why and to Whom the Legitimacy of International Law-making Institutions Matters

It is misleading to say that international law is created by states, through treaty and custom, both because this formulation overlooks the growing contribution of global governance institutions to international law-making and because various nonstate actors increasingly play a role in international law-making. The legitimacy of international law is not just a concern of states, but also of non-state groups and individual citizens, who sometimes may reasonably question the legitimacy of international institutions even though they know that their own states have consented to them. As I noted earlier, individuals and groups may still question the legitimacy of ILIs even though their state has voluntarily consented to them, not because they believe that these institutions treat weaker *states* unfairly, but rather because they believe that these institutions act unfairly toward *them* or threaten *their* welfare. To a large extent, this concern on the part of citizens reflects the growing penetration of international law into life within states. The further we depart from the picture of international laws as being created solely by states and as dealing solely with the relations of states to one another—and the more seriously we take the idea that human beings, not states, are the ultimate objects of moral concern—the clearer it becomes that a satisfactory account of the legitimacy of international law must include more than an explanation of why *states* ought to regard the international institutions through which law is made as having the right to rule. More precisely, appreciating the new face of international law shows just how inadequate the traditional framing of the question of the legitimacy of international law is. The question is much broader than "Why should states consider international law binding?"

A Deeper Sense of the Question 'Is International Law Legitimate?'

There is a still more basic issue about the legitimacy of international law. This is the question of whether or to what extent democratic state leaders and the citizens of democratic states ought to be morally committed to the project of international law—to the endeavor to build sustain an international legal order. The query here is not whether this or that international law or this or that type of ILI (e.g., treaty-law or customary law) is legitimate; rather, it concerns the moral status of the goal of developing the rule of law at the global level. This an important question, even if one concludes that international law as it now exists has a serious legitimacy deficit. Even if no existing international institutions were legitimate, we could still sensibly ask whether the project of international law makes moral sense.

Recently some American legal theorists, like some American political leaders, have answered this question in the negative, advocating what I have elsewhere called a purely instrumental stance toward international law.[10] On this view, the citizens of democratic states should direct their state leaders to support international legal institutions only when it is in the national interest to do so or when those citizens happen to have moral 'preferences' (such as the 'preference' that human rights not be violated) that are best promoted by doing so. There is no noninstrumental reason for entering into any particular international agreement or for keeping agreements already entered into, nor for contributing to the work of building and improving the international legal order.

The Ideal of the Rule of Law

The most obvious reply to the purely instrumentalist view is that there are substantial moral reasons to promote *the rule of law* at the international level. Although there is much controversy as to just what the ideal of the rule of law consists of, there is considerable consensus that the principles that constitute it include the following: the law should be general (and when there are departures from generality they should be controlled by processes that are informed by general principles); the law should be understandable and publicly proclaimed; there is a presumption against retroactive law, especially retroactive criminal law; and the administration of the law should be impartial. In a wider sense, the commitment to the rule of law is the commitment to resolving or managing conflicts by effectively institutionalizing the impartial application of publicly known general rules that are based on the assumption that there is to be an accommodation of interests. The commitment to the rule of law in this wider sense goes beyond the assertion that *if* there is to be international law it should conform to the principles that constitute the ideal of the rule of law; it is the commitment to subjecting international relations to law, in conformity to this ideal.

The traditional answer to the question "Why should we try to subject international relations to the rule of law?" was that doing so is necessary to achieve peace among states. This answer is compatible with the purely instrumental view, but it is also compatible with its rejection, if the commitment to peace is understood to be a moral duty, not merely a matter of rational prudence. Increasingly, the contemporary answer to the question is that subjecting international relations to the rule of law is necessary not only for the sake of peace among states but also for justice, where justice is understood, first and foremost, though not exclusively, as the realization of human rights.

Those who hold the purely instrumental view of international law may do so because they subscribe to a Realist theory of international relations: Realists deny that there is a noninstrumental moral obligation to promote the rule of international law because they believe that, given the nature of international relations as they understand it, international law will never be capable of making a significant contribution to justice. (In addition, they may in fact hold that the concept of justice has no application to international affairs). Given the weaknesses of Realism, which have been increasingly exposed in recent years, this reason for denying that there is a noninstrumental moral obligation to support the project of international law is hardly conclusive.

Resolving the dispute between the purely instrumentalist view and the view that there is a moral obligation to promote the rule of international law is clearly beyond the scope of the present investigation. My purpose is only to distinguish different senses of the question 'is international law legitimate' and to indicate that the deepest of these goes to the heart of our understanding of the relationship between law and justice and our predictions about the human capacity for creating lawful relationships among different societies.

Conditions an Adequate Theory of the Legitimacy of International Law Should Satisfy

The preceding analysis yields criteria of adequacy for a theory of the legitimacy of international law. Such a theory must encompass all three types of ILIs—it must provide an account of the legitimacy (or otherwise) of customary law, treaty law, and law produced by global governance institutions. It must also acknowledge that it is no longer true that states alone make international law, accommodating the fact that global governance institutions engage in rule-making that is not accurately described as the creation of law through state consent and that non-state actors, including agents of transnational, nongovernmental organizations, now sometimes contribute to the making of international law.

2. STANDARDS FOR THE LEGITIMACY OF INTERNATIONAL LAW

The Simple State Consent View

Proceeding on the assumption that institutions are the primary subject of legitimacy assessments and that the legitimacy of laws depends on the legitimacy of institutions of the institutions that make them, it may be initially tempting to say that the question of the legitimacy of international law can be answered rather simply and straightforwardly: rules are legitimate international laws if and only if they are produced through *the institution of state consent*, that is, if they are created in accordance with the procedures that states have consented to for the making of international laws, which include the requirement that states must consent to laws. The state consent view of legitimacy has been by far the dominant view among international legal theorists. Let us consider the first half of the biconditional: is state consent sufficient for legitimacy?

On the simplest interpretation of the view that state consent is sufficient, the legitimacy of treaty law is assured by the explicit consent of states, the legitimacy of customary international law is assured by a kind of implicit consent inferred from the behavior of states, and the legitimacy of law generated by global governance institutions is assured by their being created and sustained by state consent. The attraction of this view lies in an analogy with individual consent: if you and I consent to a certain arrangement as to how we shall treat each other, then surely that arrangement is legitimate. Similarly, it is said, if states consent to a certain arrangements for how their interactions are to be regulated, then it is legitimate.

There are several reasons for rejecting the view that *under current and foreseeable conditions* state consent is sufficient for the legitimacy of international laws. The consent of weaker states may be less than substantially voluntary, because stronger states can make the costs of their not consenting prohibitive. Further, in many cases states do not represent all of or even most of their people; they are not sufficiently democratic to make it reasonable to say that state consent by itself legitimizes what states consent to.

In addition, even if we focused only on treaty law—setting aside the dubious assumption that customary law reasonably can be understood as enjoying state consent—and even if all states represented all their people, it would still not follow that state consent suffices for legitimacy, for two distinct reasons. First, the problem of questionable voluntariness would still remain: the fact that a weak state is democratic does not change the fact that it is weak and therefore may face pressures that undermine the voluntariness of its consent. Second, as I have already noted, international law increasingly is not limited to rules to which states can be said to consent in a normatively substantial sense; instead, some important international law is created by global governance institutions of various sorts. Even though these institutions are created by state consent and cannot function without state support, they engage in *ongoing* governance activities, including the generation of laws and/or law-like rules, that are not controlled by the 'specific consent' of states. Hence, the problem of 'bureaucratic distance' looms large, even if the states that create these institutions are democratic; the links between the popular will in democratic states that consent to the creation of global governance institutions and the governing functions these institutions perform seem too anemic to confer legitimacy. Given the reality of bureaucratic distance, the mere fact that democratic states consented to the creation of a global governance institutions and have not withdrawn their consent does not seem sufficient to make such institutions legitimate. Finally, to the extent that non-state actors play a role in the creation of international law, state consent seems insufficient for legitimacy, unless it can be shown that the legitimacy of the contribution these non-state actors make to the creation of international law is somehow assured by state consent.

So far I have argued that, under current conditions in which (1) there is great disparity of power among states, in which (2) many states do not represent all of their people, and in which (3) there is a serious problem of 'bureaucratic distance,' state consent is not sufficient for the legitimacy of international institutions nor, therefore, for the legitimacy of the laws they make (given that the legitimacy of the latter derives from the legitimacy of the former). At this point one might argue that *in different circumstances*—where conditions (1), (2), and (3) do not obtain—state consent would be sufficient for legitimacy. In other words, we might view the claim that state consent is sufficient for legitimacy as a claim in the ideal theory of international legal order, not as a claim about what suffices for the legitimacy of international law as it is or is likely to be in the foreseeable future. Whether state consent would be a sufficient condition for legitimacy in ideal theory cannot be determined, however, until the ideal theory is laid out.

More troubling still, we cannot begin to evaluate claims about ideal theory until we specify just what an ideal theory is a theory of. The answer to the question 'Would state consent be sufficient for the legitimacy of international law-making institutions in ideal theory?" may have a different answer depending upon whether or not we assume that ideal theory is a theory for a world in which only states (as opposed to other political entities, regional or sub-state) are the primary agents for the establishment of justice.

Is State Consent Necessary for Legitimacy?

So far I have argued that, under current conditions, state consent is not sufficient for legitimacy. This leaves open the question of whether it is necessary. If we assume that state consent is a necessary condition for legitimacy under current conditions, then it appears that we must conclude that much of existing international law, perhaps especially customary international law (CIL) is illegitimate. The view that states tacitly or implicitly consent to CIL does not stand up to scrutiny. CIL norms apply to states that did not exist at the time of their emergence, even if they object to them, yet surely their objecting to them is pretty good evidence that they are not now consenting to them. To say that such states have consented to the *process* by which CIL norms emerge is equally unconvincing, given the inability of weaker states to opt out of the process or to do so without excessive costs. To summarize: if state consent is a necessary condition for legitimacy under current conditions, then a substantial portion of existing international law appears to be illegitimate.

Whether state consent is a plausible necessary condition for the legitimacy of international law in ideal theory cannot be determined unless we first have a specification of the background conditions for ideal theory, including the role of states in the overall system the ideal theory prescribes. In contrast, there is a straightforward nonideal theory argument for a norm according to which state consent is a necessary condition for the legitimacy of international law under current conditions: adherence to this norm would reduce the ability of strong states hijack the project of international law. In other words, the best reason for saying that state consent is a necessary condition for the legitimacy of international law may be that, under current and foreseeable conditions, it provides an important safeguard against the rule of the strong. Whether strict adherence to the requirement of state consent is the only feasible and adequately effective safeguard is a complex issue that cannot be pursued here. It is worth pointing out, however, that strict adherence to the requirement of state consent is a costly way of protecting against predation: it gives every state, including the most oppressive ones, a veto over any progressive change in international law.

The Demand for Democratic Legitimacy

A growing awareness of the insufficiency of state consent for legitimacy under current and foreseeable conditions, along with the widespread belief that democracy is a necessary condition for the legitimacy of the state, may explain why the debate about the legitimacy of the international legal order has shifted from a preoccupation with state consent to a debate about of the possibilities of 'global democracy.' A major focus of this discussion has been global governance institutions, in large part because they appear to be inadequately controlled by state consent or at least by the will of democratic publics and yet seem to be growing more consequential, not just for state sovereignty, but also for the well-being of individuals. Let us call the Global Democracy View the claim that at least one important type of ILI, global governance institutions, cannot be legitimate unless they are democratic in the individual-majoritarian sense. The Global Democracy View is often criticized for being utopian. The idea is that the conditions for global democracy (in the individual-electoral sense)—do not exist and are not likely to exist in the foreseeable future. This seems to me to be right, if, as the Global Democracy View holds, the requirement for legitimacy is that ILIs must be democratic in what I referred to earlier as the individual-electoral sense. Here one might either conclude that the standard of democracy now increasingly applied to states is too demanding to be applied to ILIs or one might conclude that no ILIs are legitimate, because they fail to satisfy that standard. Robert O. Keohane and I opt for the former conclusion. We argue that once the distinctive practical function of legitimacy assessments in achieving moral reason-based coordination is understood, it becomes clear that a requirement of global democracy in the individual-majoritarian sense is an unreasonably strong necessary condition in the case of global governance institutions for the foreseeable future.[11] In a nutshell, we argue that the demand for global democracy in this sense is unreasonably strong given two conditions: first, the benefits that global governance institutions provide are quite valuable and not likely to be reliably provided without them; second, the key values that underlie the demand for global democracy can be reasonably approximated if these institutions satisfy other more feasible conditions, including what we call Broad Accountability. By the latter we mean that these institutions must cooperate with external epistemic actors—individuals and groups outside the institution, in particular transnational civil society organizations—to create conditions under which the goals and processes of the institution as well as the current terms of institutional accountability, can be contested and critically revised over time, and in a manner that helps to ensure an increasingly inclusive consideration of legitimate interests, through largely transparent deliberative processes. Broad Accountability, we argue, would provide a reasonable second-best for global democracy in the individual-majoritarian sense, under current, highly nonideal conditions. Although Broad Accountability may not qualify as democracy on some accounts, it does realize some important democratic values.

Rather than recapitulate that argument in detail here, I simply want to note that even if one could argue, contrary to what Keohane and I contend, that global democracy in the individual-electoral sense is a necessary condition for the legitimacy of ILIs, *it would not be sufficient*. Even the most enthusiastic advocates of democracy at the domestic level ought to admit that the legitimacy of *any* majoritarian electoral process can be undercut if it results in serious and persistent violations of basic human rights, for example, the rights of a minority ethnic or national group. The same would be true at the global level. So, whether or not democracy (in the individual-electoral sense) is a necessary condition for the legitimacy of global governance institutions, it is not sufficient. Nor would global democracy understood as an arrangement that achieves equal political power for all states (rather than all individuals)—what I referred to in Section 1 as the state-majoritarian view—be sufficient for legitimacy, because that too is compatible with serious violations of human rights. In sum, it is difficult to imagine that any institution of governance, democratic or otherwise, at the global or the domestic level, could be legitimate if it persistently engaged in serious violations of basic human rights norms. Of course, on some understandings of democracy (whether global or domestic) respect for basic human rights is already included, but this is conflation is unhelpful. A political order could be democratic, even the very strong sense that each individual has an 'equal say' in law-making, and yet the laws could provide insufficient protection for human rights or even violate them. So, assuming that the protection of human rights is generally a necessary condition for the legitimacy of a political order, it appears that state consent, even under much more ideal conditions than those in which it now operates, is not sufficient for legitimacy.

3. HUMAN RIGHTS AND INTERNATIONAL LEGITIMACY

It is something of a commonplace that the international legal order is becoming less exclusively state-centered and more concerned with human rights. The Security Council has authorized military interventions to stop large-scale human rights violations in Bosnia and Somalia. Ad hoc tribunals and a permanent international criminal court have been created to prosecute war crimes, genocide, and crimes against humanity. The idea that state sovereignty itself is conditional on the protection of human rights seems to be taking hold.

These changes are rightly viewed as moral progress; yet they raise a fundamental issue of legitimacy that those who greet them with enthusiasm have not squarely faced. In order to be legitimate, an international legal order that takes the protection of human rights to be a fundamental goal must address a familiar challenge to the very idea of human rights: what I have elsewhere labeled *the parochialism objection*, according to which what are called *human* rights are not really universal but instead are simply reflections of one particular culture point of view (variously said to be 'Western' or 'liberal' or 'liberal individualist').

To meet this objection it is not enough to point out that most states have ratified the major human rights conditions. The question is not whether states have agreed to treat human rights norms *as if they* were universally valid but rather whether they *are* universally valid. To elide the latter distinction is to assume that state consent, under current conditions, is sufficient for legitimacy. But that claim, I have argued, is indefensible. Nor will it do to say that the international legal system includes institutions that articulate legal international human rights norms (call them IHRIs) and that ensure that these norms conform to the criteria for legality in the international legal system. By itself the legality of a putative human rights norm does nothing to establish that a human right exists. Further, nothing in the texts of human rights conventions seems to provide an adequate response to the fundamental issue of justification that the parochialism objection raises. Indeed, aside from some vague gestures toward human dignity in the Preambles, the texts scrupulously avoid the task of justification.

One might argue that the parochialism objection is hardly credible when applied to *basic* human rights norms such as the rights against enslavement, the right to physical security, the right against religious persecution, and the right to subsistence. And, indeed, it does seem implausible to say that these rights are of value only to Westerners or liberal individualists. The parochialism objection arises anew, however, once we realize that there can be serious disagreements, in some cases apparently rooted in different cultural, religious, or philosophical views, about the specific content of these rights and about how they ought to be balanced against one another in cases of conflict. For example, there may be near universal agreement that there is a human right not to be subjected to torture or to cruel and inhumane punishment, but cultural variation as to what counts as torture or cruel and inhumane punishment. In brief, even the most basic human rights norms are not self-specifying and specifications may be reasonably questioned as to whether they are parochial or not. The more fully an intuitively plausible, highly abstract human rights norm becomes legalized—that is, expressed as an international legal human right—the more vulnerable it can become to the charge of parochialism, because legalization involves, *inter alia*, greater specificity.

It is often said that the Universal Declaration of Human Rights and the various human rights treaties that followed it wisely avoided attempting a justification for the norms they asserted. To paraphrase the philosopher Jacques Maritain, it was possible to agree on a list of human rights only on the condition that almost nothing was said about how they are grounded. As an explanation of the absence of a public moral grounding for international human rights law, Maritain's remark is cogent. It does nothing to rebut the parochialism objection, however. Therefore, it also does nothing to allay the worry that an international legal order that increasingly relies on the idea of human rights in its conception of its own legitimacy, in the legitimacy assessments it makes, and in its efforts to enforce the conditions of legitimacy on other institutions, is of questionable legitimacy if it persists in doing so without being able to provide a credible public justification for the claim that it has properly identified and specified a set of genuinely universal rights.

In the end, whether such a justification becomes available will depend not only upon the further development of the moral foundations of the idea of human rights—a task which until recently most contemporary moral and political philosophers, like most international legal theorists, have avoided—but also upon improvements in the global public deliberative processes that occur within the complex array of institutions within which human rights norms are articulated, contested, and revised over time.[12] What I am suggesting is that grappling with this fundamental legitimacy problem requires an investigation of the moral-epistemic functions of these institutions. This means viewing them, not merely as venues in which antecedently justified moral norms are given legal form, but as institutions for global public deliberation that can contribute to the moral justification of human rights norms and thereby to their own legitimacy and to the legitimacy of the international legal order as a whole, so far as that order takes human rights seriously.

Notes

I am grateful to Samantha Besson, Haim Ganz, Stephen Ratner, Lukas Meyer, and John Tasioulas for their comments on earlier versions of this chapter.

1. Fernando Tesón has focused squarely on the normative sense of legitimacy and is among the first (if not *the* first) contemporary international legal scholar writing in English to advance the idea that the legitimacy of states depends upon their satisfying at least minimal standards with respect to the protection of human rights. Fernando Tesón, *Humanitarian Intervention: An Inquiry Into Law and Morality*, 3rd ed. (New York: Transnational Publishers, 2005) and *A Philosophy of International Law* (Boulder, Colo: Westview Press, 1998).

2. The rest of this section draws on Allen Buchanan and Robert O. Keohane, "The Legitimacy of Global Governance Institutions," *Ethics and International Affairs* 20, no. 2 (2006).

3. However, an institution might be operating in a perfectly just way yet be illegitimate, if it came about through serious injustice, for example, by usurping the functions of a preexisting legitimate institution.

4. By the dominant philosophical view I mean that view of the legitimacy of the state that is generally assumed in the extensive contemporary analytic philosophical literature on the question of whether there is 'a duty to obey the law.' For what may be the most developed and carefully reasoned contribution to this literature, see John A. Simmons, *Justification and Legitimacy: Essays on Rights and Obligations* (Cambridge: Cambridge University Press, 2001). Item (d) above may not be explicit in Simmon's own understanding of legitimacy, but it is included in the Weberian conception of the state as an entity that claims a *monopoly* on the use of force within a territory, and it seems clear that Simmons and others in the mainstream debate about the obligation to obey the law assume the Weberian conception. However, nothing in my central argument here depends on the claim that the dominant philosophical view includes (d).

5. It is not even clear, however, that the dominant philosophical conception of legitimacy applies to *states* as they actually are at present, as opposed to how they have been conceived in recent analytic political philosophy. The dominant philosophical conception appears to assume a unitary and unqualified sovereignty that no longer exists, if it ever did. Sovereignty is now increasingly 'unbundled' and distributed, in two ways. First, there is increasing political differentiation within states, with various forms of federalism (symmetrical and asymmetrical) and other kinds of intrastate autonomy regimes, as well as a separation of powers at both the state and federal levels. Under these conditions of complex political differentiation, there may be no definitive answer to the question 'who has exclusive authority over domain D?'—or at least no answer prior to the actual resolution of some particular conflict over authority, which may or may not occur. Yet it still makes sense to ask whether the state is legitimate. Second, there are substantial external limitations on sovereignty, including the increasingly effective institutionalization of international criminal law and international (and, in the case of the EU, regional) human rights law. These external limitations on sovereignty diminish the authority of the state even within its own territory. Given the internal dispersal of sovereignty and the external limits on it, the dominant philosophical conception of legitimacy appears to be too strong for application to the contemporary state.

6. 'Justified' in the phrase 'being justified in governing' is itself ambiguous between (a) having a liberty-right to govern, that is, it being morally permissible to govern; and (b) there being good moral reasons in favor of (the institution's) governing. I will operate with the former, weaker notion, but nothing in my argument hinges on this.

7. Simmons, *Justification and Legitimacy*, 128.

8. There are different possible interpretations of the idea that these content-independent obligations are 'weighty'. In particular, it could be argued that the right to rule implies not only that there are content-independent reasons for compliance with the institution's rules but also that these content-independent reasons are peremptory in the sense that they rule out certain kinds of reasons for not complying *ab initio*, rather than merely being weighty relative to them. On this view, if an institution that addresses a rule to one is legitimate, then the mere fact that not complying with its rule would be to one's advantage does not count as a reason that could be weighed against one's reason for compliance. The points I wish to make about the legitimacy of ILIs in this chapter do not depend upon resolving the

issue of whether the content-independent reasons for compliance are peremptory, but my assumption is that they are and this is one of the reasons for the qualifier 'substantial' in the phrase 'substantial content-independent reasons'. This is true even if 'being justified' is understood more robustly than 'having a mere liberty-right', for example, if it is taken to signify that there are strong reasons in favor of having the institution in question (for example, for prudential reasons).

9. These first two challenges to the legitimacy of ILIs are all seriously incomplete. Each merely cites an unfairness or injustice of ILIs, but then slides immediately to the conclusion that the institution is illegitimate. Something more must be said, because, as I have already noted, injustice does not entail illegitimacy. The gap here is symptomatic of a more general problem: the characteristics that appear to be relevant to legitimacy (fairness, avoidance of discrepancies between institutional goals and actual behavior, accountability, transparency, etc.) are all *scalar* (they admit of degree), yet at least in some context, the legitimacy must be regarded as a threshold concept (an institution either has it or doesn't), if legitimacy assessments are to play their practical role of distinguishing institutions that have the right to rule from those that don't. Having the right to rule, on the face of it, is not a matter of degree.

10. See, for example, Eric Posner and Jack Goldsmith, *The Limits of International Law* (Oxford: Oxford University Press, 2005).

11. Buchanan and Keohane, "Legitimacy."

12. I develop this idea of a complementary relationship between philosophical argumentation about the justification of human rights and global public deliberative processes occurring through international legal institutions in "Human Rights and the Legitimacy of the International Order" (chapter 4, this volume).

7

DEMOCRACY AND THE COMMITMENT TO INTERNATIONAL LAW

1. THE NORMATIVE AMBITIONS OF THE LIMITS OF INTERNATIONAL LAW

Jack Goldsmith and Eric Posner attempt to provide a purely "instrumental" theory of international law. There is some lack of clarity as to exactly what the instrumentalist position is. However, it includes at least two types of claims, one descriptive-explanatory, the other normative. The key descriptive-explanatory claim is that international law is best understood according to a rational choice model in which states act according to their self-interest. The instrumental theory, as I understand it, also includes the normative claim (1) that states have only self-interested reasons to comply with or help create international law. However, some of what the authors say in chapter 7, as I shall show below, suggests two additional normative claims: (2) that individuals have no moral obligation to try to cause their states to comply with international law as such, and (3) that individuals have no moral obligation to try to promote the rule of law in international relations by prevailing on their states to engage with international law in ways that are not purely instrumental, that is, not simply means for maximizing state interest.

Chapter 7 sets out the authors' views on the moral obligation—or rather lack of obligation—to comply with international law. In chapter 8 they argue that the commitment to "strong cosmopolitan state action cannot easily be reconciled with... [a] strong commitment to liberal democracy...."[1]

My focus here is on Goldsmith and Posner's normative conclusions in chapters 7 and 8, more specifically on the weakness of the arguments they offer for them and on the authors' tendency to conflate distinct normative issues and to equivocate on exactly what their normative conclusions are. However, my aim is more than criticism; I want to show how an understanding of the limitations of *The Limits of International Law* brings to the fore a question that has hitherto received too little attention: *How should those who embrace a cosmopolitan moral perspective regard international law?*

Given that most of the book is devoted to the descriptive-explanatory project, two questions inevitably arise: Why does the book include the two normative chapters, and what is the relationship between the descriptive-explanatory and normative claims?

The first thing to note in this regard is that the descriptive-explanatory chapters are not wholly non-normative. In these chapters the authors say that they are "skeptical" of the possibility of multilateral cooperation. This statement clearly has normative implications. In particular, it suggests that efforts at multilateral cooperation are likely to be futile and that it is therefore unreasonable to engage in them—unless perhaps there is some strong moral imperative to do so. The point of the latter qualification is that, although morality cannot require us to do the impossible ("ought" implies "can"), in some cases it may require us to attempt to do something that is very unlikely to succeed, if the moral stakes are high enough. (For example, we might have a moral obligation to try to rescue a lost hiker, even though we think it is unlikely he will still be alive, or we may be morally obligated to resist a genocidal regime, even if we have reason to believe that we are unlikely to prevail against it.) One connection between the "skeptical" conclusions of the descriptive-explanatory chapters and the normative claims of chapters 7 and 8 may, then, be this: The former tell us that multilateral cooperation generally and in particular the use of international law to achieve multilateral cooperation, is very unlikely to succeed, while chapter 7 tells us that there is no moral reason to buck the odds and try to achieve multilateral cooperation through international law. Chapter 8 proposes that, at least so far as we have a moral commitment to democracy, we actually have a strong moral reason *not* to pursue international cooperation through international law.

In the symposium for which this chapter was written, Goldsmith and Posner adamantly denied that they have any conscious "normative agenda" in the book. Whether the authors have a normative agenda—conscious or not—is in my judgment irrelevant to the evaluation of the book. However, it is not irrelevant to ask what the normative *import* of the book is or is likely to be taken to be. Given that they do not rest content with the descriptive-explanatory account they offer, but go on to include the two normative chapters, and imply that an attitude of "skepticism" about international cooperation through international law is appropriate, if one accepts their descriptive explanatory account, the book as a whole can be seen as a justification for a particular normative orientation toward international law. And given the current political context, it would be naive to think that readers will not ask whether that normative orientation supports what many take to be the current U.S. government's policy of treating international law as only of instrumental value, as something to be complied with when it is in the interest of the United States to do so, but as having no normative weight at all when it does not. Without claiming that this book is an attempt to provide an intellectual basis for Bush administration policy, it is accurate to say that its normative claims, if valid, would lend support to the view that it is wholly permissible for the U.S. government to take a purely instrumental stance toward international law, and that its citizens do not have a moral obligation to try to prevent their government from doing so.

2. CONFLATING SEVERAL DISTINCT OBLIGATION ISSUES

Goldsmith and Posner do not distinguish clearly between four quite different normative questions—but rather proceed as though by answering one they had answered the others.

(1) Is there a moral obligation to obey international law as such (that is, to obey a norm simply because it is an international law)?
(2) Do states have content-independent, "epistemic" reasons to comply with international laws *generally*? (One has a content-independent reason to comply with a norm if one has reason to comply with it independently of a positive evaluation of its content).
(3) Do states have content-independent, "epistemic" reasons to comply with the rules of *some* international legal norms?
(4) Is there a moral obligation on the part of individuals to try to cause their states to promote the rule of law in international affairs and to act sometimes in ways that do not maximize state interests?

At various points in the discussion in chapter 7, it is clear that the authors would respond negatively to the first two questions, though they fail to distinguish between them clearly. Whether they are attempting to provide a negative answer to the third and fourth questions is unclear. I shall argue that it is important for them to answer the third and fourth questions negatively, given the general normative thrust of chapters 7 and 8 taken together, namely, the view that it is appropriate for both citizens and states to regard international law as having merely instrumental value. I shall also argue that the arguments Posner and Goldsmith present in the two normative chapters, when considered in conjunction with the descriptive-explanatory parts of the book, fail to establish a negative answer to the third and fourth questions.

A. Is There a Moral Obligation to Comply with International Law as Such?

At times it appears that the goal of chapter 7 is only to show that *states* have no moral obligation to comply with international law as such. However, a good deal of the argument in this chapter explicitly tries to show that *individuals* have no moral obligation to try to cause their states to comply with all or most international legal norms.[2] Consider first the claim about the lack of obligation on the part of states. To establish this claim Posner and Goldsmith offer a somewhat patchy appeal to the work of philosophers, including A. John Simmons, that purports to show that individuals have no moral obligation to comply with the law as such. They suggest, not unreasonably, that at present the dominant philosophical view is that there is no moral obligation to obey the law as such, in other words that the mere fact that something is a law provides no significant moral reason to comply with it. They note that the doubts philosophers such as Simmons have about the capacity of individual consent to ground a moral obligation to comply with law as such become magnified in regard to the proposal that states have a moral obligation to comply with international law as such because they have consented. One obvious problem, as I have noted elsewhere, is that a considerable portion of international law is not grounded in state consent.[3]

Let us assume that their analysis is correct so far. The question becomes to put it bluntly, "So what?" This question is apropos because, as the philosophers upon whom the authors draw explicitly say, it is unclear that the truth of the claim that there is no moral obligation to obey the law as such has much practical significance. That is why Simmons and others refer to the claim as "*philosophical* anarchism." It does not show, for example, that individuals do not have strong moral obligations to comply with various laws. Nor should we assume that if most people do not *believe* that they have a moral obligation to comply with law *as such* the legal order will collapse—and Posner and Goldsmith provide no evidence about attitudes toward law that would back such a prediction.

The authors have two answers to the "So what?" question. First, they state that the dominant position among international legal scholars is that states have a moral obligation to comply with law as such. I am not sure that this is the dominant position, or even the majority position, among legal scholars at present. But if it is, then the authors are to be commended for joining others who have already pointed out that this is an error. However, nothing of interest follows in the text regarding states' or citizens' general normative stance toward what international law should be. It certainly does not follow either that there are no content-independent reasons for states to comply with the rules of certain international legal institutions or that there is no moral reason for individuals to try to cause their states to promote the rule of law in international affairs or to act, on occasion, in ways that do not maximize state interests. Second, Posner and Goldsmith say that:

> There is a practical reason why it matters whether states have a moral obligation to comply with international law [as such]. International law scholars who believe that states have such an obligation are as a result, optimistic about the ability of international law to solve problems of international relations, and they attribute failures to the poor design of international treaties and organizations.[4]

It is not obvious why anyone (international law scholars or otherwise) would infer from the claim that states have a moral obligation to comply with international law as such the optimistic conclusion that international law can solve "problems of international relations" if only treaties are written more carefully. One might think that the problem is that states have powerful incentives not to fulfill their obligations. It may be true that if one thought that states have a moral obligation to comply with international law as such, then it would be important to establish publicly that a given state has such an obligation, in order to try to marshal pressure to ensure that it fulfills the obligation.

In my judgment, however, the question of whether states have a moral obligation to comply with international law as such is not really the central question, quite apart from the difficulties of working out a coherent account of the state as a moral agent, capable of having moral obligations. It may be the case that states have no obligation to comply with international law as such and yet it may still be true that the project of promoting the rule of law in international affairs is morally important and that, in certain areas of international law, states have content-independent reasons to comply with international law—that is to comply irrespective of a positive evaluation of the content of the particular laws in question. It is to these other questions that I now turn. The answers to these questions do have important implications for how citizens should try to cause their states to act vis á vis international law.

B. Do States Have Content-independent Reasons to Comply with International Laws Generally?

Posner and Goldsmith set the stage for this question by referring, without much explanation, to Joseph Raz's view of authority, saying that "For Raz (1987), domestic law can have authority on epistemic grounds: the law might incorporate knowledge not available to citizens."[5] Put more accurately, Raz's view is this: One has content-independent reasons to comply with a norm if the source of the norm is such that in acting in accordance with the norms it issues we act better than we would by following reasons that apply directly to us.[6] For example, we have reason to treat the norms of the Department of Motor Vehicles (traffic laws) as "authoritative," that is, to comply with them independently of whether we evaluate their content positively, if we do better by complying with them than with deciding, in each particular case, whether to drive on the right or the left, etc.

Remarkably, Posner and Goldsmith's consideration of the relevance of Raz's notion for international law consists of just one sentence: "But, however plausible this argument may be for domestic law, it is unlikely to be true for international law."[7] This is hardly satisfactory. First of all, Raz denies that domestic law generally is such that complying with it enables us to act better than we would by acting on reasons that directly apply to us; his aim is not to use this conception of authority to show that there is an obligation or even a reason to comply with all or even most domestic laws. Second, even though it is no doubt true that states do not have content-independent reasons to comply with international laws generally (just as individuals do not have content-independent reasons to comply with domestic laws generally), states may have content-independent reasons to comply with the norms of some international legal institutions. This would be the case, for example, where the institution performs a valuable coordinating function by providing credible information to states, or supplies more accurate and impartial assessments regarding compliance with human rights treaties than states could achieve on their own. Nothing the authors have said so far rules out this possibility, and there may be a number of international legal institutions that fit this description. Consequently, Posner and Goldsmith have not established their central "instrumentalist" claim, if this is understood as the assertion that whether a state should comply with any particular international legal norm depends solely on whether doing so would maximize its interests.

Of course, the fact that states have content-independent reasons to comply with the norms of some international institutions is compatible with the authors' "instrumentalist" thesis, if "better" (in "enabling the state to act better than it would if it acted on reasons to apply directly to it") is restricted to better serving the state's long-term interest. However, the Razian conception of authority is not limited to reasons of self-interest; its notion of reliance on institutional rules (independently of a positive evaluation of the content of the particular rules) as enabling us to "act better" leaves open whether "better" means only "better serve one's own interest" or "better" should be understood to accommodate other-regarding values. That is why I included the example of an international legal institution providing better assessments of human rights violations. Although Posner and Goldsmith argue in the descriptive-explanatory chapters of the book that states *do* generally act solely to maximize their own interests, they cannot merely *assume*, in the normative chapters, that states *ought* to act only in a way that maximizes self-interest and then use this assumption to try to argue that a purely instrumental attitude toward international law is appropriate for citizens or for states. Thus, they have neither shown that states do not have content-independent reasons to comply with the norms of some international institutions, nor that when they do this it is merely an instance of the instrumental value of international law, where "instrumental" means "valuable for advancing state interests."

C. Do Individuals Have a Moral Obligation to Try to Cause Their States to Promote the Rule of Law in International Affairs?

Let me briefly recapitulate why I think the authors need to answer this question negatively. Their descriptive-explanatory account leads them to conclude that it is appropriate to be "skeptical" about the prospects for cooperation through international law. Indeed, they claim that the beneficial developments attributed to international law, such as improvement in the protection of human rights, are due to factors other than cooperation. In other words, Goldsmith and Posner try to give us reason to believe that the prospects of successful cooperative international action through international law are very poor. Then, in chapter 7, they try to block the possible rejoinder that even if the prospects for success are poor, we should try to prevail on our states to "enter into more treaties," create more international law, etc., because we have a moral obligation to try to cause our states to promote the rule of law in international relations, or because we believe that international law can be a significant instrument for attaining cosmopolitan goals. The point here is that there are some people who believe in the rule of law and think that they have a moral obligation to do what they can to help promote it in international relations. There are also others who believe that international law can play a significant role in helping to achieve moral progress, whether or not they attribute this to the notion of the rule of law or not. Because states are still, for the most part, the creators of international law, both groups will conclude that they have an obligation to prevail on their states to engage in a constructive—and not merely instrumental—way, even if they think that the odds of success are not good, *if* they believe the potential moral payoff is high and *if* they believe that the costs of investing energy in the project of influencing their states in this way, including the opportunity costs, are not too high. If Posner and Goldsmith could show that individuals have no moral obligation to try to cause their states to promote the rule of international law—or that the commitment to democracy provides a moral reason *not* to try to promote it—then they would close this loophole in the argument that because cooperation under international law is unlikely to succeed, we should not be concerned if our states take a purely instrumental posture toward international law. In current political terms, they would have shown that we should have no objection to what some say the Bush administration policy is namely using international law when it furthers our state interests, ignoring it when it does not.[8]

The main point I want to make is that nothing that Posner and Goldsmith say in chapter 7 supports the conclusion that the answer to question (4) is negative. Even if they have shown that states do not have a moral obligation to comply with international law as such, it does not follow that individuals have no moral obligation to try to cause their states to promote the rule of law in international relations or to use international law to promote moral progress in the world. Nor does the pretty obvious fact that not all areas of international law have Razian authority support a negative answer to question (4). Whether the answer to question (4) is negative or affirmative depends upon the resolution of complex issues concerning the importance of the project of establishing the rule of law which Posner and Goldsmith do not engage in this book.

More specifically, the authors do not consider why it is that some people apparently believe that there are moral reasons to promote the rule of law in international relations. To put the same point differently: Posner and Goldsmith indicate no awareness of the moral attractiveness of the ideal of the rule of law; so it is not surprising that they conclude that there is no moral obligation to try to promote the rule of law and that international law has only instrumental value.

It is beyond the scope of this chapter to provide anything approaching a satisfactory account of what is morally compelling about the ideal of the rule of law or to show that the rule of law should be promoted not only domestically, but in international relations as well. Instead, I will only sketch some of the elements of the ideal of the rule of law that have led some people to find it morally compelling. Even if I succeed in making a good *prima facie* case for why individuals ought to try to promote the rule of law, this would not be enough to show what a commitment to doing so implies for how we should try to get our states to act in their foreign relations. For one thing, the best accounts of the morally compelling features of the ideal of the rule of law are geared toward what *domestic* law can be like, as I shall presently show.[9] In my judgment, the most morally compelling features of the ideal of the rule of law have to do with the ways in which a legal system can protect *individuals'* interests and respect *individuals'* autonomy; but much of international law concerns the relations among *states* and in many cases states do not represent the interests of some or even most of their citizens. So it is not clear just how the commitment to the rule of law is to be cashed out in the international arena. Secondly, and equally importantly, it is crucial not to confuse a commitment to the rule of law with support for existing law and legal institutions, and this is especially true in the case of existing international law and existing international legal institutions—which are extremely defective in many cases *from the standpoint of the ideal of the rule of law.*

For example, it seems that some believe that the rule of law in international affairs requires strict adherence to the principle of "state equality"—that international law should stringently avoid discriminating among types of states, at least so far as the most important rights of sovereignty are concerned.[10] Robert Keohane and I have argued that this is a mistake, that those who hold this view are confusing a commitment to the rule of law, that is, a commitment to lawfulness as a normative ideal, with one particular feature of the current international legal system. We have argued that under certain conditions a rule-governed coalition of at least minimally liberal states would be the appropriate venue for making some especially problematic decisions concerning the use of force.[11] Such an arrangement would violate the "equality of states" principle in the latter's application to decisions to use force. Yet it might be better from a moral point of view and a better approximation of the ideal of the rule of law.[12]

Before pursuing these complications further, however, let me clarify the general point that whether individuals have a moral obligation to try to ensure that institutions promote the rule of law does not depend upon whether they (or the state) have a moral obligation to comply with law as such. There can be a moral obligation to promote the rule of law in spite of the fact that there is no moral obligation to obey any particular law solely because it is the law, because whether the enterprise of law is morally compelling is independent of the moral quality of any particular law and indeed independent of the particular characteristics of a given legal system. Those who believe that there are moral reasons to engage in the enterprise of law find the ideal of the rule of law morally compelling, but this does not commit them to the view that the fact that a norm is an international legal norm creates an obligation to comply with it.

Here I can only begin to indicate some of the features of the ideal of the rule of law that are thought to make it morally compelling, drawing heavily on Lon Fuller's conception of the inner morality of law as well as on H.L.A. Hart's work. The ideal of the rule of law is usually understood to include several elements, each of which is only approximated in actual legal systems, whether domestic or international: (1) laws are to be general, (2) they are to be relatively stable, thereby making possible and sustaining a framework of expectations within which individuals can plan their actions, coordinate with one another, etc., (3) to the extent that law addresses individuals, it should address them as choosers, as individuals capable of autonomy, and when it addresses corporations or other collective entities such as states, it should do so in ways that are compatible with respect for individual autonomy, (4) the basis of legal determinations is to be principled and deliberative, and the principles invoked, as well as the deliberative processes themselves, are to be both public and accessible, (5) the interpretation and administration of law are to be impartial, (6) all persons are to be equal before the law, (7) although the law may be ultimately backed by coercion, it is to provide a mode of conflict resolution that does not rest primarily on power, but on the principled and inclusive consideration of interests, and (8) overtime, the process of principled deliberation should aid in the establishment of a body of rules that is coherent, that satisfies the preceding six conditions, and that can serve as a basis for making future legal determinations.

Given this rudimentary sketch of the ideal of the rule of law, it should be clear that it bears two intimate connections with justice. First, the ideal of the rule of law *includes* some important elements of justice, in particular the notions of impartiality, nondiscrimination, and respect for persons as autonomous beings who can give and accept justifications for acting. Second, although the ideal of the rule of law does not exhaust the content of justice, an institution that does a credible job of approximating the ideal will *provide valuable resources for the pursuit of justice* more comprehensively understood, especially insofar as justice requires protection of every person's most basic interests and a commitment to oppose discrimination.

Notice that I have not said that justice requires equal consideration of persons' interests, but only that it requires protection of everyone's basic interests. This distinction is important, because I want to emphasize that one can appreciate the moral importance of the rule of law because of its connections with justice, and therefore recognize that there is a moral obligation to promote the rule of law, without in any way being committed to the very strong, strictly egalitarian view that everyone's interests—their well-being as a whole, not just their basic interests—ought to be given equal consideration. This point will be important when we examine Posner and Goldsmith's normative claims in chapter 8. Even if they succeed there in establishing that strong cosmopolitanism is incompatible with democracy, this will do nothing to show that there is no moral obligation to try to promote the rule of law, because the ideal of the rule of law does not include the egalitarian commitments that are distinctive characteristics of strong cosmopolitanism.

I have suggested that the morally compelling character of the ideal of the rule of law is most easily grasped in its application to systems of law that take individuals to be the primary addressees of legal claims, and that it is therefore more difficult to ascertain what the ideal of the rule of law demands in the case of international law, given that the primary addressees of international law are states, not persons. Nevertheless, some of the elements of the ideal, such as generality and impartiality, as well as the notion that legal determinations should be made through publicly accessible, deliberative processes, and should contribute to the development of a consistent, coherent body of rules, apply directly to international law as well.

It is worth noting that the morally compelling character of the ideal of the rule of law actually provides a reason for thinking that there can be no moral obligation to comply with law as such: If an actual law falls far enough short of the ideal of the rule of law, there may be no moral reason to comply with it at all, much less a moral reason to comply with it simply because it is law. According to an even moderately positivist conception of what the law is, something can be a law and yet depart significantly from the ideal of the rule of law.

As I have argued elsewhere, a commitment to the rule of law in international relations may, under certain circumstances, require not only noncompliance with particular international legal norms, but even the creation of new institutions that may further weaken some existing international legal institutions.[13] Precisely the same is true for domestic laws and domestic legal institutions. For example, it was respect for the ideal of the rule of law, among other things, that supported not only voiding many laws created in the Third Reich, but also restructuring German legal institutions. A commitment to the rule of law, then, whether in the domestic or international sphere, is not the same as a commitment to the status quo, especially when the status quo falls far short of the ideal of the rule of law.

Let me hasten to say that I do not believe that many areas of international law even approximate the constituent conditions of the ideal of the rule of law. That is not the point. The point, rather, is that a proper appreciation of the ideal of the rule of law implies that we have moral reasons to promote the enterprise of law and that, therefore, it is not the case that international law is only of instrumental value.

The last statement requires an important qualification: Given the morally compelling character of the ideal of the rule of law, we have a moral obligation to promote the rule of law, internationally as well as domestically—unless it can be shown that the rule of law cannot be approximated to any valuable extent in international relations, or that the attempt to approximate it would involve excessive moral costs. Of course, more extreme proponents of the realist tradition have argued that the rule of law, precisely because it includes moral elements, cannot be established in international relations, because international relations are characterized by a massive and insoluble assurance problem that makes moral behavior irrational and unsustainable. Moreover, some realists, including Hans Morgenthau and E.H. Carr, have held that the moral costs of attempting to extend the rule of law to international relations are excessive. However, in my view and that of many others, the extreme empirical assumptions on which such a realist view rests are so implausible that we are not forced to conclude that the attempt to promote the rule of law in international relations is either futile or morally counterproductive.[14] Be that as it may, Goldsmith and Posner do not present an extreme realist view, defend it against its legion critics, and then conclude that the enterprise of international law is doomed and that, therefore, there can be no moral obligation to promote the rule of law in international relations (because "cannot" implies "not ought"). Instead, they simply argue that there is no moral obligation to obey international laws as such, suggest that international law as a whole does not have authority in Raz's sense, and then erroneously suggest that individuals have no moral obligation to try to cause their states to promote the rule of law in international relations.

It should not be surprising that chapter 7 yields only these conclusions, given that the authors do not engage the issue of what is morally compelling about the ideal of the rule of law, either in this chapter or anywhere else in the book. If law generally, including international law, has noninstrumental value, this is presumably because the enterprise of the rule of law embodies important moral values and, more specifically, because some of the features of a legal system both partly embody justice and also make the law a valuable resource for the pursuit of justice. There is, in fact, a remarkable absence, in *Limits* of any appreciation for why some people value the rule of law and why those that do are likely to find unconvincing the thesis that international law is only valuable to the extent that it advances the interests of states.

3. CONFUSING DIFFERENT COSMOPOLITANISMS

In chapter 8, Posner and Goldsmith first claim they will argue against strong cosmopolitanism, which they define on the first page of the chapter as the very extreme view that states should "act internationally on the basis of global welfare rather than state welfare."[15] However, on the very next page, they claim to have refuted the quite different view that states ought sometimes to act internationally in ways that do *not maximize* state welfare. (They say that the claim that states should perform international acts that do not pass a cost-benefit test where costs and benefits considered are only those attaching to that state itself is "misplaced."[16]) Of course, strong cosmopolitanism (the view that states should pursue global interests rather than their own) and extreme statism (the view that states should exclusively pursue the maximization of their interests) are not the only alternatives. There is also a range of views that are usually called moderate cosmopolitanism, according to which states may give priority to the interests of their own people, but nonetheless sometimes ought to act to protect the basic interests of foreigners. In chapter 8, as with their treatment of the moral obligation to comply with international law in chapter 7, the authors' arguments are plausible only against the more extreme, already heavily criticized strong cosmopolitan view, and are entirely ineffective against the more plausible and increasingly widely held, moderate cosmopolitan position.

Before establishing the latter claim, however, let me note that, although the chief aim of chapter 8 is to show that strong cosmopolitanism is in "deep tension" with the commitment to democracy, there is no attempt to clarify exactly what sort of view strong cosmopolitanism is, and therefore it is difficult to tell exactly what is being argued for. Unfortunately, the authors do not avail themselves of some very useful distinctions that have been made in the burgeoning philosophical literature on cosmopolitan normative theory.

The authors fail, for example, to distinguish between cosmopolitanism as a moral view and cosmopolitanism as an institutional view.[17] Cosmopolitanism as a moral view is usually described as the claim that every person is in some fundamental sense of equal moral worth and that, consequently, fundamental moral status is not dependent on citizenship or nationality.[18] As an institutional view, cosmopolitanism is the claim that there should be a world government or some other sort of all-encompassing institutional structure in which all persons have equal membership rights. There are few takers these days for the institutional view.

Posner and Goldsmith target a view about what states should do; they want to argue that the claim that states should promote global interests rather than their own interests is both wrong-headed, because states will never do so ("cannot" implies "not ought"), and because it is in "deep tension with democracy." There are two ways one might interpret the claim that states should promote global interests "rather than" their own and hence two ways to understand what the authors mean by strong cosmopolitanism. Following the first interpretation, one takes the "rather than" literally: call this utterly self-abnegating cosmopolitanism, the view that states should disregard their own interests entirely and only pursue the global good (whatever that might be). Since nobody seems to hold this view, I will not consider it further. According to the second interpretation, strong cosmopolitanism is an *impartialist* view about how states ought to act: each state should give equal weight to its own interests (or rather, the interests of its citizens) and to the interests of every other state (the interests of their citizens).

For a number of reasons, I and many other contributors to the recent literature on cosmopolitanism reject the impartialist view and instead embrace a moderate cosmopolitan view when it comes to our prescriptions for how citizens should try to get their states to act.[19] Our view is that individuals have a moral obligation to try to get their states to do more to protect the basic interests of foreigners who are at risk, but that it is perfectly appropriate for states to act with partiality toward their own citizens.[20] Notice that being a moderate cosmopolitan in this sense does not mean that one rejects cosmopolitanism as a moral view; rather, it is because we believe that every person has fundamental moral worth—that every individual's basic interests deserve protection—that we hold that a proper appreciation of the state's rightful priority of its own citizens' welfare should not be confused with the quite different idea that the *only* legitimate function of the state is to serve its own citizens' welfare, which I earlier characterized as extreme statism. Later I will argue that extreme statism is a very implausible view of legitimate state functions.

With these distinctions among different kinds of cosmopolitan views in mind, we can now begin to assess Posner and Goldsmith's claim that it is wrong to expect states to act in a more cosmopolitan manner than they are presently doing and hence that it is wrong to hold that citizens have a moral duty to try to cause their states to do so (because "cannot" implies "not ought"). It may be true that some (moral) cosmopolitans underestimate the difficulty of changing states so that they act in more cosmopolitan ways. This can hardly be said, however, of many human rights activists (some of whom may be strong cosmopolitans in the impartialist sense and some of whom may be moderate cosmopolitans). They know, from tough experience how hard it is, and often say as much.

Nevertheless, to enlighten those cosmopolitans who underestimate the difficulties, the authors correctly point out that there are several considerations that work against democratic states engaging in costly cosmopolitan action. The first thing to notice, however, is that, taken together, these factors do not support the conclusion that states cannot engage in *more* cosmopolitan action than they presently do.

For example, Posner and Goldsmith note that it has been argued on the basis of evolutionary theory that altruism is largely an intragroup phenomenon. But there is a large gap between the latter claim and the conclusion that states cannot engage in more cosmopolitan action than at present and that therefore it is wrong for their citizens to expect them to do so. The difficulty with such slides from "is" to "cannot" to "not ought" is two-fold.

First, from the standpoint of the simple evolutionary view on which Posner and Goldsmith rely, it is not just cosmopolitan attitudes that are hard to explain; the existence of the modern state itself is almost incomprehensible. In virtually all modern states there are many laws that are designed to provide benefits for some citizens by taking resources from others, and such laws have had considerable stability, in spite of the fact that the totality of citizens, the population of the state, is nothing like the sort of primary group whose altruistic behavior evolutionary theory is supposed to explain. There seem to be two possibilities: either (a) the existence and effectiveness of such laws within the state rely importantly on altruism toward one's fellow citizens or (b) it is made possible by institutional arrangements in the absence of such altruism. If (a) is the case, then the big question for Posner and Goldsmith is this: If individuals' altruism can be extensive enough to encompass hundreds of millions of people one will never meet and with whom one has virtually no interaction, simply because they are one's fellow citizens, what reason is there to believe that altruism's limits happen to coincide with those of current state borders? If (b) is the case, then Posner and Goldsmith need to explain why institutional arrangements can compensate for lack of altruism in the case of states, but not in the case of larger domains.

The authors suggest that within states there are "thicker" forms of association and that this explains the fact of genuine domestic cooperation and the existence of domestic laws that are designed to produce results that do not benefit all but provide special assistance to some. The obvious problem with this response is that the "thicker" forms of association that exist within states typically do not encompass all citizens, but instead only exist among various subgroups (religions, ethnic groups, classes, etc.). Given how far current evolutionary theories are from explaining large-scale social cooperation, much less the modern pluralistic, multiethnic, and often multi-national state, it is not very persuasive to say that evolutionary theory tells us that we cannot expect any increase in cosmopolitan action. If evolutionary theory comes to be able to explain the existence of large modern states, it will presumably have to incorporate a larger and more complex role for institutions than it currently does. But there is no reason to think that if this is accomplished, the result will be support for the conclusion that genuine cooperation or other-regarding sentiments cannot extend across national borders.

Second, there are historical examples of people undertaking what certainly appear to be cosmopolitan actions even when it is not in their best interest to do so, and where they succeeded in enlisting large and powerful institutional resources, including those of the state, to achieve their cosmopolitan ends. One of the most remarkable is the movement first to stop the trans-Atlantic slave trade and then to abolish slavery. Individuals who largely objected to slavery on moral-religious grounds succeeded in creating a highly organized politically savvy mass movement that eventually won over the British government and enlisted the force of the British navy.[21] A significant feature of antislavery political discourse was the insistence that African slaves were moral equals, when it came to the protection of their basic interests, or at least their interest in liberty. Few abolitionists if any were egalitarians; the vast majority were probably better characterized as moderate cosmopolitans.

In response to this apparent counterexample, one might try to save the hypothesis that altruism is exclusively or primarily an intragroup phenomenon by saying that antislavery agitators succeeded in convincing people that African slaves were members of our own group, namely, humanity—recall the popular antislavery medal that depicted an African in chains, with the inscription, "Am I not a man and a brother?" But of course this would be a Pyrrhic victory, since adopting the thesis that altruism exists only with a groups is vacuous if humanity counts as a group. The point is that it is one thing to say that our evolutionary past or something else about our psychology creates obstacles to cosmopolitan sentiment and action, but quite another to draw the shamelessly convenient conclusion that we are already at the limit and that the limit cannot be moved outward.

The closest that Goldsmith and Posner come to arguing that we are already in fact at the psychological limits of altruism occurs in an instance of the rhetorical strategy of bait and switch, as when they say they will criticize an interesting position that they ascribe to prominent theorists and then attack a quite different, less plausible position that the theorists they cite do not hold. They mention Martha Nussbaum as a contemporary cosmopolitan who explores the possibility that a broadly humanistic education (along with modern electronic media and the greater interaction that globalization facilitates) can extend our sentiments to people we formerly regarded as alien. But then they quickly characterize this kind of view, quite dismissively, as "perfectibilist."[22] This, of course, is a serious misuse of the term; to believe that people can become more cosmopolitan than they presently are is not to affirm the perfectibility of man. Here the authors substitute pejorative rhetoric for argument, falsely implying that anyone who favors more cosmopolitan education is a (wide-eyed) perfectibilist.

It is crucial to understand where the burden of argument lies in this instance. Goldsmith and Posner are advancing the very strong thesis that we are presently at the limit, motivationally and institutionally, of cosmopolitan action. Setting out a list of factors that tend to make it more difficult to engage in cosmopolitan action than in self-interested action, other things being equal, is a far cry from establishing this very strong thesis.

For example, the authors assert that the people of the United States are not willing to expend wealth and lives for humanitarian intervention, without even considering recent empirical literature on the subject.[23] That literature is complex and not univocal in its conclusions, but some studies indicate that the U.S. public will in fact tolerate considerable costs of military interventions, including humanitarian interventions, under certain conditions that are far from fanciful. For example, some studies indicate that how many casualties or what other costs the public will tolerate depends in part upon whether the respondents think it was right to undertake the intervention and believe that the goal of the intervention is being successfully pursued.[24] Similarly, Goldsmith and Posner flatly state that humanitarian interventions have not increased in recent years.[25] Again, this is an empirical question that requires both careful definitions (what counts as humanitarian intervention?) and recourse to data, neither of which the authors even begin to provide. Without engaging this complex issue, one can say, however, that U.N.-sanctioned interventions that have been justified on humanitarian grounds increased significantly in the 1990s, including interventions in Bosnia, Haiti, Somalia, East Timor, and Kosovo. To summarize, the first part of chapter 8, the attempt to show that we should not expect any increase in cosmopolitan action on the part of states, is analytically confused (because it fails to distinguish between whether there are limits to altruism and whether we have reason to believe we have reached the limits), rhetorically disingenuous (because it portrays progress as perfection), and empirically weak (because it fails to engage the relevant empirical literature and instead merely asserts controversial sweeping generalizations, whose key terms, such as "humanitarian intervention," are left wholly unspecified).

4. WHY THE COMMITMENT TO DEMOCRACY SUPPORTS COSMOPOLITANISM

The second part of chapter 8 attempts to show that there is a "deep tension" between strong cosmopolitanism and the commitment to democracy. Once again we must ask: What is strong cosmopolitanism? If it is the impartialist view that individuals should try to get their states to act so as to count equally the interests of their own citizens and those of citizens of other states, then I agree with the authors that it is highly unlikely that most citizens will in fact recognize or act on this putative obligation. But, contrary to what Posner and Goldsmith say, this does not show that citizens should not try to get their states to act in a more cosmopolitan manner than they are doing now. If, as I have suggested, the more plausible form of cosmopolitanism is moderate cosmopolitanism, then the more interesting question to ask is whether moderate cosmopolitanism is "in tension" with the commitment to democracy. My conclusion will be that moderate cosmopolitanism is not in tension with democracy as a matter of principle or theory. I think this point is worth making, because, although Posner and Goldsmith say they are trying to show how problematic strong cosmopolitanism is for those committed to democracy, at times they seem to be rejecting moderate cosmopolitanism, for example, when they say that it is wrong for citizens of a democracy to expect their states to act in a more cosmopolitan manner than they do now, by ratifying more international treaties that serve the interests of foreigners, supporting the International Criminal Court, etc.

Before we proceed further, it is important to understand that even if it is true that there is a *tension* between the commitment to democracy and the commitment to moderate cosmopolitanism, it is not clear what follows from this. In particular, it does not follow that the citizens of a democracy should not try to get their governments to act in a *more* cosmopolitan manner than they presently do; nor does it even follow that government officials in a democracy should absolutely refrain from cosmopolitan action unless authorized to do so by the public. After all, there are lots of tensions in democracies: between individual autonomy and the common good, between the right to freedom of the press and the right to a fair trial, between the commitment to stable property rights and the need to rectify past injustices, for example. Furthermore, one should not assume that it is never morally permissible for state leaders to act without authorization, if the action in question would further an important moral goal or, more plausibly, avert a human catastrophe.

The tension the authors want to call to our attention exists, they believe, at both the institutional level and the level of theory or principle. With regard to the former level, they mention several institutional obstacles to the U.S. government taking cosmopolitan action. The most important obstacle, they contend, is the overarching requirement that "foreign policy must be justified on terms acceptable to voters [or, rather, to the majority of them]."[26] Because Posner and Goldsmith believe that cosmopolitan sentiments are "weak" among American voters (and other democratic publics), they believe that this is a serious obstacle. As to how "serious" they think it is, that is unclear. The authors' statement, cited above, that it is a mistake to expect states to act in a more cosmopolitan fashion than they presently do, suggests that they think it is an insurmountable obstacle. They first present certain institutional features as serious obstacles, but then slide toward the unwarranted conclusion that they are insurmountable obstacles.

Part of the problem, as I noted earlier, is that they remain content to operate with the very vague, undifferentiated notion of "cosmopolitan sentiment," neither drawing on empirical work to try to determine the conditions under which different kinds of cosmopolitan action may be supported by publics nor telling us what counts as "weak" in this context. In addition, as I have also already observed, they too readily dismiss as "perfectibilist" the prospect that cosmopolitan sentiment might be strengthened, through education and institutional change. In summary, the authors' discussion of institutional obstacles to cosmopolitan action does not support the broad claim that it is very likely to be futile for citizens of a democracy to try to get their governments to engage in more cosmopolitan action than they now do, so it does nothing to show that citizens have no moral obligation to pressure their governments to do so (on the grounds that "cannot" implies "not ought").

Exactly what the tension between democracy and cosmopolitanism derives from at the level of *theory* or *principle* is perhaps not quite so clear. The following passage suggests that Goldsmith and Posner are uncritically assuming that any departure from the purpose for which a state was founded is either unfeasible or illegitimate.

> Another crucial difference between a liberal democratic state and, say, Oxfam International, is that the state does not organize itself for the purpose of engaging in acts of cosmopolitan charity. The dominant purpose of any state is to create a community of mutual benefit for citizens and other members, and more generally to preserve and enhance the welfare of compatriots. The U.S. Constitution, for example, was designed to create a more perfect *domestic* order, and its foreign relations mechanisms were crafted to enhance U.S. welfare.[27]

Notice, first, that the authors' thesis that the "dominant" purpose of any state is to preserve and enhance the welfare of its own citizens *only* rules out strong cosmopolitanism (understood either as the utter self-abnegation or the impartialist view); it is quite compatible with moderate cosmopolitanism, and it certainly does not rule out the possibility that states can act in a more cosmopolitan manner than they currently do and still accord a proper priority to their own citizens' welfare. Second, and more importantly, the fact that a state was created for a particular purpose may tell us that there are likely to be institutional obstacles to pursuing other purposes, but it does not show that the pursuit of other purposes is unfeasible, much less inconsistent in principle or theory. The United States and other states currently pursue many activities that were not envisioned by their founders. The question is whether they ought to. The issue of when institutional goals should be expanded or otherwise revised is a very important one, but Goldsmith and Posner do not engage it. To summarize my argument thus far: Posner and Goldsmith have not shown that it is futile to expect democratic states to engage in more cosmopolitan action than they do, and they have not shown that moderate cosmopolitanism is incompatible with democracy in principle or theory. They have, however, given those cosmopolitans who underestimate the difficulty of getting democratic states to act in a more cosmopolitan manner good reason to reconsider their optimism.

I would suggest that there *is* a theoretical or in-principle tension worth considering, but that it is a tension between a certain view of democracy that Posner and Goldsmith may hold and the justifications for democracy. Since I have developed this line of thought in some detail elsewhere, I will only sketch it here.[28] The core ideas are that the more plausible justifications that are given for having democratic government rely on universalistic moral values, and that these universalistic moral values not only impose limits on majority rule domestically (in the form of entrenched individual rights, for example), but also give us reason to regard the state as something more than merely an instrument for our mutual benefit. If this is the case, then there is something deeply wrong with the assumption that the only legitimate function of the democratic state is to realize the preferences of its own citizens or to maximize their welfare. The same reasons that we have for insisting on having a democratic state also require us to acknowledge that our state should not be regarded simply as an instrument for realizing our preferences or maximizing our welfare. Just as the values that undergird democracy justify internal limitations on democratic policy, in the form of entrenched individual rights that constrain majority rule, so they also impose limitations on how democracies should act regarding foreign relations.

Goldsmith and Posner seem to assume a commitment to democracy, while saying almost nothing about the justifications for democracy. The more plausible justifications for democracy typically fall into two classes: arguments to show that democracy is the most reliable form of government for constraining abuses of government power and helping ensure that government effectively serves the interests of all citizens; and arguments to show that when individuals are subject to a system of coercively backed laws, a proper regard for equality requires that in some sense each must have an "equal say" in determining what the laws will be. When fleshed out, both types of arguments appeal to certain morally relevant characteristics that are universal among people, not possessed exclusively by those who happen to be our fellow citizens. For example, when we try to spell out why government ought to serve the welfare of all citizens, we must appeal, ultimately, to the moral importance of each citizen's basic interests; but in doing so, we will, in the end, rely on something like the idea that *any* individual who possesses certain characteristics is deserving of protection. To take only one example: when John Locke argues that government is legitimate only when it protects life, liberty, and property, he appeals to what he takes to be generic features of human beings—their capacity for rationality in particular. He says they have these rights because they are men, not because they are Englishmen. If the basic interests, protection of which justifies the existence of the state and determines the conditions of its legitimacy, are human interests common to all persons, then surely a way of thinking about the nature of the state that provides no basis for obligations to help ensure that the basic interests of all persons are protected is fundamentally flawed. Similarly, attempts to flesh out the argument that everyone subject to a system of coercively backed laws out to have a say in determining what the laws are must appeal, ultimately, to a principle of equality or of respect for autonomy that is universal in scope.

It does not follow, of course, that everyone is entitled to participate in some sort of "world-democracy." But it is hard to see how our commitment to the values of equality and autonomy that underlie our commitment to democracy in our own state could have no implications for our conception of the legitimate functions of the state, given that in our world states are the most powerful institutional resources we possess for implementing such fundamental moral values. In brief, the same values that support the commitment to democracy at least establish a *prima facie* case for regarding the state as a resource for implementing those values. But if this is so, then we cannot simply *assume* that as a matter of principle democracies are only legitimately concerned with realizing their own citizens' preferences or maximizing their interests. And we cannot, therefore, conclude that for this reason democracy is in tension with cosmopolitan state action as a matter of principle or theory. Simply to assume such a view of the legitimate functions of the state—to assume the validity of extreme statism—in an argument against cosmopolitanism is to beg the fundamental question at issue. Yet without this assumption, Posner and Goldsmith's discussion of democracy in chapter 8 cannot show that cosmopolitanism, at least in moderate forms, and democracy are in tension as a matter of principle or theory.

I will mention briefly one other reason for rejecting extreme statism, the view that the only legitimate function of the state is to realize its own citizens' preferences or to maximize their interests. This view is incompatible with some very stable and apparently widely held moral intuitions about our negative moral duties to foreigners. Taken literally, extreme statism implies that the state ought to undertake an unprovoked attack on another state, if doing so would serve its citizens' interests, unless the majority of the citizens happen to disapprove of its doing so. Thus, the view that the state ought only to act to realize its own citizens' preferences or to maximize their welfare is in direct conflict with the intuition that it is wrong to harm the innocent and that it is wrong to engage in aggressive war.

A proponent of this view of the legitimate functions of the state might attempt to avoid this unsavory implication by saying that the government's mandate to do only what serves the best interests of its citizens (or realizes the preferences of the majority of citizens) is limited by a general negative duty not to harm. The problem is that this move appears to be wholly ad hoc. In other words, once it is conceded that the state is not properly conceived as being exclusively an instrument to advance the interests of its citizens (or to realize their preferences), we must face the question of why our obligations to foreigners are limited to the duty not to harm. The objection, then, can be formulated as a dilemma. Either the proponent of this view of the legitimate functions of the state must stick to it, denying that states have any obligations whatsoever to foreigners, including negative duties not to kill or injure them in the pursuit of maximizing their own citizens' interests or realizing the citizens' preferences; or he must acknowledge that states have such negative duties, but then face the charge that he provides no basis for not recognizing some positive duties as well. And note that here, once again, the choice is not between strong cosmopolitanism, understood as the extreme view that we ought to treat the interests of foreigners as *equal* to ours, on the one hand, and rejecting positive duties to foreigners altogether, on the other. A third, more reasonable alternative is that we have some positive duties to foreigners, and that our conception of legitimate state functions should take this into account.

I conclude that Posner and Goldsmith have not shown that there is a "deep tension" between democracy and moderate cosmopolitanism as a matter of principle or theory, and that they have given us no reason to think that the institutional obstacles that they describe preclude a significant *increase* in cosmopolitan action relative to the status quo. I have also argued that the commitment to democracy in fact pushes us toward, not away from cosmopolitanism, insofar as the most plausible justifications for democracy rely on premises about the equal fundamental moral worth of all persons.

If the authors reply that their only aim was to show that there is a tension between democracy and strong cosmopolitanism, then two points are apropos. First, as I have already emphasized, by restricting their argument to an attack on strong cosmopolitanism, the authors would fail to engage what may now be the dominant type of cosmopolitan view—moderate cosmopolitanism. Second, restricting their attack to strong cosmopolitanism fails to support their central contention that we should not expect democracies to develop more cosmopolitan policies.

5. CONCLUSIONS

The Limits of International Law advances a number of provocative theses. Given the political context in which it occurs—and given the intellectual debate about international law that the current political context has stimulated—it is appropriate to ask not only whether the book succeeds in its intellectual aims, but also whether those aims, if attained, would lend support to the present posture of the U.S. government regarding international law.

The authors do argue that it is a mistake for U.S. citizens to expect their state to act in a more cosmopolitan manner. They also argue that the proper attitude toward international law—the only reasonable attitude, given their theory of how international law works—is purely instrumental, that international law is valuable only to the extent that it serves state interests. Finally, Posner and Goldsmith also suggest that there is some sort of incompatibility in principle between cosmopolitan commitments—at least serious ones—and the commitment to democracy. If all of these theses were true, then current U.S. policies that disregard certain fundamental international legal norms, including those prohibiting torture and the rendition of prisoners to countries where they will be tortured, would be more defensible than they are. This is *not* to say that the fact that the authors advance these theses shows that they support the policies in question. There are good moral and prudential arguments against such policies that are quite independent of the issue of what the proper posture toward international law is, and endorsing these arguments may be compatible with everything the authors say in *Limits*. Nevertheless, given the political context, it is important to understand that Posner and Goldsmith do not succeed in establishing any of the foregoing theses and that, therefore, those who believe that this book provides support for the policies in question are mistaken.

Nonetheless, in the normative chapters of their book, Posner and Goldsmith have succeeded in performing two commendable services: they have helped to make clear the magnitude of the political task facing those who regard the democratic state as a valuable resource for realizing cosmopolitan principles, and they have challenged those who are committed to the rule of law in international relations to articulate more clearly the basis and nature of that commitment.

Notes

1. Jack L. Goldsmith and Eric A. Posner, *The Limits of International Law* (New York: Oxford University Press, 2005), 205.

2. For example, the authors indicate that they are going to try to answer the question of "why individuals and governments should feel obligated to cause the state to comply with its legal obligations." Goldsmith and Posner, *Limits*, 189. Similarly, they ask whether "citizens have a moral obligation to cause the state to comply with its obligations," and go on to rule as implausible various bases for saying that they do have such an obligation (188). Also

the authors query whether "members of the public really have an obligation to pressure their government to maintain adhere to a treaty that could only have disastrous effects for the state and its citizens. . . ." (192).

3. See generally Allen Buchanan, *Justice, Legitimacy, and Self-determination: Moral Foundations for International Law* (New York: Oxford University Press, 2004) [hereinafter Buchanan, *Justice*].

4. Goldsmith and Posner, *Limits*, 203.

5. Ibid., 195 (citing Joseph Raz, *Government by Consent*).

6. Joseph Raz, *The Morality of Freedom* (New York: Oxford University Press, 1986), 35, 53.

7. Goldsmith and Posner, *Limits*, 195.

8. There are two reasons to think that the authors believe themselves to be establishing a negative answer to (2) as well. First, they describe their task in the book as advancing an "instrumental" theory of international law, and they clearly think that their instrumental view has an important normative component. From a normative point of view, an instrumental theory of international law is one according to which international law has only instrumental value, and this presumably means that the proper attitude toward not just individual international laws but also the *enterprise* of international law—the attempt to extend the rule of law to international affairs—is purely instrumental. In other words, not just compliance with particular international laws, but the enterprise of international law should be regarded as being valuable only to the extent that engagement with it furthers state interests. Second, the following passage, at the beginning of chapter 8, summarizes what Goldsmith and Posner claim to have established in chapter 7, and this summary refers not just to the proper attitude toward this or that particular international law but toward the enterprise of international law.

> Chapter 7 analyzed a state's moral duty to comply with international law. This chapter analyzes the state's moral duty to enter into more treaties that would benefit third-party states, give up sovereignty to institutions which promote justice such as the International Criminal Court (ICC), and, in general, act on the basis of global welfare rather than state welfare.

Goldsmith and Posner, *Limits*, 205.

9. I am indebted to Jack Goldsmith for prompting me to take this point seriously.

10. Allen Buchanan, "Between International Law Fetishism and International Law Instrumentalism" (unpublished paper, on file with the author).

11. Allen Buchanan, "Reforming the International Law of Humanitarian Intervention," in J. L. Holzgrefe and Robert O. Keohane, eds., *Humanitarian Intervention: Ethical, Legal, and Political Dilemmas* (New York: Cambridge University Press, 2003), 130–74; Allen Buchanan and Robert O. Keohane, "The Preventive Use of Force: A Cosmopolitan Institutional Proposal," *Ethics and International Affairs* 18, no. 1 (2004).

12. It is ironic that those who have rejected the proposal for a liberal coalition to make decisions concerning the use of force almost invariably say that the Security Council is the only legitimate venue for making such decisions, given that the permanent member veto is a clear (and, one might add, morally arbitrary) violation of the principle of the "equality of states."

13. Allen Buchanan, "From Nuremburg to Kosovo: The Morality of Illegal International Legal Reform," *Ethics* 117 (2001): 673; Buchanan, *Justice*.

14. Charles Beitz, *Political Theory and International Relations* (Princeton, N.J.: Princeton University Press, 1999).

15. Goldsmith and Posner, *Limits*, 205.

16. Ibid., 206.

17. Charles Beitz, "International Liberalism and Distributive Justice: A Survey of Recent Thought," *World Politics* 51 (1999): 269.

18. Kok-Chor Tan, *Justice Without Borders: Cosmopolitanism, Nationalism and Patriotism* (New York: Cambridge University Press, 2004), 35.

19. See, e.g., Buchanan, *Justice*, 1–232; David Miller, *Citizenship and National Identity* (Malden, Mass: Blackwell, 2000), 161–79.

20. Goldsmith and Posner quote only one theorist, Michael Green, who seems to hold that existing institutions, as they are, rather than individuals, have cosmopolitan moral obligations. Goldsmith and Posner, *Limits*, 207. They then proceed to mischaracteize what some have called the "institutional turn" in ethics and international affairs, lumping a number of other theorists together with Green. Contrary to Goldsmith and Posner, the "institutional turn." is not that cosmopolitans have come to the conclusion that institutions rather than individuals have obligations to alleviate poverty in other countries; it is that they have come to realize that significant amelioration of world poverty will require institutional action. Neither Thomas Pogge nor Martha Nussbaum, to take only two prominent examples, hold the view that Goldsmith and Posner attribute to Green; yet both are prominent figures in the "institutional turn." So, because many cosmopolitans do not say that institutions, rather than individuals have cosmopolitan obligations, a convincing argument against cosmopolitanism cannot focus exclusively on the question of whether states have cosmopolitan obligations. The key question is whether individuals have a moral obligation to try to get their states to act in a more cosmopolitan manner.

21. See, e.g., Adam Hochschild, *Bury the Chains: Prophets and Rebels in the Fight to Free an Empire's Slaves* (Boston: Houghton Mifflin, 2005). This book makes the case that the abolition of slavery was generally not thought to be Britain's interest at the beginning of the movement and that the cost of using the British navy (which was otherwise heavily occupied with fighting in the Napoleonic Wars) to destroy the trans-Atlantic slave trade and the cost to the Empire of abolishing slavery in the West Indies (due to an anticipated decline in profits from sugar production) were thought to be quite high at the time.

22. Goldsmith and Posner, *Limits*, 220.

23. Ibid., 214.

24. Peter D. Feaver and Christopher Gelpi, *Choosing Your Battles: American Civil-military Relations and the Use of Force* (Princeton, N.J.: Princeton University Press, 2004); Christopher Gelpi, Peter D. Feaver, and Jason Reifler, "Success Matters: Casualty Sensitivity and the War in Iraq," *International Security* 30, no. 3 (2006): 30.

25. Goldsmith and Posner, *Limits*, 220.

26. Ibid., 212.

27. Ibid., 211.

28. Allen Buchanan, "The Internal Legitimacy of Humanitarian Intervention," *Journal of Political Philosophy* 7 (1999): 71; Buchanan, *Justice*.

8

CONSTITUTIONAL DEMOCRACY AND THE RULE OF INTERNATIONAL LAW: ARE THEY COMPATIBLE?

With Russell Powell

The past two decades have witnessed a dramatic increase in the number of democratic states and also the emergence of what might be called robust international law (RIL), which increasingly claims the authority to regulate matters once considered to be the exclusive concern of the state, including the state's treatment of its own citizens within its own territory. For example, human rights law obligates States to abolish long-standing practices regarding punishment, to secure the rights of children in ways that may challenge traditional parenting practices, to change existing political processes to ensure rights of freedom of association and assembly, and to provide access for all citizens to basic education and health care. Human rights law is RIL *par excellence*, but international criminal law and some of international environmental and trade law, also now impact what were traditionally considered matters reserved for the authority of the state. International law now makes robust claims of authority over all states, including constitutional democracies.

At first blush, the relationship between democratization and RIL seems to be a harmonious one of mutual enhancement: constitutional democracies have often encouraged the development of RIL, and RIL has in turn has provided support for democratization. Yet there is a substantial body of thought according to which constitutional democracy and RIL are incompatible. The allegation of incompatibility should be disturbing, especially to liberal cosmopolitans, who have not considered the possibility that the commitment to constitutional democracy at the domestic level and a robust international legal order can be in conflict.

The nature of the alleged incompatibility is unclear, however. Five distinct incompatibilist worries ought to be distinguished. (1) Some who view the growth of RIL as a threat to constitutional democracy seem to hold that there is an incompatibility *in principle*. On this view, a state is not democratic if its citizens are subject to any political authority that is not exclusively accountable to them.[1] (2) Others hold that at least in some cases, including that of the United States, RIL is undermining constitutional democracy (i) by shifting power from the legislative to the executive and judicial branches and thereby damaging the system of checks and balances that the separation of powers provides, and (ii) by encroaching on the prerogatives of federal units (in the United States these are states, while in other countries they are provinces, cantons, etc.) to regulate important matters hitherto recognized as being within their jurisdiction.[2] (3) A third incompatibilist worry focuses on the "democratic deficit" of the global governance institutions that create RIL. The complaint is that these institutions are controlled by elites who are not democratically accountable. On this view, recognizing the authority of international law that lacks democratic accountability is incompatible with the commitment to constitutional democracy. (4) A fourth concern is the growing tendency of judges in domestic courts to draw on international law in interpreting domestic law. There are two worries here: first, that at least in some areas of RIL, including customary human rights law, the law is so undeveloped and incoherent that judges may be tempted to "cherry pick" the principles that yield the answers they prefer; second, that some areas of RIL express values that conflict with the values that underlie the domestic law of some countries, with the result that judicial borrowing from RIL for purposes of interpreting domestic law may disrupt the coherence and integrity of domestic law. (5) Finally, some charge that there has been a transfer of power from constitutional democracies to global governance institutions without appropriate democratic authorization. On this view, the fact that such institutions are created through treaties or Executive Agreements according to existing constitutionally specified procedures is insufficient, given that their operations significantly restrict the scope of popular self-government and may also alter constitutional structures.[3]

For convenience, let us use the label 'incompatibilist concerns' to cover all five complaints about the impact of RIL on constitutional democracy, while keeping in mind that they are quite distinct. Some of the complaints may apply with greater force to certain areas of RIL (such as human rights law) than to others (such as trade or environmental law). Also, the various complaints focus on different ways in which RIL can impact domestic law—from the implementation of treaties to serving as a resource for the interpretation of domestic law. Nevertheless, taken together they present a serious challenge to liberal cosmopolitan theorists, most of whom have unreflectively assumed that their enthusiasm for constitutional democracy and their commitment to RIL are in harmony. It is appropriate to label these concerns 'incompatibilist', because those who voice them do *not* suggest that they are merely pointing out that engagement with RIL involves some cost to constitutional democratic values, costs that might be worth bearing. Instead, they strongly suggest and in some cases explicitly assert that the problems they catalog are so serious—and the value of constitutional democracy so obvious and overwhelming—that the proper choice for the citizens and leaders of constitutional democracy is to refrain from acknowledging the authority of RIL.

Some theorists who take a generally positive view of the growth of RIL attempt to counter the allegation that it is incompatible with constitutional democracy.[4] They identify two sorts of reasons for the citizens and leaders of constitutional democracies to accept RIL.

The first sort of reason is cosmopolitan. The claim is that the same concern for human rights that undergirds the commitment to constitutional democracy in one's own country also speaks in favor of supporting RIL to help ensure that the basic human rights of persons everywhere are protected. International institutions can contribute to the protection of human rights, if they wield authority that can supercede that of the state. It is not clear that this response covers the full range of concerns about the impact of RIL on constitutional democracies, but it does address the type of RIL that has drawn the most critical fire, international human rights law.

The second sort of reason offered to counter Incompatibilist arguments is not cosmopolitan, though it is compatible with cosmopolitanism. The idea is that participation in international institutions that make robust claims of legal authority can and in fact does enhance constitutional democracy in three ways: (1) by providing better protection for individual rights domestically, (2) by helping to constrain the influence of special interest groups in domestic politics (e.g., when participation in the WTO enables political leaders to resist lobbying by protectionist groups), and (3) by providing technical expertise and access to "best practices" in a number of policy areas.[5] The attraction of this second response to Incompatibilist Concerns is that it meets them on their own ground, attempting to show why those committed to *their own* constitutional democracy should support RIL, independently of any cosmopolitan commitments. This second type of argument we will label the Self-regarding Compatibilist Response, to distinguish from the first, the Cosmopolitan Compatibilist Response.

Our first aim in this chapter is to evaluate the current debate on the compatibility of constitutional democracy and RIL and then to deepen it. In Section 1, we offer a more comprehensive account of the reasons, both Cosmopolitan and Self-regarding, that those who are committed to constitutional democracy have for supporting RIL. In Section 2, we spell out in detail the full range of Incompatibilist concerns and show that while some of them are readily dismissed (because they rely on mistaken views about constitutional democracy), others have considerable force. In Section 3, we argue that even the best arguments on both sides of the compatibility debate are not just inconclusive, but radically incomplete. The Compatibilists' arguments are incomplete because they merely identify various reasons in favor of the friends of constitutional democracy embracing RIL without considering whether these reasons might be outweighed by the most serious Incompatibilist Concerns, some of the most important of which they do not even acknowledge. The Incompatibilist case is equally defective. At most the weightiest Incompatibilist arguments show that RIL carries certain risks to constitutional democracies; they do not show that these risks are so serious and intractable as to make support for RIL incompatible with a sincere commitment to constitutional democracy. Incompatibilists beg the question against RIL by assuming, rather than arguing, that any alteration of existing constitutional structures or any diminution in the scope of national self-determination is unacceptable.

We then draw the implications of the analysis for the current state of liberal cosmopolitan political theory, arguing that liberal cosmopolitans have underestimated the constitutional impact of RIL and that a principled accommodation between the legal systems of constitutional democracies and a robust international legal system may require public constitutional deliberation and popular choice, that is, constitutional amendment, referenda, special national legislation, or even in some cases a new constitutional convention. One key conclusion of our analysis will be that the piecemeal, incremental development of increasingly robust international law—which, outside the European Union context, occurs without anything resembling public constitutional deliberation and popular choice—is highly problematic from the standpoint of the values that underlie constitutional democracy. Another conclusion will be that liberal cosmopolitan political theory will remain unconvincing until it provides a systematic response to the problem of reconciling the commitment to constitutional democracy with the commitment to the rule of international law. Mainstream liberal cosmopolitan political theory does not propose a world state; it advocates RIL while assuming the persistence of states. Yet it fails to provide an account how constitutional democracy and RIL can be harmonized. Such an account, we will argue, would require both a constitutional theory and a theory of political self-determination. Our ultimate aim, then, is to articulate a neglected but critical research agenda for liberal cosmopolitan theory.

1. THE CASE FOR A COMMITMENT TO RIL

A. 'Self-regarding' Reasons

i. Better Protection of the Rights of Citizens

Constitutional democracy as we shall understand it here is not mere majority rule; it is a form of governance that includes entrenched civil and political rights and various constitutional structures, including an independent judiciary and, in the case of federal states, an allocation of powers between the federal government and the governments of federal units. The system of rights and the constitutional structures serve both to facilitate and to constrain fair majoritarian voting procedures that are designed to ground legislation in citizens' preferences and to hold government officials accountable.

Even the best existing constitutional democracies may fail to provide equal protection of the human rights of some of their citizens, especially women, members of national minorities, immigrants, people of color, and gays, lesbians, and transgender people. In addition, in cases of perceived dire national emergency, such as war and terrorist attacks, every constitutional democracy is at risk for unjustifiably infringing civil rights generally, not just those of minorities.[6] Acknowledging the authority of international human rights law can provide a valuable back-up for domestic institutions for the protection of individual and minority rights. The predictable imperfection of domestic arrangements for the protection of citizens' rights, then, provides a reason for acknowledging the authority of international law when doing so affords better protection of human rights.[7]

ii. Constraining Special Interests

Constitutional democracies include various mechanisms for reducing not only the risk of tyranny of the majority but also the risk that public policy will be hijacked by powerful special interest groups. But often these domestic mechanisms are not sufficient, especially under conditions in which the special interests are concentrated and the opposition to them is diffuse. Participation in robust international legal regimes, especially in the areas of trade and environmental protection, has been shown to ameliorate this problem.[8] For example, the binding rules of the WTO against trade discrimination have made it possible for the U.S. Congress to resist the lobbying efforts of domestic protectionist interests. In such cases, the decision to submit to the authority of RIL can be an expression of the very same values that underlie the commitment to domestic constitutional mechanisms.

iii. Enhancing Democratic Deliberation

In a number of policy areas that significantly affect the quality of their own citizens' lives, states can draw on more extensive pools of experts and learn from the identification of best practices most effectively, and sometimes only, through participation in global governance institutions that claim the authority to supercede domestic law.[9] The accountability that periodic elections provide, the relative transparency of constitutional democracies, and the fact that transnational civil society organizations can operate most freely in them, together increase the likelihood that the distinctive epistemic resources that RIL can provide will actually impact domestic democratic deliberations.[10]

The possible epistemic gains from acceptance of RIL are not limited to improving democratic deliberation through the purely instrumental use of better factual information. Acknowledging the authority of RIL can also improve the quality of moral and legal argumentation that is crucial for democratic deliberation about domestic policy. This benefit is especially salient when there is a significant risk that democratic deliberation will be distorted by biases present in the dominant domestic culture—for example, the assumption that women are not suited for employment outside the home or that national minorities are 'enemies within' who are not entitled to equal citizenship status. Participation in the institutions of RIL can help expose such assumptions and can model deliberation that is not distorted by them.

B. Cosmopolitan Reasons

The three reasons above are reasons to accept RIL that should appeal to citizens of constitutional democracies because of the positive effects of such engagement on their own polities. Their force does not presuppose that the citizens of a given constitutional democracy are or ought to be influenced by cosmopolitan commitments—that is, by a direct concern for the rights and interests of persons who are not their fellow citizens. The advantage of making the case for RIL solely on the basis of such 'self-regarding' reasons[11] is clear enough: it meets the Incompatibilist Concerns on their own terms, by assuming only a commitment to one's own constitutional democracy. Nevertheless, we now want to consider cosmopolitan reasons for the citizens of constitutional democracies to accept RIL. In doing so, we will show that it is a mistake to limit the debate to 'self-regarding' reasons. First, what appear to be exclusively 'self-regarding' reasons are in some central cases rooted in cosmopolitan values. Second, to restrict the debate to 'self-regarding' reasons is to accept a very problematic assumption that Incompatibilists seem uniformly to make but fail to defend: the assumption that if there is a conflict between our commitment to our own constitutional democracy and a commitment to RIL, the former should always prevail. This assumption is problematic, we will argue, because it fails to take seriously the possibility that there can be circumstances in which the values that the commitment to RIL promotes are so important that they warrant changing the domestic constitution or tolerating some impairment of existing constitutional arrangements.

i. Protecting the Human Rights of All People

From a cosmopolitan standpoint, this is perhaps the most obvious benefit of RIL. A commitment to international human rights law and to the emerging institutions of international criminal law can enable the citizens of constitutional democracies and their political leaders to contribute to better protection of the basic interests of all persons. Just as important, pursuing the protection of the human rights of all through institutions that are accessible to all, rather than exclusively through the institutions of one's own state, is itself a public expression of the fundamental principle of cosmopolitanism: the moral equality of persons, regardless of nationality. Further, in the case of powerful countries with a history of hegemonic behavior or colonialism, unilateral efforts to promote human rights are likely to be perceived as a front for the pursuit of national interests. In contrast, the protection of human rights through international institutions may be perceived to be more legitimate and the perception of legitimacy may make it more effective.

ii. Correcting for the Inherent Bias of Democracy

The most convincing case for constitutional democracy appeals at least in part to the moral importance of the protection of basic *human* interests (not just the peculiar interests of Americans or Englishmen, etc.) that this type of polity best provides.[12] For that reason, the commitment to one's own constitutional democracy ought to be grounded at least in part in cosmopolitan values.

Even though the most convincing case for constitutional democracy appeals to cosmopolitan values, constitutional democracies are typically structured so as to ensure that political leaders are accountable only to their own fellow citizens. This is most obviously the case with regard to accountability through periodic elections: foreigners have no votes, so there is an inherent bias in democratic politics against a proper consideration of their rights and interests.

Acceptance of RIL can help correct for the inherent parochial bias of democratic politics, by requiring state policy that affects the basic interests of foreigners to take those interests into account.[13] From this perspective, acknowledging the authority of RIL is not incompatible with a commitment to constitutional democracy; it is a way of enabling those who are committed to constitutional democracy, and who rightly realize that their commitment rests at least in part on cosmopolitan values, to act consistently on that commitment.

iii. Promoting the Rule of Law

One of the chief moral attractions of the idea of the rule of law, whether domestic or international, is that the rule of law expresses a strong public commitment to *not* settling conflicts of interests and preferences by recourse to sheer power. This commitment does not rule out the resolution of conflicts by force, of course, but it does require that force not be the first resort and that when it is employed it is justified by publicly available reasons of the right sort, what might be called principled reasons, as distinct from mere threats or appeals to the interests of those who happen to be the stronger. In international relations, where disparities of power are great, the moral case for the rule of law is correspondingly strong.

There are several reasons to repudiate the rule of sheer power. The need to protect the vulnerable and to avoid unfairness are among the most obvious, but there is also the idea that respect for persons requires an appeal to their capacity to act on the basis of principled reasons rather than relying solely or primarily on their capacity to respond to threats. All of these reasons qualify as cosmopolitan, because they all assume the fundamental equal moral status of persons: all are to be treated fairly; vulnerable persons generally, not just the vulnerable who are one's fellow citizens, are to be protected; all are to be respected by appealing to their capacity for being moved by principled reasons.

These basic moral attractions of the rule of law have always been one chief element in the case for having international law (the other being the Realist idea that the system of restraint that international law provides is in the interest of every state because no state can reasonably expect to maintain a position of domination). The question is whether the basic moral values that ground the commitment to the rule of law give the citizens and political leaders of a constitutional democracy reason to acknowledge the authority of international law even within domains that were previously thought to be protected by the veil of sovereignty?

The answer may depend upon what sort of international law is involved. Consider the case of international human rights law. It is appropriate to focus on human rights law because it is the type of RIL that has been viewed with the greatest suspicion by Incompatibilists. Disputes arise as to the scope and institutional implications of particular human rights norms. Presumably the principle that conflicts should not be settled by sheer power applies to this sort of dispute; to exclude it seems arbitrary. If this is the case, then the idea of repudiating the rule of sheer power, which lies at the heart of the commitment to the rule of law, provides a reason for powerful states (such as the United States) to *not* claim the unqualified right to determine how human rights norms will be interpreted and applied to its own actions, or to the conduct of its citizens or officials. When a powerful state claims the right to do this, it is in effect asserting that it is permissible for it to be a judge in its own case, to decide whether complaints that it has failed to protect human rights are valid. Because it is a powerful state, its vulnerability to sanctions by other states or international organizations or world public opinion will be relatively inconsequential, at least in cases in which it has a strong interest in the outcome, and this means that it may be tempted to act in a biased, self-serving fashion. There will be a significant risk that the conflict will be settled by sheer power—that is, in accordance with the interest of the powerful simply because they are powerful—rather than in a principled, publicly justifiable way. At the very least, such a state bears a burden of argument to explain why the usual rule-of-law considerations that speak in favor of not being a judge in one's own case are not dispositive in case of disputes over the interpretation and application of human rights norms.[14] The point here is not that a state's merely acknowledging the authority of RIL ensures that it will in fact act accordingly; the current paucity of effective enforcement mechanisms for RIL leaves open the possibility that formal acquiescence will be accompanied by noncompliance. Rather, it is that fundamental rule of law considerations that are familiar to those who support the domestic rule of law can count as reasons to comply with RIL, reasons that have weight independently of whether there are effective enforcement mechanisms.

Of course, one could argue that at present the burden of explaining why the principle that one shouldn't be a judge in one's own case *can* be met in some areas of international law that most significantly challenge state sovereignty. Some have argued that the defects of the current International Criminal Court process are so great as to outweigh the rule of law reasons for acknowledging the authority of the Court. Our aim here, however, is not to show that the commitment to the rule of law supplies a *conclusive* reason to support any particular area of RIL, but only to show that it can provide *a* reason to support RIL, depending upon the circumstances. Moreover, when it does, the reason it supplies is one that should carry significant weight with those committed to constitutional democracy, so far as the idea of constitutional democracy includes that of the rule of law.

This conclusion requires more careful formulation to highlight an important qualification. Some of the most basic moral values that underlie the commitment to the rule of law supply reasons for states to acknowledge the authority of international law in cases where there is a risk that bias and the perquisites of power would otherwise be likely to determine the outcome, *if* the international law in question itself sufficiently embodies the ideal of the rule of law. If international law is merely the rule of the powerful by another name, disguised by empty formalities that ape the rule of law, then a commitment to the rule of law provides no reason for acknowledging the authority of that law.[15]

Stephen Ratner has argued quite forcefully that the familiar charge that international law is highly partial toward powerful states is hyperbolic at best.[16] It is not necessary to take a stand on that complex issue here, however. Instead, we wish to emphasize a distinction made earlier, between the claim that RIL is in principle incompatible with constitutional democracy and the claim that it is at present incompatible, given current practice, including the imperfect state of international law. The point is that the basic moral considerations that ground the commitment to the rule of law supply a reason for supporting the project of establishing RIL, even if at present there are areas of existing international law with respect to which the force of this reason is attenuated. Each of the other reasons noted earlier for acknowledging the authority of international law, whether cosmopolitan or 'self-regarding', is also a reason for supporting the project of establishing effective RIL. In some circumstances, the best way to support that project may be to acknowledge the authority of the law, while acknowledging its current imperfections and striving to remedy them.

The chief conclusions of this section can now be summarized. First, there are both cosmopolitan and 'self-regarding' reasons for citizens of constitutional democracies to acknowledge the authority of RIL. Second, there is no inconsistency between these reasons and some of the weightiest reasons in favor of constitutional democracy, and in some instances they are the same reasons. However, as the next section shows, there are a number of different considerations which provide reasons that cut in the opposite direction. Showing that there are weighty reasons in favor of recognizing the authority of RIL that advocates of constitutional democracy can appreciate does not amount to an argument that RIL is compatible with constitutional democracy. In that sense, the case for compatibilism is at this point seriously incomplete. We next turn, therefore, to arguments that have been offered to support the conclusion that constitutional democracy and RIL are incompatible.

2. CONCERNS ABOUT THE IMPACT OF ROBUST INTERNATIONAL LAW ON CONSTITUTIONAL DEMOCRACY

A. The Exclusive Accountability Argument

Rabkin among others complains that acceptance of RIL can involve a national government's delegation of power over its citizens to entities, namely, international organizations and courts, that are not *exclusively* accountable to those citizens and then seems to conclude that this state of affairs is incompatible with constitutional democracy.[17] Call this the Exclusive Accountability Argument.

It is important to be clear about whether this is an argument about the incompatibility of RIL with constitutional democracy or as an assertion about its incompatibility with the *U.S. Constitution's* limits on delegation. On the former interpretation, the claim begs the question at issue, by assuming that constitutional democracy requires not only that those who wield power over citizens be accountable to them (and accountable to them each equally), but also that they be accountable to them alone. On the latter interpretation, as an assertion about U.S. Constitutional law, the claim is perhaps more plausible, but does nothing to support the thesis that constitutional democracy and RIL are incompatible.

To establish the more general conclusion, one would have to show that any constitution that did not require delegated powers to be exclusively accountable to the domestic citizenry is not a genuine democratic constitution. That would require showing either that such delegation is incompatible with democracy or that it is incompatible with constitutionalism. It is hard to know even how one would begin to make such an argument, either conceptually, by trying to show that non-exclusive accountability is inconsistent with the core ideas of democracy or of constitutionalism, or empirically, by trying to show that non-exclusive accountability causes the destruction or malfunctioning of democracy or of constitutionalism. Simply to assume that constitutional democracy per se bars any delegation of political power to agencies that are not exclusively accountable to the citizens of the democracy begs the question of whether constitutional democracy and RIL are compatible.[18]

Furthermore, there is an obvious reply to the more restricted claim that delegation of authority to agents not exclusively accountable to U.S. citizens is incompatible with the American form of constitutional democracy. The U.S. Constitution authorizes the president, with concurrence of two-thirds of the Senate, to ratify treaties. In some cases, treaties set up mechanisms for dispute resolution, through arbitration by third parties who are not accountable to the citizens of the contending states or at least not accountable exclusively to them. The clause of the Constitution that authorizes treaty-making includes no suggestion that such treaties are prohibited.

B. The Unprincipled Judicial Borrowing Argument

The concern here is that domestic judges will abuse their office, picking and choosing from various bodies of international law in order to get the outcomes they prefer, if international law is regarded as a legitimate resource for the interpretation of domestic law. This objection, if valid, would not be restricted to RIL, but as a matter of fact those who advance it typically are most concerned about international human rights law, which increasingly claims robust authority. There are really three distinct concerns, though they have not been clearly distinguished in the literature. The first is that judges will undermine the rule of law by making decisions according to their preferences rather than according to principles of law. The charge is that the incoherence or underdeveloped character of international law, or of certain areas of international law, and in particular customary human rights law, facilitate unprincipled borrowing.

Second, some Incompatibilists, including Rabkin and Supreme Court Justice Scalia, gesture rather sketchily toward what might be a communitarian version of this objection.[19] Their idea is that in some cases (the United States being one of them) the cultural values that undergird a system of domestic law may be at odds with those that are expressed in international human rights law and that, when this is the case, judicial borrowing for purposes of interpreting domestic law can result in law that does not 'fit' the people to whom it is applied and which does not cohere with pre-existing domestic law. For example, Justice Scalia and others have criticized judges' recourse to international human rights law in interpreting the U.S. Constitution's ban on "cruel and unusual punishment" on these grounds.[20]

The third concern is that judges will pick and choose from international law in a way that encroaches on the proper authority of the legislative branch, thwarting legislative purpose by interpreting laws in the light of international law that runs contrary to that purpose.[21] Because there are additional ways in which engagement with RIL might derange internal constitutional structures, we will take the third version up under that general heading below. For now, let us consider the first and second versions of the complaint about unprincipled judicial borrowing: the worry that judges will use recourse to international law as an interpretive resource so as to substitute their preferences for principles and the concern that such borrowing will disrupt the normative coherence of domestic law (the communitarian concern).

Here the distinction between in principle incompatibility and incompatibility under current conditions and practices, a distinction which we introduced at the beginning of this chapter, but which has been neglected by both sides of the debate, is again pertinent. Whether domestic judicial reliance on RIL as an interpretive resource runs an unacceptable risk of excessive judicial discretion or of undermining the normative coherence of domestic law will depend on (a) how coherent the relevant RIL is and on (b) the degree of continuity between the two bodies of law.

According to some Incompatibilists, the coherence of RIL is especially problematic in the case of customary international human rights law, because of lax or at best rather indeterminate standards for what counts as customary international law.[22] If these critics are correct, it does not follow that domestic judges should forswear all reliance on RIL as an interpretive resource, but rather that they should be especially cautious about relying on those areas of RIL that lack coherence or determinacy. This particular Incompatibilist concern is not an in principle objection to treating RIL as a resource for interpreting domestic law; it would dissipate if RIL matures into a more coherent and determinate system of law.

Nor does the existence of discontinuities between domestic law and RIL provide a conclusive reason for rejecting RIL as a resource for interpreting domestic law. In some cases, the degree of continuity may be rather high, precisely because the domestic legal system has been consciously shaped in the light of international legal norms, especially in the area of human rights law. This is the case, for example, in some countries that have recently emerged from authoritarianism and in some developing countries: their constitutions deliberately seek to harmonize domestic and international law, at least so far as human rights are concerned.[23] Deliberate efforts to harmonize domestic and international law have occurred in other areas as well, including trade law, intellectual property, and the regulation of communications.

How well international law and domestic law cohere is a contingent matter and may vary across different areas of international law. So the risk that acceptance of RIL will result in unprincipled judicial borrowing cannot be a reason for thinking that constitutional democracy and RIL are incompatible in principle. Further, for the Incompatibilist to say that where coherence is lacking we should reject RIL would be to beg the deeper question as to whether the citizens and leaders of constitutional democracies have good reason to support the development of RIL, even if doing so comes at some cost to the coherence of their own legal order. If they do have good reason, then to that extent they also have reason to try to achieve greater coherence between domestic and international law, even if it means modifying domestic law. The key point is that it is wrong to assume that where RIL and domestic law do not cohere, we must accept this as an unalterable fact and cleave indefinitely to the supremacy of domestic law as it now is.

The charge that, because of deep differences in cultural values, judicial recourse to international law as a resource will produce domestic law that does not 'fit' the people to whom it is applied has limited force as an argument against acknowledging the authority of RIL, for two reasons. First, those who advance it do not clearly identify the supposed deep differences in cultural values and more importantly they do not even begin to show that such differences are relevant to *all* areas of international law that judges may treat as a resource for interpretation or to all international legal norms within any particular area of law. Second, they do not consider the possibility that in some cases cultural differences in values may diminish over time, in part through the development of international law. Instead, they beg the question by assuming that if there are cultural differences, the proper response is always to uphold the supremacy of the domestic law that expresses one side of the cultural divide.

It is no doubt true that in some cases RIL runs contrary to cultural values present in some of the countries. This is perhaps most evident in the case of human rights norms against sexual and religious discrimination: some societies contain cultural values that are extremely sexist and intolerant of religious diversity. In such cases, the 'fit' between RIL and (some) domestic cultural values may be considerably less than perfect. And *if* domestic law reflects the cultural values in question, then recourse to the latter by domestic judges may introduce some incoherence into domestic law. But what exactly is supposed to follow from this? It does not follow that those countries should deny the authority of the international norms in question or that the project of developing robust international human rights law ought not to be pursued. That would only follow if congruence with domestic cultural values or the coherence of domestic law in the short-term were overriding values. Because there is no reason to believe they are (and a number of good reasons to think they are not, including the importance of protecting human rights), the most that follows is that considerations of cultural 'fit' and legal coherence can provide *some* reason for not accepting RIL in those cases in which those considerations are relevant.

In subsection D below we consider yet another Incompatibilist Concern, one that we believe better captures the grain of truth in the communitarian version of the Unprincipled Judicial Borrowing Argument: the charge that acknowledging the authority of RIL interferes with the proper self-determination of societies, where this includes considerable discretion to arrange domestic affairs in accordance with a society's fundamental values. For now our conclusion is two-fold. First, the versions of the Unprincipled Judicial Borrowing Argument that we have considered so far do not show that there is an in principle incompatibility between constitutional democracy and RIL. Second, these Incompatibilist arguments do not show that where judicial recourse to international law as an interpretative resource runs a risk of introducing incoherence into domestic law, the proper response is to reject RIL and to repudiate the project of developing a more coherent integration of domestic and international law. (After all, some incoherence in the short-term may be the acceptable price of progress in law, here as elsewhere). None of this is to dismiss the risks of unprincipled judicial borrowing; the point rather is that that risk should be weighed against the benefits of relying on RIL and that the need to reduce the risk can be a reason for attempting to make RIL more coherent rather than for abandoning the project of establishing effective RIL.

C. The Constitutional Derangement Argument

This Incompatibilist argument focuses on the damage that acceptance of RIL can do to the internal constitutional structures of a constitutional democracy. The potential damage is of two sorts: the undermining of the constitutional allocation of power among the branches of the government, and the undermining of federalism by robbing federal units (states, cantons, provinces, etc.) of some of their proper authority.

RIL can become binding domestic law in the United States chiefly in two ways: through the ratification of treaties and when international customary law is regarded as federal common law. Some U.S. constitutional scholars charge that in either case the incorporation of RIL into domestic law diminishes the rightful authority of the legislative branch.[24]

According to the U.S. Constitution, international law created through treaties automatically becomes the "law of the land": when the United States ratifies a treaty, its provisions take precedence over both the law of the states (federal units) and prior federal law with which it is inconsistent, without the requirement of federal legislation.[25] The executive's power to make treaties is not unlimited of course, because ratification requires Senate approval; but the latter is arguably a weaker form of legislative control than in the ordinary creation of federal law.

Constitutional scholars who take this form of the Constitutional Derangement Argument seriously point out that the U.S. Constitutional provision that makes treaties federal law without federal legislation was drafted in a world in which international treaties did not include RIL—law that extends to matters previously thought to lie at the core of the protected sphere of state sovereignty, as is the case with modern human rights law.[26]

Given that the U.S. Constitution unconditionally declares the supremacy of treaty law over states' laws and inconsistent prior federal law and given the clarity of its provisions for the ratification of treaties, it is implausible to argue that RIL created by treaty is contrary to the U.S. Constitution.[27] It might still be the case, however, that the acceptance of RIL through treaty ratification effects a reallocation of power away from the legislative branch that is suboptimal from the standpoint of constitutional design and perhaps contrary to the intentions of the framers of the constitution as well.

Similarly, it can be argued that treaty-created RIL, at least in the area of human rights, reallocates power from the legislatures of the states (federal units) to the federal executive and the Senate, when human rights treaties are ratified and take precedence over the states' laws. The charge here is that the acceptance of RIL changes the constitutional structure of the federal union, by weakening self-government in the federal units. The same sort of structural change could be effected by according customary international human rights the status of federal common law. Acknowledging the authority of international human rights treaties or of customary human rights law could result in a diminution of federal units' control over the nature of punishments within their jurisdictions by prohibiting the death penalty.

Fortunately, for present purposes it is not necessary to enter the thicket of U.S. Constitutional interpretation. Instead, it will suffice to make two general points, whose significance is not limited to the peculiarities of the U.S. context. First, for States whose constitutions were drafted prior to the era of RIL and which have not been modified in the light of this development, the possibility that domestic legal acknowledgement of the authority of RIL may damage such a state's constitutional structures cannot be dismissed. The introduction of new legal norms from the outside—norms that regulate matters previously assigned by the constitution to various branches and levels of government—may well be at odds with existing constitutional design; to assume that they will be harmonious would be unduly optimistic. Second, when the acceptance of RIL does impair existing constitutional structures, the proper conclusion to draw is not that constitutional democracy is incompatible with RIL, but rather that the acceptance of RIL is incompatible with the optimal functioning of *the particular form of constitutional democracy that includes those constitutional structures.* Showing that this or that existing constitutional structure is impacted negatively by the acceptance of RIL is a far cry from establishing that constitutional democracy and RIL are incompatible, because there is a plurality of forms of constitutional democracy. Further, constitutional structures rarely if ever work either optimally or not at all; instead, they do the jobs they were designed to do with greater or lesser effectiveness. So, even when the acceptance of RIL does have a negative impact on the constitutional structures of a particular constitutional democracy, the impact may be of greater or lesser seriousness. In cases where the impact is limited, accepting some detriment to the functioning of constitutional arrangements may be a reasonable trade-off, if this is the only way to secure the important benefits that RIL can bring. For example, some loss of legislative authority on the part of the units of a federal constitutional democracy might be a reasonable price to pay, under certain circumstances, if this is necessary for achieving better protection of basic human rights. It is a different question, of course, as to when a loss of legislative authority counts as an infringement of the constitution, as opposed to a departure from previous practice regarding legislative functions, and still another as to whether, when a constitution is being infringed, it is always obligatory to change it or to eliminate the infringement.

D. The Loss of Self-determination

It is common in some quarters to lament the "democratic deficit" of global governance institutions. There are two distinct problems to be sorted out. The first is the democratic deficit problem properly speaking: the fact that the international institutions through which RIL is articulated and applied are not democratic. That problem would be solved if the institutions in question became democratic. But a second problem would remain even if the daunting task of achieving global democracy were completed.

Suppose that all of the institutions that articulate and apply RIL were democratic in a very strong sense: suppose, as Richard Falk and others have proposed, the existence of a global legislature whose members fairly represented everyone or better yet a global direct "virtual" democratic assembly in which all competent persons vote on legislation.[28] There might no longer be a democratic deficit, but a second problem would persist: if the global legislature makes RIL, law reaching into what had been the domains hitherto controlled by constitutional democracies, then the citizens of those democracies will suffer a diminution of self-governance; their political self-determination will be reduced. Regardless of whether RIL is created through democratic processes or not, it constricts the domain of self-government in constitutional democracies (and in other types of states as well).

By itself, this does not imply that RIL and constitutional democracy are incompatible; to think so would to beg the question of compatibility by assuming that in constitutional democracies self-determination must be *unlimited*. Nor does it imply that RIL should be rejected; to think so would be to assume that the preservation of the largest domain of self-determination in constitutional democracies takes precedence over all other considerations, including the benefits that RIL can bestow. The critical issue is this: when does the diminution of self-determination in a constitutional democracy become so great as to be incompatible with it warranting the title of a democracy, a territory whose inhabitants are in some meaningful sense self-governing?

To answer this question we have to delve deeper into the basis of the commitment to constitutional democracy. So far, we have emphasized only some of the values upon which the commitment to constitutional democracy rests, but there are others. One of the most important is the value of political self-determination. Constitutional democracy can enable the people of the state as a whole and, in the case of federal constitutional democracies, also territorially concentrated groups within the state, to exercise political self-determination. Political self-determination is valuable for a number of reasons which it is unnecessary to rehearse here. Because it is valuable for a number of different reasons, reasons that will have greater weight for members of various groups, and because self-determination is not an all or nothing matter, but rather comes in many forms and degrees, there is no single or easy answer to the question: how much self-determination is enough for a constitutional democracy?

An intuitively plausible reply is that we can appeal to the value of self-determination itself and simply say that the citizens of constitutional democracies should decide how much self-governance they will relinquish to global governance institutions.[29] But even if we grant that the decision to relinquish some dimensions of self-determination to a robust international legal order ought itself to be viewed as a matter of self-determination, we still need to know *how* this choice is to be made. And even if the case could be made that it is permissible or even obligatory to relinquish a great deal of self-governance to the international legal order—for example, in order to promote peace or to achieve better protection of human rights or to safeguard the environment—it would not follow that *just any way* of transferring political power is appropriate. More precisely, we need to ask whether the same values that undergird the commitment to constitutional democracy also place constraints on *how* powers of self-government can be transferred to international institutions.

One cannot assume that the ways in which RIL is actually being created satisfy reasonable constraints on the relinquishing of self-determination. To gain a sufficiently critical perspective on current practice, an analogy may be useful. There is much to be said for the idea that when existing political units come together to form a federal state, as occurred in what became the United States or when a centralized state devolves into a federal state, or when secession occurs, these are such significant constitutional changes as to require some form of democratic authorization that is more robust than the ordinary legislative process. In brief, for such major changes in the character of a polity, *public constitutional deliberation and popular choice* seem to be required.[30] Similarly, if the development of RIL continues to reduce the domain of self-determination for a constitutional democracy, the point may be reached at which proper appreciation of the value of self-determination requires public deliberation and popular choice, some sort of authorization that is more directly democratic than an ordinary legislative act or the ratification of a treaty.[31]

We now want to suggest a parallel point with respect to another Incompatibilist Concern discussed earlier: the negative impact of RIL on existing constitutional structures, including the allocation of power among the branches of government and between federal units and the federal government. If the alteration of existing constitutional structures is significant, then some especially robust form of democratic authorization is required here also.

Let us call international law that can reasonably be expected to either (a) significantly restrict a polity's self-determination or (b) alter its internal constitutional structures "Robust international law," (with a capital 'R'). Now consider three ways in which a constitutional democracy might come to be subject to Robust international law. The first, to which we have already alluded, is through public constitutional deliberation and popular choice, by processes that give more weight to the popular will than ordinary legislative processes and which are preceded by special public deliberations designed to reflect the fact that constitutional changes are at stake. Here the mechanisms for accepting Robust international law would be a new constitutional convention, constitutional amendment, or a referendum in which all citizens could vote. The second alternative is some form of special supermajority national legislation: recognition of the supremacy of international law that qualifies as constitutional change would require approval from the national legislature by considerably more than a bare majority. The distinction between this alternative and the first is perhaps less than clear: if a special national legislative act were preceded by extraordinary public deliberation, it might count as an instance of public deliberation and choice. The third alternative is a *process of accretion* in which no public constitutional deliberation or popular choice occurs and no special legislative approval is required—a process that might be characterized rather uncharitably as a constitutional democracy's slow death by a thousand cuts. The accretion can occur through a combination of Congressional-executive agreements ("fast-track" processes that by-pass the usual Senate supermajority requirement for approval of trade agreements), automatic inclusion of ratified treaties in "the law of the land," the recognition of international law as federal common law, judicial borrowing from international law, and the development of more robust global governance institutions that increasingly create policies through their own bureaucracies, without 'specific' consent from States.

The third process, that of accretion, is deeply problematic from the standpoint of the commitment to democracy: there are alterations of a constitutional democracy that could properly be called constitutional changes, but there is no point at which there is public deliberation about them that recognizes that they are constitutional changes and no process of the sort that is ordinarily thought to be appropriate for constitutional choice is invoked to determine whether to make them. Nor is there even any special national legislative act to signal that this is not just law-making or traditional treaty-making as usual.

The processes by which European Union law has evolved have included, at several critical junctures, something approaching the first model for accepting Robust international law, the public constitutional deliberation and popular choice model. But for most states, including the United States, the process of accepting RIL has been one of accretion: public constitutional deliberation and popular choice have been conspicuously absent.

Whether or not this process of accretion has in fact *already* subjected the United States and other states to Robust international law (capital 'R')—that is, whether the acceptance of international law has caused significant changes in constitutional structures or in the scope of political self-determination of sufficient magnitude to require public constitutional deliberation and choice—is perhaps open to reasonable disagreement. To make a sound judgment on this matter one would need to do two things, neither of which those who worry about the impact of international law on constitutional democracy have done. First, one would have to tell a convincing *causal* story about the actual, not just the potential, negative impact of U.S. ratification of human rights treaties or other types of international law on the powers of federal units, or on the allocation of powers between the federal, legislative, and judicial branches of government, or on the scope of the country's self-determination. Second, one would also have to provide a normative account of *which* alterations of constitutional structures and which limitations on self-determination warrant public constitutional deliberation and popular choice. Beyond that, one would also need a normative account of the proper mechanisms for public constitutional deliberation and popular choice. In brief, one would need normative accounts of both self-determination and of constitutional change that cohere with the principles and values that ground constitutional democracy.

Our objective here is not to try to provide either the causal or the normative accounts. Instead, we simply want to advance a rather commonsensical principle: where the acceptance of international law by a constitutional democracy can be reasonably expected to result in *constitutional changes*—significant alterations in constitutional structures or significant diminutions in political self-determination—then, as with other constitutional changes (such as consensual secession, accession to a federation, or devolution from a centralized state), there is a strong presumption that public constitutional deliberation and popular choice are required. The intuition that grounds this meta-constitutional principle, call it M, is both simple and robust: some political changes are so momentous that the ordinary processes for making political decisions are inadequate, and in such cases the decision ought to be made by the ultimate source of political authority, the people.

Although principle M is intuitively plausible, to our knowledge it has not been advanced by either party to the debate about the compatibility of constitutional democracy and RIL. Compatibilists have not considered it because they have ignored the impact of RIL on constitutional structures and self-determination. Incompatibilists have not considered it because they have assumed that the existing constitutional order is sacrosanct and have not been willing to take seriously the possibility that it might require modification for the sake of accommodating international law.

3. REFRAMING THE DEBATE

It should be clear at this point that even the best arguments on both sides of the debate on the compatibility of constitutional democracy and RIL are not just inconclusive but radically incomplete. Once we set aside the unconvincing arguments that purport to show that RIL and constitutional democracy are incompatible in principle, we are left with the claim that RIL can alter constitutional structures and diminish self-determination without proper democratic authorization, and that there are risks involved when judges treat international law as a resource for interpreting domestic law. But unless one assumes (implausibly) that *any* change in constitutional structures or *any* reduction in the scope of self-determination is unacceptable, or that RIL cannot be made more coherent and determinate, it does not follow that those committed to constitutional democracy should reject the project of establishing RIL. On the other side of the ledger, it is not enough, in order to allay worries about the impact of RIL on constitutional structures or on the scope of self-determination, for enthusiasts of RIL to point out that there are several weighty reasons why citizens of constitutional democracy ought to value RIL and that these are consonant with their commitment to constitutional democracy. Those reasons show that RIL can provide certain important benefits that the friends of constitutional democracy should value, but they do not address the concerns about constitutional change and loss of self-determination. The latter concerns might swamp the benefits the Compatibilists tout.

Because Compatibilists have not addressed these two most serious Incompatibilist concerns, they have not been forced to confront the question of *trade-offs* between their commitment to constitutional democracy and their commitment to promoting cosmopolitan values through RIL. In other words, Compatibilists have not considered the possibility that the commitment to constitutional democracy may have to be compromised for the sake of building a robust international legal order or vice versa. Incompatibilists have not faced the question of trade-offs either, because they assume that the existing constitutional order and democracy as they understand them are so important that no other values can compete with them.

The idea of trade-offs warrants elaboration. The recognition that trade-offs may be required rests on a kind of value pluralism, the reasonable idea that the commitment to RIL and the commitment to constitutional democracy can both be high moral priorities, without either trumping the other across the board. Once we see that both the commitment to constitutional democracy and the commitment to RIL rest on a plurality of values, it should not be surprising that tensions between the two commitments could arise.

The first step in reframing the debate in a more fruitful way is to dispense with the assumption that the question is whether constitutional democracy and robust international law are compatible. Instead, we should begin with a thorough understanding of the various tensions between the commitment to constitutional democracy and the commitment to RIL and then ask how we can best honor both commitments. To determine whether and in what way one commitment ought to be compromised for the sake of the other, however, it will be necessary to answer questions about the relative importance of a plurality of values that can only be provided by a more comprehensive political philosophy. A political philosophy that gives priority to a substantive conception of global distributive justice over democratic process, for example, might prescribe a different way of addressing tensions between the commitments to constitutional democracy and to RIL, than a theory that gave greater weight to democratic process. On the former sort of theory, some damage to domestic democratic processes might be a price worth paying for the sake of better realization of principles of global distributive justice, and the effectiveness of international institutions in promoting global distributive justice might then compensate for the "democratic deficit" that those institutions suffer.

Compatibilists have offered weighty moral reasons in favor of acknowledging RIL; incompatibilists have shown how acknowledging RIL can alter constitutional structures or diminish self-determination, and do so without proper democratic authorization. Neither kind of consideration provides *practical conclusions* in the absence of a more comprehensive political philosophy than either party to the debate has even begun to outline. We have suggested that principle M above is a plausible element of a response to the problem of resolving tensions between the commitment to RIL and to constitutional democracy. But principle M is unsatisfyingly indeterminate, without a larger background theory to determine what counts as a "significant" diminution of self-determination and what counts as a change in constitutional structures versus a shift in practice within existing structures.

We will conclude with an observation on the bearing of the debate about the compatibility of constitutional democracy with RIL on the current state of liberal cosmopolitan political philosophy. Mainstream liberal cosmopolitan theory accepts the persistence of states, even though it advocates the development of RIL to prune back state sovereignty in the name of moral equality, human rights, and global distributive justice. As liberals, liberal cosmopolitans advocate constitutional democracy at the level of the state; as cosmopolitans, they advocate RIL. What they have failed to realize is that these two commitments can be in tension, in at least two ways: first, RIL may derange internal constitutional structures and second, depending upon the process by which its authority comes to be accepted, it may constitute an undemocratic diminution of self-determination. To resolve these tensions, liberal cosmopolitan theorists must expand significantly the domain of their theorizing. They must develop mutually consistent accounts of constitutionalism, including a normative theory of constitutional change, and of the proper scope of self-determination in a world of states; and they must do so in a way that is consistent with their basic values as cosmopolitans.

Notes

The authors are grateful to Kenneth Abbot, Jeff Holzgreve, Robert O. Keohane, James Nickel, and Michael White for their extremely helpful comments on a draft of this chapter.

1. See Jeremy A. Rabkin, *Law Without Nations? Why Constitutional Government Requires Sovereign States* (Princeton, N.J.: Princeton University Press, 2005) and *The Case for Sovereignty* (Washington, D.C.: American Enterprise Institute Press, 2004). Later we criticize this 'exclusive accountability argument'. Rabkin and some others who have been labeled New Sovereigntists may also hold a related, but distinct view: the Austinian-Hobbesian dogma that any genuine polity or any genuine legal system must have a single "sovereign source," a publicly identifiable agent that is capable of both resolving any possible issue about what the law requires and of effectively enforcing its judgment in this regard. We believe that the dubiousness of this view has been sufficiently exposed and that it is not necessary to consider it here.

2. For the seminal articulation of this view, see Curtis A. Bradley and Jack L. Goldsmith, "Customary International Law as Federal Common Law: A Critique of the Modern Position," *Harvard Law Review* 110 (1997): 815–876, and "UN Human Rights Standards and U.S. Law: The Current Illegitimacy of International Human Rights," *Fordham Law Review* 66 (1997): 319–369.

3. See, e.g., Jeremy A. Rabkin, *Why Sovereignty Matters*, 2nd ed. (Washington, D.C.: American Enterprise Institute Press, 1998); John C. Yoo, "Globalism and the Constitution:

Treaties, Non-self-execution, and the Original Understanding," *Columbia Law Review* 99 (1999): 1955–2094; Curtis A. Bradley and Jack L. Goldsmith, "Treaties, Human Rights, and Conditional Consent," *University of Pennsylvania Law Review* 149 (2000): 339–468.

4. See, e.g., Robert O. Keohane, Stephen Macedo, and Andrew Moravesik, "Democracy-enhancing Multilateralism," Institute for International Law and Justice Working Paper No. 2007/4 (New York: New York University Law School, 2007); Allen Buchanan, *Justice, Legitimacy and Self-determination: Moral Foundations for International Law* (Oxford: Oxford University Press, 2003), esp. part III. Mattias Kumm, "The Legitimacy of International Law: A Constitutionalist Framework of Analysis," *European Journal of International Law* 15 (2004): 907–31; Samantha Besson, "Whose Constitution(s)? International Law, Constitutionalism, and Democracy," *Ruling the World? Constitutionalism, International Law and Global Governance*, ed. J. Dunoff and J. Trachtman (Cambridge: Cambridge University Press, 2009).

5. For what may be the best articulation of this second sort of compatibilist view, see Keohane, Macedo, and Moravcsik, "Democracy-enhancing Multilateralism."

6. See Buchanan, *Justice, Legitimacy and Self-determination.*

7. This remains true even for well-developed democracies. For instance, in *Dudgeon* v. *United Kingdom*, 4 Eur. Ct. H.R. 149 (1981), the issue before the European Court of Human Rights was whether statutes in Northern Ireland criminalizing homosexual conduct ("buggery" or "gross indecency") between consenting adults violated the right to privacy under Article 8 of the European Convention on Human Rights. The criminal statutes in question made such acts punishable by up to life in prison. The Court, however, held that the buggery laws breached Article 8 of the Convention, since there was no pressing social need to justify such a significant violation of privacy and family life. See *Lawrence v. Texas*, 539 U.S. 558 (2003) for a similar result in the United States. Likewise, in *Toonen v. Australia*, Case No. 488/1992, U.N. Hum. Rts. Comm., 15th Sess., U.N. Doc. CCPR/C/50/D/488/1992 (1994), the United Nations Human Rights Committee struck down criminal prohibitions on homosexual activity in Tasmania, holding that the word "sex" should be understood to include sexual orientation within the meaning of the International Covenant on Civil and Political Rights. See generally Keohane, Macedo, and Moravcsik, "Democracy-enhancing Multilateralism."

8. Keohane, Macedo, and Moravcsik, ibid., provide valuable concrete examples.

9. See e.g. Joshua Cohen and Charles Sabel, "Directly Deliberative Polyarchy," *European Law Journal* 3 (1997): 313–42.

10. Keohane, Macedo, and Moravcsik, "Democracy-enhancing Multilateralism."

11. The scare quotes here are to emphasize that these are not necessarily egoistic reasons, but rather are reasons that should have force for those who value their own constitutional democracy independently of any cosmopolitan considerations.

12. Allen Buchanan, "The Internal Legitimacy of Humanitarian Intervention," *The Journal of Political Philosophy* 7 (1999): 71–87; and *Justice, Legitimacy and Self-determination.*

13. This does not imply that the interests of foreigners ought to be weighed equally with those of citizens. Recognizing that the interests of foreigners ought to be taken into account is compatible with a moderate cosmopolitanism according to which the interests of citizens may be accorded priority.

14. Kristen Hessler has argued that democracies have epistemic virtues—in particular, resources for public deliberation—that create a presumption that they should have the authority to interpret human rights norms in their domestic application. This is compatible with the claim that there are circumstances in which the authority of international human rights law should supercede the authority of the state. Kristen Hessler, "Resolving Interpretive Conflicts in International Human Rights Law," *The Journal of Political Philosophy* 13 (2005): 29–52.

15. At this point an asymmetry between domestic and international law becomes salient. In well-developed domestic legal systems (except in cases of rulings by the country's highest court), if a party complains that a law or a court's judgment is simply an instance of arbitrary power in legal guise, there are established legal processes and principles that can be invoked to determine the validity of the complaint. But in international law, or at least in some areas of international law, these legal resources may be lacking and therefore the suspicion that the law is merely a disguise for the rule of power may be hard to dispel. Where this is the case, the claim that the commitment to the rule of law speaks in favor of acknowledging the authority of RIL is less compelling.

16. Stephen Ratner, "Is International Law Impartial," *Legal Theory* 11 (2005): 39–74.

17. Rabkin, *Law Without Nations?* and *The Case for Sovereignty*.

18. Note that our claim here is *not* that democracy precludes a constitution that requires exclusive accountability, but only that there seems to be no reason to assume that a democratic constitution must require exclusive accountability. Hence we are not committed to the view that if the U.S. Constitution requires exclusive accountability, then this shows that it is defective. For a detailed defense of the view that RIL is not in principle incompatible with either the idea of constitutionalism or with that of democracy, see Allen Buchanan and Russell Powell, "Fidelity to Constitutional Democracy and to International Law," in David Armstrong, ed., *The Routledge Handbook of International Law* (Cambridge: Cambridge University Press, 2009).

19. See "Transcript of Discussion between U.S. Supreme Court Justices Antonin Scalia and Stephen Breyer on 'The Constitutional Relevance of Foreign Court Decisions,'" American University, Jan. 13, 2005, available at: http://domino.american.edu/AU/media/mediarel.nsf/1D265343BDC2189785256B810071F238/1F2F7DC4757FD01E85256F890068E6E0?OpenDocument. See also *Atkins v. Virginia*, 536 U.S. 304 (2002) (Justice Scalia, dissenting); Rabkin, *Law Without Nations?* and *The Case for Sovereignty*.

20. Justice Scalia, for instance, maintains that the only legal and moral standards relevant to U.S. constitutional jurisprudence are "[t]he standards of decency of American society—not the standards of decency of the world, not the standards of decency of other countries that don't have our background, that don't have our culture, that don't have our moral views." Scalia-Breyer, ibid.

21. In the U.S. case, on the assumption that customary international law has the status of federal common law, all of these worries are exacerbated. And because federal common law takes precedence over conflicting states' laws, there is the additional concern that judge's recourse to international law undermines federalism by encroaching on the proper domain of the states' law-making authority.

22. One worry is that an overly permissive conception of what it takes to satisfy the *opinio juris* condition for the emergence of a customary norm has begun to take root—in particular, that mere pronouncements by State officials can suffice to demonstrate the subjective belief that the practice is consistent with or required by the prevailing law.

23. Attempts to harmonize domestic and international law are varied. In some countries, human rights conventions and other aspects of international law are accorded a supreme status above all domestic law including the Constitution (see e.g., the Netherlands, Belgium, and Luxembourg). For instance, under Article 91(3) of the Netherlands' Constitution (adopted in 1983), treaties that conflict with the Constitution may be approved by the Chambers of Parliament by a two-thirds vote; as per Article 94, statutes that are inconsistent with treaties are not applicable. In other countries (such as Austria and Finland), treaties that derogate from or are otherwise inconsistent with the domestic constitution may be approved by a super majority in parliament, rendering them equal or superior to the Constitution. In many states, international treaties preempt both earlier and subsequent

domestic statutes (see *inter alia* France, Portugal, Spain, Switzerland, and Greece), although a few countries only accord this status to international law concerning human rights (see e.g., Russia, Romania, and the Czech Republic). In other states, however, the major human rights conventions have the status of ordinary domestic law, applying a 'later-in-time' rule to resolve conflicts between domestic and international law (see e.g., Germany, Ireland, Italy, Norway, Poland, Turkey, United Kingdom, and the United States, *inter alia*).

24. The tripartite separation of powers is allegedly vitiated by the federal incorporation of international law in several ways. The judicial branch is said to exceed its constitutional mandates by incorporating customary international law into federal common law and by invoking foreign precedent as persuasive authority in U.S. constitutional jurisprudence. The executive is claimed to exceed its constitutionally enumerated powers by entering into 'self-executing' treaties which regulate subject matter reserved to Congress and/or to the several states. Finally, the entire federal government is held to exceed its legitimate authority by incorporating into U.S. law international norms which regulate content constitutionally reserved for state regulation. See, respectively: Bradley and Goldsmith, "Customary International Law as Federal Common Law"; Yoo, "Globalism and the Constitution"; and Rabkin, *Law Without Nations*? and *The Case for Sovereignty*.

25. See U.S. Constitution, Art. VI.

26. Yoo, "Globalism and the Constitution" (arguing that self-executing treaties are unconstitutional); Rabkin, *The Case for Sovereignty*.

27. This case is persuasively made by David M. Golove, "Human Rights Treaties and the U.S. Constitution," *DePaul Law Review* 52 (2002): 579–635; "Treaty-making and the Nation: The Historical Foundations of the Nationalist Conception of the Treaty Power," *Michigan Law Review* 98 (2000): 1075–1319.

28. See Richard Falk and Andrew Strauss, "On the Creation of a Global Peoples Assembly: Legitimacy and the Power of Popular Sovereignty," *Stanford Journal of International Law* 36 (2000): 191–219.

29. On reflection, this intuition may not stand scrutiny, because, at least in principle, it seems that the citizens of a democracy could (mistakenly) cede authority beyond the point at which it could be said that they are self-governing.

30. In order to ratify treaties of major importance, such as those which establish robust supranational organizations, many nations require special majority legislation (e.g., Greece, Austria, Finland, Croatia, *inter alia*) or constitutional revision (e.g., France), while others hold referenda (e.g., Denmark, Sweden, and Switzerland).

31. James Nickel has suggested that in some cases of acknowledging the authority of RIL what might be called tacit democratic authorization would suffice—that none of the mechanisms for public deliberation and choice we list would be required. For example, if citizens do not "punish" those officials who signed the relevant treaties, etc., by voting against them in the next election, this could count as a kind of democratic authorization. In our view, the notion of tacit democratic authorization is problematic in general, but perhaps especially problematic when it comes to such significant political changes as secession, accession, and devolution. Accordingly, we hold that there should be a presumption of a requirement of public deliberation and choice, at least for cases in which acknowledging the authority of RIL is likely to produce constitutional changes or changes in the scope of self-determination that are comparable to secession, accession, and devolution.

PART III

THE USE OF FORCE

9

THE INTERNAL LEGITIMACY OF HUMANITARIAN INTERVENTION

1. THE PROBLEM OF INTERNAL LEGITIMACY

Humanitarian intervention is often defined as infringement of a state's sovereignty by an external agent or agents for the sake of preventing human rights violations.[1] The term "infringement" in this definition is carefully chosen: the implied contrast is between infringements and violations; not all infringements are unjust, so the definition remains neutral as to whether, or under what conditions, intervention is justified.

On a stricter definition, humanitarian intervention is limited to the use of force, as distinguished from economic sanctions. Some writers add the stipulation that humanitarian intervention must be humanitarian in intent, that the sole or at least the primary goal of the intervention must be to protect the welfare and freedom of those in another state, rather than some advantage to the intervening state or its citizens.[2]

The ethics of humanitarian intervention is a complex and passionately disputed topic. Familiar issues include the following. (1) Given the centrality of state sovereignty in international law, when, if ever, is humanitarian intervention legal, and under what conditions is it morally permissible to engage in illegal humanitarian intervention? (2) When, if ever, is unilateral, as opposed to collective, humanitarian intervention morally justified? (3) Does any persistent violation of human rights justify intervention, or only extreme violations, such as genocide? (4) Even if persistent human rights violations (or violations of certain basic human rights) constitute a *prima facie* justification for intervention, what other conditions must be satisfied? (Proposals include a requirement of proportionality, such that the human rights violations that result from the intervention should be considerably less than those it is designed to prevent, and requirements of procedural justice for impartially identifying targets of intervention and for selecting disinterested agents of intervention.)

There is another fundamental issue of the ethics of humanitarian intervention that seems largely to have gone unnoticed in the contemporary scholarly debate: the problem of the internal legitimacy of humanitarian intervention.[3] This problem remains after all the familiar questions are answered satisfactorily; yet it precedes them all because, unless it can be answered affirmatively, the other questions do not arise. It is this problem that is the focus of this chapter.

The problem is this: How can the government of a state morally justify humanitarian intervention to its own citizens? Like the questions listed above, this is a question about moral justification, but unlike them it directs the question of justification inward. The other, more familiar questions concerning humanitarian intervention are questions about external legitimacy: they assume that there is no problem of internal legitimacy or, if there is, that it has been solved; they concentrate on whether intervention by one state or by a collection of states can be justified to the state that is the object of intervention, or to the community of states as a whole.

The failure to address the problem of the internal legitimacy of humanitarian intervention is a major deficiency, not only in the moral theory of intervention, but in the doctrine of human rights as well. Evolving human rights law specifies the conditions under which it is legally permissible for states to intervene to protect human rights when they choose to do so. In addition, under the basic principle that agreements are to be kept (*pacta sunt servanda*), international law recognizes that states that have signed human rights treaties have obligations under those treaties. Yet such treaties (including the International Covenant on Civil and Political Rights) only impose on signatories duties to protect the human rights of their own citizens and merely encourage states to "promote" human rights in other states.[4]

In other words, existing international human rights law does not establish clear obligations of humanitarian intervention on the part of states.[5] Human rights activists and some international legal scholars have advocated that international law should be modified so that it imposes clear obligations to engage in humanitarian intervention on states. However, it can be argued that unless humanitarian intervention is internally legitimate, the imposition of a duty of humanitarian intervention would itself be a moral wrong. Like the ethical literature on humanitarian intervention, international legal doctrine for the most part slides over the problem of internal legitimacy.

At this juncture a cautionary word is in order. The problem of the internal legitimacy of humanitarian intervention, as I have defined it, is a problem about the morality, not the legality, of humanitarian intervention. International legal writers have rightly noted that at least for some states the legality of participation in some aspects of international human rights enforcement efforts is questionable. In some cases, as with Japan and Germany, the constitution of a state prohibits the use of military force abroad, even for humanitarian intervention. It has also been argued that participation in some international efforts to implement human rights norms, including war crimes trials, may be incompatible with the stringent demands of the equal protection and due process provisions of the US Constitution.[6] The question I shall focus on here, however, is not whether humanitarian intervention is internally legal (that is, lawful according to the legal system of the state that intervenes) but whether the government can provide an adequate moral justification to its own citizens when it intervenes on humanitarian grounds.

An immediate response may well be: There is no problem here; if the intervening state is legitimate, then its legitimacy justifies its interventions to its people, at least if those interventions are justifiable externally (that is, to the target of intervention and the world community). However, this response begs the question. It assumes, without argument, that among the legitimate activities of a state are undertakings whose primary aim is to protect the rights of persons who are not its citizens. But, as I shall argue, this assumption is unjustifiable from the perspective of what is arguably the dominant understanding of the nature of the state and the role of government in liberal political thought: the idea that the state is an association for the mutual advantage of its members and that the government is simply an agent whose fiduciary duty is to serve the interests, or to realize the will of those citizens.

Exploring the problem of the internal legitimacy of humanitarian intervention leads us back, then, to what is perhaps the most basic question of political philosophy: what are states for? I shall argue that the dominant understanding of the nature of the state and the role of government, what I shall refer to as the "discretionary association" view, makes internally legitimate humanitarian intervention impossible (except, perhaps, in the special case where it is explicitly authorized by democratic processes). And I will indicate that the dominant way of thinking about justice—the view that justice is a matter of relations among members of a cooperative scheme—reinforces the discretionary association view's inability to account for the internal legitimacy of humanitarian intervention. I will also articulate the features of the "discretionary association" view that explain its perennial attraction.

However, I will then argue that humanitarian intervention can be internally legitimate. First, I will raise several serious objections to the "discretionary association view" that makes the internal legitimacy of humanitarian intervention problematic. Second, I will show that the attractions of the discretionary association view can be preserved in an alternative understanding of "the state as an instrument for justice" in such a way as to provide a solution to the problem of the internal legitimacy of humanitarian intervention.

2. THE DISCRETIONARY ASSOCIATION VIEW OF THE STATE

The internal legitimacy of humanitarian intervention is an intelligible problem regardless of what view of the state one takes, but within the dominant view of the state in liberal political thought it is an especially daunting problem. According to the dominant view, the state is a discretionary association for the mutual advantage of its members. The government is simply the agent of the associated individuals, an instrument to further *their* interests. Or, on a more complex, democratic variant of that dominant view, the state is a framework not simply for serving the interests of the citizens but also for articulating their will, through democratic processes, and the role of the government is not only to serve the citizens' interests but to realize their will (or rather the will of the majority of the citizens).

Perhaps the clearest proponent of the discretionary association view is Locke. For him the state is a discretionary association in this sense: Although there is no moral obligation to enter into political society, it is permissible and even advisable for individuals who interact together in a state of nature to avoid its "inconveniences"—especially those attendant on private enforcement of the moral rules—by forming a political society and authorizing a group of individuals to be the government, to serve as the agent of the people.[7] For Locke political association is discretionary, not only in the sense that there is no moral obligation to form a state, but also in that individuals may choose with whom they wish to associate politically. There is no suggestion of what I have referred to elsewhere as an "obligation of inclusion"—a moral duty to help ensure that all persons have access to institutions that will protect their basic rights.[8]

The very idea of a social contract so central to liberal theorizing about justice suggests the discretionary association view. The state is understood as the creation of a hypothetical contract among those who are to be its citizens, and the terms of the contract they agree on are justified by showing how observance of those terms serves *their* interests. No one else's interests are represented, so legitimate political authority is naturally defined as authority exercised for the good of the parties to the contract, the citizens of this state. Even in variants of the contract doctrine that view the parties as representatives of future generations, such as Rawls's, it is only insofar as future generations are presumed to be citizens of *this* state that their interests are considered in the making of the contract. The state is understood to be the enforcer of principles of justice, and principles of justice are thought of as specifying the terms of cooperation among those who are bound together in one political society, rather than as specifying how persons generally must be treated.

The discretionary association view usually includes a distinction between the state and the government. The justifying function of the state—what justifies the interference with liberty that it entails—is the wellbeing and freedom of its members. There is no suggestion that the state must do anything to serve the cause of justice in the world at large. What makes a government legitimate is that it acts as the faithful agent of its own citizens. And to that extent, government acts legitimately only when it occupies itself exclusively with the interests of the citizens of the state of which it is the government.

The enduring popularity of the discretionary association view is no accident. It has several signal attractions, at least from the standpoint of a liberal political philosophy. First, the discretionary association view puts government in its place. It makes it clear who is master, namely, the people. Thus the discretionary association view is a powerful expression of the idea of popular sovereignty: the government, being the instrument of the people, serves at their pleasure. The government has no independent moral status, no rights on its own account. Second, the discretionary association view implies the equal freedom of the citizens. Individuals freely decide whether to enter into association with one another. Third, the state itself—the structure of institutions that create and sustain political society—is justified because it serves the interests of the people and for no other reason. Especially at a time when states (and even subjects) were seen as the property of dynastic families whose interests they were to serve, and when rulers used their power to uphold a hierarchy of rank among subjects, these features of the discretionary association view represented a profound moral revolution in political thought.

According to the simpler version of the discretionary association view, a government that engages in what I referred to earlier as pure humanitarian intervention violates its fiduciary obligation: it fails to act in the best interest of its citizens. This failure is momentous, because it is a violation of the fiduciary duty of the government, which in turn is founded on the justifying function of the state—the fact that the state serves the interests of its citizens.

On the more complex, democratic version of the discretionary association view, the mere fact that a government engages in pure humanitarian intervention by definition shows that it acts contrary to the best interests of its citizens, but it is apparently a further question as to whether the government acts illegitimately. For the citizens might democratically authorize pure humanitarian intervention even though they are aware that it is not in their best interest. Such would be the case if the majority gave higher priority to justice than to their own interests.

One should not be too quick to assume, however, that pure humanitarian intervention is within the sphere of legitimate democratic authorization allowed by the discretionary association view. For according to this view the state is not an instrument for moral progress. It has a much more limited purpose: the advancement of the interests of its citizens. Hence a proponent of the discretionary association view might hold that the function justifying the state places an antecedent constraint on what may be authorized by democratic processes, just as a list of individual rights places an antecedent constraint on what may be decided by majority rule. On this interpretation of the democratic variant of the discretionary association view, the majority is sovereign only over choices concerning which interests of the citizens are to be given priority and how they are to be pursued. At least so long is there is one citizen who votes against it, pure humanitarian intervention is illegitimate, because the purpose of the state (the goal which unites all citizens in one political association) is limited to the advantage of those citizens, and the effective pursuit of this goal limits the sphere of legitimate democratic decision making.

It will do no good to say that democratic processes define the citizens' interests—that if the majority votes for humanitarian intervention then *ipso facto* humanitarian intervention is in the citizens' interest, and that therefore humanitarian intervention democratically approved lies within the proper sphere of state action according to the discretionary association view. Such a claim is nothing more than verbal sleight of hand. At most, democratic endorsement of humanitarian intervention establishes that the majority of citizens, not even all citizens, prefer such intervention. It does not establish that it is in the interest of all citizens or even that the majority of the citizens believe it is in their interest. Furthermore, our question is whether pure humanitarian intervention—intervention that is not in the interests of the citizens (or even in the interests of a majority of them)—can be internally justified. At the very least, the assumption that democratic authorization legitimizes pure humanitarian intervention requires a departure from a strict interpretation of the discretionary association view's central tenet, which is that the state is an arrangement for the mutual advantage of its citizens. Instead the discretionary association view would have to be reformulated as follows: the state is first and foremost an arrangement for the mutual advantage of its members; however, once the basic interests of all the citizens are secured, it is permissible, through democratic processes, to authorize actions that do not serve the best interests of the citizens.

Suppose that this modification is acceptable. Suppose, that is, that the discretionary association view can be reasonably interpreted to include an understanding of democratic authorization according to which legitimate democratic decisions are not limited to those that serve the best interests of the citizens. This only means that there are conditions under which pure humanitarian intervention is permissible. There is still nothing in the democratic variant of the discretionary association view that requires citizens ever to forgo their own interests for the sake of preventing human rights violations abroad. This is part of what is meant by calling it the discretionary association view.

If the citizens' will, duly expressed through democratic processes, is that their government should refrain from pure humanitarian intervention, then this is permissible, according to the dominant view. However, once democratic processes have expressed the people's desire not to engage in pure humanitarian intervention, pure humanitarian intervention by the government is illegitimate. From the standpoint of the discretionary association view of the state, pure humanitarian intervention is not only non-obligatory. It is in fact morally impermissible, unless there is a clear democratic mandate.

A consistent policy of avoiding pure humanitarian intervention would, of course, require that the state in question refrain from signing any human rights conventions or other agreements that create obligations of pure humanitarian intervention. Call this mode of state practice "the Swiss model."[9] From the standpoint of the discretionary association view, even on its democratic variant, there would be nothing morally defective about a world in which *every* state adopted the "Swiss model."

I noted earlier that an awareness of the problem of the internal legitimacy of humanitarian intervention is conspicuously absent in much of the contemporary scholarly literature on the ethics of intervention. However, so-called political realists, of which Hans J. Morgenthau and George F. Kennan are perhaps the most influential modern examples, have typically opposed pure humanitarian intervention.[10]

The realists have not fared well at the hands of recent moral theorists of international relations. They present easy targets, in great part because they often fail to give rigorous arguments in favor of their views and sometimes even appear muddled in their thinking.[11] My aim here is not to untangle the various threads of realist thinking in a systematic way, but only to indicate that there is one strand that is securely anchored in the discretionary association view of the nature of the state and the role of government. If this is so, then at least some realist arguments against pure humanitarian intervention cannot be convincingly refuted without rejecting a dominant paradigm of liberal political thought.

There are two quite different ways to understand the realist's antipathy to pure humanitarian intervention. According to the first, what might be called the moral nihilist view, all moral action in international relations is irrational, because the conditions for moral behavior being rational do not obtain in the international sphere.

According to the second realist view, which might be called the "fiduciary obligation" position, there is at least one moral concept that is applicable to international relations: the concept of an overriding fiduciary obligation on the part of the leaders of states to serve the interests of their peoples, even when doing so violates other putative moral principles. On this second realist view, the ruthless leader is not a stranger to morality. He is the dedicated servant of a higher morality.

Unlike the international moral nihilist or Hobbesian, the fiduciary realist does not make the mistake of assuming that there is no room for moral concepts or for rational moral behavior at all in international relations. However, the fiduciary realist view constricts the morality of international relations almost to the vanishing point. Government officials not only may but ought to transgress any moral principle for the sake of fulfilling their fiduciary obligations.

Critics of this variety of realism have been quick to point out that it is vulnerable to two serious objections. First, fiduciary obligations are not absolute. By undertaking fiduciary duties government officials do not thereby wipe the slate clean of all pre-existing obligations they may have as individuals, including obligations not to violate human rights. So the fact that government officials have fiduciary obligations to their own citizens does not show that it is permissible for them to violate other moral principles, much less that they act wrongly if they act on other moral principles. Second, at least for some states some of the time, survival is not at stake in international relations. At least the more powerful states can engage in pure humanitarian intervention without risking their survival.

These objections are telling against the fiduciary realist position as it is usually presented. But they leave one important element of the fiduciary realist position untouched—its opposition to pure humanitarian intervention. The fiduciary realist can argue as follows: It is true that fiduciary obligations are not absolute; they can be overridden by weightier obligations. From this it follows that government leaders do not have moral *carte blanche* to do whatever is necessary to further the interests of their citizens. But that is not to say that they may use the resources of the state to further the interests of individuals who are not citizens of the state, and the discretionary association view provides no explanation of why they should be allowed to do so. (Similarly, if I hire you to be my agent, it is true that you do not thereby escape other obligations you may have, but the mere fact that you have other obligations does not entitle you to use my resources to fulfill them.) Yes, the realist continues, it is quite correct to point out that not all pure humanitarian interventions put the state's survival interests at risk. But this is irrelevant to the question of pure humanitarian intervention. The fact remains that government officials ought only to serve the interests of their own states.

Fiduciary realism, stripped of the implausible assumptions to which critics have rightly objected, has the merit of taking seriously the idea that the government is the agent of the people—the people of its state—and that the fact that it is their agent makes a difference to what it may do. It is crucial to understand that this strand of realist thought is not a muddled aberration, a *sui generis* confusion or free-floating anomaly in Western political thought. It is nurtured by the dominant discretionary association paradigm, which includes the idea that the government is only an agent, bound by a fiduciary obligation. Unless we are willing to reject or modify the discretionary association view, there will be no convincing reply to the fiduciary normative realist's objection to pure humanitarian intervention.

3. THE MORAL COSTS OF THE DISCRETIONARY ASSOCIATION VIEW

Despite its several attractions, noted above, the discretionary association view is subject to four serious problems. Two have already been mentioned. It not only leaves us without a convincing reply to the fiduciary normative realist, but also implies that there would be nothing morally wrong with a world in which every state adopted "the Swiss model." In such a world, the enforcement of human rights standards abroad would be regarded as purely optional. The language of moral obligation would be out of place in debates about humanitarian intervention.

A third problem is that the discretionary association view is afflicted by a deep incoherence, if not an outright inconsistency. It justifies the state as a coercive apparatus by appeal to the need to protect *universal* interests, while at the same time limiting the right of the state to use its coercive power to the protection of a particular group of persons, identified by the purely contingent characteristic of happening to be members of the same political society.

According to the most plausible version of this view, the most important interests that states are to serve are basic human interests, not special interests that citizens of this or that particular state have but that the citizens of other states might not have. Thus for Locke, for example, government best serves the interests of its citizens by protecting life, liberty and property. If the interests whose protection justifies the state are human interests, common to all persons, then surely a way of thinking about the nature of states and the role of government that provides no basis for obligations to help ensure that the interests of all persons are protected is fundamentally flawed.

This point can be put even more forcefully if it is framed in terms of individuals' rights. According to the more influential examples of the discretionary association view such as Locke's and Rawls's, the state is to ensure that the cooperative framework it supplies works to the mutual advantage of all citizens by protecting every citizen's basic human rights. And it is the fact that the state protects all citizens' basic human rights that is supposed to justify its use of coercion: because these rights are so important for all persons as persons, the interferences with liberty that this coercion involves are justified. So on the one hand the discretionary association view bases its conception of the nature of the state and the role of government on a universalist conception of which kinds of interests are worth protecting by the coercive power of the state, while on the other hand it provides no basis for imputing any obligation to use the resources of the state to implement this universalist conception beyond the boundaries of the state. The discretionary association view rules out obligations of pure humanitarian intervention in principle at the same time that it implicitly embraces a universalist conception of the worth of the individual that recognizes no boundaries.

A fourth problem with the discretionary association view takes the form of a dilemma. Either that view must deny that states have any obligations toward citizens of other states, including negative duties not to kill or injure them wantonly, in which case it is in stark conflict both with some of our most basic and widely held moral intuitions and with one of the most basic principles of international law; or else that view must acknowledge that states have such negative duties, making it then vulnerable to the charge that it provides no reasonable basis for not recognizing some positive duties as well. Let us consider each alternative in turn.

Taken literally, the discretionary association view holds that the state may not do anything except serve the best interests of its citizens. This would mean that if it were the case that an unprovoked attack on another state would promote its citizens' interests, then the state may undertake such an attack. Such an implication is squarely at odds with what is perhaps one of our most confident and widely shared moral intuitions, namely, that it is wrong to harm the innocent. It is also in conflict with one of the most basic principles of international law, namely, that wars of aggression are prohibited. Not surprisingly, most proponents of the discretionary association view would acknowledge that a state's efforts to serve the interests of its citizens must be constrained by certain basic negative duties toward others. Let us call this the softened discretionary association view.

The difficulty is that once the discretionary association view makes this concession, it is hard to see how it can avoid going further, toward the recognition of at least some positive duties toward noncitizens. The most plausible reasons for holding that states have negative duties toward noncitizens appeal to the moral importance of human beings as such, and to the role which the fulfillment of the negative duties in question plays in protecting certain fundamental interests in liberty and wellbeing that human beings as such have. But, as has been convincingly argued in many other contexts, the protection of those fundamental interests also requires the fulfillment of positive duties as well, including duties to ensure that all have access to resources for subsistence and to basic educational opportunities. Libertarian attempts to limit duties to those that are negative either fail to appreciate that the same considerations that ground negative rights also ground positive ones or assume that the only morally significant sort of liberty is freedom from coercion. In brief, the same arguments that show that the state has positive as well as negative duties to its own citizens show that it is arbitrary to soften the harsh implications of the discretionary association view by admitting negative duties to noncitizens while denying any positive duties to noncitizens.

Suppose that the proponent of the discretionary association view could somehow avoid the objection that acknowledging negative duties to noncitizens while denying positive ones is arbitrary. The softened discretionary association view would still conflict with some rather basic moral intuitions. For example, it cannot explain what is wrong with a rich and powerful state refusing to exert even the most minimal efforts, at virtually no risk to itself, to prevent genocide in a neighboring state. In a world in which the discretionary association view were taken seriously no one could appeal to an obligation to engage in humanitarian intervention even as a *prima facie* obligation that might be overridden by practical considerations.

Whether or not the international legal system should impose legal obligations to cooperate in pure humanitarian interventions upon states that democratically decide not to engage in pure humanitarian interventions is another matter. There might be sound reasons for refraining from efforts to impose such international legal obligations. My point is that the discretionary association view makes it impossible to argue that even the most powerful and rich state has any moral obligation, no matter how limited, to cooperate in pure humanitarian intervention efforts, even when doing so is necessary to stop the most egregious violations of human rights and even when the costs of doing so are minimal.

Indeed, the discretionary association view cannot make sense of the fact that we experience the question of pure humanitarian intervention as a moral conflict. We experience a moral conflict because we feel the pull not only of moral reasons against pure humanitarian intervention, but in favor of it as well. On the discretionary association view, there are not two sides to the matter and hence there can be no conflict, because there can be no moral obligation to engage in pure humanitarian intervention.

One can, of course, construct practical arguments for why states should only attend to the interests of their own citizens and the fulfillment of negative duties toward noncitizens. One could argue that, even though there is a *prima facie* obligation to engage in pure humanitarian intervention, such intervention is never justifiable all things considered because any serious effort at pure humanitarian intervention would be excessively costly to the citizens of the intervening state, or because it is doomed to failure for lack of the resources and knowledge required for success, or because it is likely to be a disguised imperialist adventure, and not a pure humanitarian intervention at all. But we are not concerned here with whether pure humanitarian intervention meets standards of practicality. We are asking whether it can even in principle be internally justified, given the dominant liberal model of what states are for and what the role of government is. Even if all the foregoing practical problems disappeared, our question would remain.

In addition, the same features of the discretionary association view that preclude it from recognizing that the people of one state sometimes have at least a *prima facie* obligation to intervene on humanitarian grounds in another state also make it unable to account for what I take to be a relatively uncontroversial moral intuition about the ethics of immigration. According to the discretionary association view, it is simply a confusion to argue that the people of a very rich and secure state have even a *prima facie* moral obligation to accept even a small number of refugees from genocide occurring just across the border, even when their acceptance carries no risks to the people of the state. It is one thing to say that the obligation to accept political refugees is limited—for example, that a people need not accept refugees if doing so will embroil them in a war or will create ethnic conflict within their state or will undermine the dominant culture of the state. But it is quite another to say that there is no obligation at all. Yet, on the discretionary association view, there is no such obligation.

4. THE STATE AS AN INSTRUMENT FOR JUSTICE

For all of these reasons it is worth asking whether the attractions of the discretionary association view can be preserved while avoiding these costs. The chief moral cost of the discretionary association view is not that it implies that *governments* should not undertake pure humanitarian intervention except (perhaps) when explicitly authorized to do so by democratic processes. The more basic problem is that it provides no basis for believing that the *people* of any particular state have any obligation to use the resources of their state to undertake pure humanitarian intervention or to accept refugees even under the least painful circumstances. On the contrary, the discretionary association model portrays pure humanitarian intervention and the acceptance of refugees as aberrations, as inexplicable departures from what political action ought to be. Even on the democratic variant of the discretionary association view there is still a problem, as we have seen: how can a majority voting in favor of pure humanitarian intervention justify their decision to a dissenting minority, given that the justifying function of the state is to serve the interests of its citizens, not to protect the rights of others?

There is a radically different conception of the nature of the state and the role of government that avoids the moral and theoretical costs of the discretionary association view while at the same time preserving its attractions. We may call it the "state-as-the-instrument-for-justice" view. It rests upon the premise that there is a natural duty of justice that requires us to help ensure that all persons have access to institutions for the protection of their basic moral rights.[12]

In *A Theory of Justice* Rawls articulates a natural duty of justice as having two parts: "first, we are to comply with and do our fair share in just institutions when they exist and apply to us; and second, we are to assist in the establishment of just arrangements when they do not exist, at least when this can be done with little cost to ourselves."[13] The duty is said to be natural in the sense that individuals have it independently of any special undertakings and independently of the institutional roles they may occupy.

The scope of the second clause is perhaps not altogether clear. It could mean that we are to help establish just institutions that will apply to us, where no just institutions now apply to us. Or it could mean that we are to help establish justice institutions for all persons.

In fact, three different understandings of the second clause can be distinguished. In each case the qualifier "if one can do so without excessive costs" is to be understood as being included (for brevity I will not repeat it each time).

NDJ1: Each person has a duty to contribute to the creation of just arrangements to include himself and his fellow citizens.

NDJ2: Each person has a duty to contribute to the creation of just arrangements to include himself and all those with whom he will interact (which may include some who are not his fellow citizens).

NDJ3: Each person has a duty to contribute to the inclusion of all persons in just arrangements.

It is the third, most demanding understanding of the "natural duty of justice" upon which I will focus. It alone provides a secure foundation for an obligation of pure humanitarian intervention, and only it provides a convincing solution to the problem of the internal legitimacy of pure humanitarian intervention.

The natural duty of justice (hereafter understood as NDJ3) is such a fundamental principle that it may seem impossible to provide an argument for it that does not assume at least one premise that is more controversial than the principle itself. However, even if no convincing argument can be presented for it, it has considerable intuitive appeal, at least if, as I have suggested, it is understood as imposing a limited obligation, not an obligation to help ensure that all have access to just institutions regardless of cost. Given its intuitive appeal, showing that the natural duty of justice provides the basis for a view of the nature of the state and the role of government that avoids the costs of the discretionary association view while preserving its attractions would be a valuable exercise, even if no argument for it could be supplied. Nevertheless, although I cannot attempt to provide a conclusive case for the natural duty NDJ3 here, I will indicate one plausible line of argument in support of it.

Before doing so, however, I would like to emphasize that proponents of the discretionary association view typically do not provide explicit arguments to support it. Instead, support for the discretionary association view is indirect. Its plausibility appears to depend solely upon what it implies: namely, that citizens are free and equal; that the state is to serve their interests, rather than the interests of the ruler or the citizens of some other state; and that the government is merely their agent, with no rights or moral standing of its own. Yet these attractive implications, I shall argue, also follow from what I have referred to as the instrument for justice view.

Perhaps the best way to argue for the natural duty of justice is to tease out the incoherence of denying that this duty exists while at the same time affirming that persons as such have rights. I take it that the assertion that persons as such have rights means that we all have a duty to treat persons in certain ways, and that this duty is owed to persons because it is grounded in the nature of persons. Different moral theories may provide somewhat different accounts of what it is about persons that is the source of their rights and hence of our duties toward them (Kantian theories, for instance, hold that it is the capacity for moral agency.) But what is important is that the duties that correlate with the rights of persons as such are *owed to* persons. They are not merely duties *regarding* persons (such as we would have if, for example, the sole basis for moral constraints on the way we may treat people were the commands of God or the relationships we happen to have toward persons).

To say that persons as such have certain rights, then, means that because of certain characteristics that all persons have they are entitled to certain treatment. But if this is so, then surely one ought not only to respect persons' rights by not violating them. One ought also to contribute to creating arrangements that will ensure that persons' rights are not violated. To put the same point somewhat differently, respect for persons requires doing something to ensure that they are treated respectfully.

Consider the alternative. Suppose that the ground of our duties regarding persons were external to them—that we are required to treat them in certain ways only because God commands us to do so, for example. We would have duties regarding persons but not owed to them. In this case there would be no incoherence or oddness at all about acknowledging that we are obligated to treat persons in certain ways while at the same time denying that we have any obligation whatsoever, no matter how limited, to help ensure that others treat them similarly. For although God *might* command us to see that our fellows treat persons as he commands us to treat them, he also might not.

Alternatively, suppose that the ground of one's duty not to violate persons' rights lay only in some relationship one happens to bear to them, such as being a fellow citizen or being co-participants in some international economic arrangement for our mutual advantage. If some such relationship were the sole basis of the duty, then one would not have a duty to persons as such to respect their rights, and there would be no presumption that there is a duty to help ensure that all persons rights are respected.

In contrast, if the basic moral rights of persons are grounded in the morally important characteristics that all persons possess, then it is difficult to maintain a separation between respecting persons' rights and making some effort to see that their rights are respected. At the very least, the same appreciation for the nature of persons that is supposed to ground their most basic rights and hence our duty to respect those rights carries a presumptive duty to help ensure that all persons can live in conditions in which their basic rights are respected, at least if we can do so without excessive costs to ourselves.

I would not presume to assert that these considerations provide an unassailable foundation for the natural duty of justice. But let us suppose, for the sake of drawing out the implications of this duty for how we conceive of the nature of the state and the role of government, that each of us has an obligation to help ensure that all persons have access to rights-protecting institutions. The extent of what we are actually required to do to fulfill that obligation will vary with the costs of fulfilling it. If this is the case, then those individuals who are politically organized, who can collectively command the resources of a state, will have greater capacity to help ensure that others have access to a justice-protecting regime, without excessive costs.

With this greater capacity comes greater responsibility for alleviating the condition of other persons whose rights are imperilled. As individuals commanding only our own private resources, there may be little that any of us can do to help ensure that all persons can live in a rights-protecting regime. But when we are organized in a state our collective capacity for promoting just institutions abroad is greatly enhanced. And if we live in a powerful and rich state, there will surely be cases in which our collective resources can be used to further the cause of justice in the world, without excessive costs to us.

Because it is a natural duty, NDJ3 places a constraint on how we may use our institutional resources, upon what we may do with the state, and hence what our government, our agent, may do. Given the fact that having a state of our own enables us to act on the natural duty, we are not morally free to use our state merely as a framework for *our* mutual advantage. Thus if we were to adopt the "Swiss model," we would fail to acknowledge the natural duty of justice and ignore the fact that in our world at present states are the chief instrumentalities by which individuals can help ensure that all persons have access to institutions that protect their rights.

This is not to say that the sole legitimate purpose, or even the primary legitimate purpose of particular political associations is to promote justice for all of humanity. Because the natural duty includes an excessive cost proviso, it can accommodate the idea that citizens may rightly show partiality to their own interests. (Moreover, there are sound practical reasons for first seeking to establish justice locally, within the boundaries of existing states, working from within them.[14]) But what the natural duty does imply is that the state cannot be viewed simply as an arrangement for the mutual benefit of its members alone. And this suffices to rebut the fiduciary realist's claim that humanitarian intervention is in principle illegitimate.

The assumption that there is a natural duty of justice allows us to develop a view of the state that preserves the attractive implications of the discretionary association view, while avoiding its moral and theoretical costs. If we suppose that there is a natural duty of justice (NDJ3), then we must acknowledge that those who collectively control effective political institutions have responsibilities to others and that consequently the state is not merely an association for the mutual advantage of its members, but a resource for ensuring that all persons' rights are protected. Given this view of the state, we can explain the moral conflict we feel when we consider the pros and cons of pure humanitarian intervention.

A view of the state as an instrument for justice is clearly compatible with what is probably the single most attractive feature of the discretionary association view: a proper understanding of the status of government—that government is simply an agent, not a moral being with rights of its own. It also captures the idea that citizens are free and equal by affirming that all persons' rights matter. For even though the state-as-the-instrument-for-justice view places some constraints on the use of state resources for enhancing the condition of the citizens, it does not do so in the name of any assumption of unequal worth. On the contrary, the constraints it imposes follow from the assumption that all persons are of equal moral worth and that consequently all are entitled to protection of their rights. Finally, the state-as-an-instrument-for-justice view, like the discretionary association view, rules out any arrangements that sacrifice the interests of the citizens for the sake of benefitting anyone else, whether it be the rulers or the citizens of some other state. For according to the instrument for justice view, the proper business of the state is to benefit its members, within the constraints imposed by the natural duty of justice, and these constraints recognize that there are limits on the costs that the citizens of one state must bear to protect the rights of other persons.

Acknowledging that there is a robust natural duty of justice that requires citizens to use their state's resources to help ensure that all have access to a rights-protecting regime is an important theoretical advance in the doctrine of human rights. But from this alone it does not follow that it would be legitimate for the international legal system to *enforce* a duty on the part of states to contribute to the establishment of justice for all persons. For the natural duty of justice might be viewed as an imperfect duty rather than an enforceable one—merely an indeterminate and hence unenforceable duty to do something to help provide just institutions for all persons. Although I can only sketch the argument here, I will conclude by suggesting that a conscientious effort to act on the natural duty of justice will require states to work together to create international legal institutions that will articulate determinate duties and assign them to states in such a way as to distribute fairly the costs of ensuring that all persons have access to rights-protecting institutions. If this were accomplished, the enforcement of duties of humanitarian intervention would be morally justifiable.

Notes

1. See, for example, Jack Donnelly, "Human Rights, Humanitarian Intervention and American Foreign Policy: Law, Morality, and Politics," *Journal of International Affairs* 37 (1984): 311.

2. See, for example, Fernando Tesón, *Humanitarian Intervention*, 2nd ed. (Irvington-on-Hudson, N.Y.: Transnational Publishers, 1992), 1–6.

3. I borrow the term "internal legitimacy" from Ronald Sanders. In an unpublished paper Sanders distinguishes between internal and external legitimacy. On his view, a state is internally legitimate if its citizens (or the majority of them) accept it as having rightful political authority. My use of the term does not follow his, however. I only use it to focus on which party the justification for humanitarian intervention is directed toward.

4. Article 2, Part II, International Covenant on Civil and Political Rights (1966), in James Nickel, *Making Sense of Human Rights* (Berkeley: University of California Press, 1987), 212.

5. As opposed to those that might be generated by other more specific treaties into which states have entered.

6. Alfred Rubin, *Ethics and Authority in International Law* (Cambridge: Cambridge University Press, 1997), 93.

7. John Locke, *Second Treatise of Civil Government*, ed. C.B. Macpherson (Indianapolis, Ind.: Hackett, 1980), 1–2.

8. Allen Buchanan, "The Morality of Inclusion," *Social Philosophy and Policy* 10 (1993): 242–47.

9. This label is not intended to suggest that Switzerland actually pursues a purely self-interested foreign policy (all the time). The point rather is that this country, whether rightly or wrongly, has the reputation of sufficiently approximating such a policy to make the label a handy one.

10. George F. Kennan, *Realities of American Foreign Policy* (Princeton, N.J.: Princeton University Press, 1954); Hans J. Morgonthau, *In Defense of the National Interest* (New York: Knopf, 1952), and *Politics Among Nations*, 5th ed. (New York: Knopf, 1973).

11. For excellent critiques of realist thinking, see: Marshall Cohen, "Moral Skepticism and International Relations," *Philosophy and Public Affairs* 13 (1984): 299–346; and Charles Beitz, *Political Theory and International Relations* (Princeton, N.J.: Princeton University Press, 1979), 15–50.

12. The remainder of this section draws on my paper "Political Legitimacy and the Natural Duty of Justice" (unpublished).

13. John Rawls, *A Theory of Justice* (Cambridge, Mass.: Harvard University Press, 1971), p. 334.

14. For an illuminating and systematic elaboration of this important point, see Jeremy Waldron, "Special Ties and Natural Duties," *Philosophy and Public Affairs* 22 (1993), 22–30.

10

BEYOND THE NATIONAL INTEREST

1. THE DOMINANCE OF A DOGMA

Few would deny that the national interest should play a major role in foreign policy. But often much stronger assertions about the national interest are made or, more frequently, uncritically assumed to be true. The strongest of these, and the one explicitly endorsed by many state leaders, diplomats, and theorists of international relations, is that a state's foreign policy always ought to be determined exclusively by the national interest (the *Obligatory Exclusivity Thesis*).

"Foreign policy" here is understood very broadly, to encompass the state's policies of making war and seeking peace, its posture toward international law, its participation in the global economy through trade treaties, treaties concerning communications infrastructures, participation in international financial regimes, the provision of aid to other countries, including its support of international organizations that attempt to alleviate suffering in countries afflicted by war and natural disasters, and so forth. Hans Morgenthau, one of the most influential international relations theorists of the twentieth century, unambiguously proclaimed the supremacy of the national interest, asserting that it should be "the one guiding star, one standard thought, one rule of action" in foreign policy.[1]

Taken literally, Morgenthau's assertion presupposes that every foreign policy decision affects the national interest one way or the other. Since this is a dubious presupposition, and because I am interested in evaluating the more plausible versions of the idea that the national interest should reign supreme in foreign policy, I will understand the Obligatory Exclusivity Thesis as acknowledging that some decisions may not affect the national interest one way or another and as permitting other considerations to guide policy when this is the case.

Let us say, then, that the Obligatory Exclusivity Thesis is that whenever a policy maker or decision maker has the opportunity to act in a way that furthers the national interest, he or she ought to do so, where "furthering" means maximizing—doing what is best, so far as the national interest is concerned. The Obligatory Exclusivity Thesis implies that where the national interest conflicts with other values, the national interest should always take precedence.

A somewhat weaker claim about the supremacy of the national interest is the Permissive Exclusivity Thesis: It is always permissible for a state's foreign policy to be determined exclusively by the national interest. If a state chooses, it may subordinate all other values to the pursuit of the national interest in any case, in which there is a conflict of values.

To many people who are not diplomats, state leaders, or international relations theorists, even the weaker Permissive Exclusivity Thesis will seem counterintuitive because it seems to allow the most extreme selfishness, allowing a state to refrain from all action to promote the well-being of foreigners or to protect them against the grossest human rights violations even if it could be done at little cost, unless such action best promotes the national interest. It is doubtful, for example, that most citizens of the United States believe that their country's humanitarian aid to famine victims in Ethiopia was justified only if it was the policy choice among those available that maximized U.S. national interest. This is not to say that they believe that the United States should supply foreign aid to the detriment of its more important interests, but rather that some foreign aid is justified even if alternative uses of the same resources would be more beneficial to the United States.

If this is a widely held view, then it is at odds with what appears to be the dominant view among diplomats and state leaders, and probably among international relations theorists as well. The quote from Morgenthau above shows that he endorsed the Obligatory Exclusivity Thesis, and similar quotes could be produced from other prominent international relations theorists. Given that many thoughtful scholars of international relations tend to accept it, the Obligatory Exclusivity Thesis must be taken seriously, even if it seems obviously false to most of us.

My focus in this chapter, however, is on the weaker Permissible Exclusivity Thesis, for two reasons. First, it is less demanding and to that extent should be easier to justify than the Obligatory Exclusivity Thesis; second, if I can show that the Permissive Exclusivity Thesis is indefensible, this will count against the Obligatory version as well: if it is not permissible to do something, then it cannot be obligatory to do it.

In addition to the Permissive Exclusivity Thesis, there are several other claims about the relationship between the national interest and foreign policy worth considering, especially if, as I shall argue, the Permisive Exclusivity and Obligatory Exclusivity Theses ought to be rejected. There is another, more important reason to sort out these various assertions, to determine exactly what is being said about the relationship between foreign policy and the national interest: the popularity in some quarters of the Permissive Exclusivity Thesis may be due to a failure to understand just how extreme it is and a tendency to confuse it with the weaker claims. So clarification must precede evaluation. The following theses about the relationship between foreign policy and the national interest need to be distinguished.

The Permissive Exclusivity Thesis: It is permissible for foreign policy to be determined exclusively by the national interest, whenever there is a policy choice that would have some effect, one way or the other, on the national interest.

The Permissive Protection Thesis: Whenever acting otherwise would cause a serious setback to the national interest, it is permissible for foreign policy to be determined exclusively by the national interest (that is, by what would best reduce the prospects of a serious setback to the national interest).

The Permissive Survivalist Thesis: Whenever acting otherwise would constitute a serious risk to the national survival, it is permissible for foreign policy to be determined exclusively by what will best secure the nation's survival (what maximizes the nation's survival prospects).

Earlier I surmised that many ordinary citizens if asked probably would reject the Permissible Exclusivity Thesis, if only because they believe that humanitarian foreign aid is sometimes justified independently of whether it furthers the national interest at all, much less maximizes it. Nevertheless, at times it appears that there is a rather widespread acceptance of the Permissible Exclusivity Thesis. More specifically, the hypothesis that this thesis is being tacitly assumed explains the severe constraints under which public discussion often proceeds on a wide range of issues from immigration, to humanitarian intervention and preventive war, to international environmental initiatives and regional trade agreements, to participation in or resistance to the process of developing an international criminal court. In all of these cases, the issue is frequently posed, at least in the media and among politicians, as the question of which course of action would be in the national interest.

One should not assume that this shows that public opinion is inconsistent. Instead, it may be the case that although few ordinary citizens actually subscribe to the Permissible Exclusivity Thesis (which applies across the board in foreign policy), many tacitly assume that on certain occasions or in certain areas of foreign policy such as decisions concerning especially important trade agreements or military action abroad, the national interest should reign supreme. They may in fact subscribe not to the Permissible Exclusivity Thesis, but to one or both of its weaker relatives, the Permissible Protection Thesis or the Permissible Survivalist Thesis. Beginning with the stronger thesis I will examine all three claims about the proper role of the national interest in foreign policy.

Recognizing the apparent conflict between the exclusive pursuit of the national interest and commonsense morality, those I shall call *Accommodationists* attempt to make the Permissible Exclusivity Thesis more palatable by showing that properly understood the national interest requires acting in the interests of individuals and groups beyond the state's borders and allows concern for human rights to play a significant role in foreign policy. The accommodationist strategy is to show that the pursuit of national interest, while parochial in principle, is cosmopolitan in practice.

In this chapter I subject the Permissible Exclusivity Thesis to critical examination. I argue that if there are any human rights, then a weighty burden of argument is on those who subscribe to it, not on those who reject it. I then argue that this burden of argument has not been borne—that attempts to justify the Permissible Exclusivity Thesis fail. (An interesting feature of these attempted justifications is that they are almost invariably presented as justifications for the stronger Obligatory Exclusivity Thesis and would support it if sound.) My conclusion will be that those state leaders, diplomats, and international relations theorists who claim to believe in human rights but endorse the Permissible Exclusivity Thesis are in an untenable position. I also show that the accommodationist strategy does not support the Permissible Exclusivity Thesis: if the justifications for the Permissible Exclusivity Thesis fail, then the fact that acting on it would generally not involve failure to respect human rights abroad does nothing to justify the thesis. In addition, I show that even the weaker theses about the supremacy of the national interest are dubious. I conclude by indicating how the character of discourse about foreign policy is transformed, once we embrace the proposition that the pursuit of national interest ought to be constrained by a commitment to protecting the human rights of all persons.

2. ATTEMPTS TO JUSTIFY THE PERMISSIBLE EXCLUSIVITY THESIS

Before proceeding to a critical examination of arguments to support it, I want to stress that the Permissible Exclusivity Thesis needs to be supported. There is nothing natural or commonsensical about the assertion that foreign policy may be—much less ought to be—guided exclusively by the goal of maximizing the national interest. To the contrary, on its face this thesis is diametrically opposed to the acknowledgment that there are human rights—rights that all persons have regardless of whether they are our fellow citizens. It is also apparently at odds with the commonsense belief that a rich and powerful state such as the United States from time to time ought to act charitably toward less fortunate peoples by supplying aid in times of disaster, even if, strictly speaking, justice does not require it. Because the Permissible Exclusivity Thesis itself takes no position on what the national interest is, one cannot assume congruence between pursuit of the national interest and respect for human rights or the promptings of charity.

It is also important to understand that proponents of the Permissible Exclusivity Thesis are wrong if they assume that it only allows the subordination of concerns about the human rights of persons in *other* countries to the pursuit of the national interest. The Permissible Exclusivity Principle asserts that it is permissible, in the domain of foreign policy, to do whatever is necessary to further the national interest, including violating the most basic human rights of anyone whose rights stand in the way of that goal, whether or not he is a fellow citizen. Taken literally, the Permissible Exclusivity Principle is a much more radical doctrine than might first appear.

This neglected point warrants elaboration. It is a mistake to assume that the national interest in any area of policy, including foreign policy, is always congruent with the interest of every citizen. Indeed, to the extent that it makes sense to speak of a national interest as something to be pursued in its own right, it must be something distinct from the interests of each of the citizens, and this means that the national interest and the interests of a particular citizen or group of citizens can be in conflict. Although foreign policy decisions are directed toward preserving or altering relationships between the state and institutions or groups beyond its borders, there can be circumstances in which a particular foreign policy that is directed toward the national interest may be very harmful to some citizens. For example, it might be in the national interest to sacrifice a group of citizens who are being unjustly imprisoned by a foreign power.

And notice that the Permissible Exclusivity Thesis does not require that the nation's survival must be at stake or that sacrificing the interests of these citizens is necessary to avoid a major setback to the national interest. The Permissible Exclusivity Thesis says that it is permissible for foreign policy—not just foreign policy that exclusively affects foreigners (if there ever is such a thing)—to aim exclusively at furthering the national interest, and this implies that it is permissible to do whatever is necessary to best promote that interest.

From this it follows that the most basic interests of citizens may be sacrificed for the sake of any gain with respect to the national interest, not just in extreme cases in which the national survival is at stake or major interests are seriously at risk. Unlike the Permissible Protective Thesis and the Permissible Survivalist Thesis, the Permissible Exclusivity Thesis is unqualified: it asserts that it is permissible to do whatever best serves the national interest and in so doing assumes no threshold magnitude for the benefit to be gained.

So the Permissible Exclusivity Thesis does not recognize the sanctity of human rights at home while denying it abroad; it is thoroughly impartial in subordinating all values, including the protection of human rights in any venue, to the national interest, so far as foreign policy is concerned. Moreover, although I will not press the point further, I think it will be clear that the justifications for the Permissible Exclusivity Thesis would, if sound, entail that human rights at home, as well as abroad, may be subordinate to the national interest.[2] The same reasons that purportedly justify disregarding the human rights of foreigners would, if valid, justify the same treatment for citizens.

In addition, the Permissible Exclusivity Thesis would allow wars of aggression against harmless, rights-respecting countries—if, for example, the national interest (not just the national survival or the need to avoid a major setback to the national interest) required expropriating their oil. Given how abhorrent its apparent implications are, the Permissible Exclusivity Thesis requires a justification.

Before articulating and criticizing attempts to bear this burden of justification, let me make clear the limitations of my critique of the Permissible Exclusivity Thesis. It is not my aim here to refute those who deny that there are human rights. My goal is to show that if there are any human rights then it is not the case that it is permissible for the exclusive goal of foreign policy to be the furthering of the national interest.[3] The targets of my criticism are those who believe they can consistently endorse Permissible Exclusivity and at the same time acknowledge that there are human rights.

The Fiduciary Realist Justification for Permissible Exclusivity. This is the first of three attempts to justify the assertion that foreign policy may be exclusively directed toward maximizing the national interest. Fiduciary Realism holds that the overriding moral obligation of state leaders is to act to maximize the national interest, by virtue of their role as fiduciary.

Proponents of this view often assume that the state leaders are entrusted with serving the well-being of the people of the states they lead, and then use the term "the national interest" as if it were synonymous with the well-being of the people. Later I will criticize this usage, pointing out that on some interpretations the national interest and the interest of the people of the state as a whole are not only distinct but in conflict. But for now I want to show that regardless of which way we interpret "the national interest," the Fiduciary Realist Justification does not justify the Permissible Exclusivity Thesis.

According to the Fiduciary Realist Justification, what is justifiable and even obligatory for state leaders is impermissible for others who do not occupy this role. The proper conduct for state leaders is not to act amorally; they are to serve steadfastly a higher moral principle, subordinating all other values, personal or private, to it. Their fiduciary duty is to conduct foreign policy with an exclusive concern for the national interest. According to this view, exclusive pursuit of the national interest is obligatory and hence trivially it is permissible.

Much more must be said to make this view at all credible, for the simple reason that becoming a fiduciary does not wipe the moral slate clean. If I agree to become your guardian or your financial counselor or your doctor, this does not relieve me of all preexisting moral obligations, and it certainly does not extinguish those obligations that are the correlatives of human rights.

Even a fiduciary role as basic as that of parent does not relieve one of such fundamental moral obligations. There are limits—some of them provided by human rights—as to what a parent may do to save her child. She may not kill someone else's child and take its liver to transplant into her own dying child, for example. So if the Fiduciary Realist argument is to succeed, it must show that this particular fiduciary role—the role of state leader—is profoundly different.

It is at this point that the second term in the phrase "Fiduciary Realism" comes into play. To make the case that state leaders ought to or may subordinate all values to the pursuit of the national interest, it is necessary to embrace a set of empirical beliefs about the world of international relations that is associated with Realism or what might be called Hobbesian Realism. The adjective "Hobbesian" is appropriate because this version of Realism portrays the condition of states in the international system as being like that of individuals in Hobbes's state of nature. (However, Hobbes himself appears to have held that the predicament of states in the international system is not as dire as that of individuals in the state of nature. If that is so, then a Hobbesian conception of international relations is not Hobbes's view of international relations.)

The term "Realism" is used in various ways. I have no wish to provoke a fruitless debate about what "the real Realist view" is. Instead, although I will characterize a position that I believe has as good a claim as any to be called Realist, my main concern is with the position, not the label. The goal is to set out the cluster of beliefs about the facts of international relations that would give credibility to the claim that state leaders as fiduciaries may act exclusively in the national interest so far as foreign policy is concerned.

The view I have in mind portrays the world of international relations as a massive assurance problem. Even if any one state were willing to curb its pursuit of self-interest, it would be irrational to do so under the conditions that obtain in international relations, that is, in the absence of assurance that its self-restraint will not be taken advantage of by other states.[4]

These conditions are said to be as follows: (a) there is no global sovereign, no supreme arbiter of conflicts capable of enforcing rules of peaceful cooperation; (b) there is (approximate) equality of power, such that no state can permanently dominate all others; (c) the fundamental preference of states is to survive; (d) but, given conditions (a), (b), and (c), what is rational for each state to do is to strive by all means available to dominate others in order to avoid being dominated; and (e) in a situation in which all states strive to dominate, without constraints on the means they employ to do so, moral principles are inapplicable.

Contemporary political scientists sometimes utilize a somewhat different conception of Realism which, though consistent with and grounded in the four assumptions stated above, may warrant making explicit. "For political realists, international politics...is a struggle for power but, unlike domestic politics, a struggle dominated by organized violence."[5] On this view relations among states are thoroughly competitive; military competition is the dominant form of international competition; states function as unitary actors whose dominant issue is military security; and whatever cooperation exists among states is derivative on the struggle for military security. In that sense there is only one issue for every state: how to achieve security against hostile force; all other issues matter only so far as they bear on this.

As entrenched as Hobbesian Realism still is in certain quarters, it is untenable. Its sweeping empirical generalizations about international relations are far from being self-evident truisms; they are indeed disconfirmed by a balanced view of the facts. My aim here is not to provide a thorough refutation of Hobbesian Realism but only to sketch the outlines of such a critique in sufficient detail to show that this view of international relations is too flawed to serve in a justification of the Permissible Exclusivity Thesis.

Some of the most interesting work in international relations in the past two decades provides considerable evidence that international relations are not a Hobbesian war of each against all. There are stable patterns of peaceful cooperation, some bilateral, some multistate, some regional, others genuinely global. These include financial regimes, trade agreements, structures for scientific cooperation, environmental accords, and international support for human rights, economic development, labor standards, and disaster relief.

Furthermore, as Keohane and Nye and other critics of Realism point out, it would be dogmatic and inattentive to the facts to say that in all these cases cooperation is derivative on the competition for military dominance.

The issues that concern states are not so hierarchically structured (with military security at the apex of the pyramid) as the Hobbesian Realist assumes. Extensive cooperation occurs in a number of areas in which military security is not a concern.

Survival is not an issue, much less the paramount issue, in many contexts of state interactions. (Consider, for example, relations between Britain and the United States over the last 120 years or so, or relations among most Western European states over the last 50 years.) Nor is it true, as the Hobbesian Realist claims, that states are roughly equal in power and hence in vulnerability. Powerful states can afford to take risks in efforts to build cooperation, and they also face lesser risks of others defecting from cooperative commitments because the costs of betraying their trust may be very high. Furthermore, the information revolution greatly facilitates the communication upon which trust depends.

Perhaps most important, contrary to the Hobbesian Realist, state preferences are neither fixed nor are they uniform among states. The positive (that is explanatory, as distinct from normative) liberal theory of international relations marshals impressive evidence for the thesis that state preferences (more precisely the preferences expressed by state leaders in foreign policy) vary, depending upon the internal character of the state and its domestic society.[6] Of equal significance is the fact that state preferences change over time as a function of the activities of various groups within the state, particularly as these interact with and are empowered by transnational and international governmental and nongovernmental organizations and institutions.

For all of these reasons, Hobbesian Realism's picture of the world of international relations is sufficiently inaccurate to undercut the argument that state leaders have an absolute fiduciary duty to act only in the national interest. Unless all of the very stringent conditions that characterize the Hobbesian conception of international relations obtain, appeals to the nature of international relations cannot support the conclusion that the state leader should act as a fiduciary to serve the national interest without constraint.

The results of my examination of Fiduciary Realism as a justification for the Permissible Exclusivity Thesis can now be summarized. Fiduciary Realism contends that even if respect for human rights should constrain action in other areas of human life, foreign affairs is an exception, because the overriding obligation of the state leader, as a fiduciary, is to further the national interest. This view that as a fiduciary the state leader ought exclusively to pursue the national interest cannot rest merely on the claim that he or she is a fiduciary, since assuming fiduciary duties does not wipe the moral slate clean; in particular, being a fiduciary does not relieve one of the most fundamental moral obligations, including those that are the correlatives of human rights. So if this particular fiduciary is to be in the morally unique position of subordinating all other obligations to the obligation to serve the national interest, it must be because of something special, indeed unique, about the circumstances in which the fiduciary must pursue that goal.

Hobbesian Realism is an attempt to show that the circumstances in which the state leader acts have this special character, but Hobbesian Realism rests on untenable empirical generalizations about the world of international relations. And once Hobbesian Realism is abandoned, there seem to be no grounds for the assertion that the fiduciary role of state leader absolves him of all moral obligations apart from the obligation to serve the national interest.

There is another flaw in the Fiduciary Realist justification for the Permissible Exclusivity Thesis. It lies not in a mistaken understanding of the facts about international relations, but rather in the assumption that the national interest is of such unique moral importance that it makes sense for state leaders to make it the exclusive goal of their endeavors. Consider just how strong the Permissible Exclusivity Thesis is: it entails that pursuing an additional increment of benefit for a nation that is already exceptionally rich and already enjoys excellent protection of human rights *always* should have priority over every other end, including making great improvement in the well-being of the world's worst-off people.

The proponent of Permissible Exclusivity might reply that even if maximizing the national interest is not the most fundamental goal morally speaking, it is the only proper goal for state leaders, who are after all fiduciaries for their peoples. To do otherwise would be to violate the terms of the social compact by which state leaders are empowered to serve as leaders.

This reply begs the question. What is at issue is how we ought to understand the state leader's fiduciary role and in particular whether her obligation to pursue the national interest (or the interests of the people of her state as a whole) is to be understood as absolute or constrained in some way by concern for the human rights of persons in other states. What the proponent of Permissible Exclusivity needs—but has failed to supply—is a cogent account of why, despite the fact that the goal of maximizing the national interest is not a morally fundamental goal, state leaders, as fiduciaries, ought to treat it as if it were. The answer cannot be that this is what they are expected to do as the executors of foreign policy, because our question is what the goal of foreign policy should be.

It will do no good for the advocate of Permissible Exclusivity to appeal to a particular conception of the nature of the state that I have criticized elsewhere, according to which the state is nothing more than an association for the mutual benefit of its own citizens.[7] On this conception, the role of the state leader, as a fiduciary whose overriding obligation is to further the national interest, follows from the nature of the state. She is to serve exclusively the interest of her fellow citizens in all she does, including the conduct of foreign policy, because of what the state is: an instrument whose sole legitimate function is to benefit its citizens. The state leader is simply the agent the state apparatus employs to further the interests of the citizens in the area of foreign policy.

This move merely pushes the normative question back a stage, for now we must ask: why should we conceive of the state as an association for the exclusive benefit of its citizens? If there are human rights, this is not how we should conceive of the state, instead, the state should be thought of as a resource, not only for furthering the interests of its own citizens, but also for helping to ensure the protection of human rights. This is fully compatible, of course, with holding the sensible view that citizens have a special claim on the resources of their state, up to the point that it secures for them an adequate or even a generous level of protection of their human rights.

It is important to understand why asserting that the state is an association for the exclusive benefit of its citizens in defense of the Exclusive Permissibility Thesis begs the question. Precisely what is at issue is whether the state should be regarded exclusively as an instrument for furthering the interests of its citizens or as a resource upon which valid claims of cosmopolitan justice also can be made. What is needed to support Permissible Exclusivity is an argument for *why* the state should be regarded exclusively as an association for the benefit of its members, not a dogmatic essentialist declaration that that is just what the state is.

The Hobbesian Realist view of international relations can be seen as an attempt to provide a reason why the state ought to operate, at least in its foreign policy, exclusively as an association for the benefit of its citizens: no other course of action is rational, given the life-or-death anarchic struggle among states. In other words, even if in principle the state's resources should be used to promote the human rights of persons beyond its borders, in practice we never reach the point where it is rational to do so, due to the Hobbesian nature of international relations. So if it is admitted that it is appropriate for the state leader to attend first to securing adequate protection of human rights for her own citizens, this is all the Hobbesian

Realist needs—if we accept his characterization of international relations. If international relations are a violent anarchic struggle for power among states, the only way a state can achieve an *adequate* level of human rights protection for its own citizens is to make the national interest its exclusive concern in foreign policy. In brief, the Hobbesian Realist can concede that *when the national survival is not at stake*, pursuit of the national interest should not take precedence over human rights, but then quickly add that given the nature of international relations, *the national survival is always at stake.*

However, we have seen that the bleak Hobbesian view of international relations is sufficiently inaccurate that it cannot support such a morally problematic view of the state, nor, consequently, of the role of the state leader as fiduciary. Survival is not always at stake; issues of foreign policy do not all hang together, with every other issue being connected to survival. So our earlier conclusion stands: the Fiduciary Realist justification for the Permissible Exclusivity Thesis fails.

There are, of course, different understandings of the fiduciary role of state leaders, or more generally, government officials, depending upon how the national interest is understood. So far I have marshaled criticisms of the Permissible Exclusivity Thesis that do not depend upon which particular conception of the national interest is employed. Later I will explore the multiple ambiguities of "the national interest" and show that once they are appreciated the Permissible Exclusivity Thesis looks even less cogent; but at this juncture I will only contrast two different understandings of "the national interest."

The Hobbesian Realist understands the national interest in a very determinate, narrow way, as physical security through military dominance. In contrast, some hold that the national interest is the interest of the nation, understood as an ethnonational (or, in the case of fascism, racial) group. The idea here is that the national interest is the interest of the nation living its distinctive kind of life, pursuing its special destiny, and so forth. When combined with the premise that the interest of the nation is the highest moral value, this does entail Permissible Exclusivity. But of course the needed premise is repugnant, both because no rational explanation has ever been given of why the interest of the nation is the highest moral value and because of the atrocities committed by those who proclaim that it is.

Moreover, to hold that the interest of the nation is the supreme moral value is to deny that there are human rights, and I have already stated that I am not concerned with that position in this chapter. Nevertheless, in evaluating the Permissible Exclusivity Thesis we do well to keep in mind the outrages that have been committed in its name.

The Instrumental Justification for Permissible Exclusivity. The second attempt to show that even though there are human rights, it is permissible for foreign policy to be determined exclusively by what best promotes the national interest concedes that although the national interest is not the supreme moral value, conditions in international relations are such that those who conduct foreign policy should act as if it is. Like the Fiduciary Realist Justification, this argument holds that it is irrational to subordinate the national interest to any other concern, though for a different reason. The Instrumental Justification is analogous to arguments that try to show that overall utility is maximized, not by pursuing it directly, but by following rules other than the principle that utility is to be maximized. The Instrumental Justification for Permissible Exclusivity concedes that in principle the pursuit of the national interest ought to be constrained by consideration for the human rights of foreigners, but also holds that under the conditions prevailing in international relations the best outcomes for everyone (or at least for most of humanity) will occur if each state aims exclusively at maximizing the national interest in foreign policy.

For the Instrumental Justification for Permissible Exclusivity to work, it must include a convincing explanation of why respect for the human rights of humanity at large will be achieved by each state exclusively pursuing its national interest. The needed explanation presumably would be of the invisible hand variety—the world-political analog of the theory of the ideal market.

The theory of the ideal market explains how self-interested individuals can achieve mutually beneficial outcomes—but only when a constellation of robust conditions is present, including secure property rights, access to (perfect) information about goods and services, the absence of monopoly, and zero transaction costs. It is difficult to imagine what the analogous conditions would be in the case of international relations, especially since states are quite different from actors in a market.

The fatal weakness of the Instrumental Justification for Permissible Exclusivity is that the needed explanation has not been produced, and it is doubtful that it could be. There are too many obvious instances in which the exclusive pursuit of the national interest results in disregard for the human rights of persons in other states, without off-setting gains in the protection of human rights of others. The difficulty, then, is that there is neither a theory to show why a global harmony of interests would be achieved through the interactions of exclusively self-interested states under certain ideal conditions, nor any reason to believe that if the theory were produced our world would sufficiently approximate these ideal conditions to make the Instrumental Justification for Permissible Exclusivity credible.

Hans Morgenthau offers an interesting twist to the Instrumentalist Justification, one that has the advantage of not requiring an invisible hand explanation. According to Morgenthau, it will be better for humanity, not just for the people of a particular state, if each state exclusively pursues its own interest, because any attempt to shape foreign policy by moral values will lead to moral imperialism and ultimately to fanatical, highly destructive conflicts among states.

Morgenthau thus provides a different reason than that offered by the Hobbesian Realist for why the state ought to be regarded simply as a resource for pursuing the interests of its own citizens, as an association exclusively for their mutual benefit. He holds that this is how the state should be understood because a more ambitious role for the state will lead to disaster for all.[8] Ironically, Morgenthau's defense of the Permissive Exclusivity Thesis is cosmopolitan: it is for the good of humanity that states should exclusively pursue the national interest in their foreign policies.

Morgenthau appears to assume that (1) each society has its own view of morality, that there is little or no commonality of values among societies, and that (2) once a state attempts to guide its foreign policy by morality rather than the national interest, it will eschew tolerance and attempt to enforce its views on other states regardless of costs to others and ultimately to itself.

However, he presents no evidence to show that there are as many moralities as societies, that there is no significant commonality among different societies' moral points of view. He merely observes that the cosmopolitan, aristocratic value system that was previously shared by (Western) diplomats disappeared with the advent of democratization, without considering the possibility that there is growing global culture of basic human rights that represents a minimal moral consensus.

Given that a shared morality performs certain functions that all societies need (they are after all, human societies), it would be very surprising if different societies had as little in common as Morganthau assumes. Indeed we should expect some congruence of basic moral principles across societies, given the roles that morality plays in human life: in particular, coordinating behavior and providing relatively peaceful means for resolving or avoiding the more common mutually destructive conflicts that can occur wherever human beings go about the basic tasks that all humans must perform.

As Stewart Hampshire has observed, there is a lethal tension in the view that there is a fundamental diversity in basic ethical principles, because for something to count as a *basic* ethical principle it must be grounded in and responsive to human interests (rather than in the parochial interests that some humans happen to have).[9] By the most basic ethical principles Hampshire means those that prohibit behavior resulting in the worst harms to which human beings—all human beings—are vulnerable. But if this is so, then it is hard to see how different societies, so long as they are societies of human beings, could disagree greatly in their most basic ethical principles.

More important, Morgenthau's argument overlooks the fact that there is an apparently broadening global culture of basic human rights, evidenced not only by human rights treaties signed by states, but by the growing power of transnational organizations to exert pressure on states to comply with these treaties.[10] It is true that there is disagreement about the precise contours of even some of the least controversial human rights and much controversy about whether some rights—especially those recognizing robust economic entitlements—really are human rights. But none of this should blind one to the fact that there is considerable consensus on a minimal, core conception of human rights that include the rights against slavery and involuntary servitude, the rights to physical security of the person, including the right not to be tortured or to be subject to arbitrary arrest, and the right not to be excluded from political participation on the basis of race.

In addition, this growing consensus on basic human rights operates within an international institutional framework that places significant constraints on the moral imperialism that Morgenthau rightly dreads, in at least two respects. First, the idea of human rights still functions within a state-centered system that values state sovereignty very highly and an international legal system that prohibits humanitarian intervention without UN Security Council authorization and also prohibits aggressive war. Second, due to the admission of newly liberated colonial peoples in the 1960s and 1970s to the United Nations and to the institutions of international law and politics generally, and due to the growing appreciation for cultural diversity in the most developed and powerful states, it is more difficult for any state to try to impose on the world its own peculiar conception of morality.

Morgenthau also wrongly assumes a sharp distinction between the national interest and a society's moral values. This is to proceed as if the national interest is something exogenously determined, as if a group's interest is in no way shaped by its conception of its relationship to the realization of its moral values. But if the national interest and the society's moral values are not so separable, then the attempt to avoid what Morgenthau takes to be the risks of a morally guided foreign policy by cleaving to the pursuit of national interest is doomed.

Finally, Morgenthau overlooks the possibility that one way to reduce the risk of moral imperialism and hence the destruction it causes is to establish international legal structures that recognize the importance of diversity by helping to secure for all persons the rights to freedom of religion and freedom of conscience as well as a prohibition against aggressive war. Yet for these structures to function effectively, they require support from states, especially powerful ones, and sometimes in circumstances that do not best promote the national interest.[11] Reducing the risk of moral imperialism may in fact be incompatible with the exclusive pursuit of the national interest.

Presumably what Morgenthau had in mind when he warned against forsaking national interest for morality was the danger of states attempting to impose grand ideologies like fascism or communism through total war. But the risk of efforts to guide foreign policy by a modern conception of human rights that accords priority to the most minimal, widely accepted human rights and recognizes the value of diversity of cultures within the constraints of that minimum is clearly much lower.

Even if one state—say the world's one superpower—were to attempt to impose its own conception of justice or of the good society on the world, there is little reason to believe that it would do so at the risk of total war in an era of nuclear and other weapons of mass destruction. U.S. "moral imperialism," even during the Cold War, operated within the constraint of a fundamental commitment to avoiding a war among the great powers. To take only one example: fear of a nuclear confrontation with the Soviet Union or a large-scale conventional war with China led U.S. foreign policy makers to observe rather severe constraints on the use of military force to prevent South Vietnam from being controlled by communists.

Moreover, in the current context in which the most serious violent conflicts occur within states, Morgenthau's assertion that we reduce the risk of violence by setting aside concern for human rights and pursuing only the national interest rings hollow. Today the subordination of human rights and other moral concerns to national interest often takes the form of the oppression of national minorities. The pursuit of national interest, rather than being an effective strategy for peace as Morgenthau envisioned it, has proved to be a recipe for violent internal conflict that often spills across borders. (One might overlook this fundamental point if one wrongly believed that each state contains one nation and that therefore the pursuit of the national interest serves the interests of everyone in the state.)

Morgenthau's admonition to states to stick to the pursuit of national interest might be sound advice for a world in which the major threat to human well-being is horrendously destructive competition for world domination among states driven by intolerant, totalizing ideologies, unconstrained by a global culture of human rights, by international institutions prohibiting aggressive war and upholding the sovereignty of states, and by a resolve on the part of the most powerful states to avoid global total war; but this is not to say that it is wise counsel for our world.

The flaw in Morgenthau's defense of Permissible Exclusivity is that it wrongly assumes that the only alternatives are (1) the exclusive pursuit of national interest (somehow defined in a morally neutral way) and (2) unconstrained moral imperialism. So Morgenthau's argument from the risk of pursuing moral values in foreign policy does not justify the Permissible Exclusivity Thesis.

The Epistemic Justification. Recent statements by U.S. National Security Advisor Condoleezza Rice suggest another argument for Permissible Exclusivity, though as with the Fiduciary Justification, the conclusion actually stated seems to be the stronger Obligatory Exclusivity Thesis.[12] She asserts that U.S. foreign policy should be based on "the firm ground of national interest" rather than on "the illusory interests of the international community." Taken at face value, this appears to be an assault on a strawman, since virtually no one advocates that U.S. foreign policy should be determined solely or even mainly by the interests of the international community, if this means whatever interests all or most states have in common. Perhaps instead Rice is trying to make a point about the epistemic accessibility of alternative goals for policy: the national interest is concrete and knowable (and in that sense "firm ground"), whereas moral values—at least those that are not encompassed by U.S. national interest—are indeterminate and a matter of unresolvable controversy (hence "illusory"). Therefore, pursuit of the national interest is the only practicable goal for foreign policy.

Now presumably Rice would concede that at least in the case of the United States a commitment to protecting the human rights of its own citizens is an important constituent of the national interest. If this is so, then pursuit of the national interest requires that we know what is conducive to the human rights of Americans, and this in turn requires that we have some fairly clear idea of what human rights are and what respecting them requires. But if the goal of protecting our fellow citizens' human rights is sufficiently determinate to guide policy, why is a direct concern for the human rights of others an unsuitable consideration for policy?[13]

Of course there can be complicated issues about what policy best promotes human rights, especially in societies with different cultures and political systems from our own But there is nothing in principle more determinate about the goal, simply because it is to be pursued abroad.

This is certainly true for the most basic human rights. For example, though it would be more difficult to achieve, the goal of ensuring that all people are free from slavery or have enough to eat or are not subject to arbitrary arrest and torture by the police is no more an indeterminate end than doing the same for Americans. No doubt there often will be special difficulties in knowing how best to bring about this end in societies quite different from ours, but it would be very implausible to hold that we so seldom have sufficient knowledge about what would improve the human rights of people abroad that we ought to banish concern for their human rights from foreign policy discourse and cleave only to the pursuit of our national interest.

There is one interpretation of "national interest" that might be thought to lend some plausibility to the claim that it is a better goal for foreign policy because it is more determinate and knowable. If *national interest* can be reduced to *national survival*, then there is something to be said for the view that *when national survival is at stake*, the first order of business is to act in the national interest, that is, to do what is necessary to ensure the national survival. And there may be circumstances in which we can know just which set of actions are necessary. On this interpretation of the Epistemic Justification for Permissible Exclusivity, the point is that sticking with basics—and what could be more basic than survival?—is a firmer basis for foreign policy than pursuing more ambitious and less determinate goals.

If this is what is meant, then what is being advanced is an argument for the much weaker Permissible *Survivalist* Thesis, the claim that when the national survival is at stake, it is permissible to do whatever is necessary to secure it, not an argument for the Permissible Exclusivity Thesis, which does not limit the scope of the permission to matters of survival. This is a distinction of great practical importance because much mischief is done by proceeding as if whenever the national interest is at stake the national survival hangs in the balance. The point of the critique of Hobbesian Realism is that this is not so.

However, whether we take the Epistemic Argument at face value, as an argument for the stronger Permissible Exclusivity Thesis, or as an argument for the Permissible Survivalist Thesis, it has several serious flaws. First, as the current U.S. situation shows, it will often not be possible to know just what should be done to ensure the national survival and hence the national interest so far as survival is an important component of it (assuming, which seems dubious, that global terrorism really is a threat to America's survival—as opposed to a threat to her extraordinary dominance, high standard of living, and the exceptional sense of security her citizens have enjoyed until recently). Should the United States focus on destroying the terrorist group Al Qaeda? Invade Syria? Exert more pressure for a Mid-East peace settlement? Become independent of foreign oil? Provide substantial economic aid to countries that are likely to spawn terrorism? If all of the above, which should be given priority?

To take another example, consider the predicament of Britain in 1940 after the fall of France. Was it so clear that the national survival of Britain required fighting on alone after the fall of France, as opposed to negotiating a settlement with Hitler that would have preserved Britain and the Empire and bought time to enlist American support if Hitler violated the agreement? In some, perhaps many cases, it may be easier to know whether a particular policy will promote or adversely affect the human rights of persons in some other country than to know what best promotes our own survival prospects.

Second, there is one respect in which guiding foreign policy by a concern for human rights is *less* epistemically demanding and *more* determinate than subordinating policy exclusively to national interest, at least if the latter is understood to include more than survival. Working with other states and international and transnational organizations to ensure that all persons enjoy the most basic human rights is a much more *minimal* goal than maximizing the national interest. The latter presents a moving target; so long as the state and its citizens can be made better off, the task is never complete. In that sense, the national interest is indeterminate.

There is one more interpretation of the claim that the national interest is a more determinate, and hence more suitable goal, than any other, including the protection of human rights. On this reading the national interest is identified with the state's *power*, understood as the capacity to achieve our ends, especially by being able to get others to do what we want, whatever our ends happen to be.

The difficulty with this way of trying to support Permissible Exclusivity is twofold. First, it is not clear that the maximization of power is a determinate goal—instead it appears to be a moving target that is never reached. So from the standpoint of epistemic accessibility it is hardly a winner. Second, taken literally the goal of maximizing power is irrational: rather than maximizing one's assets for action a rational agent will attempt to achieve an appropriate balance of acquiring and maintaining assets for future action (investment) and making choices that reduce assets for future action (consumption). But if the goal is to optimize (not maximize) power, it seems farfetched to say that optimizing, that is, selecting the proper tradeoff between the pursuit of power and its use to achieve one's goals, is more epistemically accessible than any other goal, especially the protection of basic human rights. Knowing when to use the power one has and when to seek more power, when one cannot do both simultaneously, is often not easy. It may in fact be more difficult than knowing how a particular foreign policy decision would affect basic human rights of persons in another country.

For Rice's argument to work, it would not only have to do a much better job of showing that the national interest is a more determinate and hence a more practical goal for policy than any other. It would also have to show that the national interest is so much more epistemically accessible as a goal for foreign policy than any other consideration, including concern for basic human rights, that a rational agent would opt for pursuing the national interest, no matter what the opportunity costs—regardless of what would be lost by narrowing the scope of policy in this way.

Of course, how much would be lost from a moral point of view will depend upon whether and how frequently the exclusive pursuit of national interest will mean acting in ways that detract from the protection of human rights. The accommodationist strategy, which I examine in the next section, is to argue that in general the pursuit of national interest, properly conceived, is congruent with the protection of human rights. For now I wish only to emphasize that there is no reason to believe that in general, the national interest is a "firmer ground" for foreign policy than a commitment to basic human rights in the sense of being more determinate and hence easier to know how to achieve.

Once we realize that the common situation for policy choice is not one in which survival is at issue, we can begin to see just how indeterminate and epistemically problematic the national interest is, quite apart from the fact that if it is to be maximized there is no end to what its pursuit requires. The "nation" must either be a misleading label for the citizenry as a whole or it must refer to a group of individuals united by a shared national identity (a nation in the ethno-national or racial sense), where this implies a common understanding of the history of the nation, an aspiration for self-government, and whatever other characteristics distinguish nations from mere collections of citizens, cultural groups, and so on.

Consider the former alternative, that the nation whose interests is to be furthered is the citizenry of the state as a whole. Not only is it not clear what the interest of the citizenry as a whole is; there is much dispute, including much moral controversy, about how it ought to be understood. For utilitarians the interest of the citizenry as a whole is determined by aggregating the gains and losses for each citizen with respect to every policy option. What is in the national interest understood in this way is whatever maximizes utility for that whole group. But for those who regard rights as fundamental moral considerations, maximizing the interest of the whole group of citizens must be constrained by respect for the rights of individuals and perhaps minority groups as well. The firm ground of national interest, understood as the interest of the citizenry, turns out to be a place-holder for the most basic disputes in political theory, those that concern the proper way to understand the common good so far as this is to be the object of state policy.

On the second alternative "nation" means what it says, referring not just to the citizens of a state, but to a particular kind of group, one whose members are co-nationals in the sense of being united by a common identity that includes a shared belief in the nation's history, its distinctive character, etc. Though we commonly speak of nation-states, and pretend that the interest of the state is the same as the interest of a nation, almost all states contain more than one nation in this sense, and all contain a plurality of cultural, political, and religious as well as socioeconomic groups, with distinct and sometimes conflicting interests. So the question immediately arises: why should the goal of foreign policy privilege the interest of the nation and thereby relegate the interests of all these other groups to an inferior status?

The Permissible Exclusivity Thesis provides a powerful weapon for so-called nation-building, which in virtually every case is nation-breaking, the destruction of all national groups except the one that has captured control of the state, and of all religious and cultural groups as well. Given the weakness of the justifications for Permissible Exclusivity, the fact that its acceptance carries this potential for grave harm is a strike against it.

If we jettison the fiction of the nation-state and realize that the state virtually always contains more than one nation, as well as various other sorts of groups that are important sources of identity and well-being for individuals, how exactly is the state leader or maker of foreign policy to know what the national interest is? The *national interest* in the multinational, multicultural state may prove to be exceedingly elusive—unless it is taken to be consticuted primarily by the protection of every citizen's basic human rights. In what sense, then, is the national interest "firmer ground" than a commitment to human rights, where human rights are understood as providing a moral minimum to which all persons are entitled? If the national interest consists of the protection of all citizens' basic human rights plus the protection of appropriate group rights for minorities, it is even less plausible to say that it is a more determinate goal than respect for the basic human rights of foreigners.

I conclude that the Epistemic Justification for the Permissible Exclusivity Thesis also fails. It either construes the national interest narrowly as survival, in which case it relies on the same distorted Hobbesian characterization of international relations that undermines the Fiduciary Realist Justification, or it construes the national interest more comprehensively, in which case the national interest is ambiguous, disputable, and far from being an especially determinate goal for foreign policy.

3. THE ACCOMMODATIONIST STRATEGY

I noted earlier that the Permissible Exclusivity Thesis itself is neutral as to whether adherence to it will in fact involve disregard for human rights. The Fiduciary Realist, Instrumental, and Epistemic arguments attempt to justify Permissible Exclusivity *independently* of whether it can be shown that exclusive pursuit of the national interest can accommodate respect for human rights. I have argued that each of these arguments is flawed. I now turn to attempts to show that even if in principle the implications of the Permissible Exclusivity Thesis are morally unacceptable, in practice they are benign.

The central point is that even if the accommodationist strategy succeeds in showing that acting on the Permissible Exclusivity Thesis does not have morally unacceptable consequences, this is *not* a justification for it. The fact (if it is a fact) that acting on the Permissible Exclusivity Thesis need not involve disregard for the rights of persons in other countries only rebuts one argument *against* Permissible Exclusivity—namely, that its consequences are morally repugnant—it does not supply a reason *for accepting* Permissible Exclusivity. In fact, the accommodationist, if she knows what she is about, is not concerned with justifying Permissible Exclusivity; instead she addresses her claim that the pursuit of national interest and morality are congruent to those who are already convinced that there is a strong if not conclusive case for exclusively pursuing the national interest.

I now want to distinguish two different types of views that might lead one to pursue the accommodationist strategy. The first, which I shall call the human rights accommodationist view, holds that there are human rights—that all persons, whether they are our fellow citizens or not—can make valid claims of justice on us, that there are certain fundamental obligations that we owe to all persons as such.

Because they believe there are human rights, accommodationists of this sort believe that a direct concern for human rights *should* guide foreign policy; but they also believe that in fact states will exclusively pursue the national interest. So they try to persuade state leaders that it is in fact in the national interest to pursue a foreign policy that respects the human rights of foreigners. For example, the human rights accommodationist argues that the ability of the United States to secure the national interest depends in part upon whether the world perceives its actions to be legitimate and that this in turn depends upon whether those actions exhibit a degree of impartiality and hence regard for the human rights of persons generally, not just Americans. Human rights accommodationists do not endorse the Permissible Exclusivity Thesis—they reject the position that states *should* exclusively pursue the national interest. But because they believe that this is what states will do, they opt for second-best, trying to convince state leaders that the best way to further the national interest is to do what they would do if they took human rights seriously, independently of any contribution they might make to the national interest.

The second sort of accommodationist may be called subjectivist. Subjectivist accommodationists are skeptical about human rights—unwilling to endorse the assertion that persons as such have fundamental moral claims on us. Instead, they operate on the assumption that at least the people of their own country do in fact care about the well-being and freedom of foreigners, perhaps to such an extent that this concern is partly constitutive of their identity as a people and therefore is a component of the national interest.[14]

Subjectivist accommodationists can concede that this concern for others is often expressed in the language of human rights and that this form of discourse attributes entitlements to others, not just preferences on our part for their welfare. However, they are skeptical about the moral objectivism implied by the language of human rights. Subjectivist accommodationists prefer simply to note that we do care about foreigners, and that our sense of ourselves as a people includes the awareness that we do. The subjectivist accommodationists' goal is to show that the pursuit of the national interest is not in fact in conflict with honoring this component of our identity, that indeed so far as our national interest depends in part upon that identity we ought to include concern for foreigners in our foreign policy. This position warrants the label "subjectivist" because it treats the apparent commitment to human rights as in fact nothing more than a very deep preference for taking the welfare of foreigners into account. If we can be said to have obligations to foreigners at all (other than those we undertake through promises, treaties, etc.), this can only mean that we ought to treat them in certain ways in order to be true to who we are—assuming that we are people who do care deeply about them. The second sort of accommodationism, then, is compatible with an outright denial that there are any human rights. Unlike the human rights accommodationists, subjectivist accommodationists can wholeheartedly embrace the Permissible Exclusivity Thesis; for them it is not a second-best.

Yet as with the human rights accommodationist, subjectivist accommodationists should not be seen as offering a justification for Permissible Exclusivity. Both assume that Permissible Exclusivity is the dominant view and simply seek to reconcile its acceptance with the pursuit of a foreign policy that shows some respect for human rights abroad. Human rights accommodationists seek this reconciliation because they believe that the best hope for human rights, in a world in which states will in fact exclusively pursue the national interest, is to persuade state leaders that the national interest requires respect for human rights. Subjectivist accommodationists seek this reconciliation because they want to convince those who happen to care about the well-being and freedom of foreigners that they can act on this concern while exclusively pursuing the national interest—that there need be no conflict between acting on the concern they happen to have for foreigners and the national interest. Neither does anything to establish that Permissible Exclusivity is the correct view. Neither mitigates the fact that the arguments for Permissible Exclusivity are insufficient to establish it.

Here it might be objected that there is a third way to understand the accommodationist strategy that *does* serve to justify Permissible Exclusivity. One way we justify a principle of action is to show that following it would lead to outcomes that we independently believe to be right. Thus if it can be shown that the pursuit of the national interest does in fact require a foreign policy that respects the human rights of foreigners this will count toward the justification of Permissible Exclusivity.

The difficulty with this way of understanding the accommodationist project will be familiar to those who know the literature on utilitarianism. The mere fact (if it is a fact) that maximizing social utility would require treating people fairly does not show that utilitarianism is the correct view, if the same moral intuitions that tell us that people ought to be treated fairly are based on principles of justice explain why maximization of social utility is not itself a fundamental moral goal.

Hence the fact (if it is a fact) that following the principle of utility would yield the right answers does nothing to justify utilitarianism, if the moral principles that best fit our firmest moral intuitions about particular cases imply that even when utilitarianism gets the answer right it does so for the wrong reason. To borrow an example from Rawls: even if it could be shown that as a matter of fact, utilitarianism would prohibit slavery (because there would in fact be few if any cases in which the well-being of the masters would exceed the misery of the slaves), *that* is not why slavery is wrong; it is wrong because it violates a fundamental principle of the equality of persons that cannot be reduced to the utilitarian principle that everyone's preferences are to be counted.[15] In brief, what is fundamentally wrong with slavery is not that it fails to maximize utility, but that it violates the most basic rights of persons as autonomous beings. Similarly, if we believe that the chief reason the good of foreigners should count is that they have human rights, the fact (if it is a fact) that the pursuit of national interest is compatible with taking their good into account does nothing to show that Permissible Exclusivity is the correct fundamental principle.

The central point here is that our belief that others have moral claims on us is not a brute intuition. We can back it up with an account of the moral importance of the basic, common interests of human beings that ground their rights, an account that does *not* portray the importance of these interests as being dependent upon the contribution which protecting them makes to furthering the national interest. But because that is so, the mere fact (if it is a fact) that the exclusive pursuit of national interest would honor those claims does nothing to justify the Permissible Exclusivity Thesis.

4. EXPLAINING THE POPULARITY OF THE PERMISSIBLE EXCLUSIVITY THESIS

Given the weakness of the putative justifications for the Permissible Exclusivity Thesis, we need an explanation of its popularity. It is not so hard to explain why state leaders would find Permissible Exclusivity attractive and encourage its acceptance by their fellow citizens. Because of the elasticity of the notion of national interest, acceptance of Permissible Exclusivity greatly augments the power of state leaders, since it allows them to pursue the national interest without constraint, whenever faced with a decision that will affect the national interest one way or another. And for leaders who seek to base their power on appeals to nationalism, the idea that all that matters is the national interest provides them with a powerful resource for manipulating public opinion and sentiment—and for mobilizing co-nationals against supposed enemies within or outside the state. To explain the appeal of the Permissible Exclusivity Thesis to others, especially to those who are not already motivated by a deeply felt nationalism, may be somewhat more difficult.

The more general appeal of Permissive Exclusivity may be mainly negative: it looks attractive because what is assumed to be the alternative is so unpalatable.

There are two different assumptions about what the alternative is that cast Permissive Exclusivity in a comparatively favorable light. But neither assumption, I shall argue, is plausible.

Sometimes those who support Permissive Exclusivity proceed as if the only alternative is a kind of starry-eyed utopianism, an attempt to implement principles of justice right here and now, without regard for the realities of power and the fallibilities of human beings.[16] However, to assume that this is the only alternative to exclusive pursuit of the national interest is either to confuse appeals to morality with moralizing or to overlook the distinction between ideal and nonideal normative theory that those who take human rights seriously can and often do observe.[17]

As a pejorative term, "moralizing" presumably refers to naive attempts to change behavior solely by appeals to moral principles, perhaps combined with a tendency to see issues that are not truly moral issues as being so. Plainly, those who appeal to the importance of human rights and their relevance to foreign policy need not be guilty of these errors. The most effective human rights activists demonstrate by their behavior that appeals to morality alone do not suffice, but must be accompanied by efforts to create additional incentives for moral behavior (for example, by lobbying with the European Union to make better protection of human rights a condition for admission of new states). And a moral view that focuses on the most basic human rights as minimal standards can hardly be accused of injecting morality into all areas of human life. So the charge that appealing to human rights as a constraint on the pursuit of the national interest is *moralizing* is not cogent.[18]

It is also a mistake to assume that those who believe that human rights should play a role in foreign policy naively believe that actions we could undertake now in the name of morality will produce a perfectly just world or that they are unaware that premature or ill-crafted efforts at reform can be counterproductive. Those who take human rights seriously need not neglect the distinction between ideal and nonideal theory.

Ideal theory specifies the general principles that a just world order would conform to; nonideal theory proposes second-best principles for our far-from-ideal world and attempts to show how we should go about the task of moving closer toward the ideal situation. To recognize the distinction between ideal and nonideal theory is to acknowledge that how we strive for justice must take considerations of feasibility into account.

In fact the ideal/nonideal distinction is often tacitly invoked by human rights advocates when they are confronted with the question of how to respond to human rights violations. For example, many human rights activists acknowledge that although female genital mutilation (at least when it involves total excision of the clitoris) is a violation of human rights, nothing whatsoever follows from this about the advisability of attempting to force people to stop engaging in the practice. They understand that attempts to force this reform, especially if they originate from outside the cultures in which clitidorectomy is practiced, may well be counterproductive and are also likely to be implemented in ways that show disrespect for people in other cultures that are still suffering the effects of colonialism.

In other words, one can acknowledge that certain practices violate basic human rights, but also recognize that efforts to end them must be informed by considerations of feasibility broadly understood. Believing that human rights should matter in foreign policy need not entail stupidity or callous disregard for history and cultural context.

There are, of course, many mistakes that advocates of reform in the name of justice can make if they fail to take seriously the distinction between ideal and nonideal theory and along with it the distinction between being justified in condemning a practice and being justified in intervening to change it. But the fact that this is so does nothing to establish that states should only pursue the national interest and never allow moral considerations to shape their foreign policy.

It may be that contemporary proponents of Permissible Exclusivity overestimate the danger that any commitment to human rights will result in stupidly destructive utopianism because they subscribe to an interpretation of the causes of World War II associated with T. H. Carr's extraordinarily influential views in the second edition of *The Twenty Years Crisis*. On this reading of Carr, his point is that the utopianism (or moralizing idealism) of the Western powers in the interwar years gave fascism room to grow until it became such an obviously grave threat that there was no alternative but total war to extirpate it. According to this account, the leaders of the world's most powerful democracies committed two profound errors: first, they underestimated how ruthless the fascists were, naively thinking that appeals to moral principles would constrain them, when in fact only force would have been effective; second, the fact that they had scruples concerning human rights or other moral values, while the fascists did not, put them at a disadvantage in the deadly game of power politics.

If this is the reason for assuming that any current attempt to constrain pursuit of the national interest by respect for human rights is mistaken, it is almost laughably inadequate. First, it is implausible to hold that a chief source of the Western powers' failure to nip fascism in the bud was fastidiousness about human rights or a naive belief in the power of appeals to morality. A more plausible hypothesis is that a combination of other factors were at work: the unwillingness of politicians to press for the huge sacrifices that rearmament would entail during a period of unprecedented economic depression, the willingness to sacrifice weaker countries in hope that it would sate the fascists' appetites, the lack of a clearly articulated and institutionally embodied global culture of human rights, and the absence of an unambiguous, firmly entrenched international legal prohibition on aggressive war. It is simply a mistake to assume that what lead to World War II was a naive faith on the part of Western leaders and diplomats that fascism could be contained by piously intoning principles of justice or a blind devotion to human rights.

A more likely hypothesis is that it was the failure to take serious measures to protect human rights, not a concern about them, that encouraged the fascists. Indeed, it can be argued that appeals to the national interest served to rationalize allowing other countries to be crushed by the fascists. (To paraphrase Chamberlain: Who are the Czechs to us?)

Second, even if had been shown that a major cause of World War II was a failure of those who believed in human rights to appreciate how ruthless the fascists were and how immune they were to moral appeals to desist from their aggressions or a blind devotion to human rights that overlooked questions of feasibility, this would hardly be sufficient to establish the grand, sweeping generalization that it is always permissible to subordinate respect for human rights to the pursuit of the national interest. To draw such a large conclusion from one case would be to over-interpret the data to an astonishing degree.

There is another explanation of the popularity of the Permissible Exclusivity Thesis that does not rest upon the false assumption that the only alternative to exclusive pursuit of the national interest is a stupidly self-defeating, moralizing utopianism. It assumes, instead, that we are faced with a choice between exclusive pursuit of the national interest and a thoroughly impartial cosmopolitanism that allows no special priority at all for the national interest. This view assumes that once we concede that the national interest should not be the end all and be all of foreign policy, we have committed ourselves to something that most would find quite unpalatable: the position that our national interest should be fully subordinate to the demands of global justice, that our state should count our interests no more than the interests of foreigners, and that consequently we must be prepared to sacrifice our national interest for the sake of morally improving the world.

Like the claim that anyone who believes that the pursuit of national interest should be constrained by regard for human rights is a stupidly self-defeating, moralizing utopian, this is a caricature of the position it attacks. To deny that the national interest may always take precedence over human rights concerns one need not embrace the equally extreme position that the national interest counts for nothing or should always be subordinate. For one thing, given that the world is divided up into states—and given the absence of a world government capable of promoting the interests of humanity—there is good reason for having a division of moral labor in which individual states are held primarily responsible for the welfare of their own citizens.

However, this is not to say that states must be understood as having an unconstrained mandate to maximize the national interest no matter what. When a state has secured an adequate level of human rights protection for all its citizens, it can no longer plausibly plead that the fate of those in other countries is none of its concern. For those who have the good fortune to live in states where human rights are generally well protected to continue to devote all the resources of their state exclusively to maximizing their own well-being when many in other states lack minimal protection for their most basic human rights is not compatible with taking human rights seriously.

The choice, then, is not between the Permissible Exclusivity Thesis and a thorough-going impartial cosmopolitanism that rejects any special place for the national interest. Once this simple point is acknowledged, it is no longer possible to justify Permissible Exclusivity by claiming that the alternative to embracing it is unacceptable.

Notice, also, how unpersuasive it would be to argue that once we admit considerations other than the national interest into the foreign policy debate, we will be on a slippery slope toward the excesses of human rights utopianism or thoroughly impartial cosmopolitanism. If history is any indication of what the future will be like, the danger is not that states will neglect the national interest in an ecstasy of self-sacrificial cosmopolitanism. On the contrary, the greater risk is that they will continue in systematically devaluing the claims of persons in other states.

The popularity of the Permissible Exclusivity Thesis both reflects and supports this self-interested bias. Rejecting Permissible Exclusivity opens up the possibility for direct advocacy of a moderate cosmopolitanism, with the hope that at least to some small extent this may counteract the tendency toward exclusive preoccupation with the national interest.

5. THE RETREAT FROM PERMISSIBLE EXCLUSIVITY: EVALUATING THE WEAKER NATIONAL INTEREST THESES

The results of my analysis thus far can be summarized: (1) Both the Obligatory and the Permissible Exclusivity Theses require a justification, because they evidently allow what we ordinarily regard as extremely immoral behavior, including the violation of the most basic human rights. (2) The putative justifications for the Permissible Exclusivity Thesis—the Fiduciary Realist, Instrumental, and Epistemic arguments—do not succeed. (3) Even if the accommodationist strategy succeeds—even if it can be shown that judicious pursuit of the national interest will take the human rights of foreigners seriously—this does not justify the Permissible Exclusivity Thesis. (4) If the Permissible Exclusivity Thesis is not justified, then *a fortiori* the stronger Obligatory Exclusivity Thesis, which implies it, is not justified. (5) If one believes in human rights, then one cannot consistently endorse the Permissible Exclusivity Thesis (nor, *a fortiori*, the stronger Obligatory Exclusivity Thesis). I also argued that (6) rejecting the Permissible Exclusivity Thesis does not commit one to either of two unpalatable alternatives: stupidly counterproductive, moralizing utopianism or an extreme cosmopolitan position that allows no preference at all for the interests of one's own state or its citizens. Now I want to examine briefly two related, but much weaker and accordingly more plausible theses about the role of national interest in foreign policy that I distinguished earlier: the Permissible Protection Thesis and the Permissible Survivalist Thesis.

Consider first the Permissible Protection Thesis, which asserts that in foreign policy it is always permissible to do whatever is necessary to avert a major setback to the national interest. If this thesis is correct, then there is no need to examine the Permissible Survivalist Thesis, since a threat to survival surely counts as a major setback to the national interest if anything does. If the Permissible Protection Thesis is correct, then the correctness of the Permissible Survivalist Thesis follows trivially.

As a general statement about what is permissible for any state to do, the Permissible Protection Thesis is implausible, unless it is combined with the qualification that *national interest* is restricted to *legitimate interests*. To see why this is so, consider the following example.

Through a long process involving repeated, large-scale violations of basic human rights, a state has come to have a national interest in preserving a system of colonial domination upon which its exceptional prosperity depends. In fact, the state is unlikely to survive without these ill-gotten gains; if it loses its colonies it will likely fragment into two or more states and the economic well-being of its people will probably decline severely. Moreover, if the state disintegrates, then the nation that controls it (the dominant nationality) will suffer a very serious setback to its interests; it will no longer control its own state but will be forced to accommodate the interests of other nationalities in one or the other of the multinational states that are likely to emerge from the disintegration. Finally, suppose that the state's leaders are faced with a stark policy choice: if they pursue policy A they will be able to preserve their colonial rule and with it the state and the dominance of the nation; if they pursue policy B, which is to cooperate in the peaceful liberation of the colonies, the state will be imperiled and the nation that dominates the state will suffer a major setback to its interests. According to the Permissible Protection Principle, it is permissible for the state leaders to choose option A; but if there are human rights and if the colonial domination from which the state and the nation is now profiting involves violations of them, then it may be wrong to choose option A.

The point of this example is that illegitimate national interests cannot trump human rights. So unless one is willing to deny that there are human rights, one must reject the Permissible Protection Thesis.

This is not to say that the need to avert a major setback to the national interest can never justify acting in a way that has adverse consequences for the human rights of foreigners. To take the human rights of foreigners seriously does not entail that regard for their human rights must always be overriding. For example, if the "serious setback to the national interest" is a dangerous erosion of the state's ability to protect its own citizens' human rights, then a reasonable preference for ourselves and our fellow citizens may allow a foreign policy choice that avoids this "setback to the national interest" even at the expense of forgoing the protection of the human rights of foreigners. Similarly, rejection of the Permissible Protection Principle is consistent with acknowledging that if our country is unjustly attacked (or perhaps even only credibly threatened with dire harm), it is permissible for us to respond with lethal force and to act in other ways that would otherwise count as clear violations of human rights were it not for the fact that we are victims of aggression. Yet even in such cases a kind of proportionality principle is applicable:

only the most serious setbacks to *the more important legitimate national interests* would justify policies that are prejudicial to the basic human rights of foreigners who have done us no wrong.

So unless the Permissible Protection Principle is significantly revised by restricting it to efforts to protect legitimate national interests of exceptional importance, it is not consistent with taking human rights seriously. The Permissible Protection Principle itself is unacceptable.

Consider now the Permissible Survivalist Principle. It suffers the same defect that afflicts the unqualified version of the Permissible Protection Principle: it fails to distinguish between legitimate and illegitimate interests. Even the interest in national survival can be illegitimate in the sense of having little or no moral weight to counterpoise against our obligations regarding human rights. Could anyone (other than a Nazi) believe that the survival of the Third Reich was an absolute value, that it was permissible to subordinate all other values, including human rights, to its preservation? Political entities are not super-persons, with the rights of persons writ large; they are institutional structures to serve human welfare. But even persons do not have an unlimited right to do whatever is necessary to survive.

Suppose that the "national interest" as it occurs in the Permissible Survivalist Thesis refers not to the state as in my example of the Third Reich, but either to (a) the citizenry as a whole or to (b) the nation (understood as a group that shares a national identity, which may or may not be coextensive with the totality of the citizenry). Consider alternative (a). On this interpretation the Permissible Survivalist Thesis says that it is permissible to do whatever is necessary to prevent the bulk of the citizenry from perishing. On the face of it, even this seems wrong, since it overlooks the fact that in some cases the citizens of a state may be at risk because of their own wrongdoing, as when they have unjustly attacked another state which then responds with lethal force. It would be quite another matter to hold that to preserve themselves from destruction by an aggressor, to ward off their unjust destruction, the people of a state may do to the attacker whatever is necessary—though the just war tradition would deny even this much weaker claim. But even if we set aside the reservations of the just war tradition and accept the claim that it is permissible for a state to do whatever is necessary to preserve its citizenry when they are not responsible for being in peril, as when they are unjustly attacked, this is a much weaker claim than the thesis that it is permissible to act exclusively in the national interest whenever the citizenry's survival is at stake (regardless of how they got into that predicament) and weaker still than the claim that it is obligatory to do so. But as I have already noted, it is the stronger claims that, though unsubstantiated, dominate thinking in international relations.

According to (b), the alternative interpretation of the Permissible Survivalist Thesis, it is permissible to do anything that is necessary to ensure the survival of the nation, where the nation is understood as a group sharing a national identity, rather than simply the citizenry as a whole, as in interpretation (a). There is still an ambiguity, however: "survival of the nation" could mean either physical survival of the persons constituting the nation or survival of the national identity. The national identity might cease to exist even though most or even all the members of the group physically survive, as would occur, for example, if the national identity included a religious affiliation and the entire group converted to another religion or was permanently prevented from practicing its own.

Regardless of whether "survival of the nation" means the physical survival of the persons constituting the nation or survival of the national identity, the Permissible Survivalist claim is still implausible, if we assume that there are human rights, for reasons already noted. No one has an absolute right to his or her own physical survival, much less to the survival of his or her nationality; to think otherwise is to deny that others have human rights. For if others have human rights, these impose constraints on what we may do, even what we may do to ensure our own survival. (To modify an earlier example: I may need your kidney to survive, but from this it does not follow that it is permissible for me to rip it out of you.)

If others have rights, then at most one has a right to defend oneself against unjust attacks or against attacks for which one bears no culpability. And what is true of individuals would appear to be true of groups: What it is permissible for a group, whether it is a collection of individuals who are the citizens of a state or a group sharing a national identity, will depend, among other things, upon whether that group, acting through its representatives, provoked the threat by acting unjustly. So unless it is seriously qualified, the Permissible Survivalist Thesis, like its stronger relatives, is not justified. I conclude that both of the weaker relatives of the Permissible Exclusivity Thesis are dubious at best.

6. THE NATIONAL INTEREST AND HUMAN RIGHTS

Those who assert that foreign policy should be or may be determined exclusively by what would best promote the national interest typically do not deny that there are human rights. Instead, they assume or argue that there is something about the domain of international relations that creates an exception to the general moral priority that should be accorded to human rights. Those who try to support the supremacy of the national interest by appeal to Fiduciary Realism hold that the ubiquitous struggle for military domination among states extinguishes what would otherwise be our obligations to respect the human rights of foreigners; they do not typically say that human rights-based obligations are inapplicable in the domestic sphere. Those who employ the Instrumental Justification do not assert that in relations with our fellow citizens or our families or friends we will produce outcomes that are beneficial for all concerned by exclusively pursuing our own interests; they only claim that all will be better off if states exclusively pursue their own interests in their dealings with other states. In Morgenthau's version of the Instrumentalist Justification for Permissible Exclusivity the explanation of why attempts to act morally will result in misery for humanity in this particular domain of human activity assumes that there are irreconcilable differences in the basic moralities of different states and that in the absence of a global umpire to keep the peace, allowing moral concerns to play a role in foreign policy will inevitably lead to mutually destructive moral fanaticism. So he too is at pains to show that there is something unique about international relations that calls for ignoring moral obligations that apply in other areas of life. Similarly, those who try to justify the supremacy of the national interest by arguing that it provides a more determinate goal than the commitment to human rights does presumably do not deny that it is appropriate to try to protect human rights within the state. So they too must be assuming that there is something distinctive about the domain of international relations that makes it inappropriate to do there what it is appropriate to do domestically. Their view must be that we simply cannot have sufficient knowledge of what respect for human rights requires in our treatment of those beyond our borders to allow human rights concerns to be incorporated into foreign policy.

I have argued that all of these putative explanations of what makes appeals to human rights inapplicable in international relations fail. If I am right about this, then those who advocate the supremacy of the national interest in foreign policy must either abandon that position or deny that there are human rights. The position that there are human rights but that foreign policy may abrogate them whenever they conflict with the national interest is untenable, as is the assertion that human rights may be abrogated whenever respecting them would risk a major setback to the national interest, and the even weaker claim that appeals to the national survival always trumps respect for human rights.

My main aim in this chapter was to criticize the stronger versions of the view that the national interest should reign supreme in foreign policy, the Permissible Exclusivity Thesis and the Obligatory Exclusivity Thesis, because these are the dominant positions among diplomats, state leaders, and probably international relations theorists as well. I want to emphasize that the soundness of my criticisms of these two assertions is independent of the success or failure of my criticism of the weaker claims, the Permissible Protection Thesis and the Permissible Survivalist Thesis. Nevertheless, it is an important result of the analysis that even the weaker theses are dubious.

7. LIBERATING THE DISCOURSE OF FOREIGN POLICY

Once we jettison the dogma that foreign policy should or even may exclusively further the national interest, our orientation to the world beyond our borders undergoes a transformation. This is not to say that foreign policy decisions become easier, only that they can now take into account the full range of relevant values. Instead of asking only "Is humanitarian intervention (or a more permissive immigration policy or a preventive war against terrorist or their allies, or the creation of an international criminal court) in our national interest?" we can now ask: "Would this policy choice promote human rights and can it be pursued in a way that is compatible with according a reasonable priority to our more important legitimate national interests?" In other words, once we are freed from the unwarranted constraint of assuming that only the national interest matters, we can begin to face the difficult but necessary question of how we are to balance a concern for the human rights of others with a proper special regard for our own country's welfare. We can now at least ask whether a genuine commitment to the human rights of all persons is compatible with continuing to guide policy exclusively by the goal of forever improving our own situation in a world in which so many people beyond our borders do not even approximate our standard of human rights protection. Once we dispense with the dogma of the supremacy of the national interest, we can begin to ask the right questions.[19]

Notes

1. Hans Morgenthau, *In Defense of the National Interest* (New York: Knopf, 1952), 242.

2. Some who advocate Permissible Exclusivity might deny that it allows or requires the state to disregard the rights of its own citizens for the sake of pursuing the national interest in foreign policy. They would then have to show why it is acceptable in foreign policy to disregard the human rights of foreigners though wrong to violate the human rights of citizens. For reasons that will become clearer as my argument unfolds, this will prove exceedingly difficult to do, because the putative justifications for Permissible Exclusivity do not allow such a distinction between the effects of foreign policy on foreigners and on citizens. However, the criticisms of Permissible Exclusivity that follow do not assume the literal interpretation—that it requires the subordination of citizens' human rights as well as those of foreigners.

3. For a presentation of various arguments for the existence of human rights, see Allen Buchanan, *Justice, Legitimacy, and Self-determination: Moral Foundations for International Law* (Oxford: Oxford University Press, 2004).

4. The remainder of this section draws on Allen Buchanan, *Justice, Legitimacy, and Self-determination: Moral Foundations for International Law*, ch. 1.

5. Robert O. Keohane and Joseph Nye Jr., *Power and Interdependence*, 3rd ed. (Boston: Addison Wesley Longman, 2000), 20.

6. Anne-Marie Slaughter, "International Law in a World of Liberal States" and "International Law and International Relations Theory: A Dual Agenda," *American Journal of International Law* 6 (1993): 503–38; Andrew Moravscic, "Taking Preferences Seriously: A Liberal Theory of International Politics," *International Organization* 51 (1997): 513–54.

7. Allen Buchanan, "The Internal Legitimacy of Humanitarian Intervention," *Journal of Political Philosophy* 7 (2000): 71–87.

8. Hans Morgenthau, *Politics among Nations: The Struggle for Power and Peace*, 6th ed., revised by Kenneth W. Thompson (New York: Knopf, 1985).

9. Stewart Hampshire, *Innocence and Experience* (Cambridge: Harvard University Press, 1989), 90.

10. Thomas Risse, Stephen C. Ropp, and Kathyrn Sikkink, eds., *The Power of Human Rights: International Norms and Domestic Change* (Cambridge: Cambridge University Press, 1999), 199.

11. This point is due to Martha Nussbaum.

12. Condoleezza Rice, "Promoting the National Interest," *Foreign Affairs* (January–February 2000): 79.

13. Rice suggests that the national interest of the United States includes (or consists of?) spreading freedom and democracy through the adoption of market economies. But freedom and democracy are not more determinate goals than the protection of human rights, if only because the more credible attempts to spell out what freedom and democracy are rely upon the conception of human rights. (For example, the sort of freedom we ought to promote is not license to do whatever one wants, but liberty constrained by respect for the human rights of others). Nor is marketization an especially determinate goal, since there is not only an indefinite range of options featuring greater or lesser constraints on market activities and market outcomes, but many different institutional arrangements for achieving the needed constraints as well.

14. Joseph S. Nye Jr., *The Paradox of American Power: Why the World's Only Super-power Can't Go It Alone* (Oxford: Oxford University Press, 2002), 163. Given his views in earlier works, it is doubtful that Nye endorses the subjectivist accommodationist position. His aim in *The Paradox of American Power* is to show that the U.S. national interest is best served by wisely using and cultivating "soft power" along with hard power. He presents his case in such a way as to appeal to the widest audience, and in so doing articulates what I call the subjectivist accommodationist position, though he stops short of endorsing it.

15. John Rawls, *A Theory of Justice* (Cambridge: Harvard University Press, 1971), 8, 245.

16. See, for example, Jonathan Haslam, *No Virtue Like Necessity: Realist Thought in International Relations since Machiavelli* (New Haven, Conn.: Yale University Press, 2002).

17. For one clear example among many of Realist theorists of international relations who fall to distinguish acting from moral principles from moralizing, see John J. Mersheimer, *The Tragedy of Great Power Politics* (New York: W. W. Norton, 2001), 22–24. Like many other Realists, including Haslam (*No Virtue*), Mersheimer seems to relish making derisive remarks about those who recommend that foreign policy should take human rights seriously, even suggesting that their advice to policy makers is morally irresponsible. So far as this harsh condemnation of departures from the exclusive pursuit of the national interest is based on the gross conflation of efforts to take human rights seriously in foreign policy with stupidly counterproductive moralizing utopianism, such Realists themselves may better deserve to be called moralizers than those they criticize. For one might argue that they are guilty of indulging in self-righteous moral indignation, of harshly condemning others for being morally irresponsible—and doing so on the basis of arguments that trade on confusions so egregious that one would be tempted to call them deliberate, if one were as quick to make negative moral judgments about others as these writers are. The Realist conflation of concern about morality with moralizing has, after all, been exposed many times before over a period of many years; yet writers like Haslam and Mersheimer continue to make this mistake. See for example, Marshall Cohen (note 18).

18. Marshall Cohen exposes this confusion between morality and moralizing (or moralism). "Moral Skepticism and International Relations," *International Ethics: A Philosophy and Public Affairs Reader*, ed. Charles Beitz et al. (Princeton, N.J.: Princeton University Press, 1985), 6–7.

19. I am grateful to Jeff Holzgrefe, Robert O. Keohane, and Martha Nussbaum, who generously provided valuable comments on a draft of this chapter.

11

INSTITUTIONALIZING THE JUST WAR

Momentous events, especially wars and revolutions, have a way of awakening theorists from their slumbers (dogmatic or otherwise). The U.S. invasion and occupation of Iraq has stimulated a vigorous scholarly debate over the justification of preventive war and forcible democratization. Justifications for preventive war and forcible democratization both challenge the Just War Norm (henceforth JWN), according to which war is permissible only in response to an actual or imminent attack.[1] Preventive war justifications hold that it can be permissible to make war to avert a temporally distant harm; forcible democratization justifications hold that it can be permissible to make war to achieve a temporally distant good, namely, democracy.

However, the debate has proceeded within the confines of a rarely stated framing assumption: that the key question is whether to abandon the JWN in favor of a more permissive norm regarding the use of force.[2] I shall argue that the assumption that the choice is between competing norms is mistaken. The proper choice is between adherence to the JWN and the creation of new institutions that would allow for a more permissive norm. Not just alternative norms but also alternative combinations of norms and institutions need to be evaluated.

The chief practical aim of Just War Theory is to constrain war making. The *jus ad bellum* part of Just War Theory tries to do so by articulating norms which, if adhered to by state leaders, would constrain their decisions about whether to go to war. However, constraint on the resort to war can be achieved not only by state leaders adhering to narrowly drawn norms, but also by a division of labor between more permissive norms and institutions designed to reduce the risks that reliance on more permissive norms would otherwise entail. Therefore, focusing only on competing norms rather than on combinations of norms and institutions makes sense, but only does so, if one assumes either (1) that the validity of norms does not depend upon institutional context, or (2) that existing institutional resources for constraining war are negligible *and* the creation of new institutional resources is either not feasible or not worth the cost.

In Section 1 I argue that the first assumption is false. Section 2 explains the best rationale for the JWN: it rules out war to avert temporally distant harms or to achieve temporally distant goods in recognition of the fact that reliance on such inherently speculative justifications entails extraordinary risks of error and abuse. I then explain how adherence to the highly constraining JWN as a way of avoiding these extraordinary risks comes at a high cost, given certain assumptions about the new conditions of terrorism. Next, I argue that the attempt to avoid these costs by simply abandoning the JWN in favor of a more permissive norm that allows preventive force is a mistake, because it ignores the extraordinary risks that the JWN's prohibition on preventive war is calculated to avoid I show that the proper choice is not between adhering to the JWN and abandoning it in favor of a more permissive norm, but rather between adhering to the JWN and adopting a more permissive norm embedded in an institutional framework that ameliorates the risks of a more permissive norm. I then argue that which option is better depends both upon the costs of continuing to adhere to the JWN and the feasibility and costs of creating institutions that would make reliance on a more permissive norm acceptable. Next, I show that whether it is worthwhile to try to create institutions in which a more permissive norm would be valid cannot be decided by philosophical argument alone, but requires empirically based institutional analysis. In order to make clear that these results are not confined to the controversy over preventive war, but have broader implications for how we conceive of theorizing the morality of war, I then examine the proposal that the JWN should be relaxed so as to allow for war to achieve democracy. I show that here, as in the case of preventive war, the controversy cannot be resolved simply by comparing alternative norms. Whether the JWN's blanket prohibition of wars of democratization should be adhered to depends upon whether the extraordinary risks involved in the use of the Forcible Democratization Justification can be adequately ameliorated by embedding a more permissive norm in new institutional arrangements, and whether the costs of continued adherence to the JWN are sufficiently high to warrant the costs of developing such institutions. Taken together, these explorations of preventive war and forcible democratization support the conclusion that some of the most serious controversies about the morality of war cannot be resolved without an inquiry into the feasibility and desirability of institutional change.

Section 3 draws the implications of this conclusion for the broader question of the viability of Just War Theory. I argue that Just War Theory assumes that institutional resources for constraining war are negligible and that therefore this way of thinking about war *cannot* answer the question of whether the JWN should be abandoned in favor of a more permissive norm embedded in a system of institutional safeguards. I then conclude that there are two ways to interpret this result. On one interpretation, Just War Theory has a much more limited domain than one might think: it is only a theory of the morality of war for the circumstances in which institutional resources for constraining the decisions of state leaders are negligible. If institutional resources significantly improve, then we have moved beyond the domain of Just War Theory. This interpretation is plausible, if one assumes that the domain of Just War Theory is *war* in the following technical sense: armed conflict among states that are in a state of nature vis à vis one another, where one important feature of the state of nature is lack of institutional capacity. On the second interpretation, Just War Theory has a more ambitious aim: to provide an account of the morality of large-scale military conflict among states, covering both situations in which there is significant institutional capacity and situations in which there is not. If my arguments are sound, then Just War Theory is either not a comprehensive moral account of large-scale armed conflict, or it is comprehensive but mistaken. Either it is limited to a domain in which institutional resources are negligible and can tell us nothing about what norms would be valid under different circumstances or whether we should try to build institutional capacity; or it purports to cover a domain that includes institutional as well as noninstitutional circumstances, but fails to take seriously the fact that the validity of norms can depend upon institutional context.

Finally, I argue that once the relationship between the validity of norms and institutions is understood, it becomes clear that contemporary just war *theorizing* is methodologically flawed, because it is insufficiently empirical. In arguing in favor of the Traditional Norm, theorists often implicitly employ empirical premises about the bad consequences of abandoning the Traditional Norm in favor of a more permissive one. However, their empiricism is arbitrarily incomplete. They fail to appreciate the fact that the risks of abandoning the JWN are not fixed, but can vary depending upon institutional context. So, if Just War Theory is to be a comprehensive theory of large-scale military conflict, Just War theorizing must become more empirical. Arguments for and against proposed use-of-force norms must include factual premises about how various institutions work and about the feasibility and costs of creating them. This methodological implication is of considerable consequence; it means that a comprehensive Just War Theory cannot rely exclusively on philosophical argument as it is usually understood. The integration of moral philosophy and institutional analysis is required.

1. HOW THE VALIDITY OF NORMS CAN DEPEND ON INSTITUTIONS OR THEIR ABSENCE

Whether a norm is valid can depend upon institutional context. Where we can rely on the police and courts to protect us from attacks by other individuals, a more narrowly drawn norm of justified self-defense is valid, other things being equal; where we must depend solely on our own efforts, there may be more latitude as to the measures we may take to protect ourselves.

Conversely, where appropriate institutions are present, a more permissive norm may be valid than would be the case if these institutions did not exist. For example, it may be appropriate for police to have wider search or surveillance powers when there is reliable judicial review of their activities and where every citizen has access to competent legal counsel than where these institutional safeguards are lacking.

It is the latter connection between institutions and norms I wish to emphasize. Constraints on agents can be achieved not only by their adherence to narrowly drawn norms but also by a combination of more permissive norms and institutions. This simple point has large implications for how to think about the morality of war. The next section draws out those implications in dialectical fashion, by critically evaluating the current controversy about the justification of preventive war and forcible democratization.

2. PREVENTIVE WAR AND FORCIBLE DEMOCRATIZATION

Some critics have assumed that the Bush Administration's appeal to the idea of preventive force in order to justify the invasion of Iraq in March of 2003 relies on a form of argument that enjoyed considerable popularity (at least among state leaders) during the eighteenth and nineteenth centuries in Europe, when the idea of the balance of power was ascendant. According to David Luban, this form of argument relies on the following premises:

(1) Some state of affairs X (e.g., the balance of power in Europe) preserves some important value V ("European liberties") and is therefore worth defending even at some cost; and

(2) to fight early, before X begins to unravel, greatly reduces the cost of the defense of V, while waiting does not avoid war (unless one gives up V) but only results in fighting on a larger scale at worse odds.[3]

On Luban's reading, the Bush Administration's version of this argument substitutes "U.S. dominance" (remaining the one hyperpower) for "the balance of power."

Let us call a preventive war justification that relies on these two premises the Traditional Preventive War Justification. Luban argues persuasively against this justification that its acceptance would be likely to lead to many wars and lead us to regard war as *ordinary*, that is, to fail to appreciate the almost incomprehensible, distinctive evil of war. To use this argument, he concludes, is simply too risky. However, as is usually the case with those who employ consequentialist reasoning to determine which just war norms are valid, he provides no explicit account of the relationship between the nature of the argument and the characteristics of the agents that are likely to employ it to spell out exactly what those risks are.[4]

Nor does Luban consider the possibility that the risks in question are not fixed, but instead vary, depending upon the institutional framework within which the justification is deployed to justify the act of going to war. In that sense, Luban, like virtually all Just War Theorists, is incompletely empirical in his theorizing. He acknowledges the relevance of empirical assumptions by relying on arguments about the consequences of adopting this or that norm, but he does not recognize that the validity of norms can depend upon institutional context. Finally, though he suggests that the Traditional Preventive War Justification ought not to be used, he does not consider the role that institutional constraints might play in preventing its use, for example, by institutionally backed rules of public deliberation that explicitly exclude it. Instead, he again remains within the noninstitutionalist strictures of Just War Theory, apparently relying upon the persuasive effects of an institutionally disembodied consequentialist argument on the conscience of state leaders or on right-minded citizens who may then exert pressure on their leaders to behave properly.

Two Distinct Justifications for Preventive War

Some Bush Administration statements are consistent with the Traditional Preventive War Justification. However, some of the Administration's rhetoric suggests a more restricted and plausible appeal to preventive force. The Bush "National Security Strategy" can be read as claiming that under the new conditions of terrorism, the right of self-defense encompasses the use preventive force: "...the United States...will not hesitate to act alone, if necessary, to exercise our right of self-defense by acting preemptively against...terrorists, to prevent them from doing harm against our people and our country."[5] The reason given for acknowledging this expanded right of self-defense is straightforward. We now live in a world in which weapons of mass destruction are widely available and can be deployed covertly and suddenly, and in which there are agents who are willing to use them against innocent persons and who are not subject to the 'logic of deterrence' to which state leaders typically conform. Under these new conditions, the Administration concludes, preventive force in self-defense is justifiable.

On a charitable interpretation, this passage from the National Defense Strategy appeals to what I shall call the *Preventive Self-defense Justification*, according to which preventive war can be justified as an exercise of the right of self-defense, but only when the target against whom they engage in preventive war is *wrongfully imposing a dire risk.* On this view, the right of self-defense allows preventive war, but it does not allow preventive force to be used whenever using it would prevent some harm or other and waiting to address the harm at a later date would be more costly and risky. Instead, the Preventive Self-defense Justification limits the resort to preventive war in two crucial ways. First, unlike The Traditional Preventive War Justification, it does not allow appeal to anything so broad as the preservation of "important values," or even to the prevention of harms, but instead limits action to the prevention of the most serious of harms. In the case of states, this would mean something much more serious than economic loss or loss of military dominance.[6] Second, the risk of harm must be *wrongfully imposed.* The mere fact that B poses a threat to A, even a dire threat, does not justify A's acting to prevent the threat from being realized. For example, if A has already unjustly attacked B, A is not justified in attacking B again to prevent B from rallying its forces and attacking A, even if the threat B poses is dire. In this case, B poses a dire threat to A, but not a wrongfully imposed dire threat.

Once the distinctive character of the Preventive Self-defense Justification is understood, it becomes clear that the Traditional Preventive Force Argument is not properly described as invoking the right of self-defense at all. Not all action to protect "important values" counts as self-defense.

Consequentialist and Rights-based Arguments against Preventive Self-defense

There are two main arguments against the thesis that the right of self-defense allows preventive war under certain circumstances. The first, consequentialist objection is analogous to Luban's complaint about the Traditional Preventive Force Justification: the use of such a justification for war is too risky. The second, rights-based objection is that preventive war necessarily violates the rights to life of those against whom it is waged because, by hypothesis, they have not (yet) done anything wrong and therefore retain the right to life that the "innocent" have. Later I will argue that the consequentialist objection to the Preventive Self-defense Justification, as typically framed, is incomplete, because it fails to consider whether the risks of using this justification could be adequately ameliorated by appropriate institutions. First, however, I want to focus on the rights-based objection.

The most obvious rebuttal to the rights-based objection is that it is not true that the target of preventive force, by hypothesis, has done nothing wrong. On the preventive force justification under consideration, he has done something wrong: he has wrongly imposed a dire risk on another, even though the harm is not imminent.

Both the law of conspiracy and the law of attempts provide useful analogies for understanding how a wrongly imposed dire threat need not be imminent. In both cases, the elements of the crime capture the idea that the agents in question have done something wrong, but in neither case must there be an imminent harm. In the law of conspiracy, two or more persons, working in concert, must have formed a "specific intention" and a plan to commit a crime, and (in most jurisdictions) something must have been done toward carrying out the plan.[7] In the law of attempts, the individuals must have taken some substantial step toward committing a crime, but this need not result in the crime being imminent.[8]

Of course, both the law of attempts and that of conspiracy can sometimes be poorly framed in statute and there can be abuses in the enforcement of each as well. Nevertheless, there is nothing in the basic conception of either type of law that entails that enforcement of them, even with lethal force in extreme circumstances, *necessarily* involves violations of the rights of those against whom they are applied. In neither case can it be said that force is being used against someone who has not yet done anything wrong. If this is so, then there is no fundamental moral bar to holding that force can sometimes be justified in order to avert a future wrongful harm that is not yet imminent.[9]

In the case of enforcing the law of conspiracy and attempts, force is employed only under the direction of judicial institutions; private enforcement of such laws would be so risky as to be morally impermissible. What this shows is that a justification for preventive self-defense that draws on the analogy of conspiracy and attempts would have to include recourse to institutions that would adequately ameliorate the risks of private enforcement in the absence of an international judiciary. Later I shall sketch such an institution.

An articulated account of the self-defense justification for preventive war would have to spell out precisely what counts as wrongfully imposing a dire risk, and make a fully convincing case that this does not require imminent harm. My aim here is not to produce such an account. Instead I have tried only to say enough to indicate its plausibility and by doing so make it clear that one cannot disregard the possibility of preventive self-defense by merely asserting that it necessarily violates the rights of the target because the target, by hypothesis, has not yet done anything wrong.

Why Imminence Is Not Necessary

Luban offers his consequentialist criticism of the much less plausible Traditional Preventive Force Justification and then goes on to propose a more constraining justification for preventive war. According to Luban, preventive war is justifiable only when it is necessary to avert a harm that is "probabilistically imminent," though this need not involve being temporally imminent. In other words, Luban retains the Traditional Norm according to which a state may make war only to stop an occurring or imminent attack, but construes imminence expansively, to cover *both* temporally proximate and temporally distant harms, if they are "all but certain."[10] He then suggests that this criterion for justified preventive war is equivalent to restricting the Traditional Preventive Argument to cases where the target of preventive war is a "rogue state," on the assumption that the characteristics that define rogue states make it "all but certain" that they will act aggressively at some point in the future.[11]

Luban wrongly assumes that what justifies preventive force is the existence of an "imminent" threat, by which he means an "*all but certain*" prospect that something like what I have called a dire harm will occur. This analysis omits something that is essential to the idea of the right of self-defense and that accounts for the plausibility of the claim that preventive war, if it can be justified at all, is justifiable only in cases of self-defense: namely, that the dire risk to be averted is *wrongfully imposed*.

A harm's being imminent in the sense of being "all but certain" does nothing to justify using preventive force of any kind, much less preventive war. Consider the following variation on the case discussed above. A unjustly attacks B and then attacks B again, to prevent B's launching an "all but certain" lethal attack (in justified self-defense) against A.[12] The fact that B's acting to harm A is "all but certain" does nothing to justify A's second attack on B, and this is true even if the harm B would inflict on A is as serious as possible. Conversely, preventive force may be justified to avert a harm that is considerably less than "all but certain" if the harm is sufficiently great and the imposition of the risk of that harm is deeply wrong. For example, if I viciously plan to kill you and you have good evidence that I am committed to carrying out the plan, you may be justified in using lethal force against me, if this is the only way to prevent your murder, even if my plan is considerably less than foolproof. To expect you to refrain from using force to protect yourself unless the risk of deadly harm I wrongly impose on you is "all but certain" would be to construe the right of self-defense in a way that places an unreasonable burden of restraint on the innocent to protect themselves, at least in circumstances in which you cannot rely on effective help from others. Of course, if you and I happen to live in a society with an effective police and court system, you do not have to rely exclusively on your own actions to protect yourself from my sinister plan, and under these conditions a more restricted understanding of your right of self-defense may be compelling.

It can be argued that even the rather constrained legal right of individual self-defense that presupposes such backup institutions does not require anything so strong as Luban's notion of "all but certain" harm. However, even if it did, matters are quite different on the international scene, where at present there is nothing approaching an effective police force.

The results of the argument of this section thus far can be summarized as follows. (1) Luban's consequentialist criticism of the Traditional Preventive Force Argument is cogent (though for the reasons noted, incomplete). (2) The Preventive Self-defense Justification, explicated in terms of the use of force is to avert a wrongfully imposed dire harm, is more plausible than Luban's attempt to accommodate preventive war within the constraints of the Traditional Norm by stretching the notion of imminence. (3) The Preventive Self-defense Argument cannot be ruled out on the grounds that it allows the use of force against those who have not done anything wrong, because it limits the use of preventive force to circumstances in which the target has in fact already done something wrong (by initiating the execution of an aggressive plan). (4) So, because the "rights-based" objection fails, if the Preventive Force Justification is unsound, the argument against it must be consequentialist in nature. The next step, then, is to explicate the Preventive Self-defense Justification in its most plausible form and then develop more carefully and evaluate the objection that it is too risky to use. To do this it is first necessary to understand how the new conditions of terrorism are supposed to make the idea of preventive self-defense more plausible.

The Significance of the New Conditions of Terrorism

As I observed earlier, the Bush Administration National "Defense Strategy" suggests that the new conditions of terrorism call for an expanded understanding of the scope of the right of self-defense, one that encompasses preventive war. How are the "new conditions" supposed to change the scope of the right of self-defense? The New Conditions Argument would go like this:

(1) The scope of the right of (national) self-defense depends upon what risks of harm a country can reasonably be expected to bear by forgoing actions that it could undertake to protect itself against wrongfully imposed dire risks.
(2) Under the "new conditions," it is unreasonable to expect a country, in its efforts to protect itself against wrongfully imposed dire risks, to restrict itself to using force against presently occurring or imminent attacks (i.e., to adhere to the Traditional Norm and thereby foreswear preventive war).
(3) (Therefore,) under the new conditions, the scope of the right of self-defense does *not exclude* preventive action.

Notice that the appeal to the new conditions of the "war on terrorism" *cannot* establish the conclusion that the United States (or any country) is morally justified in using preventive force in order to defend itself whenever it deems such force to be necessary to avert a wrongfully imposed dire risk, much less any harm that is "all but certain." At most, it only establishes a much weaker conclusion: that a *blanket prohibition* on the use of preventive force in self-defense is unacceptable. In other words, a proper appreciation of the "new conditions" at most implies that there may be circumstances in which the use of preventive force is morally justifiable as an exercise of the right of self-defense. It does not specify what the conditions are.

In fact the New Conditions Argument does not even establish that the JWN's blanket prohibition on preventive self-defense should be abandoned, unless the crucial premise (2) can be supported. What is clear is that the "new conditions" increase the costs of adherence to the JWN. However, from that it does not follow that those increased costs are unreasonable. Whether they are unreasonable depends upon how high the costs of abandoning the JWN are likely to be. Even if the costs of adhering to the JWN are now high, due to the "new conditions," the costs of abandoning it may be higher still, unless something is done to ameliorate the extraordinary risks of relying on the Preventive Self-defense Justification.

The problem with simply assuming premise (2) is that doing so ignores the reason why the JWN's prohibition of preventive war seemed plausible in the first place. Recall that, as Luban and others have argued, the best justification for the JWN is that adherence to it avoids the extraordinary risks that are entailed by relying on inherently speculative justifications such as the Preventive Self-defense Justification. Given how serious those risks are, we cannot assume that because the costs of adhering to the norm that avoids them have *increased*, adherence to that norm is no longer justified.

We seem to be in a very difficult situation, then. On the one hand, due to the "new conditions," the costs of adhering to the JWN have increased; on the other hand, the costs of abandoning the JWN so as to allow preventive war are high. Whether we should adhere to the JWN or abandon it in favor of one that permits preventive self-defense depends upon a comparison of these costs. However, it is not clear that anyone is in a position to make an accurate comparison.

I now want to argue that there is a way out of this impasse. It may be possible both to avoid the extraordinary risks of adopting a new norm according to which preventive self-defense is sometimes permissible and to avoid the costs of adhering to the JWN in the "new conditions." One can have one's cake and eat it, too, if a more permissive norm than the JWN can be properly embedded in an institutional arrangement that adequately reduces the risks that attend the inherently speculative character of the Preventive Self-defense Justification.

My aim in this chapter is not to make a rock-solid case for this institutionalist solution to the problem of preventive war. I only want to show that the controversy over the justifiability of preventive war cannot be resolved without considering the possibility of an institutional solution and that doing this requires moving beyond the framing assumptions of Just War theorizing. Nevertheless, to make it clear what an institutionalist solution would look like and to show that it should not be dismissed out of hand as unrealistic, I will sketch a proposal for institutionalizing decisions concerning preventive self-defense that Robert O. Keohane and I explored recently. We outline the main features of an appropriate institution that would make it permissible for leaders to appeal to the right of self-defense in order to justify preventive war.[13] Instead of recapitulating the details of that argument here, I will sketch only the main features of this institutionalist approach, adding some important premises that were overlooked or not sufficiently emphasized earlier, and then see whether it can be extended to encompass the second major challenge to the JWN as well, the Forcible Democratization Justification.

The key idea is that for preventive force to be justified as an exercise of the right of self-defense, the decision to use preventive force must be made within a multilateral framework designed to reduce the special risks of error and abuse that are involved in attempts to justify the use of force by appeal to speculative reasoning about possible future harms (more precisely, wrongfully imposed risks of temporally distant dire harms).[14]

The special risks involved in relying on the idea that self-defense can include preventive war are due to the way the inherently speculative character of this justification interacts with the cognitive and moral limitations of the agents who are likely to invoke it. Because the harm to be averted is speculative, there are ample opportunities for honest mistakes in prediction, bias in the interpretation of evidence and hence in estimating both the magnitude and the probability of the anticipated harm, and hence for self-deception as well as deception of others.

In addition, those who occupy the role of state leader are subject to incentives that encourage them to overestimate risks to their own country and to underestimate the costs of the preventive action (especially the costs to foreigners), or even to misrepresent deliberately the facts in order to justify aggressive actions under the cover of self-defense. To the extent that the leader is held accountable only to her own citizens, she is likely to construe her fiduciary obligation to act in the "national interest" in a near absolute fashion, sharply discounting, if not simply disregarding, the interests of foreigners. Even if the leader acknowledges that she ought to take the interests of foreigners seriously, from her standpoint there is a marked asymmetry between two kinds of possible errors she might make. Failing to prevent a serious harm to her own people is politically much more damaging than engaging in unnecessary preventive action, at least if the costs of the latter fall chiefly on foreigners.

These special risks of justifying war by appeal to preventive self-defense are exacerbated if two conditions are satisfied. First, the agent has *congruent interests*, interests that speak in favor of engaging in the action in question independently of whether the preventive self-defense justification itself provides adequate support for the action. In the Iraq case, congruent interests most likely included some or all of the following: deterring other present or future "strongman" rulers in the Middle East from undertaking actions that are deemed contrary to U.S. interests; disabling potential threats to Israel; demonstrating to the world that the United States has and is willing to use overwhelming military power and dispelling the common assumption that the U.S. government will not undertake military operations that involve significant casualties to U.S. troops; and having permanent military bases in the Middle East to protect U.S. access to oil, especially after anti-U.S. terrorism made the continued presence of large numbers of U.S. troops in Saudi Arabia untenable. Second, the agent is not willing to appeal to the congruent interests in publicly justifying the action in question.

In cases in which an agent has significant congruent interests, but is not willing to publicly appeal to them to justify her actions, there is a risk that the agent will proclaim to others, and perhaps even come to believe, that the justifying conditions specified in the justification the agent publicly embraces are satisfied, when in fact they are not. Under these conditions, the risk is that the justification will become a mere rationalization for furthering congruent interests that the agent is not willing to appeal to publicly. Call this the *Mere Rationalization Risk.*

In the Iraq case, both of the conditions for the Mere Rationalization Risk seem to have been satisfied. The Bush Administration persisted in its appeal to the right of preventive self-defense even after the renewed International Atomic Energy Agency inspections found no evidence of nuclear weapons and in spite of the fact that the UN team headed by Hans Blix reported that it had found no biological or chemical weapons and was receiving greater cooperation from Iraqi officials. The fact that the Bush Administration persisted in the Preventive Self-defense Justification in spite of this evidence that it had initially overestimated the risk of Iraqi WMDs suggests that it believed that invading Iraq would serve other important interests. If these other interests included any of those listed above, it is hardly surprising that the Bush Administration would not have been willing to cite them in a public justification for going to war. It is one thing to tell the people of the United States that they must go to war to protect themselves from a devastating terrorist attack, quite another that they must do so to protect Israel from a potential threat or to convince the world that the United States is willing to use its overwhelming military force or to secure military bases in Iraq because a large U.S. presence in Saudi Arabia is no longer an option.

Where the decision maker has strong congruent interests that she is not willing to invoke in public justification, there is a risk that the decision will be made on the basis of motivated false beliefs (in this case about the presence of WMDs in Iraq). Where the type of justification the decision maker employs gives extraordinary opportunities for the sorts of errors of judgment that motivated false belief encourages, as is the case with the inherently speculative Preventive Self-defense Justification, the risk is all the higher.

The Bush Administration could have reduced these risks in either of two ways. First, it could have accepted the French government's proposal to postpone the invasion for a several months while Blix's inspections continued. Doing this would have provided a safeguard against possible biases or errors in its initial intelligence concerning the presence of WMDs in Iraq, thereby reducing the risk that the decision to go to war would be the result of motivated false belief, facilitated by the presence of strong congruent interests the Administration was not willing to appeal to in a public justification. Second, if, as some argued, weather conditions made postponement of the invasion impractical, the Administration could have pre-committed to a post-invasion evaluation of its actions by an impartial body empowered to impose costs on the United States if it turned out that there was a serious discrepancy between the evidence the Administration cited to justify preventive war and the facts that came to light after the invasion. By doing neither, the Bush Administration failed to take seriously the extraordinary risks of reliance on the Preventive War Justification. Later I will argue that once the complexities of the Forcible Democratization Justification are understood, it becomes clear that it too carries an extraordinary risk of being a mere rationalization.

In the earlier paper Keohane and I argued that the special risks of relying on preventive self-defense justifications can only be adequately reduced by requiring that the decision to engage in preventive action to be made through a multilateral institutional procedure that ensures the accountability of both the party that proposes preventive force and those who are to approve or disapprove its request for authorization to use it. Ensuring accountability requires that the party proposing to use preventive force must agree, ex ante, to an ex post evaluation of its actions by a comparatively impartial body that will have full access to the occupied territory. If the evaluation is negative, significant costs must predictably fall on the party that proposed the use of preventive force. For example, that party must bear a greater proportion of the costs of the war and of post-war reconstruction and / or have less of a say in how the reconstruction is carried out.

The standard of evaluation employed ex post would not require that all the statements the proposer of preventive force makes ex ante be fully accurate, because the possibility of nonculpable errors cannot be eliminated. Instead, the comparatively impartial body undertaking the evaluation would focus on whether the decision ex ante was reasonable all things considered, employing something like the legal notion of due diligence or the concept of reasonable belief that is employed in the law of individual self-defense.

Two points bear special emphasis. First, the case for creating such an institution is comparative. The relevant question is not whether it would produce perfect decisions but rather whether it would be an improvement over the status quo. Furthermore, its being an improvement does not depend upon the possibility of creating and empowering a strictly impartial body to make the post-conflict evaluation, but rather upon whether such a body would be sufficiently impartial to create incentives for better decision making. Including representatives of reputable transnational nongovernmental organizations, in particular human rights organizations, would be one way to combat partiality. Second, the accountability regime Keohane and I sketch does not operate through enforcement of norms, where this means compliance through coercion. Hence it does not require the currently utopian assumption that sovereign states will consent to anything resembling an international criminal court with police powers capable of defining and enforcing a norm specifying what counts as aggressive war. Instead, it is designed to build on the incentives that states actually have and to utilize the prospects of costs other than coercive enforcement, in order to improve decision making.

At this point it might be objected that state leaders would not allow themselves to be constrained in these ways, that they would not cooperate in the creation of such institutions. Whether this is so is an empirical question, but it is worth noting that there are two incentives for creating such an institution, or at least not blocking efforts to create it, to which even the most ardent practitioners of

Real Politik may be subject. First, because the use of the Preventive Self-defense Justification is so subject to error and abuse, any state leader who invokes it faces a serious credibility problem. Unless this credibility problem is solved, the state that invokes the Preventive Self-defense Justification may find it difficult to secure military allies or cost-sharers. Subjecting itself to an accountability regime for making decisions about the use of preventive force or forcible democratization can help a state solve its credibility problem. Second, in democratic countries the demand for the creation of such institutions could become a focal point for the efforts of citizens who are concerned, both on moral and prudential grounds, about the risks of invoking the Preventive Self-defense Justification. Determining the conditions under which these incentives will dominate is, of course, an empirical matter.

Keohane and I argued that this sort of accountability mechanism, along with procedural requirements designed to foster principled deliberation, can elicit more accurate information about risks and benefits and reduce the risk of strategic behavior, deception, self-deception, and manipulation. We emphasized that such an institution should be multilateral on the commonsensical grounds that no country, including and perhaps especially the world's one hyperpower with its complex geopolitical interests, can be trusted to determine unilaterally when preventive force would be justifiable as a matter of self-defense.[15]

Two Basic Strategies for Achieving Responsibility in Justification

There are, then, two quite different ways in which one can take into account the extraordinary risks of relying on the Preventive Self-defense Justification for war. First, one can do what the JWN advocates: adhere to a blanket prohibition on preventive force. The attraction of this response is that it simply takes one especially risky kind of justification off the table. As the New Conditions Argument shows, however, under present conditions the costs of continued adherence to a blanket prohibition are considerable. Alternatively, one can invoke a more permissive norm, thus avoiding the increased costs of adhering to the JWN, but try to reduce the extraordinary risks of preventive self-defense by embedding the more permissive norm in a decision-making process that includes appropriate safeguards. This second response recognizes that striking the right balance between restraint and the ability to prevent harm can require a kind of division of labor between the content of a norm regarding self-defense and the institutional arrangements within which the norm is to be invoked. What is disturbing about the Bush Administration's reliance on the Preventive Self-defense Justification is that it abandoned the protection against the special risks of preventive action that are provided by the traditional Just War Theory blanket prohibition *without* any acknowledgment that doing so entailed serious risks, and apparently without taking any measures to reduce them.

Keohane and I not only argued that institutional innovation is a *necessary* condition for justified preventive self-defense; we also opted for the institutionalist solution (though we stopped short of endorsing one particular institutional arrangement). We did so because we assumed that under the "new conditions," the costs of the alternative strategy of barring all appeals to preventive self-defense were too great.

Our argument was incomplete. As I have already indicated, it is not enough to note that the costs of continued adherence to the JWN have increased, due to the new conditions, and that a new institutional arrangement could avoid those costs as well as reduce the risks of relying on the JWN. That might be so, yet it might still be the case that we should continue to adhere to the JWN, if the costs of abandoning it were higher still. That would be the case if the costs of building a new institution were sufficiently high or if there were a significant risk that the new institution would not perform as intended.[16]

For present purposes, I need not defend the assumption that the costs of continued adherence to the JWN are intolerably high. My aim here is not to endorse the institutionalist option in this case, but rather only to demonstrate its plausibility in order to show how taking the relationship between norms and institutions seriously transforms thinking about the morality of war. The crucial point is that the controversy over preventive war cannot be resolved conclusively without a serious consideration of the institutional alternatives to the status quo. Because Just War Theory simply assumes that institutional resources are negligible, it is inherently conservative. Because Just War theorizing does not take up the burden of an empirical inquiry into the feasibility of institutional change and the comparative costs and benefits of adhering to norms designed to function in the absence of institutions versus developing new institutions, it is methodologically flawed.

I now want to bolster these conclusions by applying the institutionalist approach to another challenge to the JWN; the attempt to justify war to create democracy. Again, my purpose is not to resolve the controversy, but rather to show that it cannot be resolved within the cramped framing assumptions of Just War Theory but instead requires supplementing abstract philosophical argumentation with empirically based institutional design. As with preventive self-defense, it will not be necessary to show that institutional innovation would make forcible democratization justifiable. Instead, I need only make a strong prima facie case that institutionalization is necessary for justifiability.

The Second Challenge to the Traditional Norm: The Forcible Democratization Justification

This justification expands greatly what are generally recognized as the conditions for justified armed humanitarian intervention. Instead of restricting those conditions to actual or imminent massive violation of basic human rights, it asserts that armed humanitarian intervention of the most destructive sort, a full-scale war to topple a regime and occupy an entire country, can be justified if undertaken for the sake of creating democracy.

The structure of the problem is the same as that of preventive war. On the one hand, the inherently speculative character of the justification carries extraordinary risks. Adhering to the Traditional Norm avoids these risks by taking the Forcible Democratization Justification off the table, just as it rules out preventive self-defense as a justification for war. However, avoiding these risks in this way comes at a cost: we are not allowed to use military force to break the yoke of tyranny.

Here, too, the proper question to ask is not whether the Traditional Norm should be replaced with a more permissive one that allows forcible democratization, but whether (1) there is a feasible institutional arrangement that could adequately ameliorate the extraordinary risks of using a forcible democratization justification, and whether (2) the costs of continued adherence to the JWN, which excludes forcible democratization, are sufficiently high, relative to the costs of creating the new institution, that we should bear the costs of institutional innovation.

No amount of philosophical argumentation, by itself, can answer this question. As in the controversy over preventive self-defense, an approach that combines moral philosophy and empirically informed institutional analysis is required. To show that this is so, however, it is first necessary to explain why continued adherence to a use-of-force norm that excludes forcible democratization entails serious costs and then to show that there is no basic moral obstacle to forcible democratization.

Taking Cosmopolitan Commitments Seriously

It may be tempting for those who consider themselves cosmopolitans to dismiss the Forcible Democratization Justification simply because it has been invoked by what they take to be an extremely anticosmopolitan administration to justify what they take to be an unnecessary war. This temptation ought to be resisted. Cosmopolitans should try to distinguish between the question of whether forcible democratization was justified in the case of Iraq from the more general question of whether the Forcible Democratization Justification can be properly institutionalized so as to ameliorate its extraordinary risks, and whether the costs of adhering to a blanket prohibition on forcible democratization are sufficiently high to warrant opting for the institutionalist solution.

To the extent that cosmopolitans hold the following beliefs, they should not simply dismiss the idea of forcible democratization. First, sovereignty, and hence immunity from external force, is conditional; states earn it by doing a credible job of protecting basic human rights. Second, democracy is the most reliable arrangement for securing basic human rights.[17] Third, "one-off" humanitarian intervention to stop violence that has already become large-scale is often insufficient, merely postponing the killing until the intervener has withdrawn. Fourth, to the extent that cosmopolitans are heirs of the liberal theorists of revolution of the seventeen and eighteenth centuries, they believe that a people may go to war to establish its own democratic institutions. But if war is morally permissible for the sake of establishing democracy for ourselves, could not war to establish democracy in another country that is so thoroughly repressive as to make revolution virtually impossible also be a moral option? Finally, if, as I have already argued, the JWN that war is only justifiable in response to actual or imminent attack is not a fundamental moral principle but at most a contingent moral rule, one whose validity may vary with institutional context, then there is all the more reason to take seriously the idea that there may be circumstances in which going to war to create the form of government that best protects human rights would be justified.

For all these reasons the Forcible Democratization Justification cannot simply be dismissed, at least not by cosmopolitans. Instead, the proper course of action is to articulate the justification carefully, take stock of its special risks, try to determine whether feasible institutional arrangements could adequately reduce them, and then determine whether the costs adhering to a norm that takes forcible democratization justifications off the table are sufficiently high to warrant the costs of developing the new institutional arrangements.

In the discussion that follows I do not attempt to set out all the conditions that would have to be satisfied if forcible democratization were to be justifiable. Instead, I want to say just enough about them to make it clear that using this sort of justification carries extraordinary risks and that the only reasonable prospect for adequately ameliorating these risks would be to create new institutions to structure the decision-making process. In other words, I want to show that institutional innovation would be a *necessary* condition for relaxing the JWN to allow for forcible democratization, not that the best course of action is to start building the new institutions. This will suffice to confirm my chief conclusion: that theorizing about the morality of war must go beyond philosophical argumentation as traditionally understood to include empirically based reasoning about institutional alternatives. If it turns out that the sorts of institutions that would be required are not feasible, given the array of power and interests in our world, then the conclusion to be drawn is that war for democratization is not morally justified.

Justifying Forcible Democratization

The Forcible Democratization Justification presents war as a necessary means to achieving a good for the people of the country that is to be invaded. However, merely focusing on the good to be achieved for them is clearly inadequate: to justify attacking the nondemocratic leaders of the state and those who support them, more than the prospect of providing a benefit to the people is needed. As in all cases of justifying war, those who are the targets of military action must be, in Jeff McMahan's phrase, "liable" to have military force used against them.[18]

For the Forcible Democratization Justification to get off the ground as a distinct justification for making war, it must be the case that those who rule undemocratically *are forcibly preventing the people from creating democratic institutions.* For brevity, let us call those who meet this description Despots. The question, then, is whether being a Despot makes one a legitimate target for war making even in the absence of the sorts of massive violations of human rights under which ordinary humanitarian intervention can be justified.

At least in the mainstream of the liberal tradition, it is thought that the people themselves can be justified in going to war against Despots; that is, that revolution as forcible democratization *from within* can be justified. The assumption is that simply by ruling undemocratically and forcibly resisting the people's efforts to create democracy, one can become a legitimate target of war making by the people themselves. (The most obvious explanation of why being a Despot makes one liable to revolutionary force is that Despots violate the people's right of self-government, either as a collective right or as the right of each individual to participate in self-government.) So unless one is willing to deny that there is a right to revolution against Despots, then one must acknowledge that being a Despot can make one a legitimate target of war making. Conversely, unless revolution against Despots is justifiable, it is hard to see how one could begin to make the case for forcible democratization. I will simply assume, for the sake of the argument to follow, that revolution against Despots can be justified.

At this point there are two opposing views to be considered. According to the first, being a Despot only makes one a legitimate target of war making *by those whose right of self-government one is violating.* According to the second, under certain circumstances being a Despot can also make one a legitimate target of war making *by others* than those whose right of self-government one is violating, if those others act so as to vindicate the right of self-government of one's victims. Call the former the *Constrained View* and the latter the *Permissive View.*

Assuming that revolution against Despots can be justifiable, the Constrained View must be false, for it would rule out making war to support a democratic revolution under conditions in which all of the oppressed people have explicitly requested such support. The question, then, is whether there are circumstances other than those of explicit authorization in Despots are legitimate targets of war making by external forces.

Notice that the worry about whether attacks on a Despot by external forces are justified where there is no explicit authorization is *not* that such attacks would violate the rights of the Despot. Clearly, whether the Despot's rights are violated could not be affected by authorization one way or the other, for the simple reason that the moral barrier against attack that all persons originally enjoy cannot be removed merely by someone else's granting permission to a third party to attack them. Instead, the worry about unauthorized intervention to secure democracy for an oppressed people is that it involves unwarranted paternalism toward or failure to show proper respect for the intended beneficiaries.

What must a would-be forcible democratizer do, then, to avoid unwarranted paternalism, in circumstances in which their explicit authorization of his action is not possible? I am not sure how to answer this question, but it seems to me that at minimum the would-be forcible democratizer would have to have good reason to believe that the intended beneficiaries could reasonably accept the risks that the forcible democratization process poses for them. Call this the *Respect* (or *Antipaternalism*) *Principle.*

The attraction of the Respect Principle is apparent. Generally speaking, it seems wrong to impose serious costs on others in order to provide them with benefits, unless they consent to one's doing so or at least unless one has good reason to believe that they would or at least reasonably could regard the ratio of benefits to costs as acceptable. There are three basic grounds for this presumption. The first is a healthy appreciation of the fallibility of even the most sincere benefactors and of the tendency for the insincere to disguise themselves as benefactors. The second is a more basic commitment to respecting individual autonomy. The third is instrumental: if popular support for democratization is lacking, then resistance to military occupation and forcible institution building will likely be greater and in consequence the project of democratization may involve unacceptably high human costs or may fail altogether.

The point of the Respect Principle is *not* that one may never act to secure human rights without the consent of all of those whom one's actions will affect. The claim is much narrower: to impose costly benefits on a people one should have credible evidence that they could reasonably regard this trade-off as acceptable.[19]

It could be argued that another principle must be satisfied if forcible democratization is to be justified: the would-be forcible democratizer must reasonably believe that the benefits to the intended beneficiaries will significantly exceed the costs to them. Call this the Beneficiary Proportionality Principle. This principle seems reasonable, given that the purpose of the war is to bring the benefits of democracy to the people whose country is invaded. The assumption is that democracy will make them significantly better off. But if the process by which democracy is brought about is too costly to them, democracy will not make them better off. So unless the Beneficiary Proportionality Principle is satisfied, the war is futile on its own terms.

However, the two principles could point in opposite directions. Suppose the would-be forcible democratizer judges that the expected costs to the intended beneficiaries would be excessive, but the intended beneficiaries find the costs acceptable. My inclination is to say that this is not a problem, because the Respect Principle is the appropriate criterion and that the Beneficiary Proportionality Principle should only be invoked as a proxy for the Respect Principle under conditions in which it is difficult to determine more directly what costs it would be reasonable for the intended beneficiaries to accept.[20] The idea would be that, in the absence of credible evidence of what sorts of costs they would find acceptable, imposing costly benefits on a people is morally permissible only if there is strong evidence that the expected costs to them will be exceeded significantly by the expected benefits to them.

Fortunately, it is not necessary for me to support this intuition here. Instead, I will proceed on the weaker, quite plausible assumption that forcible democratization would only be justified if either the Benefit Proportionality or the Respect Principles is satisfied. The next step is to explore the special risks of relying on the Forcible Democratization Justification, understood as including the requirement that at least one of these principles must be satisfied.

The Risks of Using the Forcible Democratization Justification

As with the Preventive Self-defense Justification, the risks of this justification result from the interaction between its speculative character and the characteristics of the agents that are likely to employ it. To ensure that the Benefit Proportionality or Respect Principles are satisfied requires empirical predictions, under conditions of considerable uncertainty, and this creates considerable opportunities for error, bias, deception of others, and self-deception. To make a sound judgment that either principle is satisfied, one must have something like a causal theory of forcible democratization, although all the causal links need not be clearly specified. Unless one has at least a basic grasp of the conditions under which forcible democratization can succeed, one cannot make credible estimates either of what the costs of the effort to the beneficiaries are likely to be or whether those costs could be reasonably accepted by them.

Now it could be argued with considerable persuasiveness that at present no one is in possession of a causal theory of forcible democratization capable of grounding the predictions that are necessary for determining whether the Benefit Proportionality or Respect Principles are satisfied ex ante, that is, at the time when the would-be forcible democratizer is supposed to be determining whether they are satisfied. Nonetheless, let us suppose for the sake of argument that there is credible information about the circumstances in which forcible democratization is more likely to succeed. Even if this is so, there will clearly be considerable opportunity for honest errors of judgment, as well as deception and manipulation of evidence. Everything said earlier about the inherent risks of the speculative character of the Preventive Self-defense Justification applies, perhaps with even greater force here. When the would-be forcible democratizers have ulterior motives for going to war that they are loathe to cite in public justifications, the possibility of motivated false belief exacerbates these risks.

This last factor should not be underestimated. It is very likely that any state that is willing to incur the human and material costs of going to war will have additional motives beyond that of humanitarian concern for those upon whom it proposes to bestow the blessings of democracy.

In addition, there is another feature of the Forcible Democratization Justification that carries special risks. This justification is open-ended in a way that the Preventive Self-defense Justification is not. The end to be achieved in the case of the Forcible Democratization Justification is less determinate in two ways than the end to be achieved in the case of the Preventive Self-defense Justification. First, 'democracy' refers to a range of governance institutions, whereas in the Preventive Self-defense Justification the end for which war is undertaken is the removal of a wrongfully imposed risk of a dire harm. In the former case, the indeterminacy of the end facilitates what might be called *goal substitution*. If the forcible democratizer has congruent interests, then she may be tempted to pursue their realization under the cover of achieving democracy, and this is easier to accomplish, other things being equal, if the end is indeterminate. In consequence, it may be harder for third parties to detect that goals other than democracy are driving, and in fact distorting or undercutting, the putative democratization effort until very late in the game. The would-be forcible democratizer, then, may have strong incentives for not clarifying the nature of the goal ex ante. Furthermore, failure to specify the goal may only increase the opportunities for erroneously believing, or deceitfully saying that one believes, that the Beneficiary Proportionality and Respect Principles are satisfied when in fact they are not.

Second, the end is temporally indeterminate. Given the lack of a serviceable causal theory of how democracy is to be produced, no timetable can be given for when the end will be achieved. If democracy is not achieved in three years, the forcible democratizer can say that it will likely take five or more, and so on. To put the same point differently, the use of the Preventive Self-defense Justification, as we have explicated it, requires the justifier to identify a rather concrete harm to be averted, to link that future harm to something the target of preventive action has already done in such a way that the "wrongful imposition of a dire risk" condition is satisfied, and to say something determinate about how the harm would come about if preventive action were not taken. Unless all of this is done, the case for preventive self-defense is not made. But if it is done, then the agent invoking this justification has in effect created some of the conditions that are necessary for her being held accountable. The case of Iraq illustrates the point nicely: if the claim is that war is necessary to prevent WMDs from falling into the hands of terrorists, but no WMDs are found and there is no evidence that they were spirited away in the nick of time, then this counts toward discrediting the justification.

It is quite different in the case of going to war to create democracy. Failure to produce democracy is not evidence that the justification has failed, at least not for a very long time. Even after the nondemocratic government is deposed, the would-be democratizer can argue that ongoing armed resistance comes from antidemocratic forces and that antidemocratic "wreckers" are impeding the development of new institutions. In that sense, the agent who uses the Forcible Democratization

Justification incurs less risk of being exposed as insincere and less risk of being held accountable than an agent who uses the Preventive Self-defense Justification. Furthermore, if democracy is never achieved, the agent who invoked the latter justification has a ready excuse that is likely to have considerable rhetorical appeal, especially if there is widespread prejudice toward the culture and character of the intended beneficiaries: she can blame the failure on the intended beneficiaries' lack of political will or on ignorance.

The twin indeterminacy of the end in the Forcible Democratization Justification therefore diminishes the accountability of those who employ it and to that extent encourages goal substitution and other forms of self-deception or deception of others. To put the same point differently, the nature of the justification itself reduces the expected costs to the justifier of misusing the justification. This makes using the justification riskier, other things being equal.

This brief exploration of the risks of relying on the Forcible Democratization Justification is not intended to be exhaustive. However, it should suffice to establish that the risks of using the Forcible Democratization Justification are so great that its use could be morally permissible only if credible measures were taken to reduce them. Once these risks are understood, it seems clear that credible measures would have to include institutionalizing the decision-making process. As noted earlier, Keohane and I have argued in detail, a necessary condition for justified preventive self-defense is that the decision to engage in preventive action must be made within an institutional framework aptly designed to reduce the special risks of this kind of justification. The institutionalist conclusion applies a fortiori to the Forcible Democratization Justification, because it is, if anything, even more subject to error and abuse than the Preventive War Justification. If this is the case, then the Traditional Norm should not be abandoned in favor of a more permissive norm that allows forcible democratization unless the new norm would be embedded in a system of institutional safeguards.

The analysis thus far indicates that at minimum the needed institutional safeguards would have to do two things. First, they would have to cope with the risks associated with the indeterminancy of the goal of democratization. Second, they would have to ensure reliable predictions of the sort necessary for a credible effort to determine ex ante whether the Beneficiary Proportionality and Respect Principles are satisfied. I now want show how an accountability regime for making use-of-force decisions that include decisions to make war to create democracy might achieve these two objectives.

Making the Goal More Determinate

In order to reduce the risks associated with the indeterminancy of the goal, an institution for making responsible decisions concerning forcible democratization would need to do at least three things: (1) specify benchmarks for progress toward democratization; (2) provide mechanisms for monitoring progress, according to the benchmarks; and (3) attach significant costs to failure to make appropriate progress. Furthermore, such an arrangement could only be expected to work if it were multilateral or at least included adequate provisions for independent and comparatively impartial monitoring of progress according to antecedently specified benchmarks.

In order to specify benchmarks for progress toward democratization, the vague concept of democracy would have to be made more determinate. The state or coalition proposing war for forcible democratization would be required to specify what sort of democracy they aim to help create. From a cosmopolitan standpoint the aim is presumably some form of constitutional democracy, with an independent judiciary and other institutions for protecting the rights of individuals and, where appropriate, minorities as well. The task here is to steer a course between a conception of democracy that is so indeterminate as to create the risks of mere rationalization or goal substitution and one that is specified in such a narrow way as to invite the criticism that the forcible democratizers are imposing their own parochial conception of democracy on a people who may have good reason to reject it.[21]

Institutionalizing the Benefit Proportionality and Respect Principles

Ensuring the reliability of the sorts of empirical predictions that one would have to make in order to do a credible job, ex ante, of determining whether the Benefit Proportionality and Respect Principles are satisfied would require two things. First, one would have to know enough about how forcible democratization works to formulate a set of conditions under which the prospects for successful forcible democratization are good. These conditions need not be understood as being either jointly sufficient or individually necessary for success. Instead, they might be more like what Rawls refers to as "counting principles": the more of them are satisfied and the greater the extent to which they are satisfied, the more likely the effort will succeed.[22]

Second, there would have to be a way of helping to ensure that the criteria were accurately applied to the assessment of the case at hand. Presumably this would require the application of the "counting principles" by a comparatively impartial body, that is, someone other than the state / (or states) that is / (are) proposing forcible democratization. There would have to be an accountability mechanism similar to the one Keohane and I propose for preventive war decisions, to create incentives for the would-be forcible democratizer to make the case for action on the basis of reliable predictions concerning the costs and benefits. Similarly, whether relevant states would agree to participate in such an institution would depend upon a number of factors, including how much state leaders value the credibility that participation in it would bring and the extent to which politically effective domestic groups see their state's participation as worthwhile on prudential and / or moral grounds.

At present there is considerable controversy as to the conditions under which forcible democratization is likely to occur.[23] That it *can* occur is clear from the fact that it *has* occurred in at least three cases: Japan, Germany, and Italy after World War II.[24] Simply for purposes of illustration, let us consider a hypothesis about what a plausible list of "counting principles" would look like: the prospects for forcible democratization are greater the more of the following criteria are satisfied and the greater the degree to which they are satisfied, other things being equal.[25]

(1) The current regime (that is, the despotism that is to be toppled and replaced by a democracy) is foreign.
(2) There is a fairly recent history of democracy.
(3) The current regime has just suffered a total defeat in a war caused by its own aggression (Germany, Japan, and Italy).
(4) Economic development is sufficient for a substantial middle class and literacy rates are high (Germany, Japan, and Italy).

If the current regime is an alien imposition, the people in question presumably will be more likely to cooperate with, or at least not as vigorously resist, an invasion to topple it than if it were their "own" regime. If there is a history of democracy, then that is some reason to hope that it can take root again or at least to believe that there is no essential incompatibility between democracy and the dominant culture of the country. If the current regime has been totally defeated in a war caused by is own aggression, the population may be more receptive to the fundamental political change, even if it is imposed by recent enemies. Some theorists have suggested that condition 4 may be more important for preventing a newly established democracy from deteriorating than for creating democracy in the first place. Perhaps the point is that high literacy rates enable more effective participation in democratic processes and that where there is a substantial middle class significant numbers of people will be economically secure enough to continue to support democratic processes even when short-term results are not optimal from their point of view. If this is the case, then condition 4 is relevant to the question of whether forcible democratization is likely to create a stable democracy.

At most, only one of these conditions, the fourth, was satisfied in the case of Iraq. In fact, it is not even clear that it was satisfied. By the time the war was launched, the level of economic development had declined seriously, due to a combination of a decade of sanctions and gross mismanagement on the part of the Baathist regime.

What is striking is that nothing in the actual decision-making process that led to the invasion of Iraq required U.S. leaders take a stand on what conditions improve the prospects for successful forcible democratization, much less to provide any evidence that such conditions were present in Iraq. Suppose, instead, that the decision to engage in forcible democratization had been made in an institutional framework that (1) required the public articulation of the favorable conditions for forcible democratization and the marshalling of evidence of that at least some of them were satisfied in the case at hand; and (2) facilitated a critical, impartial evaluation of the criteria and the evidence; and (3) attached significant costs to a negative evaluation. Such an arrangement would reduce the extraordinary risks of relying on the Forcible Democratization Justification.

My aim in this section has not been to develop either a comprehensive moral theory of forcible democratization or to advance an institutionalist solution to the risks that reliance on the Forcible Democratization Justification entails. Instead, I have tried to show that as in the case of preventive self-defense, the moral controversy cannot be resolved without a consideration of the ways in which institutional innovations might cope with the special risks of this type of justification, and to establish that appropriate institutionalization of the decision-making process is a necessary condition for justified forcible democratization.

My aim is not to show that the institutional approach outlined here is likely to be adapted by the most powerful states either at present or in the future. If it turns out that the institutional demands for morally permissible decisions to engage in preventive self-defense or forcible democratization will not be met, then my argument supports the conclusion that preventive self-defense and forcible democratization are not justifiable. If the institutions in question cannot be realized, then continued adherence to the JWN's blanket prohibitions will be vindicated.

Institutions and the Ethics of Leadership

The institutionalist approach I have articulated in this chapter has important implications for how we ought to conceive of the ethics of leadership. A cogent theory of the ethics of leadership will include principles for evaluating the conduct of leaders that are grounded in reasonable assumptions about what we can expect of leaders. If a leadership role itself makes the individual who occupies it especially vulnerable to certain sorts of moral failings or cognitive errors, because of the social expectations that constitute the role, the requirements of staying in power, or specific features of the institutions within which leaders function, then our moral evaluations of leaders ought to take this into account. Otherwise, evaluations will be unrealistic and unfairly blaming.

It is a mistake, however, to assume that the special moral risks of the leadership role are fixed. Both the character and the gravity of these risks can vary, depending upon the institutional context in which the leader functions. Constitutional theory is grounded on this simple point. Appropriate institutional checks and balances can reduce the risks attendant on leadership roles in various branches of government.

More generally, properly designed institutions can reduce the moral risks of leadership by protecting leaders from moral lapses or cognitive errors that facilitate unethical decisions that would otherwise be likely to occur. This could be achieved in either or both of two ways. First, institutions that require leaders to justify their actions to the public, to parties in other branches of government, or in the case of multilateral institutions, to other leaders, could simply prohibit appeals to certain types of justifications, on the grounds that they are too risky. (The idea that institutions can constrain the types of justifications that may be employed is not new, of course. Every legal system employs it. Only certain kinds of arguments, those that appeal to established legal principles, are permitted to be used in legal proceedings.) Second, especially risky types of justifications might be allowed, but only if they are deployed within a properly designed set of institutional safeguards to reduce these risks to acceptable levels. The ethics of leadership should take institutions seriously, then, not only in order to make fair evaluations of the performance of leaders in the light of the contributions institutions can make to the risks that leaders labor under, but also in considering how institutional arrangements can improve the performance of leaders.

A disturbing feature of the scholarly discussion of the justifiability of the U.S. invasion of Iraq and of the more general issues of preventive war and forcible democratization the invasion raised is the absence of any consideration of the ethics of leadership. Justifications are treated more as abstract objects, as sets of propositions, than as actions performed by justifiers. One implication of my analysis here is that what might be called the *ethics of justification* ought to be central to moral theorizing about war. Decisions to go to war are made by state leaders, and state leaders are subject to incentives and motivations that can make their recourse to certain kinds of justifications for going to war extremely dangerous; and the dangers, at least to some extent, are knowable. So leaders should be judged not simply for their actions, but also for the sorts of justifications they invoke for them. Similarly, arguments intended to justify war ought to be evaluated not only according to the truth of their premises and the validity of their inferences, but also according to the epistemic and moral demands their proper use makes on the sorts of agents that are likely to employ them.

3. THE LIMITS OF JUST WAR THEORY

Through a critical examination of two challenges to the traditional just war norm, I have made the case for rethinking the framing assumptions of traditional thinking about the morality of war. I have argued that the validity of use-of-force norms can depend upon institutional context and that the validity of the Just War Norm that war is only justified in response to an actual or imminent attack is at best contingent. This latter highly constraining norm, which rules out preventive force and forcible democratization, may be quite plausible where institutional resources for constraining war are negligible. The attraction of the JWN is that it avoids the extraordinary risks of the Preventive Self-defense and Forcible Democratization Justifications by taking these justifications off the table. However, here, as elsewhere, risk reduction is not costless. When circumstances change, costs that previously were tolerable may become excessive. The question then arises as to whether the old norm is still valid.

Whether it is, I have argued, cannot be determined without going beyond the noninstitutionalist framing assumption of Just War Theory. The proper question to ask is not whether the Traditional Norm ought to be replaced with a more permissive one, but rather whether we should continue to adhere to the JWN or create new institutions within which reliance on a more permissive norm would be morally responsible. The key point is that constraint can be achieved not only by narrowly drawn norms, but also by a combination of institutional safeguards and more permissive norms. Whether we should stick to the old norm or institutionalize a more permissive one depends upon two factors: whether the new norm-institution package would be morally better than the status quo and the feasibility and costs of creating the new institution. Among the costs to be considered is the possibility that the effort to create a new institution may weaken support for the old, more constraining norm, without in fact producing an institution that adequately ameliorates the special risks of resort to preventive self-defense or forcible democratization justifications.

Once the interdependence of norms and institutions is understood, the inadequacy of Just War Theory becomes clear. If the domain of Just War Theory is limited to large-scale military conflict under conditions in which institutional resources are negligible, then it cannot tell us whether we should create new institutions for the sake of adopting better norms, and its approach to the morality of war is inherently and arbitrarily conservative. If the domain of Just War Theory is simply large-scale military conflict, then the Traditional Norm, whose plausibility depends upon the assumption that constraint is to be achieved without reliance on institutions, is not adequately supported. To show that the JWN is valid, it is necessary to engage in empirically grounded institutional reasoning. Philosophical argument, although necessary, is not enough. A defensible theory of the morality of war must integrate moral reasoning with institutional theory.

Notes

I am indebted to Robert O. Keohane for many insights that helped stimulate me to write this chapter and to Keohane, Jeff McMahan, Christopher (Kit) Wellman, and the editors of *Philosophy and Public Affairs*, for valuable comments on earlier drafts.

1. I proceed on the assumption that the dominant stream of contemporary Just War Theory endorses this norm. In its earlier versions, Just War Theory included the idea that war could be waged to punish wrongs. However, in recent times the idea of war as punishment has fallen into disfavor, for good reasons. Nonetheless, one might argue that what

I have called the *Just War Norm* includes an exception: war may be waged (as a last resort) to rectify wrongful conquest. Whether this is an exception depends upon how one construes "armed attack" in the JWN. If this includes an unjust occupation as an ongoing attack on the people of the unjustly conquered state, then war to rectify wrongful conquest is not an exception to the JWN but rather is encompassed by it. If one believes that this is an implausible construal of "armed attack," then the JWN can be reformulated to include this exception. The two justifications I am concerned with in this chapter, the Preventive Self-defense Justification and the Forcible Democratization Justification, are challenges to the JWN regardless of whether it is understood to cover war to rectify unjust conquest or not.

2. An exception is Allen Buchanan and Robert O. Keohane, "The Preventive Use of Force: A Cosmopolitan Institutionalist Perspective," *Ethics and International Affairs* 18 (2004): 1–22.

3. David Luban, "Preventive War," *Philosophy and Public Affairs* 32 (2004): 207–48, at p. 220.

4. Richard Miller's valuable discussion of humanitarian military intervention is a notable exception. Richard W. Miller, "Respectable Oppressors, Hypocritical Liberators: Morality, Intervention, and Reality," in *Ethics and Foreign Intervention*, ed. Deen K. Chaterjee and Don E. Schied (Cambridge: Cambridge University Press, 2003), 215.

5. "National Security Strategy of the United States of America September 2002," p. 6: available at http://www.globalsecurity.org/military/library/policy/dod/nds-usa_mar2005. This document misleadingly uses the term 'preemptive,' which in standard international legal usage refers to efforts to thwart an *imminent* attack, to cover preventive self-defense, that is, defensive action against a temporally distant anticipated harm.

6. Luban's view of justified preventive war, which I critique below, incorporates something like the notion of a dire harm, but does not include the crucial requirement that the risk of harm must be wrongfully imposed.

7. Arnold H. Lowey, "Conspiracy," in *Criminal Law in a Nutshell* (St. Paul, Minn.: West Group, 2000), 260; and Joshua Dressler, "Inchoate Offenses," in *Cases and Materials in Criminal Law*, 2nd ed. (St. Paul, Minn.: West Group, 1999), 765.

8. Russell Powell, "The Law and Philosophy of Preventive War: An Institution-based Approach to Collective Self-defense in Response to Mega-terrorism" (unpublished manuscript), builds on the Institutionalist approach to preventive force developed in Buchanan and Keohane and argues that the law of attempts is the more useful analogy because, unlike the law of conspiracy, it does not require two or more parties working in concert. Powell's paper provides valuable critical overview of the international legal issues regarding preventive force.

9. It might be argued that there is still a problem: at least some of the enemy soldiers who may be targeted by the preventive action may not, in any significant sense, be part of the conspiracy. I argue that there are two distinct conditions under which such individuals may be legitimate targets: when they are culpable for putting themselves at the disposal of governments whose behavior indicates that are likely to engage in conspiracies to commit aggression or when the unjust harm that will occur if preventive action is not taken is so great that it is justifiable to attack them in spite of their lack of culpability, given that reasonable efforts have been made to apprise them that the action about to be taken against them is not an unjust attack but rather a justified preventive action and that they have been given the opportunity to surrender or step aside. Allen Buchanan, "The Justification of Preventive War," in *Preemption: Military Action and Moral Justification*, ed. Henry Shue and David Rodin (Oxford: Oxford University Press, 2007).

10. David Luban, "Preventive War," 230.

11. Ibid., 229–31.

12. I thank Jeff McMahan for this example.

13. Buchanan and Keohane, "Preventive Use of Force."

14. Ibid., 10–16.

15. In saying that preventive self-defense is justifiable only if the decision to use it is made within such institutional constraints, we were *not* endorsing the view that preventive force is only justified if the decision to use it receives Security Council authorization. On the contrary, we argued that the Security Council does not satisfy the accountability requirements we outline, chiefly because there is no effective accountability for the exercise of the permanent member veto.

16. I am indebted to Rachel Zuckert for making this point clear to me.

17. Some might object to this assumption, contending that nondemocratic states *can* do a creditable job of protecting basic human rights, in spite of the fact that the most massive violations of citizens' basic human rights by their governments in modern times have been perpetrated by dictatorships, not democratic governments. The plausibility of this objection depends in part upon how high one sets the bar for being democratic. If one's definition of 'democracy' includes the requirement that major government officials are subject to accountability through periodic elections, then a strong case can be made that even basic human rights are insecure where democracy is not present. See, for example, Amartya Sen's empirically based argument that famines do not occur in democracies. Amartya K. Sen, *Poverty and Famines: An Essay on Entitlement and Deprivation* (New York: Oxford University Press, 1981); "Development: Which Way Now?" *Economic Journal* 93 (1983): 745–62; Amartya K. Sen and Jean Dreze, *Hunger and Public Action* (Oxford: Clarendon Press, 1989). See David Beetham, *Democracy and Rights* (Cambridge, England: Polity Press, 1999), 89–114. (It may not be an accident that Rawls's example of a nondemocratic state that protects basic human rights is an *imaginary* society, "Kazanistan." See John Rawls, *The Law of Peoples* [Cambridge, Mass.: Harvard University Press, 1999], 5, 64.) In my judgment, the view that basic human rights are insecure without democracy is sufficiently plausible to make worthwhile the project of trying to ascertain the conditions under which forcible democratization would be justified.

18. Jeff McMahan, "The Ethics of Killing in War," *Ethics* 114 (2004): 693–733.

19. Any attempt to determine whether the Antipaternalism Principle is satisfied is complicated by the fact that the costs of successful forcible democratization are likely to be disportionately borne by the present population, while the benefits largely will accrue to later generations. Notice, however, that this problem is not unique to forcible democratization from without. It also arises for revolution. Furthermore, support for democratic revolution is not likely to be anywhere near unanimous even among those now living. These reflections raise an interesting question whose exploration must await another occasion: is forcible democratization from without significantly more morally problematic than democratic revolution? I am indebted to an editor of *Philosophy and Public Affairs* for prompting me to consider this issue.

20. An editor of *Philosophy and Public Affairs* suggested this idea to me.

21. In particular, it would be important not to allow the goal of democratization to be replaced with that of creating a particular kind of democratic society that the forcible democratizer happens to favor, for example, one that features relatively unregulated markets or one that cooperates in the forcible democratizer's geopolitical projects or is willing to sell the forcible democratizer oil at favorable prices. The difficulty of specifying, without overspecifying, the notion of democracy should not be underestimated. The institutional arrangements would have to avoid two errors: making the goal of democracy so indeterminate as to invite goal substitution, on the one hand, and making it so determinate ex ante

as to deprive the forcible democratizers of the ability to make reasonable revisions of their initial plans for how to achieve democracy during the process of implementation, on the other. I thank Christopher Griffin for this point. In addition, there is the thorny problem of how the democratization should take into account input from the people themselves as to what particular form of democracy they want, independently of whether what they want is in fact judged to be optimal by the democratizing force.

22. John Rawls, *A Theory of Justice* (Cambridge, Mass.: Harvard University Press, 1971), 415–16.

23. The literature on democratization indicates that there is a great deal of uncertainty as to the conditions under which democracy is likely to occur. For contrasting prominent views, see the following works: Fareed Zakaria, *The Future of Freedom: Illiberal Democracy at Home and Abroad* (New York: W. W. Norton, 2003); Samuel P. Huntington, *The Third Wave: Democratization in the Late Twentieth Century* (Norman: University of Oklahoma Press, 1993); Adam Przeworski, Michael E. Alvarez, Jose Anonio Chibub, and Fernando Limong, *Democracy and Development: Political Institutions and Well-being in the World, 1950–1990* (Cambridge: Cambridge University Press, 2000).

24. Detlef Junker, ed., *The United States and Germany in the Era of the Cold War, 1945–1990, A Handbook, Vol. I: 1945–1968* (New York: Cambridge University Press, 2004); John W. Dower, *Embracing Defeat: Japan in the Wake of World War II* (New York: W. W. Norton/New Press, 1999).

25. I am grateful to Robert O. Keohane for suggestions about what should be included in the list of "counting principles."

12

JUSTIFYING PREVENTIVE WAR

1. RETHINKING THE MORALITY OF PREVENTIVE WAR

Preemptive war aims to avert an imminent harm. Preventive war aims to avert a harm that is more temporarily distant. Mainstream just war theory concedes that preemptive war can sometimes be justified, although its permissibility in international law is contested. Both mainstream just war theory and international law prohibit preventive war.[1]

1.1. The Prima Facie Case for the Justifiability of Preventive War

On the face of it, the idea that preventive war can be justifiable, at least when it is waged in self-defense, seems quite commonsensical. As Jeff McMahan has pointed out, there is a straightforward sense in which all self-defensive action is preventive. When you strike a person who is currently attacking you, your aim, so far as you are acting in self-defense, is to avert any *further* harm the attacker may do you; it is too late to defend yourself against the harm he has already caused. There seems to be no obvious bar to using force to defend oneself against an unjust harm that will occur further in the future rather than the harm that one expects in the next few seconds when an attack is already underway. Of course, one might be more likely to be mistaken about whether someone is going to attack in the distant future than about whether he is going to attack in the next moment, but that would only warrant special caution; it would not rule out preventive action.

At least in the case of individual self-defense, then, it seems that mere temporal distance is not sufficient to cancel the right of self-defense, understood as the right to use proportional force, when necessary, to avert the unjust infliction of a serious harm on oneself. If the use of lethal force can be justified to avert an imminent harm, then presumably it can be justified to avert a harm that is just slightly more temporally distant than an imminent harm, and so on.

McMahan reinforces this intuition by appeal to a hypothetical case, the Paralysis Example.[2] You find conclusive evidence that a villain has a well-thought-out plan to murder you when you become paralyzed and are unable to defend yourself, a few weeks from now. For whatever reason, you are not able to rely on the police or others to protect you; you can only avert the lethal unjust harm by using lethal force against the villain even though the harm he intends to inflict on you is not imminent. McMahan concludes that under these circumstances you would be morally justified in using preventive lethal force in self-defense. This conclusion seems to be cogent.

McMahan's example is one of individual self-defense, not war. Robert O. Keohane and I offer an example in which collective preventive force sufficient to count as an act of war seems intuitively justifiable.[3] In the Lethal Virus case, country A has good evidence, from multiple reliable sources, that an international terrorist group that has already committed several deadly attacks on innocent populations has in its possession a lethal and extraordinarily contagious virus (for which there is presently no treatment) which it will eventually release in a major city. There is no reason to believe that the release of the virus is imminent, but there is good reason to believe that once the virus leaves the terrorists' remote mountain stronghold the chances of intercepting it are poor. A missile strike against the remote mountain stronghold, which lies within the borders of country B, will destroy the virus and only kill members of the terrorist organization. Surely under these circumstances it would be justifiable to use lethal force preventively and the fact that force would be deployed collectively against a group, rather than by an individual against another individual is immaterial.

If there is doubt that a large-scale military action against a nonstate terrorist group counts as war, consider instead the following case. Country A has recently engaged in aggressive war against country C and all indications are that its commitment to aggression continues unabated. Country B has very good evidence that it is next on country A's target list and also has good evidence that A has only refrained from attacking B so far because A has not yet completed a packet of new missiles that can evade B's missile-defense system, utterly destroy B's power to resist A's invasion, and kill many of B's people. B also has good evidence that unless it destroys several facilities that make an especially critical part for the missile system now, the critical part will be distributed to a large number of well-protected missile-production facilities around country A and that B's chances of preventing A's missile attack will be poor. The missile attack, if it occurs, will be at least six months from now so the harmful attack is not imminent; but to prevent it, B must strike now.

Such examples suggest that the point McMahan invokes the Paralysis Example to make is not confined to individual acts of self-defense. Preventive war seems to be morally justifiable.

2. ARGUMENTS AGAINST PREVENTIVE WAR

The Paralysis Example, the Lethal Virus example, and the Missile Attack example at the very least show that a strong argument is needed to rule out the justifiability of preventive war. In fact, two types of arguments are advanced by those who deny that preventive war is justifiable: those that contend that the inherently speculative character of the preventive-war justification makes it too subject to error and abuse, and those according to which, quite apart from the problems of error and abuse, preventive war is unjust, because it involves a violation of the rights to life of the targets of preventive action, since, by hypothesis, they have not (yet) done anything wrong. The former type of argument is usually called consequentialist, the latter rights-based.

The strength of the consequentialist objection is its refusal to be seduced by highly sanitized, rare examples like those of the Lethal Virus and Missile Attack examples. These examples are highly sanitized in that they assume highly accurate information about the intentions and capabilities of the target of preventive action and also assume, implicitly, that there is no reasonable prospect for averting the future attack without using preventive force. (Similarly, one should be wary of attempts to justify torture simply by appealing to the intuitive permissibility of torturing an individual whom one *knows* (not merely suspects) to be a terrorist who possesses information which, if one can get it, *will* (not may) allow one to avert the destruction of millions of innocent people).

2.1. The Bad Practice Objection

However, the consequentialist label is misleading, because it lumps together two different objections based on the inherently speculative character of the preventive-war justification, only one of which is consequentialist in any interesting sense. The first objection, which more properly warrants the title 'consequentialist', appeals to the supposedly bad consequences, not of the particular preventive act, but of the general acceptance of a principle that allows preventive war. The idea here is that because the preventive-war justification is inherently speculative, the general acceptance of a principle allowing preventive war would lead to intolerable abuse and error. Too many wars would be undertaken on the basis of false or unjustified predictions of future harm or because the prospect of future harm would be used as a pretext for aggressive war, or both. Call this the 'bad practice' objection. The second objection that is lumped together with it under the label 'consequentialist', unlike the bad practice objection, does not rely upon any prediction about the bad consequences of the general acceptance of a principle that allows preventive war. Rather, it holds that, given the inherently speculative character of the preventive-war justification, it is morally irresponsible for state leaders to invoke it to undertake anything so morally momentous as war. Call this the 'irresponsible act' objection.

As it stands, the 'bad practice' objection is not in fact an argument to show that it is wrong to engage in preventive war; at most it shows that general acceptance of a principle that allows preventive war would be wrong. To make it an argument that shows that it is wrong to engage in preventive war, one would need to add one or the other of two premises, each of which is highly disputable: (*a*) it is always wrong to act on a principle which, if generally accepted, would produce unacceptable results, or (*b*) every case in which a country engages in preventive war in fact significantly increases the probability that other states will come to accept the principle that preventive war is justified (and thereby will contribute to a bad practice).

The difficulties with premise (*a*) are well-known from the critical literature on the role of generalization principles in ethical judgment. The most obvious problem is that there are innumerable acts that are permissible even though it would be disastrous if everyone did them—for example, devoting one's life to the solution of the Trolley Problem, or closing one's eyes for one minute at a particular time of day.

Premise (*b*) is too sweeping a generalization to be plausible. Whether a particular country's engaging in preventive war will significantly increase the probability that others will engage in preventive wars will depend on a number of contingent factors. The relevant question, however, is not whether it will significantly increase the probability of preventive wars, but rather whether it will significantly increase the probability of *unjustified* preventive wars. To assume that an increase in the probability of any preventive wars, just or unjust, is unacceptable, is to beg the question at hand, namely, 'Is preventive war ever justified?'

Whether a particular case of preventive war will significantly increase the probability of unjustified preventive wars in the future may depend upon how the particular case is generally regarded. Especially if there is a well-entrenched norm against preventive war, a single instance may not increase the probability of future occurrences, if the country engaging in preventive war makes a convincing case that the circumstances warranted an exception to an otherwise sound prohibition against prevention. A plausible justification, along with an acknowledgment that the general prohibition is sound, may avoid a significant increase in the chance of unjustified preventive war.

It is worth making explicit why premise (*b*) is formulated using the notion of *significantly* increasing the probability of future (unjustified) preventive wars. The point is that we cannot assume that if a particular preventive war does increase the probability of future unjustified preventive wars, it is thereby impermissible. A small increase in the probability of future unjust preventive wars might be an acceptable price to pay to prevent a sufficiently awful harm.

Any state contemplating engaging in preventive war should, of course, take seriously the possibility that its action will be taken to have precedential value and should also be aware that others may either unwittingly or deliberately misrepresent the character of the act they take as a precedent. For example, under certain circumstances, a country might be justified in engaging in preventive war, but only because of exceptional circumstances; yet other countries might believe or claim to believe that a more general precedent was being set, that a broader permission to engage in preventive war was being established, one that did not limit permissible preventive war to the exceptional circumstances. As I suggested earlier, however, how great this risk of 'false precedent' is in any particular case will depend upon several factors, including how well-entrenched the prohibition against prevention is and how good a job the country engaging in prevention does in making the case that its action was justified only because of exceptional circumstances and that those circumstances are very unlikely to be repeated. Although it may be true that the most powerful, influential countries run the greatest risk of setting a dangerous precedent by their actions, they are also the ones that are best able to shape the content of the precedent that is set.

Once we see how problematic premises (*a*) and (*b*) are, it becomes clear that the first 'consequentialist' argument against preventive war, the 'bad practice' argument, at best gives reason to be very cautious about engaging in preventive war, not conclusive reasons against its justifiability. It may be that those who have argued against preventive war by appealing to the fact that the preventive-war justification is prone to error and abuse, but who have done so without making explicit and defending either premise (*a*) or premise (*b*), have failed to distinguish clearly between two quite different tasks that might be pursued under the heading of just war theorizing. The first is to determine the moral status of various acts of war; the second is to formulate appropriate constitutive rules for a morally defensible practice of war-making. (Jeff McMahan has noted this crucial distinction and made it clear that his just war theorizing is concerned primarily with the former task). Unless supplemented with a convincing defense of either premise (*a*) or premise (*b*), the 'bad practice' objection cannot show that any particular act of making preventive war is wrong. As it stands, the 'bad practice' argument is only plausible as an objection to the general acceptance of a principle allowing preventive war, whether as a formal principle of international law or as constitutive rule of an informal practice.

It is important to understand that this first objection *cannot* provide a conclusive argument against general acceptance of a principle allowing preventive war. For as Robert O. Keohane and I have argued elsewhere, appropriate institutions for making the decision to use preventive force may significantly reduce the risk of abuse and error, both in the decision itself and with respect to its precedential effects. Whether a practice that allows preventive war under certain circumstances would be an unacceptable practice depends upon how the practice is institutionalized.[4] If institutional safeguards can adequately address the problem of abuse and error, then the practice may be morally acceptable.

2.2. The Irresponsible Act Objection

This second argument does not rely, even implicitly, on premise (*a*) or premise (*b*). It is at least the right sort of argument to show, not just that general acceptance of a principle that allows preventive war is wrong, but that it is wrong to engage in preventive war.

The intuitively plausible idea behind the 'irresponsible act' argument is that, other things being equal, the higher the stakes in acting and in particular the greater the moral risk, the higher are the *epistemic requirements* for justified action. The decision to go to war is generally a high stakes decision par excellence and the moral risks are especially great, for two reasons. First, unless one is justified in going to war, one's deliberate killing of enemy combatants will be murder, indeed mass murder. Secondly, at least in large-scale modern war, it is a virtual certainty that one will kill innocent people even if one is justified in going to war and conducts the war in such a way as to try to minimize harm to innocents. Given these grave moral risks of going to war, quite apart from often substantial prudential concerns, some types of justifications for going to war may simply be too subject to abuse and error to make it justifiable to invoke them.

The 'irresponsible act' objection is not a consequentialist objection in any interesting sense. It does not depend upon the assumption that every particular act of going to war preventively has unacceptably bad consequences (whether in itself or by virtue of contributing to the general acceptance of a principle allowing preventive war); nor does it assume that it is always wrong to rely on a justification which, if generally accepted, would produce unacceptable consequences. Instead, the 'irresponsible act' objection is more accurately described as an agent-centered argument and more particularly an argument from moral epistemic responsibility.

The 'irresponsible act' objection to preventive war is highly plausible if—but only if—one assumes that the agents who would invoke the preventive-war justification are, as it were, *on their own* in making the decision to go to war preventively. In other words, the objection is incomplete unless the context of decision-making is further specified. Whether the special risks of relying on the preventive-war justification are unacceptably high will depend, *inter alia*, upon whether the decision-making process includes effective provisions for reducing those special risks. Because the special risks are at least in significant part epistemic—due to the inherently speculative character of the preventive war-justification—the epistemic context of the decision is crucial. Because institutions can improve the epistemic performance of agents, it is critical to know what the institutional context of the preventive-war decision is, before we can regard the 'irresponsible agent' objection as conclusive. Like the 'bad practice' argument, this second objection to preventive war is inconclusive because it does not consider—and rule out—the possibility that well-designed institutions for decision-making could address the problems that would otherwise make it irresponsible for a leader to invoke the preventive-war justification.

3. THE INSTITUTIONAL APPROACH TO PREVENTIVE WAR

Robert O. Keohane and I have argued that a multilateral *accountability regime* could significantly reduce the special risks of the preventive-war justification, chiefly by providing incentives and deliberative processes that would elicit accurate information about the supposed risk to be averted by preventive action and reduce the risk that the preventive-war justification would be invoked to rationalize aggressive action.[5] The institutional arrangement we favor includes the following key elements. First, it must be multilateral, for the simple reason that no single state can be counted on fully to take into account the legitimate interests of others, especially when contemplating the use of military force. Secondly, the institutional procedure for making the preventive-war decision must satisfy conditions of *ex ante* accountability: all the relevant issues and options (including the nonmilitary options) must be explicitly discussed, under conditions that promote principled deliberation and reduce the risks of strategic bluffing, and under the assumption that the current decision will have precedential value for future cases. All parties to the discussion are to have equal standing to make proposals and to challenge proposals and justifications offered by others. In addition, the decision-making body must include diverse interests; it should not be restricted, for example, to states from one geographical area or only to rich states. We also believe, though this is not essential to the general idea of our proposal, that only states that meet minimal standards of democratic governance and that do not have a recent record of serious violations of basic human rights should be allowed to participate in the institution. (Here it is worth emphasizing that these conditions are intended only as a rather minimal filter; membership would not be restricted to a few states, to 'Western style' democracies, or to the most powerful or 'developed' countries). Thirdly, there must be effective provisions for *ex post* accountability. The state or coalition of states that engage in preventive war must come back to the decision-making body with a full report of their actions. They must also allow an impartial commission, appointed by the decision-making body or some other appropriate body (e.g., a well-respected international agency or nongovernmental human rights organization) unhindered access to the site of the military action as soon as possible. The aim of these requirements is to hold the states that engage in authorized preventive action accountable for the validity of the justifications they offered *ex ante* for using preventive force, including especially the accuracy of the information about the risk to be averted that they presented in making the case for preventive action.

3.1. Attaching Costs to Flawed Decision-making

Meaningful accountability can only be achieved, we argue, if significant costs are attached to a negative *ex post* evaluation, by an impartial body, of the justification given *ex ante* for using preventive force. For example, those who engaged in the preventive action would be required to compensate those whom they harmed and to bear all or most of the cost of repairing damage to the target country's infrastructure caused by the preventive attack. In addition, they would not be allowed to control the political situation in the target country or to determine the allocation of aid or the awarding of contracts to firms offering services for the reconstruction effort. Just as important, a negative evaluation *ex post* would impose significant reputational costs, one effect of which would be to make it more difficult for the states in question to convince the decision-making body to authorize preventive action in the future.

3.2. Feasibility

Although I cannot develop the argument at length here, Keohane and I also argue that such an institutional arrangement should not be dismissed as utopian. Potential wielders of preventive force would have a strong incentive to submit to the constraints of the accountability regime: doing so would solve what might otherwise be an insurmountable credibility problem and by gaining credibility they would be much more likely to secure military allies and cost-sharers. States that are not themselves likely to propose preventive action but who appreciate its special risks and wish to restrain the action of powerful states would also have an incentive to help create the needed institution. Finally, domestic forces that are concerned to constrain their own country's recourse to force generally, and who are especially impressed by the dangers of preventive action, would have an incentive to pressure their governments to participate in the accountability regime and, to the extent that they must be responsive to domestic constituencies, this would in turn give the government an additional reason to participate. In these ways, the creation and maintenance of an accountability regime could become a focal point for coordinated action by actors with diverse and even conflicting interests.

This institutional approach to just war theory relies upon the idea of the division of labor, in two distinct ways. First, achieving responsible decision-making is seen as a matter of getting the right combination of norms and institutions. With better institutions, it may be possible to replace a blanket norm prohibiting preventive war under any circumstances with a more nuanced norm that allows preventive war if the decision to engage in it is reached through an appropriate institutional process. Secondly, there can and presumably should be a division of labor between domestic and international (or regional) institutions. The weaker a state's own institutions for deciding to go to war are, the greater the need for guidance provided by multilateral institutions, other things being equal, and vice versa. In this regard the case of preventive-war decisions may be the limiting case in which the risks of abuse and error are so high that it is hard to imagine how domestic decision-making institutions could ever be sufficient, even if they were much more effective than those that now exist. The general point, however, is that the answer to the question of whether preventive war is justified depends upon the institutional context and both domestic and multilateral institutions must be taken into account.

In a more recent paper that builds on this work with Keohane, I have argued that whether the reduction of the risk of error and abuse that an accountability regime of the sort we outline would achieve is sufficient to make it responsible to invoke the preventive-war justification depends upon the costs of continuing to adhere to the prohibition on preventive war.[6] For present purposes, the most important conclusion of this institutionalist approach is that preventive war can be justifiable under conditions in which, relative to the costs of maintaining the prohibition on preventive war, the special risks of invoking the preventive-war justification are adequately reduced by appropriate institutional arrangements that are not only feasible but can be created without excessive cost. In brief, the 'irresponsible act' objection to preventive war does not show that preventive war is never justifiable; it only shows that it is irresponsible to invoke the preventive-war justification under conditions in which appropriate institutional arrangements for making the preventive-war decision are not available or, if available, are not utilized.

The institutional approach also provides a rebuttal to the 'bad consequences' objection. A country that subjected its attempt to justify preventive war to the institutional procedure we prescribe would not be guilty of invoking a justification whose general acceptance would produce unacceptable consequences. Nor is there reason to believe that a decision to engage in preventive war that was made according to the sort of institutional procedure Keohane and I outline would increase the incidence of erroneous or abusive uses of the preventive-war justification; on the contrary, the availability of the procedure would both increase the probability that those who complied with it would make good decisions and provide a basis for criticizing and constraining those who decided on preventive war without going through the procedure.

The accountability regime we recommend could form the basis of a morally defensible practice regarding preventive war.

The results of the analysis so far can be summarized as follows. Neither the 'bad consequences' nor the 'irresponsible act' objections show that preventive war is unjustifiable. Both objections can be met if the decision to engage in preventive war is made within an institutional framework that adequately addresses the special risks of error and abuse which the inherently speculative character of the preventive-war justification involves. So, if preventive war is morally prohibited depends upon whether the other, 'rights-based' objection is sound. I now want to argue that there are in fact two quite different 'rights-based' objections and then evaluate them in turn.

4. TWO RIGHTS-BASED OBJECTIONS TO PREVENTIVE WAR

4.1. The Simple Rights-based Argument

This objection to preventive war asserts that there is a morally crucial difference between using force against a presently occurring or imminent attack, on the one hand, and using force preventively on the other. In the former cases, the target of preventive action has done or is doing something wrong (already struck a blow or is in the process of striking one, e.g. by launching missiles or mobilizing troops for attack). In the latter case, the target of preventive force has not done anything wrong, so attacking him violates his right not to be attacked.

The simple rights-based objection begs the question at issue, namely, whether it can ever be justifiable to use lethal force to prevent an attack that is neither presently occurring nor imminent. There is a right not to be unjustly attacked, but the question is whether that right is violated by preventive force.[7]

Reflection on the law of conspiracy indicates that using force against someone who has not yet committed a wrongful harm need not violate his rights. The elements of conspiracy include a specific intention to do wrongful harm and an agreed plan of action to produce the harm. In many jurisdictions there is also the requirement that some initial step to implement the plan has been taken. There is no time limit on the execution of the plan, so the wrongful harm need not be imminent. The law of conspiracy explains how someone can have done something wrong, namely, imposed an unjust risk on others, without actually harming or being about to harm. And to the extent that we believe that enforcement of the law of conspiracy, including the use of deadly force when necessary, is justified, it seems that the moral plausibility of the law of conspiracy refutes the simple rights-based argument against preventive war.

The analogy with the law of conspiracy takes us only so far, however. It only shows that if something like the elements of the crime of conspiracy were present in the case of a state or a terrorist group conspiring to commit a massive unjust harm, it would be justifiable to use force to arrest and punish them, and to use lethal force against them if they resisted arrest, if this were necessary to stop them. In the domestic case, the use of lethal force against conspirators is a last resort and is administered by public officials subject to judicial scrutiny and other forms of accountability, while in the preventive war this is not the case.

It should be clear that this objection to the use of the analogy with the crime of conspiracy to indicate the moral justifiability of preventive war *only* applies to recourse to preventive war that is not constrained by appropriate institutional safeguards. Rather than being an objection to the institutional approach to preventive war, it merely highlights the virtues of that approach, agreeing with the latter's fundamental assumption that the special risks of invoking prevention as a justification for the use of force requires that we subject the decision-making process to a system of institutional safeguards. Thus, to the extent that an institutional scheme (such as the one Keohane and I propose) provides accountability comparable to that which exists in a domestic system in which the law of conspiracy is enforced under the scrutiny of an independent judiciary, the conspiracy analogy holds. In both the domestic case and in the international accountability regime, there is an independent, principled, and comparatively impartial determination of whether the use of force against conspirators is justified. Of course, the accountability regime is not identical to a domestic judicial determination, but it would be a mistake to assume that there is only one way to achieve the needed accountability. The key point is that where the decision to use preventive force is properly constrained by institutions properly designed to reduce the special risks of preventive force justifications and where the target of prevention has imposed an unjust risk, the use of preventive force need not violate the target's rights.

4.2. The Failure to Discriminate Objection

There is a more subtle and serious rights-based objection to the justifiability of preventive war. Unlike the simple rights-based objection, it does not make the mistake of assuming that *those who conspire harm* are not liable to attack unless the harm is imminent. Instead, the claim here is that even if the decision to make preventive war is undertaken within the sort of accountability regime that Keohane and I recommend and even if the analogy with the crime of conspiracy is sound, preventive *war* is not justifiable, only preventive attacks against the *conspirators* is justifiable.[8] The point of this objection is that the conspiracy analogy can only show that those who conspire are imposing an unjust risk on us, and that consequently it is only they who are morally liable to preventive attack, but that when we make preventive war we will be unjustly attacking some, perhaps many, enemy soldiers who had no part either in devising the malevolent plan nor in taking an initial step toward its execution. Indeed, when we engage in preventive war, we will be attacking soldiers who do not even know that they are at war or are about to be at war. Call this the 'failure to discriminate' rights-based objection.

In my judgment, this is the most serious moral objection to preventive war. Yet I do not think it is capable of showing that preventive war is never justifiable. To gauge the force of the failure to discriminate objection we need to distinguish carefully among several different cases of preventive war-making.

Case 1: The Missile Site. The leaders of country A plan to launch a surprise nuclear attack against country B from a missile base in the interior of country A. If country B waits till the missiles are fully operational it runs a high risk of utter destruction, because once launched the missiles cannot be intercepted. The missiles can be destroyed, and the threat averted, by a missile attack on the site. The personnel at the missile site know that the purpose of the construction is to launch an aggressive attack.

This case is the least difficult. The failure to discriminate objection does not apply, because the only people who will be killed by the attack on the missile site can properly be described as being among the conspirators.

Case 2: The Underground Missile Site, The same scenario as in Case 1, except that the missile base is deep underground and cannot be destroyed by air attacks. The only way for country B to avert the deadly nuclear attack is to invade country A and destroy the missiles from the ground before they are operational. However, to reach the missile site, the troops of country B will have to fight and defeat soldiers of country A. These soldiers are not conspirators—they do not know the conspiracy exists—and they will not be involved in the execution of the conspiracy, that is, the arming and firing of the missiles. These soldiers of country A might be called 'innocent obstacles' to successful preventive action on the part of B.

Notice that in this case it may not be plausible to describe the unwitting enemy soldiers as 'collateral damage,' and to invoke the doctrine of double effect. The problem with this characterization is that it seems a stretch to say that their deaths are the merely foreseen but unintended consequence of destroying the missiles. Instead, it might be more accurate to say that one intends their death as a means of averting the threat of nuclear attack. Nor can one easily say that they are being killed by not being *targeted*. In these respects, the 'innocent obstacles' in Case 2 are *not* like neighboring noncombatants who are killed by strategic bombing of military targets. So neither the distinction between the targeted and the nontargeted, nor the appeal to the doctrine of double effect convincingly removes the worry that they are unjustly killed.

Nonetheless, the case can be made that it can be justifiable to launch a preventive war that will require the killing of such 'innocent obstacles', if an appropriate institutional procedure for making the decision to engage in preventive war is followed *and* if the following conditions are satisfied: (*a*) the attack on the 'innocent obstacles' is necessary to avert the harm, (*b*) conscientious efforts are made to reduce the harm to the 'innocent obstacles', even if this involves significant costs to country B, and (*c*) a strong proportionality requirement is satisfied, that is, the harm to be averted by the preventive action is not only very great but significantly greater than the harm to the 'innocent obstacles'.

If these conditions were satisfied, it would be implausible to say that in attacking the 'innocent obstacles' the forces of country B are treating them as mere means or disregarding the fact that they are not among the conspirators. Instead, a more accurate characterization would be that this is a case of 'moral necessity', of conscientiously choosing the lesser evil to avert a much greater evil. Furthermore, satisfying the second condition would require reasonable efforts to inform the 'innocent obstacles' that the attack was going to be made, as a last resort, to thwart the future unjust attack rather than as an act of aggression, to urge them to surrender, and to give them credible assurances that they will be treated well if they do surrender. Thus one major concern about preventive action would be allayed: it would not be the case that the soldiers who were attacked would not know that they were at war or about to be at war.

If an institutional procedure like the one Keohane and I recommend were followed, and the fact that it was being followed were widely publicized, this would lend credibility to the effort to inform the 'innocent obstacles' that the coming attack was a justified act of prevention, not aggression. In addition, the same multilateral accountability regime within which the decision to make preventive war was made could help provide credible assurances that if the 'innocent obstacles' surrendered, they would be treated well.

It seems implausible to maintain the permissibility of inflicting 'collateral damage' on *non*military personnel and at the same time to insist on the absolute impermissibility of using military force against *military* personnel who continue to stand in the way of the removal of a massive unjust threat even after they have been put on notice that they will be liable to attack if they do not step aside. It might be the case that efforts to inform the 'innocent obstacles' that they are about to be attacked and ought to step aside would give the conspirators a lethal advantage by prompting them to step up the efforts to make the missiles operational. However, at this point we are no longer in the realm of preventive war, but rather war to stop an imminent attack. I conclude that in situations like Case 2, preventive war could be morally justified.

Case 3: a broad-based, public conspiracy. Country A has over the last decade become increasingly militant and aggressive. The government publicly acknowledges aggressive aims (it demands *Lebensraum* for its growing population or claims a right to the better-resourced lands of neighboring infidels) and the recruiting and training of the military includes the unambiguous message that the army is not just for defense, but for attack—for the creation of an empire, for example. It is, in fact, common knowledge among the general population that the military forces are being built up for the purpose of conquering other countries. The government of country A, in cooperation with the leaders of A's military, is conspiring to commit aggression against the first of what they hope will be a series of victims. They have a definite plan of attack, with a specific intent to do unjust harm on a massive scale, and they have taken an initial step to execute the plan. However, most members of the military, including those who would be killed or hurt by a preventive attack to thwart the aggression, do not know of the existence of the plan; they only know—or at least ought to know—that their country has aggressive goals and that they, as members of the military, will be called on to carry them out. Under these conditions, even if many members of country A's military are not themselves involved in the conspiracy, that is, are not apprized of the specific plan of aggression against the first country on the 'hit list', it seems a stretch to say that they are 'innocent obstacles' to preventing the aggression, for two reasons. First, at some future point, unless prevented from doing so, they *will participate* in the aggressive action; hence they are not merely obstacles to be overcome in order to get at those who will commit aggressive action. Their government leaders and military commanders are counting on their participation; it is an essential component of the plan. Second, A's military personnel know—or should know—that they are part of a military apparatus that is directed toward future aggression, even if they are unaware of any specific plans. Hence it is profoundly misleading to say they are innocent and to suggest that they have the same moral status as innocent civilians who happen to stand between opposing armies. It is important to emphasize that Case 3 is not fanciful. It is a fairly accurate description of the condition of the German Army in 1938 and possibly as early as 1936.

With some hesitation, I now want to focus more closely on the question of the innocence or, more accurately, the nonculpability, of military personnel. I hesitate because I am sensitive to the inhuman demands that are put on ordinary soldiers in wartime and because I am also aware that soldiers are usually quite young and subject to powerful pressures, psychological and often more tangibly coercive, to join the military and, when they are members of it, to obey orders.

Such sensitivity to the predicament of ordinary soldiers can go too far, however, in effect either robbing them of agency altogether or tacitly assuming that acting morally never requires one to bear great costs. Becoming a soldier is a morally risky act and at this point in human history everyone of normal intelligence and who is not a child, ought to know that fact. To become a soldier is to have good reason to believe that one may be called upon to kill other human beings, some of whom will most likely be innocent.

Quite apart from the fact that many soldiers are not conscripts, it will not suffice to reply that conscripts, at least, have no choice. In some cases they do have a choice, though choosing not to serve may be costly. In each of the major wars of the twentieth century, some conscientious individuals refused to fight, even when conscripted, and many more could have chosen to do so, but did not, either because they unreflectively responded to the call of 'patriotism' or because they were unwilling to bear the costs of refusal. Furthermore, it is not the case that the costs they would have borne, had they refused, were always so great that it was morally permissible for them not to refuse.

Moral theories may falter when confronted with the question of just how much cost an individual should bear to avoid wrongfully harming others. For most theories, there will be cases in which the costs of refusing to be a soldier can become so high that it is said that the individual 'had no choice'. But not every individual's situation is like that when he is confronted with the prospect of becoming a soldier. It is a peculiar feature of much contemporary just war theorizing that it expects soldiers fighting in a just cause to bear considerable risk to minimize harm to noncombatants, while at the same time proceeding *as if* becoming a soldier is never a matter of choice, *as if* soldiers cannot act wrongly in carrying out orders, no matter how unjust their cause, so long as they observe the principles of *jus in bello*, and *as if* it is unreasonable to expect soldiers to bear significant costs in refusing to carry out ('lawful') orders when they fight in an unjust cause.[9]

To become a soldier—and not be willing to disobey orders to do wrong—is to become a weapon to be wielded by others. In many cases, one will have very good reason to believe that in becoming a soldier one will become a weapon that will be used to do grave wrong. Such is the case if one becomes a soldier in a militant dictatorship that has exhibited a pattern of unjustified violence toward minorities in one's own country or aggression against other countries. It can be not only better, but even morally obligatory, to suffer punishment or even death, rather than become a weapon to be wielded at the discretion of unaccountable, vicious leaders, bent on massive violations of basic human rights.

There is one more way of responding to the second, more sophisticated 'rights-based' objection to preventive war which I will only sketch here. It depends upon a clear-eyed rejection of the idea that morality can literally be 'rights-based'. On this view, rights, including the right to self-defense, are not basic in the system of morality. Instead, one must argue for the existence of rights by appealing to the idea that there are certain interests that are so morally important that they can ground obligations owed to persons. Rights are interest-based, both in the sense that one must argue to claims about the existence of rights from premises that present certain interests as being so morally important that they deserve extraordinary protections, and in the sense that disputes about the content of rights have to be settled ultimately to appeals to the nature and moral importance of the interests in question.

In my judgment, an interest-based conception of rights must accommodate the idea of fairness, more specifically, the idea that there are limits on the self-restraint that an individual should be expected to exercise in trying to protect his basic interests when he has done nothing wrong to put those interests at risk. This is nowhere more apparent than in the case of the right of self-defense. The right of self-defense, as a moral right, is ascribed to all persons out of recognition of the equal moral importance of every person's interests in survival and in avoiding serious bodily injury. In determining what the contours of the right of self-defense are—in particular, in determining whether in some circumstances it encompasses the right to use preventive force—we need to consider carefully the fact that a blanket prohibition on preventive self-defense could, under unusual but realistic circumstances, place an unjustifiably severe constraint on an individual's ability to protect his own legitimate, vital interests. The intuitive appeal of examples like McMahan's Paralysis case or the Lethal Virus case and Missile Attack cases described above is that they reveal that under certain conditions it would be unfair to expect a person or a group to refrain from using force in self-defense until the lethal harm became imminent. It would be unfair in the sense that understanding the contours of the right of self-defense in this way would impose an excessive burden of self-restraint on individuals or groups faced with the threats as described.

In a world in which our predictions are fallible and in which the intentions and abilities of potential attackers are not fully known to us, there are two risks involved in formulating the content of the right of self-defense: if the right is formulated too broadly, that is, if the domain of rightful self-protective actions is drawn too expansively, innocent or at least nonculpable individuals are put at excessive risk of being killed or wounded through the actions of those who can invoke the right of self-defense thus defined; if the right is formulated too narrowly, then staying within its limits makes individuals and groups excessively vulnerable to being killed or wounded by others and to that extent demands unreasonable self-restraint on their part. Even if we cannot formulate a clear, crisp principle of fairness in the distribution of the risks of liability to physical attack, I believe that what is guiding our intuitions in the Paralysis, Lethal Virus, and Missile Attack cases, and what undergirds our sense that the law of conspiracy is morally permissible, is a sense that a right of self-defense that strictly excluded the use of preventive force would impose an excessive burden of self-restraint on us in some situations where our vital interests are threatened. Similarly, one could argue that it is fairer (or at least less unfair), that *soldiers* who are not conspirators but rather obstacles should be killed in a preventive action needed to thwart a lethal aggressive conspiracy, than that the intended victims of the conspiracy should suffer the threatened harm out of regard for the lives of the obstacles, if they have taken all reasonable steps to alert the latter to their role in the conspiracy and given them the opportunity to step aside.

In the case of the individual or group that is faced with either taking no steps to avert a lethal unjust harm or attacking 'innocent obstacles', under conditions where they have been warned to step aside, and credible efforts have been made to reduce the harm to them if they don't step aside, it would be unreasonable to say that the ensuing harm to the 'innocent obstacles' would represent an unfair distribution of risk. It would ring hollow to claim that those seeking to avert the unjust harm plotted by the conspirators have not gone far enough in constraining their opportunities for self-protection, that instead of acting to avert the unjust harm they should simply let the conspiracy come to fruition out of respect for the interests of the 'innocent obstacles'. If they warn the 'innocent obstacles' to step aside and fulfill the other conditions I listed above, and if they have come to the decision to use preventive force through the sort of institutional process Keohane and I describe, they have *already* borne quite significant burdens of restraint and it would be quite false to say they are treating the 'innocent obstacles' as mere means to their own survival. Moreover, and this is crucial, we are assuming that those who are going to use preventive force in self-defense have not provoked the anticipated attack—that they are not responsible for being the target of the conspiracy. Under these conditions, if harm must fall on one party or the other—either the targets of the conspiracy must suffer lethal harm or the 'innocent obstacles' must suffer lethal harm—it is less bad, and fairer, that the latter should suffer the harm.

Similarly, the law of individual self-defense holds that one can be justified in killing a wholly innocent person, if one had good reason to believe that he posed an imminent lethal threat and that using lethal force against him was necessary to avert it. The best explanation for the moral appeal of a legal right of self-defense whose content is spelled out in this way, is that the reasonableness criterion represents a fair distribution of the risks of harm between potential victims and possible attackers. My suggestion is that the same considerations of fairness speak in favor of rejecting the claim that the use of preventive force can never be justified, except against those who are conspirators, and never against those they *use* in their conspiracies. It is implausible to say that, given the pressures to become soldiers that individuals sometimes face, fairness requires that soldiers may never be attacked preventively unless they are active participants in a wrongful conspiracy.

5. CONCLUSION

In this chapter, I have attempted to strengthen the institutionalist approach to the justification of preventive war advanced in two earlier papers (see n. 2). My focus has been on the refutation of the claim that preventive war as such is unjust because it involves violations of the rights of at least some of those who are targeted in the preventive action. I have argued that even the strongest version of the 'rights-based' objection, properly understood, shows only that preventive war *may* involve the killing of soldiers who cannot be said to be imposing an unjust risk of massive harm and that even when it does it still may be justified. I have shown that there are some cases of preventive war against which 'rights-based' objections do not arise (those of Type 1 and 3 above), and argued that there are others (those of Type 2 above) in which the killing of enemy soldiers is less morally problematic than the infliction of 'collateral damage' on noncombatants, and hence is morally permissible, if the infliction of 'collateral damage' is. My conclusion is that even the strongest 'rights-based' objection is incapable of supporting the assertion that preventive war is never morally permissible and that properly designed institutions provide an effective reply to the consequentialist objections.

I wish to end, however, on a note of caution. Nothing I have said suggests that any preventive war that has been waged in the past, including the recent US invasion of Iraq, has been morally justified. The core idea of the approach to preventive war I have defended in this chapter is the insistence that efforts to justify preventive war involve especially grave risks and that these risks can only be adequately addressed through the construction of novel institutions, not through the mere extension of traditional methods of decision-making to the perilous domain of preventive action.

Notes

1. This is not to say, of course, that there are no endorsements of preventive war in the just war tradition. The claim is more modest, namely, that in general thinkers in that tradition have tended to find preventive war unacceptable.

2. Jeff McMahan, "Preventive War and the Killing of the Innocent," in Richard Sorabji and David Rodin, eds., *The Ethics of War: Shared Problems in Different Traditions* (Aldershot, UK and Burlington, Vt.: Ashgate Publishing, 2006), 173–74.

3. Allen Buchanan and Robert O. Keohane, "The Preventive Use of Force: A Cosmopolitan Institutional Perspective," *Ethics and International Affairs*, 18, no. 1 (2004): 4.

4. Ibid., 1–22.

5. Ibid.

6. Allen Buchanan, "Institutionalizing the Just War," *Philosophy and Public Affairs* 34, no. 1 (2006): 21.

7. This and the following paragraph draw on Buchanan and Keohane, "Preventive Use of Force," 6–7.

8. Steven Lee, "A Moral Critique of the Cosmopolitan Institutional Proposal," *Ethics and International Affairs* 19, no. 2 (2005): 105.

9. Jeff McMahan challenges this all too common view in "The Ethics of Killing in War," *Ethics* 114 (July 2004): 693–733.

13

FROM NUREMBURG TO KOSOVO: THE MORALITY OF ILLEGAL INTERNATIONAL LEGAL REFORM

1. THE PROBLEM OF ILLEGAL REFORM

Optimism about practice and in theory.—Most would agree that the international legal system has undergone significant moral improvement since 1945. The veil of sovereignty has been pierced: a burgeoning human rights law affirms that how a state treats its own population is no longer its own business only. Slavery, genocide, and aggressive war are prohibited. More states than ever before are democratic. Some scholars even argue that international law is moving toward recognition of a right to democratic governance as a human right.[1] The prodemocracy intervention in Haiti, the expulsion of Iraqi forces from Kuwait, and the NATO intervention in Kosovo have all been praised as valuable steps toward an international system that takes as primary the protection of the rights of individuals rather than the interests of states. Widely discussed goals for further improvement include better compliance with human rights norms; a more consistent, effective, and morally defensible international legal response to secession and other self-determination conflicts; more effective support for democracy; impartial and effective procedures for the prosecution of war crimes; and greater equality among states as actors in the creation and application of international law. The spate of normative writings on secession, self-determination, humanitarian intervention, and on the hypothesis that democratic states do not make war on one another indicates both approval for progress already achieved and the expectation of more progress to come.[2]

Lawlessness in the name of progress.—Yet what some hail as progress others decry as illegal acts that threaten the rule of law, betray a lack of sincerity regarding fidelity to law, and manifest a disturbing willingness to impose subjective, personal moral standards on others. To take only two prominent examples, international legal scholars J. S. Watson and Alfred Rubin condemn humanitarian intervention and attempts to enforce human rights norms through the operation of international war crimes tribunals as illegal acts parading under the guise of legality.[3] In addition, they suggest that the source of the illegal reformist's error may lie in his willingness to impose his own subjective view of what morality requires upon others. Such allegations raise a fundamental issue of much greater generality and import than debates over the legal status or the desirability of any particular change in the international legal rules: under what conditions, if any, is it morally justifiable to engage in acts that violate existing international law in order to bring about supposed moral improvements in the system of international law?

Distinguishing illegal acts of legal reform from mere conscientious lawbreaking.—Notice that this question is not the same as "Under what conditions, if any, is it morally justifiable to violate international law?" The case of NATO intervention in Kosovo illustrates the distinction. The chief justification U.S. and NATO officials gave for the intervention was that it was necessary to prevent a humanitarian disaster—to stop the massive human rights violations perpetrated by Serbs upon Kosovar Albanians. It appears that the preponderance of international legal opinion is that the intervention was illegal, and it is revealing that U.S. State Department officials were told to avoid the issue of legality in their public statements, presumably because it would be impossible to make a convincing case that the intervention was legal.

In addition to this chief justification, there was the suggestion, on the part of some leaders, including U.S. Secretary of State Madeleine Albright, that the NATO intervention was a first important step toward establishing a new customary norm of international law, according to which humanitarian intervention can be permissible without Security Council authorization. According to this second line of justification, violating existing law was justified to initiate an improvement in the international legal system.

The chief justification presents the illegal action as a necessary exception to law-abidingness in the name of justice, without in anyway implying that the system as a whole, or even the particular rule that is violated, is in need of improvement. Employing this justification is fully consistent with believing that the existing rule that requires Security Council authorization for humanitarian intervention is a good rule, even that it is the best rule possible. The second justification is quite different: it justifies the illegal intervention as an act directed toward reforming the system. Its implication is that the existing rule requiring Security Council authorization is not optimal, and that a new norm of humanitarian intervention, according to which Security Council authorization is not needed, is morally preferable.

There is a further difference: an agent who invokes the first justification need not have any commitment to the rule of law; he might, for example, be an anarchist. In contrast, a person who breaks the law with the aim of improving the legal system thereby shows that he values the contribution that a system of law can make to justice. So illegal acts directed toward legal reform are of special interest because, on the one hand, they seem more respectable by virtue of being directed toward improving the system (unlike acts that evidence a total disregard for the rule of law) while, on the other hand, they raise the question of how those who are committed to the rule of law can be willing to break the law. Because my concern in this chapter is with the justification of illegal acts directed toward the moral improvement of the international legal system, not with the question of when it is morally justifiable to break the law, I will not canvass the voluminous literature on the obligation to obey the law (which has focused on domestic law) and then try to determine to what extent its results apply to the case of international law.

Answering the question of when, if ever, illegal acts directed toward improving the international legal system are morally justified is a contribution to the nonideal moral theory of international law. Ideal theory prescribes and justifies the most fundamental principles that an international legal order ought to satisfy. Nonideal theory includes two parts: principles for dealing with noncompliance with the prescriptions of ideal theory and principles for determining the morally accessible ways of making the transition from our nonideal state to a satisfaction of the ideal theory's prescriptions. It is the second part of nonideal theory that includes our question.

Distinguishing illegal acts of international legal reform from the standard case of civil disobedience.—At this point one might well ask: why restrict the question to *international* law? As the considerable normative literature on civil disobedience shows, the morality of illegal acts for the sake of improving a legal system is hardly a new topic and has been explored thoroughly in regard to domestic legal systems. (For example, Dr. Martin Luther King, Jr., broke state segregation laws to stimulate legislators and the courts to eliminate them and thus make the system of law more just.) Nevertheless, for three reasons the question has particular bite in the case of international law.

First, the illegal acts that are most likely to contribute to the moral improvement of the international legal system differ markedly from acts of civil disobedience, at least when the latter are most clearly morally justifiable. From the standpoint of moral justification, the least problematic case of civil disobedience is that in which the lawbreaker violates the law openly and accepts the predictable legal penalty for her act, thus showing respect for law at the same time she violates a particular law. But as I shall elaborate below, in the typical case illegal acts directed toward reform of the international legal system are perpetrated by actors who will not be subject to legal penalty, not simply because the international legal system is weak in enforcement capacity but because the lawbreaker will tend to be a powerful state or coalition against whom punitive action is not likely to be taken.[4]

Second, and more important, compared to the better specimens of developed legal systems, the international legal system is both more in need of improvement and less endowed with resources for relatively expeditious lawful improvement. Therefore the question of the morality of illegal acts directed toward system reform is likely to be more acute and to arise more frequently in the international case.

Third, the illegal acts we are concerned with are not committed by private individuals or groups of private individuals as in the case of civil disobedience; they are state actions and this raises the stakes of the decision to act illegally. Illegal acts committed by states are, other things being equal, more of a threat to the perceived legitimacy of the system than those committed by private individuals.

The sort of illegal reformist act I shall focus on is exemplified by the NATO action in Kosovo: an illegal act of humanitarian intervention, justified as a contribution toward making the international legal system better from a moral point of view. However, the fundamental question this chapter addresses is both wider and narrower than that of the justification of humanitarian intervention: wider, because although the examples I discuss are illegal acts of humanitarian intervention my broader concern is with the more general class of illegal acts directed toward legal reform; narrower, because it is only illegal acts *directed toward legal reform* that I explore and not all acts of humanitarian intervention fit this description.[5]

Limited resources for lawful moral improvement.—The ways in which international law can be made significantly limit the options for lawful reform of the system. There are two chief sources of international law: treaty and custom. If the target of moral improvement is to prohibit a form of behavior engaged in by more than a few states or to create a new norm that allows behavior that previously would have been a violation of the rights of sovereignty that all states enjoy, reform by treaty may be a very slow process at best. Suppose that the goal of reform is to establish a norm of international law that not only requires states to "promote" human rights within their own borders and to supply periodic reports on their progress in doing so to some international body (as the major human rights covenants stipulate), but that also authorizes armed intervention to halt massive human rights violations that occur in domestic conflicts when less intrusive means have failed. Many states will refuse to sign such a treaty. Others may sign but postpone ratification indefinitely. Others may sign and ratify, but weaken the force of the document by stating "reservations" regarding some clauses (thereby exempting themselves from their requirements) or by stating "understandings" which interpret burdensome clauses in ways that make them less threatening to state interests.

As an avenue for moral improvements that are both significant and timely, the process by which international customary law is formed is hardly more promising. In briefest terms, new norms of customary law are created as the result of the emergence of a persistent pattern of behavior by states, accompanied by the belief that the behavior in question is legally required or authorized (the *opinio juris* condition). However, there are several aspects of this process that significantly limit the efficacy of the customary route toward system improvement. First, international law allows states to opt out of the new customary norm's scope by consistently dissenting from them. Second, how widespread the new pattern of state behavior must be before a new norm can be said to have "crystallized" is not only disputed but probably not capable of a definitive answer. Third, even if a sufficiently widespread and persisting pattern of behavior is established, the satisfaction of the *opinio juris* condition may be less clear and more subject to dispute. Pronouncements by state leaders may be ambiguous or mixed, in some cases indicating a recognition of the behavior in question is legally required or authorized, in other cases appearing to deny it.

Given these limitations, the efforts of the state or states that first attempt to initiate the process of customary change are fraught with uncertainty. If the new norm they seek to establish addresses a long-standing and widespread pattern of state behavior, and one in which many states profess to be legally entitled to persist, other states may not follow suit. Or, if other states follow suit, they may do so for strictly pragmatic reasons and may attempt to ensure that a new customary rule does not emerge by officially registering that they do not regard their behavior as legally required (thus thwarting satisfaction of the *opinio juris* condition).

The crucial point is that new customary norms do not emerge from a single action or even from a persistent pattern of action by one state or a small group of states. Thus the initial effort to create a new customary norm is a gamble. A new norm is created only when the initial behavior is repeated consistently by a preponderance of states over a considerable period of time and only when there is a shift in the legal consciousness of all or most states as to what the law is. At any point the process can break down. For example, if one powerful state dissents from an emerging norm, other states may decide that it is prudent to register dissent as well or to refrain from pronouncements that would otherwise count as evidence for satisfaction of the *opinio juris* requirement. For all of these reasons, significant and timely reform through the creation of new customary norms of international law is difficult and uncertain.

That reliance on change through the establishment of new custom is a formidable obstacle to fundamental social change has long been recognized. All of the great proponents of the modern state—the state with legislative sovereignty—from Bodin and Hobbes to Rousseau, recognized the severe limitations that adherence to the evolution of customary law imposed on the possibilities for reform. Only the power to issue and enforce rules that can overturn even the most deeply entrenched customary norms in domestic society would suffice; thus the insistence on legislative sovereignty. But in the international legal system there is as yet nothing approaching a universal legislature. Nor is there a process of constitutional amendment. To summarize: heavy reliance on customary law, absence of both a universal legislature capable of overturning custom and a constitutional amendment process, and the obvious limitations of the treaty process together result in a system in which lawful reform is more difficult than in developed domestic systems.[6]

Although they are quite different mechanisms for the creation of international law, treaty and custom have this in common: they both rely heavily on states' acceptance of norms as binding. Indeed, the idea that state consent (whether explicit, as in the case of treaties, or tacit, as with custom) is essential is the predominant view of what is distinctive of international law. There are well-known difficulties in the idea that customary norms enjoy the consent of all states (in particular, not opting out cannot properly be regarded as tacitly consenting), and there is also the problem that international law counts as consensual agreements that are far from voluntary on the part of one party (peace treaties signed under duress by the losers in war are said to be consented to by them). Nevertheless, there is a substantial kernel of truth in the assertion that the system exists through state consent: the mechanisms of treaty and custom result in a system in which it is extremely difficult for anyone to impose norms that the majority of states oppose.

This broadly consensual nature of international law undoubtedly brings some benefits. For example, it may make it more difficult for a hegemon to hijack the international legal system for its own purposes. Nonetheless, what might be loosely called the state consent supernorm comes at a steep price: it makes timely moral reform difficult in a system which few would deny needs improvement.

Illegal acts directed toward system reform: Three examples.—To clarify what is at stake in the issue of the morality of illegal legal reform, consider the following hypothetical cases.

> *Case 1.*—Bowing to sustained international pressure, Iraq agrees to grant autonomy (limited self-government, not full independence) to the Kurdish people in its northern region. But as with its 1970 autonomy regime for the Kurds, Iraq violates the agreement. A multinational force "endorsed" by a UN General Assembly Resolution but not empowered by a decision of the Security Council intervenes to restore the Kurds' autonomy and to create a monitoring mechanism to provide early warning if Iraq seeks to violate the autonomy arrangement in the future.
>
> *Case 2.*—A new genocide erupts in Burundi. A coalition of French and American forces quickly intervenes, disarms the perpetrators of genocide, arrests the leaders of the genocide, and turns them over to an international genocide tribunal. Neither the Secretary General of the UN, nor the Security Council, nor the General Assembly endorse this intervention, but they do not condemn it either.

Case 3.—A small Latin American country has just achieved its first truly democratic election. But then a group of fascist colonels in its armed forces overthrows the newly elected government by force and "permanently abolishes" democracy. A coalition of key members of the Organization of American States intervenes militarily and restores the elected government.

Were these events to occur there is little doubt that many members of the general public and perhaps a majority of international legal theorists would view at least some of them favorably, as contributions toward a more morally sound international order in which human rights and democracy are better protected than at present. No doubt some theorists would portray these events as the first hopeful steps toward establishing new, more morally enlightened norms of international customary law. They would hope that these types of actions would be repeated and that eventually new norms would crystallize.

Permissive versus obligatory norms.—These examples indicate another feature of the process of customary norm creation. The same type of behavior (e.g., intervention to prevent genocide, as in case 2) might exemplify the content of either a permissive or an obligatory norm of intervention. In the former case, the new customary norm would be established only after the emergence of a sustained pattern of intervention, accompanied by the belief that the intervention was legally permissible under international law; in the latter, only if the pattern of behavior were accompanied by the belief that intervening is obligatory. Presumably, as a broad generalization the establishment of a new permissive customary norm should be less difficult, to the extent that it does not impose affirmative duties on states but only increases the scope of their lawful discretionary action and in that sense does not represent a radical change in a system that has traditionally left much to the decisions of states. However, this generalization is subject to an important exception: if the new permissive norm in effect cancels a preexisting prohibition against nonconsensual action toward other states, as is the case with a permissive norm of humanitarian intervention, then it represents a very significant change and one which states may resist.

Avoiding the "What is law?" question.—My aim in articulating the three examples above is not to take a firm position on the question of whether any particular effort to improve the international legal system is illegal. I believe that it is relatively uncontroversial that in at least some of the three cases, if not all three, the act in question would be deemed uncontroversial by the preponderance of experts in international law. The choice of particular examples is not important, however. The key point is this: given the relatively undeveloped state of international law—in particular, its inadequate protection of basic human rights and its limited resources for timely and lawful change in the direction of more adequate protection—there are opportunities for acts which are both illegal and highly desirable as steps toward morally improving the system. To raise the question of the morality of illegal international legal reform, we need not agree on a definitive and comprehensive solution to the hoary question, 'What is international law?' or 'When is a norm an international law?'

Facing the question of illegal acts of reform squarely.—Critics such as Watson and Rubin are right to suggest that too often those who endorse what they regard as acts of reform evade the question of whether illegal acts are morally justifiable by assuming, without good reason, that the acts in question are not really illegal.[7] Without resolving complex debates about what the law is, I wish to confront head-on the question of whether and if so under what conditions illegal acts of reform are morally justified.

Some of the most important moral improvements in the international legal system have resulted, at least in part from illegal acts. Consider one of the great landmarks of reform: the outlawing of genocide. To a large extent this was an achievement of the Nuremburg War Crimes Tribunal (though at the time the term 'genocide' was not part of the legal lexicon). However, a strong case has been made by a number of respected commentators that the "Victors' Justice" at Nuremburg was illegal under existing international law. In particular, it has been argued that there was no customary norm or treaty prohibiting what the Tribunal called "crimes against humanity" at the time World War II occurred. But quite apart from this it has been argued that even if (contrary to what some commentators say) aggressive war was prohibited at the time the Second World War began, there was no international law authorizing the criminal prosecution of individuals for waging or conspiring to wage aggressive war.

There is no denying that the Nuremburg Tribunal contributed to some of the changes in international law that we regard as the epitome of progress—not just the prohibitions of genocide and aggressive war but also the international recognition of the rights of human subjects of medical experimentation.[8] Nonetheless, it can be argued that at least some of the punishments meted out at Nuremburg were illegal.

It can also be argued that a series of illegal actions over several decades played a significant role in one of the other most admirable improvements in the international legal system: the prohibition of slavery. In the late eighteenth and early nineteenth centuries Britain used the unrivaled power of its navy to attack the transatlantic slave trade.[9] Britain's strategy included illegal searches and seizures of ships flying under other nations' flags, as well as attempts to get other countries to enforce their own laws against commerce in human beings. It is highly probable that what success Britain had in persuading other states to cooperate in efforts to destroy the slave trade was due in part to its willingness to use illegal force. The destruction of the slave trade was a milestone in the development of a growing human rights movement that eventually issued in the international legal prohibition of slavery, but which also expanded to include other human rights.

Once the pivotal role of such illegal acts is acknowledged, it is unconvincing to appeal to the moral progress that has already been achieved in international law to support the assumption that significant continued progress will be achieved with reasonable speed and without illegality. On the contrary, given the system's limited resources for lawful change—and the fact that it is still a state-dominated system in which many of the most serious defects calling for reform lie in the behavior of states—the question of the morality of illegal reform is inescapable.

2. THE CONDEMNATION OF ILLEGAL REFORM EFFORTS

Two issues: Fidelity to law and moral authority.—We can now proceed to evaluate the position of those, such as Watson and Rubin, who condemn what they take to be illegal acts done in the name of the moral improvement of the international legal system. Such critics raise an issue that is as fundamental as it is neglected: under what conditions, if any, is it morally justifiable to breach international law in order to try to improve the system from a moral point of view? To answer this question, I shall argue, we must answer two others: (1) what is the moral basis of the commitment to bringing international relations under the rule of law? and (2) under what conditions, if any, can an agent's judgments about what justice requires count as good reasons for imposing rules on others? In order to answer question 1, we need an account of *fidelity to law* that enables us to determine how the would-be reformer should weigh the fact that his proposed action of reform is illegal. In order to answer question 2, we need an account of *moral authority* (or what Rawls calls legitimacy) that enables us to determine if the would-be reformer is justified in imposing on others a norm to which they have not consented and which some would reject. A satisfactory answer to the first question is needed to counter the charge that advocates of illegal acts directed toward system reform show lack of due respect for law while purporting to improve it. A satisfactory answer to the second question is needed to refute the allegation that advocates of illegal acts directed toward system reform are wrongly seeking to impose their own "subjective" moral views on others. I address the issue of fidelity to law in the remainder of this section; in Section 4, I address the issue of moral authority.

Unfortunately, critics like Watson and Rubin have done a better job of raising the issue of the morality of illegal legal reform than of resolving it. It is fair to say that both authors assume, more than argue, that illegalities in the name of system reform are not morally justified. At the very least, the exact character of their complaint is not clear. It is possible to begin the task of appreciating the condemnation of illegal acts of reform by reconstructing a simple argument on their behalf. Call it the Fidelity Argument. It purports to explain why the fact that the reformist's act is illegal counts decisively against the morality of the act.

1. One ought to be committed to the rule of law in international relations.
2. If one is committed to the rule of law in international relations, then one cannot consistently advocate (what one recognizes to be) illegal acts as a means of morally improving the system of international law.
3. Therefore, one ought not to advocate illegal acts as a means of morally improving the system of international law.

3. BASES FOR FIDELITY TO LAW

The first step is to clarify the phrase 'the rule of law' in the argument in order to understand just why honoring the commitment to the rule of law is important. There are in fact two quite different ways in which critics of illegal reform may be understanding 'the rule of law' in the Fidelity Argument. According to the first, 'the rule of law' refers to a normatively rich ideal for systems of rules. According to the second, 'the rule of law' means something that may be much less normatively demanding, namely, a system of rules capable of preventing a Hobbesian condition of violent chaos. Let us see how the Fidelity Argument reads under these two interpretations.

Fidelity to the ideal of law.—According to the first interpretation, the rule of law is an ideal composed of several elements: laws are to be general, public, not subject to frequent or arbitrary changes, and their requirements must be reasonably clear and such that human beings of normal capacities are able to comply with them.[10] These requirements help ensure that a system of law provides a stable framework of expectations, so that individuals can plan their projects with some confidence and coordinate their behavior with that of others. But there is another element of the rule of law as a normative ideal which on some accounts is of single importance: the requirement of equality before the law. The precise import of this requirement is, of course, subject to much dispute, but the core idea is that the law is to be applied and enforced impartially.

If we read 'the rule of law' in the Fidelity Argument as referring to this normatively demanding ideal, as including the requirement of equality before the law, then the argument is subject to a serious and obvious objection. The difficulty is that the international legal system falls short of the requirement of equality before the law. The most powerful states (such as China, the United States, and the Russian Federation) not only play an arbitrarily disproportionate role in the processes by which international law is made and applied but also are often able to violate the law with impunity.

According to the first interpretation of the Fidelity Argument, it is our moral allegiance to the rule of law as a normative ideal that is supposed to be inconsistent with advocating or committing what we believe to be illegal acts even if they are directed toward reforming the system. But to the extent that the existing system falls far short of the ideal of the rule of law in one of its most fundamental elements, the requirement of equality before the law, allegiance to the ideal exerts less moral pull toward strict fidelity to the rules of the existing system. Indeed, allegiance to the rule of law as an ideal might be thought to make illegal acts *morally obligatory* in a system that does a very poor job of approximating the requirements of the ideal. More specifically, a sincere commitment to the rule of law might be a powerful reason for committing illegal acts directed toward bringing the system closer to fulfillment of the requirement of equality before the law, if there is no lawful way to achieve this reform.[11] The point is that one cannot move directly from the commitment to the rule of law as an ideal to strict fidelity to existing law. Whether a commitment to the rule of law as an ideal precludes illegal reform actions will depend in part upon the extent to which the existing system approximates the ideal.

Notice also that the critics' second complaint has little force against illegal acts of reform directed toward making the system better satisfy the requirements of the ideal of the rule of law, especially that of equality before the law. To say that the core accepted elements of the rule of law are merely the personal moral views of the reformers, and that it would therefore be illegitimate to impose them on others, would be extremely inaccurate. Not only are they widely accepted, but unless they are assumed to be highly desirable it is hard to make sense of the idea of fidelity to the law as a moral ideal. In the next subsection we will see that the illegitimacy issue—the question of when an agent is morally justified in imposing moral standards on those who do not accept them—has more bite when the moral principles motivating illegal acts of reform are more controversial.

Substantive justice.—There is another reason why a simple appeal to the ideal of the rule of law cannot show that illegal reform acts are not morally justifiable: the extent to which a system of rules exemplifies the ideal of the rule of law is not the only factor that determines the moral pull toward compliance. Approximation of the ideal of the rule of law is a necessary, not a sufficient, condition for our being obligated to comply with legal norms, even if a deep commitment to the ideal of the rule of law is assumed. A system might do a reasonably good job of exemplifying the elements of the rule of law and still be seriously defective from the standpoint of substantive principles of justice. For example, the system might be compatible with, or even promote, unjust economic inequalities, depending upon the content of the laws of property and the extent to which the current distribution of wealth is the result of past injustices. Similarly, the elements of the ideal might be satisfied, or at least closely approximated, in a system that failed to meet even the most minimal standards of democratic participation. The elements of the rule of law prevent certain kinds of injustices and help ensure the stability and predictability that rational agents need, but this is not to say that they capture the whole of justice. And if justice is to enjoy the kind of moral priority that is widely thought to be essential to the very notion of justice, then one cannot assume that illegal acts directed toward eliminating grave injustice in the system are always ruled out by fidelity to the ideal of the rule of law. Since many, indeed perhaps most, extant theories of justice include more than the requirements of the rule of law, it would be very misleading to assume that any illegal action for the sake of reforming the international legal system by making it more just must be the imposition of the reformer's subjective view of morality or merely personal views.

Nevertheless, a more subtle form of the moral authority issue remains: even if it is true that most or even all understandings of justice take it to include more than an approximation of the ideal of the rule of law, there is much disagreement about what justice requires, and it is appropriate to ask what makes it morally justifiable for an actor to try to impose on others the conception of justice she endorses. I take up the moral authority issue in Section 4.

Earlier I suggested that an approximate conception of the ideal of the rule of law would include the requirement of equality before the law. Some might disagree, limiting the ideal of the rule of law to the other elements listed above. If they are right then this is further confirmation that the rule of law is not the only value that is relevant to assessing the weight of our commitment to fidelity to law. For if equality before the law is not to be included in the ideal of the rule of law, then there is a strong case for including it among the most basic and least controversial principles of justice, at least for those who value the role that law can play in securing justice. But if so, then whether it is morally permissible to violate a law to improve a legal system must surely depend in part on how unjust the system is.

The legitimacy of the international legal system.—The international legal system not only tolerates extreme economic inequalities among individuals and among states, it legitimizes and stabilizes them in manifold ways, not the least of which is by supporting state sovereignty over resources.[12] In addition, the international legal system is characterized by extreme political inequality among the primary members of the system (states). As already noted, a handful of powerful states wield a disproportionate influence over the creation and above all the application and enforcement of international law. Indeed, it is not implausible to argue that the extreme and morally arbitrary political inequality that characterizes the society of formally equal states robs the system of legitimacy. By a legitimate system I mean one whose institutional structures provide a framework within which its authorized actors are morally justified in making, applying, and enforcing laws.

To make a convincing case that these defects deprive the international legal system of legitimacy would require articulating and defending a theory of system legitimacy.[13] That task lies far beyond the scope of the present discussion. However, this much can be said: the more problematic a system's claim to legitimacy, the weaker the moral pull of fidelity to its laws, other things being equal. Neither Watson nor Rubin addresses the issue of whether illegal acts of reform may be justified if they hold a reasonable prospect of significantly improving the legitimacy of a system whose legitimacy is at the very least subject to doubt. However, we shall see later that there is a way of understanding their opposition to illegal reform as resting on a conception of system legitimacy that emphasizes adherence to the state consent supernorm, the principle that to be international law, a norm must enjoy the consent of states.

Given the existing international legal system's deficiencies from the standpoint of what is either a cardinal element of the ideal of the rule of law or a basic, widely shared principle of justice, namely, equality before the law, and from the standpoint of a fairly wide range of principles of distributive justice, and given that the extreme political inequality among the states poses a serious challenge to the legitimacy of the system, it is implausible to assert that a commitment to the rule of law, as a moral ideal, rules out all illegal action for the sake of reform. The very defects of the system that provide the most obvious targets for reform weaken the moral pull of strict fidelity to its laws.

So far my analysis only shows that there is no simple inference from allegiance to the ideal of the rule of law to the moral unjustifiability of illegal acts directed to system reform. It does not follow, of course, that everything is morally permissible in a system as defective as the international legal system so long as it is done in the name of reform. An important question remains: given that a commitment to the ideal of the rule of law does not categorically prohibit illegal acts of reform, under what conditions are which sorts of illegal acts of reform morally justified? As a first approximation of an answer, we can say that, other things being equal, illegal acts are more readily justified if they have a reasonable prospect of contributing toward (*a*) bringing the system significantly closer to the ideal of the rule of law in its most fundamental elements, (*b*) rectifying the most serious substantive injustices supported by the system, or (*c*) ameliorating defects in the system that impugn its legitimacy.

The rule of law as necessary for avoiding violent chaos.—Our first interpretation of 'the rule of law' in the Fidelity Argument understood that phrase in a normatively demanding way: to be committed to the rule of law is to respect and endeavor to promote systems of rules that satisfy or seriously approximate a robust conception of the equality of law. We saw that on this interpretation the connection between being committed to the rule of law and refusing to violate existing international law is more tenuous and conditional than the critics of illegal reform assume. The second interpretation of 'the rule of law' as it occurs in the Fidelity Argument owes more to Hobbes than to Fuller. The idea is that even if international law falls far short of exemplifying some of the key elements of the ideal of the rule of law and even if it is seriously deficient from the standpoint of substantive justice and legitimacy, it is all that stands between us and violent chaos.[14] On this interpretation of the Fidelity Argument, we are presented with an austere choice: abstaining from illegal acts of reform or risking a Hobbesian war of each against all in international relations.

This is a false dilemma. As a sweeping generalization, the claim that illegal acts of reform run an unconscionable risk of violent anarchy is implausible. It would be more plausible if two assumptions were true: (*a*) the existence of the international order depends solely upon the efficacy of international law and (*b*) international law is a seamless web, so that cutting one fiber (violating one norm) will result in an unraveling of the entire fabric.

The first assumption is dubious. It probably overestimates the role of law by underestimating the contributions of political and economic relations and the various institutions of transnational civil society to peace and stability in international relations. But even if the first assumption were justified, the second, "seamless web" assumption is far fetched. History refutes it. As we have already noted, there have been illegal acts that were directed toward and that actually contributed to significant reforms, yet they did not result in a collapse of the international legal system.

Respect for the state consent supernorm.—Some critics of illegal reform, including Watson and Rubin, are especially troubled by the willingness of reformers to violate what these critics believe is an essential (constitutional) feature of the existing international legal system: the state consent supernorm, a secondary rule according to which law is to be made and changed only by the consent of states.[15] (As was noted earlier, the requirement of state consent here is understood in a very loose way to be satisfied either by ratification of treaties or through conformity to norms that achieve the status of customary law.) The question, then, is this: why is the state consent supernorm of such importance that illegal acts of reform that violate it are never morally justified? There appear to be three answers worth considering: (1) only if the state consent supernorm is strictly observed will violent chaos be avoided, because only state consent can render international law *effective*; (2) state consent is the only mechanism for creating effective norms of peaceful relations among states that is capable of conferring *legitimacy* upon international norms; or (3) the state consent supernorm ought to be strictly adhered to because doing so reduces the risk that stronger states will prey on weaker ones.

Thesis (1): The general claim that compliance with legal norms can only be achieved if those whose behavior is regulated by the norms consent to them is clearly false. In the case of domestic legal systems, virtually no one would assert that consent to every norm is necessary for effectiveness. So if the importance of consent is to supply a decisive reason against acts of reform that violate the state consent supernorm in international law, it must be because there is something special about the international arena that makes consent necessary if law is to be effective enough to avoid violent chaos.

If the Realist theory of international relations were correct, it would provide an answer to the question of what that something special is. According to the Realist theory, the structure of international relations precludes moral action except where it happens to be congruent with state interest. The importance of creating norms by state consent, on this view, is that it provides a way for states, understood as purely self-interested actors, to promote their shared long-term interests in peace and stability. Unless Realism is correct, it is hard to see why we should assume that consent is necessary for effective law in the international case, while acknowledging, as we must, that it is not necessary for effectiveness in domestic systems.

Realism has been vigorously attacked, most systematically by contributors to the Liberal theory of international relations. Because I believe these attacks are telling, I will not reenact now all too familiar argumentative battles between Realists and their critics. Instead, I will focus on the second and third versions of the argument that a proper appreciation of the consensual basis of existing international law precludes justifiable acts of illegal reform.[16]

Thesis (2): This is the view that what is morally attractive about the existing international legal system is not just that it avoids the Hobbesian abyss, but that it does so by relying upon the only mechanism for creating and changing norms of peaceful interaction that can confer legitimacy upon norms, given the character of international relations.[17] (A legitimate norm, here, is understood as one that it is morally justifiable to enforce.) The underlying assumption is that the members of the so-called community of states are moral strangers, that the state system is a mere association of distinct societies that do not share substantive ends of a conception of justice, rather than a genuine community.[18] In the absence of shared substantive ends or a common conception of justice, consent is the only basis of legitimacy for a system of norms. Within domestic societies, there are moral-political cultures that are "thick" enough to fund shared substantive ends or conceptions of justice and hence to provide a basis for legitimacy without consent; but not so in international "society." But if state consent is the only basis for legitimacy in the international system, then illegal acts of reform that violate the state consent supernorm, such as illegal interventions to support democracy or to prevent massive violations of human rights in ethnic conflicts within states, strike at the very foundation of international law and hence are not morally justifiable, at least for those who profess to be committed to reforming that system.[19]

The most obvious defect of this line of argument is that its contrast between international society as a collection of moral strangers and domestic society as an ethical community united by a "thick" culture of common values is overdrawn. Especially in liberal societies, which tolerate and even promote pluralism, whatever it is that legitimates the system of legal rules, it cannot be shared substantive ends or even a shared conception of justice. What Thesis 2 overlooks is that democratic politics in liberal domestic societies includes deliberation—and heated controversy—over which substantive ends to pursue, not simply over which means to use to pursue shared substantive ends. In particular, liberal domestic societies often contain deep divisions as to conceptions of distributive justice, with some citizens espousing "welfare-state" conceptions and others "minimal state" or libertarian conceptions. Yet such societies somehow manage to avoid violent chaos and also appear to be capable of having legal systems that are legitimate.

An advocate of Thesis 2 might respond, relying on Rawls's views in *Political Liberalism* and *The Law of Peoples*, that the members of liberal societies do share what might be called a core conception of justice—the idea that society is a cooperative venture among persons conceived as free and equal—but that there is no globally shared core conception of justice. Hence adherence to the state consent supernorm is necessary in international law, but not in domestic law.

There are three difficulties with this response. First, divisions within liberal domestic societies, especially concerning distributive justice, may be so deep that we must conclude either that (*a*) there is no shared core conception of justice or that (*b*) if there is it is so vague and elastic that it cannot serve as a foundation for a legitimate system of legal norms. (Even if it is true that welfare state liberals and libertarians both hold that society is a cooperative endeavor among "free and equal" persons, their respective understandings of freedom and equality diverge sharply.) Second, and more important, even if it is, or once was, true, that value pluralism among states is much deeper than within them, there is evidence that this may be changing. As many commentators have stressed, international legal institutions, as well as the forces of economic globalization, have contributed to the development of a transnational civil society in which a culture of human rights is emerging. This culture of human rights is both founded on and serves to extend a shared conception of basic human interests and a conception of the minimal institutional arrangements needed to protect them.[20] Moreover, the canonical language of the major human rights documents indicates a tendency toward convergence that may be as good a candidate for a core shared conception of justice as that which Rawls attributes to liberal societies: the idea that human beings have an inherent equality and freedom. So even if it is true that a system of legal norms can be legitimate only if it is supported by a common culture of basic values or a shared core conception of justice, it is not clear that international society is so lacking in moral consensus that state consent must remain an indispensable condition if norms are to be legitimate.

There is a third, much more serious objection to the proposition that illegal acts of reform that violate the state consent supernorm are morally unjustifiable because they undermine the only basis for legitimacy in the international legal system: due to the very defects at which illegal acts of reform are directed, the normative force of state consent in the present system is morally questionable at best.

What is called state consent is really the consent of state leaders. But in the many states in which human rights are massively and routinely violated and where democratic institutions are lacking, state leaders cannot reasonably be regarded as agents of their people.[21] Where human rights are massively violated, individuals are prevented or deterred from participating in processes of representation, consultation, and deliberation that are necessary if state leaders are to function as agents of the people capable of exercising authority on their behalf.

But if state leaders are not agents of their peoples, then it cannot be said that state consent is binding because it expresses the people's will. How, then, can the consent of individuals who cannot reasonably be viewed as agents of the peoples they claim to represent confer legitimacy? Illegal acts directed toward creating the only conditions under which state consent could confer legitimacy cannot be ruled out as morally unjustifiable on the grounds that they violate the norm of state consent.

This is not to say that the requirement of state consent, under present conditions, is without benefit or that the benefits it brings are irrelevant to the question of whether the system is legitimate. It can be argued, as I have already suggested, that adherence to the state consent supernorm has considerable instrumental value, quite apart from the inability of state consent as such to confer legitimacy on norms. This is the point of the third thesis about the importance of the state consent requirement.

Thesis (3): This account of why the state consent supernorm is so important as to preclude illegal acts of reform that violate it is much more plausible than the first two. It does not assume that any violation of the norm of state consent poses an unacceptable risk of violent chaos, nor that state consent is supremely valuable because only it can achieve peace through norms that are legitimate. The proponent of Thesis 3 can cheerfully admit that law can be effective without consent and that under existing conditions state consent is in itself incapable of conferring legitimacy on the norms consented to. Instead, her point is that adherence to the state consent supernorm is so instrumentally valuable for reducing predation by stronger states upon weaker ones that it ought not to be violated even for the sake of system reform. Thesis 3 relies on the empirical prediction that if the international legal system fails to preserve the formal political equality of states by adhering to the state consent supernorm, the material inequalities among states will result in predatory behavior and in the violations of individual human rights as well as rights of self-determination which predation inevitably entails.[22]

It is no doubt true that the state consent supernorm provides valuable protection for weaker states. But even if this is so, it does not follow that acts of reform that violate the state consent supernorm are never morally justifiable. Acts of reform that are very likely to make a significant contribution to making the system more egalitarian—that contribute to increasing the substantive political equality of states, thereby reducing the risk of predation—may be morally justified under certain circumstances, even if they violate the state consent supernorm.

Another way to put this point is to note that the instrumental argument for strict adherence to the state consent supernorm is very much a creature of nonideal theory. At least from the standpoint of a wide range of theories of distributive justice, the existing global distribution of resources and goods is seriously unjust. But presumably these injustices play a major role in the inequalities of power among states. If the system became more distributively just, the inequalities of power that create opportunities for predation would diminish, and with them the threat of predation and the instrumental value of the state consent supernorm.

What this means is that there is nothing inconsistent in both appreciating the value of adherence to the state consent supernorm as a way of reducing predation and being willing to violate it in order to bring about systemic changes that will undercut the conditions for predation. The difficulty for the responsible reformer lies in determining when the prospects for actually achieving a significant reform in the direction of greater equality or justice are good enough to warrant undertaking an action that may have the effect of weakening what may be the best bulwark against predation the system presently possesses. While the instrumental (antipredation) argument may be powerful enough to create a strong presumption—for the time being—against violating the state consent supernorm, it is hard to see how it can provide a categorical prohibition on illegal acts of reform.

Furthermore, observing the state consent supernorm is not the only mechanism for reducing the risk of predation. The theory and practice of constitutionalism in domestic legal systems offer a variety of mechanisms for checking abuses of power. For example, a norm requiring that individual states or groups of states may intervene in domestic conflicts to protect human rights only when explicitly authorized to do so by a supermajority vote in the UN General Assembly would provide a valuable constraint on great power abuses.

The results of this section can now be briefly summarized. I have argued the notion of fidelity to law cannot provide a decisive reason for refraining from committing illegal acts directed toward reforming the international legal system. A sincere commitment to the ideal of the rule of law is not only consistent with illegal acts of reform; it may in some cases make such acts obligatory. Further, it is not plausible to argue that illegal acts of reform always constitute an unacceptable threat to peace and stability. Finally, I have argued that being willing to commit an illegal act of reform need not be inconsistent with a proper appreciation of the need to provide weaker states with protection against predation. I now turn to the other main challenge to illegal international legal reform: the charge that reformers wrongly impose their own personal or subjective views of morality upon others.

4. MORAL AUTHORITY

The charge of subjectivism.—Opponents of illegal reform such as Watson and Rubin heap scathing criticism on those who would impose their own personal or subjective views of morality or justice on others. The suggestion is that those who endorse violations of international law, and especially those who disregard the state consent supernorm, are intolerant ideologues who would deny to others the right to do what they do. It is a mistake, however, to assume as these critics apparently do, that the only alternatives are subjectivism or strict adherence to legality.

Internalist moral criticism of the system.—An agent who seeks to breach international law in order to initiate a process of bringing about a moral improvement in the system need not be appealing to a subjective or merely personal view about morality. Instead, she may be relying upon moral values that are already expressed in the system and, to the extent that the system is consensual, upon principles that are widely shared. In fact, it appears that some who were sympathetic to NATO's intervention in Kosovo, including UN Secretary General Kofi Annan, believed that this intervention was supported by one of the most morally defensible fundamental principles of the international legal system, the obligation to protect human rights, even though it was inconsistent with another principle of the system, the norm of sovereignty understood as prohibiting intervention in the domestic affairs of Serbia-Montenegro.[23] To describe those who supported the intervention by appealing to basic human rights principles internal to the system as ideologues relying on a merely personal or subjective moral view is wildly inaccurate.

Two views of moral authority.—Since the appearance of Rawls's book *Political Liberalism* there has been a complex and spirited debate about the nature of what I have called moral authority. Two main rival views have emerged. According to the first, which Rawls himself offers, moral authority, understood as the right to impose rules on others, is subject to a requirement of reasonableness. It is morally justifiable to impose on others only those principles that they could reasonably accept from the standpoint of their own comprehensive conceptions of the good or of justice, with the proviso that the latter fall within the range of the reasonable.[24] Rawls has a rather undemanding notion of what counts as a reasonable conception of the good or of justice: so long as the view is logically consistent or coherent and includes the idea that every person's good should count in the design of basic social institutions, it counts as reasonable. As I have argued elsewhere, Rawls's conception of moral authority counts as reasonable grossly inegalitarian societies, including those that include systematic, institutionalized racism or caste systems or systems that discriminate systematically against women.[25] The point is that on Rawls's view grossly and arbitrarily inegalitarian social systems count as reasonable because the requirement that everyone's good is to count is compatible with the good of some counting very little. To that extent, Rawls's conception of reasonableness is at odds with some aspects of existing international human rights law, including the right against discrimination on grounds of gender, religion, or race.

The root idea of the Rawlsian conception of moral authority is respect for persons' reasons in the light of what Rawls calls "the burdens of judgment." To acknowledge the burdens of judgment is to appreciate that due to a number of factors reasonable people can disagree on the principles of public order. Like Rubin and Watson, Rawls is concerned about those who assume that their belief that certain moral principles are valid is sufficient to give them the moral authority to impose those principles on others. In that sense, Rawls's reasonableness condition is an attempt to rule out the imposition of purely personal or subjective moral views.

However, Rawls's reasonableness criterion does not rule out imposing moral standards that others do not consent to. What people *can* reasonably accept, given their moral views, and what they actually *do* accept or consent to may differ. So, according to the Rawlsian conception of moral authority (or in his preferred term, legitimacy), acts of reform that violate the state consent supernorm are not necessarily unjustifiable, even if we slide over the problem of inferring the consent of persons from the consent of states.

Rawls's conception of moral authority focuses almost exclusively on one aspect of being reasonable, or of showing respect for the reasons of others: humility in the face of the burdens of judgment. Its only acknowledgment that reasons must be of a certain quality to warrant respect and toleration is the very weak requirement of logical consistency or coherence. A quite different conception of moral authority acknowledges the burdens of judgment and also affirms that part of what it is to respect persons is to respect them as beings who have their own views about what is good and right but places more emphasis on what might be called *epistemic responsibility* as an element of reasonableness.[26] According to this view, respect for persons' reasons does not require that we regard as reasonable any moral view that meets Rawls's rather minimal requirements of logical consistency or coherence and of taking everyone's good into account in some way. In addition, to be reasonable, and hence worthy of toleration, a moral view must be supportable by a justification that meets certain minimal standards of rationality. In other words, to be worthy of respect, moral views must be supported by reasons and reasoning that is of a certain minimal quality that goes beyond logical consistency or coherence. In particular, it must be possible to provide a justification for a moral view that does not rely on grossly false empirical claims about human nature (or about the nature of blacks, or women, or "untouchables") and which does not involve clearly invalid inferences based on grossly faulty standards of evidence. The intuitive appeal of this more demanding conception of what sorts of views are entitled to toleration lies in the idea that respect for persons' reasons requires that those reasons meet certain minimal standards of rationality, the underlying idea being that it is respect for persons' reasoning, not their opinions, that matters. According to this conception of moral authority also, it is mistaken to assume that anyone who tries to reform the international legal system by performing acts that are violations of its existing norms is thereby imposing on others her purely personal or subjective moral views. The charge of subjectivity should be reserved for those views that do not meet the minimal standards of epistemic responsibility. Different versions of this view would propose different ways of fleshing out the idea that epistemic responsibility requires more than mere logical consistency or coherence.

My aim here is not to resolve the debate about what constitutes moral authority (though I have argued elsewhere that the epistemic responsibility view is superior to the Rawlsian view).[27] Instead, I have introduced two rival conceptions of moral authority, in order to show that both create a space between rigid adherence to existing consensual international law and the attempt to impose purely subjective, personal moral beliefs in violation of existing law. So even though it is correct to say that purely subjective or merely personal moral views cannot provide a moral justification for illegal acts of reform, it does not follow that anyone who breaks the law is merely acting on a subjective or personal view.

Watson and Rubin are quite correct to question the moral authority of proponents of illegal reform. Merely believing that one is right in itself is not a sufficient reason for doing much of anything, much less for violating the law or trying to initiate a process that will result in imposing laws on others without their consent. But they are mistaken to assume that those who advocate illegal acts of system reform must lack moral authority, and they offer no account of moral authority to show that illegal reformists must or typically will lack moral authority. In addition, as I have already argued, quite apart from whether either the Rawlsian conception of moral authority or the epistemic responsibility conception is correct, those who brand all proponents of illegal reform "subjectivists" entirely overlook the fact that in some cases, perhaps most, the reformer's justification is internalist, appealing to widely shared moral principles already expressed in the system. It does not follow that these internal values of the system are beyond criticism, but they are not purely subjective or merely personal; instead, they are widely held, systematically institutionalized values. In appealing to the internal values of the system in order to justify an illegal act, the reformer is doing precisely what reformers (as opposed to revolutionaries) do: trying to see that the system does a better job of realizing the values it already embodies and is supposed to promote. The proper lesson to draw from Watson and Rubin's worries about moral subjectivism is that the justification of illegal acts of reform must rest upon a conception of moral authority, not that no justification can succeed.

5. TOWARD A THEORY OF THE MORALITY OF ILLEGAL LEGAL REFORM

Guidelines for determining the moral justifiability of illegal acts of reform.— In Section 1, I located the problem of illegal reform in the part of nonideal normative theory of international law that deals with how we are to move toward the institutional arrangements prescribed by ideal theory. We are now in a position to articulate some of the key considerations that such a nonideal theory would have to include. My aim here is not to offer a developed, comprehensive theory of the morality of transition from the nonideal to the ideal situation but only to sketch some of its broader outlines so far as it addresses the problem of illegal acts of reform. To do this I will list a set of guidelines for assessing the morality of proposed illegal acts directed toward the moral improvement of the system.

The guidelines are derived from the preceding analysis of the objections to illegal acts of reform. While none of those objections rules out the moral justifiability of illegal acts of reform, they do supply significant cautionary considerations that a responsible agent would take into account in determining whether to engage in an illegal act aimed at reforming the system. Finally, I will clarify the import of the guidelines and demonstrate their power by applying them to the recent NATO intervention in Kosovo.

An important limitation of the guidelines should be emphasized: they are not designed to provide comprehensive conditions for the justification of intervention. Instead, they are to be applied to proposals for illegal interventions once the familiar and widely acknowledged conditions for justified intervention are already satisfied. Among the most important of these familiar conditions is the principle of proportionality, which requires that the intervention not produce as much or more harm (especially to the innocent) than the harm it seeks to prevent. Much of the criticism of NATO's intervention in Kosovo focuses on the failure to satisfy this requirement. My concern, however, is with the special justificatory issues raised by the illegality of an act of intervention that is understood as being directed toward system reform. To respond to these justificatory issues, I offer the following guidelines.

1. Other things being equal, the closer a system approximates the ideal of the rule of law (the better job it does of satisfying the more important requirements that constitute that ideal), the greater the burden of justification for illegal acts.
2. Other things being equal, the less seriously defective the system is from the standpoint of the most important requirements of substantive justice, the greater the burden of justification for illegal acts.
3. Other things being equal, the more closely the system approximates the conditions for being a legitimate system (i.e., the stronger the justification for attempts to achieve enforcement of the rules of the system), the greater the burden of justification for illegal acts.
4. Other things being equal, an illegal act that violates one of the most fundamental morally defensible principles of the system bears a greater burden of justification.
5. Other things being equal, the greater the improvement, the stronger the case for committing the illegal act that is directed toward bringing it about; and if the state of affairs the illegal act is intended to bring about would not be an improvement in the system, then the act cannot be justified as an act of reform.
6. Other things being equal, illegal acts that are likely to improve significantly the legitimacy of the system are more easily justified.
7. Other things being equal, illegal acts that are likely to improve the most basic dimensions of substantive justice in the system are more easily justified.
8. Other things being equal, illegal acts that are likely to contribute to making the system more consistent with its most morally defensible fundamental principles are more easily justified.

The rationale for the guidelines.—The basic rationale common to all the guidelines is straightforward. They provide a way of gauging (*a*) whether any given illegal act can accurately be described as being directed toward reform of the system and if so (*b*) whether committing it is compatible with a sincere commitment to bringing international relations under the rule of law. The guidelines articulate the considerations that an ideal agent who is committed to pursuing justice through legal institutions, but cognizant of the deficiencies of the existing system, would take into account in determining whether to commit or endorse an illegal act of legal reform. This characterization of such an agent is intended to be abstract, allowing for the fact that different agents may have different views about what justice requires. Thus the guidelines are intended to provide concrete guidance without presupposing a particular theory of justice.

Guideline 1 captures the idea that for those who are committed to the rule of law, the fact that a system closely approximates that ideal provides a presumption in favor of compliance with its rules. Guideline 2 is a reminder that satisfying the formal requirements of the ideal of the rule of law is not sufficient for assessing the moral quality of a legal system and hence for determining the weight of the presumption that we ought to comply with its rules. In addition to satisfying or seriously approximating the ideal of the rule of law, a legal system ought to promote justice. The elements of the rule of law supply important constraints on the sorts of rules that may be employed in pursuit of the goal of substantive justice, but they are not the only factor relevant to assessing the moral quality of the system—how well the system promotes the goal of substantive justice also matters. In the case of the international legal system, it is relatively uncontroversial to sav that the most widely accepted human rights norms constitute the core of substantive justice (to call this a subjective or purely personal view would be bizarre). To the extent that the protection of human rights is an internal goal of the international legal system, the appeal to substantive justice is an appropriate consideration in determining whether illegal action is morally justifiable and cannot be dismissed as the imposition of purely personal or subjective moral views.

Guideline 3 rests on the assumption that the conditions that make the system legitimate, including preeminently its capacity to promote substantive justice within the constraints of the ideal of the rule of law, give us moral reasons to support it and that consequently we should be more reluctant, other things being equal, to violate its rules if it scores well on the criteria of legitimacy.

Guideline 4 follows straightforwardly from the fundamental commitment to supporting the international legal system as an important instrument for achieving justice. The reformer, by definition, is someone who is striving to bring about a moral improvement in the system. Accordingly, she must consider not only the improvement that may be gained through an illegal act but also the need to preserve what is valuable in the system as it is.

Guideline 5 is commonsensical, stating that the justifiability of the illegal act of legal reform depends upon whether, and if so to what extent, the state of affairs the act is intended to bring would constitute an improvement in the system. In the case of an illegal act intended to help create a new customary norm, this means that the new norm must actually be an improvement over the status quo.

Guideline 6 acknowledges a fundamental tension in the enterprise of trying to develop a morally defensible system of law: on the one hand, a person who seeks to reform a legal system, qua reformer, values the indispensable contribution that law can make to protecting human rights and serving other worthy moral values; on the other hand, she appreciates that the enterprise of law involves the coercive imposition of rules and that for this to be justified the system must meet certain moral standards. What this means is that the project of trying to develop the legal system to achieve the goal of justice must be accompanied by efforts to ensure that the system has the features needed to make the pursuit of justice through its processes morally justifiable. Thus guideline 6 acknowledges the distinction between justice and legitimacy and emphasizes that anyone who is committed to working within the system to improve it should take the legitimacy of the system itself as an important goal for reform.

Guideline 7, like guideline 3, emerges from my criticism of those opponents of illegal reform who make the mistake of thinking that conformity with the ideal of the rule of law is all we should ask of a legal system. There I argued that whether a legal system achieves or at least is compatible with the substantive requirement of justice is relevant to determining the system's moral pull toward compliance. My discussion of alternative views of moral authority showed that while Watson and Rubin are correct to condemn those who would attempt to impose subjective, that is, purely personal conceptions of substantive justice on the legal system, illegal reform for the sake of improving the substantive justice of the system is compatible with recognizing a requirement of moral authority and hence with acting from moral commitments that are not subjective in any damaging sense.

Guideline 8 is also intuitively plausible. A reformer who commits an illegal act that can reasonably be expected to make the system conform better to its own best principles is acting so as to *support* the system and to that extent the presumption against acting illegally that supporters of the system should acknowledge is weaker.

A word of caution is in order. The guidelines proceed on the assumption that content can be given to the idea of improving the system morally and they employ the notion of justice. However, they are not intended to provide a comprehensive moral theory nor to supply content for the notion of justice. They are designed to provide guidance for a responsible actor who both values the rule of law in international relations and is aware of both the system's need for improvement and the difficulties of achieving expeditious change by strictly legal means. It is inevitable that different agents may reach different conclusions about whether a particular illegal act directed toward system reform is morally justifiable, just as conscientious individuals can disagree as to whether a particular act of civil disobedience in a domestic system is morally justified. In some cases these different conclusions will be the result of different understandings of justice. But without having settled all disputes about what justice is, it is still possible to show that an actor sincerely committed to the rule of law in international relations, and who believes the existing system is worthy of efforts to reform it, can consistently perform or advocate illegal acts of reform. And it is possible to develop guidelines for responsible choices regarding illegal acts of reform.

NATO intervention in Kosovo, a test case.—To cover a wide range of possible illegal acts of reform the guidelines must be abstract. To appreciate their value and to clarify their meaning I will apply them to NATO's intervention in Kosovo. I will assume that according to the preponderance of legal opinion, this was an illegal act. I noted in Section 1 that two quite different justifications were given for the intervention: the primary justification offered was that the intervention was morally justified (even if illegal) as the only means of preventing major violations of human rights; the other justification was that the intervention was a first step toward establishing a new, more enlightened customary norm of humanitarian intervention that allows intervention without Security Council authorization. My concern in this chapter is with the second justification, because it more clearly meets the description of an illegal act directed toward morally improving the system. How does this illegal act, justified in this way, fare with regard to the eight guidelines for assessing the moral justifiability of illegal acts of system reform?

It would be difficult to argue that guidelines 1, 2, or 3 weigh conclusively against NATO's intervention in Kosovo. As I have already noted, the existing system of international law departs seriously from the ideal of the rule of law, at least so far as this includes the principle of equality before the law, falls far short of satisfying substantive principles of justice, including those, such as human rights norms, that are internal to the system, and can be challenged on grounds of legitimacy because of the morally arbitrary way in which international law is often selectively applied in the interest of the stronger.

From the standpoint of guideline 4, the intervention in Kosovo initially looks problematic, simply because of the charge that its illegality consisted in the violation of one of the most fundamental principles of the system, the norm of sovereignty articulated in Articles 2(7) and 2(4) of the UN Charter, which forbid armed intervention except in cases of self-defense or the defense of other states, in cases of aggression.[28] However, guideline 4 refers to the most morally defensible fundamental norms. If the new customary norm of intervention that the illegal act is intended to help establish would in fact constitute a major improvement in the system, it would do so by restricting state sovereignty, and this implies that the norm of sovereignty in its current form is not fully defensible. In other words, the reformist rationale for acting in violation of the existing norm of sovereignty so as to help establish a new customary norm of intervention is that the existing norm of sovereignty creates a zone of protected behavior for states that is too expansive, at the expense of the protection of human rights. The more dubious is the moral defensibility of the principle of the system that the illegal act violates, the less force guideline 4 has as a barrier to illegal action. In cases where the establishment of a new norm through illegal action would constitute a major improvement *because* the existing norm that is violated is seriously defective, guideline 4 poses no barrier to illegal action. So whether guideline 4 counts for or against NATO's intervention in Kosovo depends upon whether the change the illegal act is aimed at producing would in fact be a major moral improvement in the system, which is addressed in guidelines 5–8.

Consider next guideline 5. Recall that the act in question is aimed at the establishment of a new customary norm and that the process by which new customary norms are created is a complex, multistaged one in which there are many opportunities for failure. Above all, it is important to remember that whether a new customary norm of intervention will arise will depend not just upon what NATO did in this case but upon whether a stable pattern of similar interventions comes about, upon whether states persistently dissent from the propriety of such interventions, and upon whether those who contribute to establishing a stable pattern of similar interventions do so in a way that satisfies the *opinio juris* requirement. Given these inherent uncertainties of the effort to bring about moral improvement through the creation of a new customary norm, an actor contemplating an illegal act of reform of this sort should be on very firm ground in judging that the new norm would in fact be a major improvement. In the next subsection I will argue that this condition was not met in the case of NATO's intervention in Kosovo.

It is tempting to assume that from the standpoint of substantive justice, the Kosovo intervention scores high because the establishment of a norm authorizing intervention into internal conflicts to prevent massive human rights violations would constitute a major improvement in the system. Moreover, the charge of subjectivism (lack of moral authority) rings hollow in this sort of case because, as Kofi Annan suggested, the protection of human rights is a core value that is internal to the system. However, whether or not the NATO intervention can be described as an act of illegal reform that would, if successful, bring about a major improvement in the system depends upon the precise character of the norm that this illegal act is likely to contribute to the establishment of—and upon whether a norm of this character would be likely to be abused.

What sort of new norm of customary law?—From the standpoint of its justifiability as an illegal act directed toward improving the system, just how the illegal act is characterized matters greatly. It is not sufficient to characterize the NATO intervention as an act directed toward establishing a new norm of humanitarian intervention in domestic conflicts. Such a characterization misses both what makes the act illegal and what is supposed to make it an act directed toward improving the system by helping to establish a new norm of intervention: the fact that it was undertaken without UN authorization. Those who endorse the act, not simply as a morally justifiable act but as an act of reform calculated to contribute to the creation of a new norm, are committed to the assertion that the requirement of Security Council authorization is a defect in the system. And the fact that the intervention proceeded without Security Council authorization is the chief basis for the widely held view that the intervention was illegal.

For purposes of evaluating the justifiability of the NATO intervention as an illegal act directed toward reforming the system, then, the characterization of the act must at least include the fact that it occurred without Security Council authorization. But something else must be added to the characterization: the fact that the intervention was undertaken by a regional military alliance whose constitutional identity is that of pact for the defense of its members against aggression. Those who undertook the intervention and their supporters emphasized that it was conducted by NATO, presumably because they thought that this fact made the justification for it stronger than would have been the case had it been undertaken by a mere collection of states. Note that this appeal to the status of NATO as a regional defensive organization recognized by international law cannot refute the charge of illegality. According to Article 51 of the UN Charter, military action, including action by regional organizations as identified in Article 52, is permissible without Security Council authorization only in cases of the occurrence of armed attack against a state or a member of such an organization.[29] So the question remains: would a new customary norm permitting regional military organizations, or those that qualified as such under Article 52, be a moral improvement in the international legal system?

The answer to this question is almost certainly negative. A military alliance such as NATO is not the sort of entity that would be a plausible candidate for having a right under international law to intervene without UN authorization. The chief difficulty is that such a norm would be too liable to abuse. To appreciate this fact, suppose that China and Pakistan formed a regional security alliance and then appealed to the new norm of customary law whose creation NATO's intervention was supposed to initiate to justify intervening in Kashmir to stop Hindus from violating Muslims' rights in the part of that region controlled by India. It is one thing to say that NATO's intervention was morally justified as the only way of preventing massive human rights violations under conditions in which Security Council authorization was not obtainable. That justification for illegality makes no claims about the desirability of a new rule concerning intervention and is quite consistent with the view that despite its defects the rule requiring Security Council authorization is, all things considered, desirable under present conditions. The justification we are concerned with makes a stronger and much more dubious claim, namely, that the current rule requiring Security Council authorization ought to be abandoned and replaced with a new rule empowering regional defense alliances to engage in intervention at their discretion. Perhaps the current rule of intervention ought to be rejected, but it is very implausible to hold that adopting this new rule would be an improvement.

To conclude that the NATO intervention looks dubious from the standpoint of guidelines 5–8, then, is an understatement. The problem is not just that the change in customary law that the NATO intervention was supposed to contribute to is not a sufficiently important improvement to justify violating a fundamental norm of the system but that it is very doubtful that this change would be an improvement at all. In other words, the NATO intervention fails even to meet the threshold condition of being a plausible candidate for an illegal act of reform. So even if it scored better than it does on the other guidelines, the illegality of the act cannot be excused by appealing to the need to reform the system.

I conclude that the morality of the NATO intervention in Kosovo, understood as an illegal act directed toward improving the international legal system, is extremely doubtful. This criticism is valid independently of the cogency of the most widely publicized objection to the intervention, the charge that it violated the principle of proportionality that any intervention, legal or illegal, should satisfy because instead of stopping the ethnic cleansing of Albanians it actually accelerated it.

6. CONCLUSIONS

My chief aim in this chapter has been to identify, and to begin the task of developing a solution for, an important but neglected problem in the nonideal part of normative theory of international law: the justification of illegal acts aimed at morally improving the system. I have also shown the inadequacy of a simple and common response to the problem—the charge that such acts are impermissible because they are inconsistent with a sincere commitment to the rule of law or betray a willingness to act without moral authority by imposing purely personal or subjective views of morality. By exploring the complex array of factors that are relevant to determining whether an illegal act of reform is morally justified, I hope to have vindicated the concerns of those such as Watson and Rubin that such illegalities bear a serious burden of justification, while at the same time showing that to reject illegal reform out of hand is to fail to appreciate the complexities of the issue. This seemingly narrow inquiry has had a valuable result of much greater significance: facing the problem of the justification of illegal reform head-on, rather than pretending that reform efforts are legal by stretching the concept of legality, forces us to probe more deeply into the nature of the international legal system and the conditions for its legitimacy.

Notes

I am indebted to David Miller, Benedict Kingsbury, and an anonymous reviewer at *Ethics* for their astute and constructive comments on an earlier version of this chapter. I also thank Alex Aleinikoff, David Luban, Jane Stromseth, and other members of the legal theory workshop at the Georgetown University Law Center for their extremely helpful and generous comments on an earlier version of this chapter. I am also grateful to Alexsander Jovie, Courtney Campbell, Angelo Corlett, Michael Phillips, and Anthony Ellis for their insightful comments on a version of this chapter presented at a conference on humanitarian intervention at Portland State University (October 2000). Kristen Hessler and Avery Kolers also provided valuable comments on an early draft.

1. Thomas Franck, "The Emerging Right to Democratic Governance," *American Journal of International Law* 86 (1992): 46–91.

2. For a valuable critical exposition of the different ways of formulating the democratic peace hypothesis, the evidence for it, and the criticisms of it, see Bruce Russett, *Grasping the Democratic Peace: Principles for a Post–Cold War World* (Princeton. N.J.: Princeton University Press, 1993).

3. J. S. Watson, "A Realistic Jurisprudence of International Law," *The Yearbook of World Affairs* (London: London Institute of World Affairs, 1980), 265–85; Alfred P. Rubin, *Ethics and Authority in International Law* (Cambridge: Cambridge University Press, 1997), esp. 70–206.

4. There may, however, be domestic legal and/or political repercussions.

5. As an example of an illegal act directed toward reform that is not an act of intervention, consider the United States' unilateral declaration in 1976 of a prohibition against using fishing nets that are dangerous to dolphins in a 200-mile zone (far exceeding its territorial waters). The morality of such illegal acts directed to reform on international law in the name of protecting species or environmental protection is an important topic that merits a separate treatment.

6. The foregoing picture of international law's limited resources for lawful moral reform is, of course, a sketch in broad strokes. There are more subtle modes by which international law can be changed. For example, judicial bodies (such as the International Court of

Justice) or quasi-judicial bodies (such as the UN Human Rights Committee) can achieve reforms under the guise of interpreting existing law. However, as a broad generalization it is fair to say that these modes for effecting moral improvements are both limited and slow.

7. Watson, "Realistic," 271–72; Rubin, *Ethics*, 124.

8. The Nuremburg Code, which prohibits experimentation on human subjects without consent, was drafted as a direct result of the prosecution of the Nazi doctors for their inhumane experiments on unwilling human subjects. See German Territory under Allied Occupation, 1945–1955: U.S. Zone, Control Council No. 10, *Trials of War Criminals before the Nuremberg Military Tribunals* (Washington, D.C.: U.S. Government Printing Office, 1949), vol. 2, 181–82; William J. Bosch, *Judgment on Nuremburg: American Attitudes toward the Major German War-crimes Trials* (Chapel Hill: University of North Carolina Press, 1970).

9. Rubin, *Ethics*, 97–130; Reginald Coupland, *The British Anti-slavery Movement* (London: Oxford University Press, 1993), 151–88. Note that in adducing this example, I am not assuming that the motives of the British government were pure, only that one justification for the forcible disruption of the transatlantic slave trade that could have been given was that these illegal actions would contribute toward a moral improvement in the international legal system. Whether those who instigated the policy of disrupting the transatlantic slave trade were motivated by humanitarian concerns or not is it relevant.

10. Lon L. Fuller, *The Morality of Law* (New Haven, Conn.: Yale University Press, 1964), 33–39.

11. The problem of achieving greater equality among states is a complex one. One cannot assume that the best or only way to achieve greater equality is by greater democratic participation in the making and application of international law. One alternative would be a system of constitutional checks on actions of more powerful states. For example, international norms specifying when humanitarian intervention is justified might be crafted to reduce the risk that powerful states would abuse them, by requiring very high thresholds of human rights abuses before intervention was permitted, and by requiring international monitoring of the process of intervention to facilitate ex post evaluation of whether the requirement of proportionality was met, etc. I am indebted to T. Alexander Aleinikoff and David Luban for emphasizing this point (personal communications).

12. Henry Shue, *Basic Rights*, 2d ed. (Princeton, N.J.: Princeton University Press, 1980), 131–52; Thomas Pogge, "An Egalitarian Law of Peoples," *Philosophy and Public Affairs* 23 (1994): 195–224.

13. There are two quite different conceptions of legitimacy that are often confused in the writings of political theorists. The first, weaker conception is that of being morally justified in attempting to exercise a monopoly on the enforcement (or the making and enforcement) of laws within a jurisdiction. The second, stronger conception, often called 'political authority', includes the weaker condition but in addition includes a correlative obligation to obey the entity said to be legitimate on the part of those over whom jurisdiction is exercised. I have argued elsewhere that it is the former conception, not the latter, that is relevant to discussions of state legitimacy in the international system. I would also argue that this is true for legitimacy of the system. Allen Buchanan, "Recognitional Legitimacy and the State System," *Philosophy and Public Affairs* 28 (1999): 46–78.

14. Watson can perhaps be interpreted as endorsing this version of the Fidelity to Law Argument. He strongly emphasizes that international law will only be effective in constraining the behavior of states if it is consensual and rejects illegal acts of reform as being incompatible with the requirement of consent (Watson, "Realistic," 265, 270, 275). The chief difficulty with this line of argument is that while it would be extremely implausible to say

that there must be perfect compliance with law for it to be effective, Watson does nothing to indicate either what level of compliance is needed for effectiveness or what counts as effectiveness.

15. Rubin, *Ethics*, 190–91, 205, 206; Watson, "Realistic," 265, 270, 275.

16. The literature exposing the deficiencies of the various forms of Realism in international relations is voluminous. Of particular value are Charles Beitz, *Political Theory and International Relations* (Princeton, N.J.: Princeton University Press, 1979), 3–66; and writings of the liberal theory of international relations by Anne-Marie Slaughter, "International Law in a World of Liberal States," *European Journal of International Law* 6 (1995): 503–38; and Andrew Moravcsik, "Taking Preferences Seriously: A Liberal Theory of International Politics," *International Organization* 51 (1997): 513–53.

17. Terry Nardin, *Law, Morality, and the Relations of States* (Princeton, N.J.: Princeton University Press, 1983), 5–13; John Rawls, *The Law of Peoples* (Cambridge, Mass.: Harvard University Press, 1999), 51–120.

18. Nardin acknowledges that states do share some ends, e.g., the flourishing international trade, but his view seems to be that what is distinctive about international law is that it binds together states in the absence of shared substantive ends.

19. Watson, "Realistic," 268.

20. For a valuable exposition and defense of the idea of a global culture of human rights, see Rhoda E. Howard, *Human Rights and the Search for Community* (Boulder, Colo.: Westview, 1995), 1–20.

21. Fernando Tesón, *The Philosophy of International Law* (Boulder, Colo.: Westview, 1998), 39–41.

22. Benedict Kingsbury, "Sovereignty and Inequality," *European Journal of International Law* 9 (1998): 599–625.

23. Kofi Annan, Speech to the General Assembly, September 20, 1999, p. 2 (September 20, 1999; SG/SM/7136 GA/9569: Secretary-G).

24. John Rawls, *Political Liberalism* (New York: Columbia University Press, 1993), 136–37.

25. Allen Buchanan, "Justice, Legitimacy, and Human Rights," in Victoria Davion and Clark Wolf, eds., *The Idea of Political Liberalism* (Lanham, Md.: Rowman & Littlefield, 2000), 73–89.

26. Thomas Christiano, "On Rawls's Argument for Toleration" (unpublished paper); Allen Buchanan, *Justice, Legitimacy, and Self-determination: International Relations and the Rule of Law* (New York: Oxford University Press, 2004).

27. Buchanan, "Justice, Legitimacy, and Human Rights," and *Justice, Legitimacy and Self-determination.*

28. For a valuable review of the evidence that current international law prohibits armed humanitarian intervention, even with Security Council authorization, see Lori Fisler Damrosch, "Changing Conceptions of Intervention in International Law," in Laura W. Reed and Carl Kaysen, eds., *Emerging Norms of Justified Intervention* (a collection of essays from a project of the American Academy of Arts and Sciences) (Cambridge, Mass.: American Academy of Arts and Sciences, Committee on International Security Studies, 1993), 93–110.

29. Barry E. Carter and Phillip R. Trimble, eds., *International Law: Selected Documents* (Boston: Little, Brown, 1995), 14–15.

INDEX